THE
VERGE

THE
VERGE

REFORMATION, RENAISSANCE, AND FORTY YEARS THAT SHOOK THE WORLD

—⦿—

PATRICK WYMAN

TWELVE

NEW YORK   BOSTON

Grand Central Publishing
Hachette Book Group
1290 Avenue of the Americas, New York, NY 10104
grandcentralpublishing.com
twitter.com/grandcentralpub

First Edition: July 2021

Grand Central Publishing is a division of Hachette Book Group, Inc. The Grand Central Publishing name and logo is a trademark of Hachette Book Group, Inc.

The publisher is not responsible for websites (or their content) that are not owned by the publisher.

The Hachette Speakers Bureau provides a wide range of authors for speaking events. To find out more, go to www.hachettespeakersbureau.com or call (866) 376-6591.

Library of Congress Cataloging-in-Publication Data
Names: Wyman, Patrick, author.
Title: The verge : Reformation, Renaissance, and forty years that shook the world / Patrick Wyman.
Other titles: Reformation, Renaissance, and forty years that shook the world
Description: First edition. | New York : Twelve, 2021. | Includes bibliographical references and index.
Identifiers: LCCN 2021006600 | ISBN 9781538701188 (hardcover) | ISBN 9781538701171 (ebook)
Subjects: LCSH: Europe—Biography. | Europe—Economic conditions—15th century. | Europe—Economic conditions—16th century. | Europe—History—1492-1517.
Classification: LCC D106 .W96 2021 | DDC 940.2/10922—dc23
LC record available at https://lccn.loc.gov/2021006600

ISBNs: 978-1-5387-0118-8 (hardcover), 978-1-5387-0117-1 (ebook)

Printed in Canada

MRQ-T

10 9 8 7 6 5 4 3 2 1

For my parents

Contents

A Note on Money
and Currencies

Europeans of this period utilized a bewildering array of coins and currencies. Gold, silver, and copper of various types and denominations all played roles in everyday economic activity, as did "units of account," currencies that effectively existed only in accountants' ledgers. In the short term, these currencies' value fluctuated constantly, and playing the shifting exchange rates from place to place was one of the central activities of banking and finance. Over the period covered in this book, however, their value was stable enough to get a handle on their relative worth.

The (quite literal) gold standard for currency throughout the later Middle Ages and early modern period was the Venetian ducat. It weighed 3.56 grams and was nominally 24 carats fine. By the 1490s, it was the baseline for all the other major gold coinages of western Europe. The Florentine florin was essentially equivalent (3.54 grams), as were the fine gold cruzados of Portugal and the excelentes of Castile and Aragón (23.75 carats, but 3.74 grams), and the English half-noble and French gold écu (3.5 grams). The exception was the Rhine or Rhenish gulden, an alternative standard for much of northern and central Europe, which was 19 carats fine and a bit lighter. A ducat was worth about 1.82 Rhinegulden.

The ducat and florin equivalent are the major currencies this book employs, but several others warrant a mention. The first of these are maravedis, the silver coinage, or more often money of account, employed in Spain. One ducat was worth about 375 maravedis. Another is English shillings and pounds, a silver-based system; around the year 1500, one ducat was worth 4 shillings 7 pence (20 shillings to a pound, 12 pence to a shilling). The last is the Ottoman akçe (plural akça), also a silver coin, 60 of which were equal to a single ducat.[1]

1 ducat =
1 florin
1.82 Rhinegulden
375 maravedis
4 shillings 7 pence (4*s*/7*d*)
60 akça.

Relative Worth Around 1500

1. A master mason working in Bruges at this time made about 11 Flemish groten per day. At an exchange rate of 65–75 groten to the ducat, it took that mason six or seven days of work to make a single ducat.[2]
2. The average daily wage for an arquebusier serving in the standing forces of Spain between 1500 and 1530 was 40 maravedis. At 375 maravedis to the ducat, it would take about ten days of work to make a single ducat. For a pikeman, it was 30 maravedis, or two ducats for twenty-five days of work.[3]
3. At the siege of Vienna in 1529, Suleiman the Magnificent offered 1,000 akça per man to his Janissaries as an inducement to an assault on the city, almost 17 ducats. That sum was in addition to their regular wages.

4. Around 1500, an unskilled day laborer in Florence made 10 soldi per day. A florin—the equivalent of a ducat—was worth 140 soldi, so it took fourteen full workdays for a day laborer to make a florin or ducat.[4]

5. In 1505, English merchant John Heritage bought 42 tods of wool, a total weight of 1,176 pounds, for £23 2s. That came out to about 64 ducats.

6. In Venice in 1508, printer Aldus Manutius spent more than 200 ducats per month to keep his print shop—staffed by about fifteen employees—in operation.

7. Swabian mercenary Götz von Berlichingen and his brother were paid 2,000 Rhinegulden by Margrave Friedrich of Brandenburg for their military services as men-at-arms, with retainers serving under them, after a lengthy campaign. That is about 1,100 ducats.

8. In 1492, Christopher Columbus's expedition cost 2 million maravedis in total. That comes out to about 5,300 ducats.

9. Jakob Fugger personally loaned Charles V 543,585 florins in 1519–20 to bribe his way to the throne of the Holy Roman Empire. The total cost, including loans from other parties, came to 850,000 florins.

THE
VERGE

Deus enim et proficuum (For God and profit)
—A common phrase written in the
accounts of medieval merchants

INTRODUCTION

May 6, 1527

A bell clanged in the distance, sending its mournful tones into the early morning gloom. No light came over the horizon to illuminate the distant hills through which the river Tiber snaked, down toward the ancient city of Rome. The bell tolled over and over, an incessant pealing coming from the heights of the Capitoline Hill.

It broke what should have been an otherwise still and silent dawn. That morning was anything but. The bell was just one source of noise shattering the peace. Inside the city, the sound of pounding feet was closely followed by carts rattling and scraping down the darkened streets, loaded with barrels of gunpowder, stacks of iron cannonballs, crossbow bolts, and bags of shot for matchlock arquebuses. The din echoed off the half-buried remnants of baths, temples, arenas, and circuses, the legacy of Rome's long and illustrious past. Bleary-eyed and barely dressed, stumbling through the streets, thousands of Romans shaken out of bed and now hefting a variety of weapons made their way toward the walls.

Outside the walls, worn boots tramped over cropped pastures and the first green shoots of spring grain rising out of the fertile soil. Men stumbled in the murky dawn, the hilts of their swords scraping against steel breastplates, leather scabbards slapping against their thighs. The long wooden shafts of pikes cracked against one another, held upright as their wielders made their way into something resembling formation. Little flashes of flame appeared as arquebusiers struck flint into tinder to light match-cord, lengths of slow-burning fuse soaked with chemicals that would spark their firearms and send heavy lead balls toward their targets.

All of them were lean and dirty. Months of marching, covering hundreds of miles on the journey south from Lombardy, had hollowed out their cheeks. So too had gnawing hunger. Rain, mud, and pounding sunshine had taken its toll on their formerly flashy clothing, leaving the bright stripes of their shirts faded and copious holes amid the slashed hose.

Fear and excitement warred on their filthy, sunken faces. What kind of treasures waited for them in Rome? Gold, silver, precious gems—the assembled wealth of Christendom siphoned from all across Europe into the coffers of the pope, cardinals, and bishops: all of it theirs for the taking, if they could make it over the walls, past the defenders, and into the city; if no cannonball or lead shot tore through their fragile flesh; if no sword or pike or crossbow bolt ended their lives. So many great ifs, and to pass the time, to keep the bile down, the soldiers chattered in varied tongues. Castilian, Catalan, Swabian German, the Italian varieties of Milan and Genoa, and many more melded into a low buzz.

Hooves thudded onto the trampled ground. Up rode a man in a white coat over his suit of plate armor, bright and distinctive in the morning gloom. His face was lean and handsome, the chin under his helmet fringed with a neatly trimmed beard. The man shouted as he rode along the lines, calling out to men he recognized to encourage them. He had known some of the Spanish veterans for years, fought with them in the dreadful slaughter at Pavia two years before, and he reminded them of that towering victory. Most of the Germans were newer arrivals, *Landsknecht* mercenaries recruited in Swabia and the Tyrol, who had marched south over the Alps the past fall, but the man in white understood them just as well.

In theory, this army owed its loyalty to the Holy Roman Emperor, Charles V. The man in white, however, was Charles, Duke of Bourbon, a French nobleman who had defected to the emperor's service. He commanded this army—again, at least in theory.

The reality was different. Charles V had ordered the army's recruitment, drawing on the fearsome *Tercios*—regular Spanish soldiers recruited, trained, and maintained—already stationed in Italy, along with an assortment of short-term but highly competent Germans and Italians. Practically all of them were professionals who fought for money, veterans of prior campaigns who knew very well the business of war. The problem was that none had been paid for months, if not years. Their loyalty to the emperor had frayed along with the lack of wages. So too had Bourbon's control over them. The respected but aged Tyrolean nobleman who had recruited the Germans and brought them over the Alps, Georg von Frundsberg, had suffered an apoplectic fit when his *Landsknechte* mutinied for lack of pay. Only the promise of plundering Rome's riches had kept the force of mercenaries together for this long.

The Duke of Bourbon had no illusions about any of this. The force gathered outside Rome's imposing walls sat on the cutting edge of military technology and tactics, which they'd honed over decades of constant warfare. Gunpowder handguns, dense formations of pikemen, cannon, and hard-won, bloody experience had transformed the art of battle over the past decades, but nothing had shifted more than scale. This was a large army, roughly twenty-five thousand men, and it was far from the most imposing of the era. All had been recruited in a highly competitive and lucrative market for their services.

Assembling them was not the problem, however: Paying them was. Now tens of thousands of angry, hungry, and highly skilled soldiers waited, chomping at the bit, just outside the holiest city in western Christendom.

Bourbon came to a stop next to a German he recognized. The man was a follower of Martin Luther, he knew, and thus had little affection for Pope Clement VII, who was currently holed up inside Rome. The duke joked about the riches of priests and the rewards to come, and the *Landsknecht* laughed. Many of the Germans held Lutheran sympathies. They would relish the opportunity to separate the unworthy clergy from their ill-gotten fortunes, an added bonus on top of the necessities of plunder for their own survival. The makeshift ladders they carried, bobbing upward amid the pikes, would be their route to a righteous redistribution of wealth.

Spurring his horse onward, Bourbon raised his voice for all of his polyglot followers to hear. He would be the first man to scale the wall, he promised. Nobody in the army doubted him— the duke's bravery was the only reason the army had even held together this long.

Gunfire crackled and cannons boomed, an eruption of noise coming down from the walls. A group of Spaniards were already beginning their assault some distance away, and soon Bourbon and the rest joined them. Three spots along the defenses looked particularly promising, and the attackers had enough troops to test all three. For the moment, however, the advantage lay with the citizens of Rome. White smoke billowed from cannon and arquebuses, drifting in great clouds along the parapets and hiding the flashes of flame that lit the morning gloom. The sulfurous odor permeating the battlefield reminded the more pious among them of the reek of Hell.[1]

Cannonballs and arquebus shot ripped through the milling attackers, littering the open fields and the base of the fortifications with corpses as the Spaniards and Germans tried to force their ladders up against the walls and climb into the city. The defenders, a motley assortment of Roman citizens and Swiss mercenaries, hurled rocks and gunfire down on them. "Jews, infidels, half-castes, Lutherans," they called, adding their worst insults to the hail of shot.[2]

Thick banks of fog, rising from the marshes around the Tiber, rolled up to the walls. Rome's gunners lost sight of the *Landsknechte* and Spanish regulars. Bourbon sensed that the moment had arrived. Conspicuous in his white coat, as he shouted and waved the Germans onward with one hand while holding the ladder with the other, an arquebus ball tore through his armor and lodged in his torso. The duke fell, his white coat turning a violent shade of red. His soldiers cried out, a collective howl of anguish. First one, then a whole crowd of *Landsknechte* began retreating from the city walls as cries of "Victory!" followed them from the battlements.

For a moment, it seemed like the defenders were right. But the duke's soldiers were professionals. And they were desperate. It would take more than the death of their beloved commander to stop them. One more push brought them forward to the walls, the light of dawn barely cutting through the fog that kept the city's cannons from firing. The Germans and Spaniards absorbed the incoming gunfire, climbed their hastily constructed ladders, and surmounted the parapets. The defense collapsed. Within hours, Rome had fallen.

The carnage at the walls was fearful, but as morning gave way to afternoon, far more carnage would come. The invaders quickly overran the few pockets of Roman resistance and butchered the militia who stood and fought. The remaining Swiss made their last stand in the shadow of an ancient obelisk near the Vatican. All but a few perished. Their captain, Roïst, nearly died on the spot, but a few survivors carried him home. The attackers followed them, broke into Roïst's house, and killed the captain in front of his wife.

Unlike the Swiss, most of the defenders did not linger, instead fleeing for the safety of Castel Sant'Angelo, Pope Clement VII among them. He had spent the morning of the assault praying in the Vatican and barely escaped via the covered bridge that connected his palace to the castle before the enemy soldiers broke in. Thousands of refugees pounded at the gate, begging to be admitted before the horror of the sack engulfed them. One elderly cardinal made it in through a window; another had himself hauled up over the walls in a basket suspended from cables. They were the lucky few. The portcullis dropped, leaving the rest outside the safety of the castle. Bourbon's soldiers, less their leader, had the last holdouts surrounded.

Looking out from Sant'Angelo, Pope Clement could see the smoke rising over his city. Shattering glass, breaking wood, crackling flames, and sporadic gunfire—and above it all, the piercing screams of fleeing citizens—filled the streets and alleyways as evening descended on Rome.

The emperor's army slaughtered indiscriminately while establishing control, killing the sick and infirm at the hospital of Santo Spirito along with a group of orphaned children. These were only a few among many hundreds of unarmed civilians. For many of the imperial soldiers now wandering the streets of Rome, it was not their first sack, and before long, murder gave way to something far more deliberate and systematic. After all, a dead prisoner was a dead end. A live captive had value. And they could always kill him later.

Come evening, flames illuminated the city, throwing light

onto scenes of horrific violence. Mounds of corpses surrounded the high altar of St. Peter's Basilica. One group of Spaniards captured a Venetian resident in the city and began pulling out his fingernails one by one to force him to divulge the location of his valuables. People threw themselves from open windows to get away from the attackers breaking into their homes. Another group of Spanish professionals refused to share the loot they had found in an abandoned shop with a coterie of Germans, who promptly locked the Spaniards inside and burned the shop to the ground. Blood and mud commingled in the gutters, the pillaging soldiers trampling dead bodies underfoot as they moved from one target to the next.

When the dawn finally came, it illuminated a city in the throes of convulsive, bloody brutality.

The Lutheran sympathizers among the German *Landsknechte* did not pass up the opportunity to carry out a bit of religious score-settling. One group slaughtered an elderly priest who refused to grant Communion to an ass. Another beat a pro-imperial cardinal as they dragged him through the streets, even though the clergyman was a supporter of the emperor—their nominal employer—in his ongoing quarrel with the pope. Others trampled Communion hosts underfoot. Lutheran arquebusiers used holy relics as targets, shooting lead balls into ornate reliquaries and the sacred heads of mummified saints. They stripped the city's many churches of their riches and dumped piles of ancient bones into the streets. The papal tombs in St. Peter's were ripped open, their decaying occupants thrown down among the more recently deceased, whose blood was still pouring out on the tiles of the holiest place in Christendom. The cavalry eventually used the basilica as a stable for their horses. The head of Saint Andrew and the veil of Saint Veronica, two of the holiest relics in Christendom, were thrown in the gutter. *Landsknechte* plundered the city's many monasteries, which contained treasures accumulated over centuries of pious donations.

The Portuguese ambassador, sent by Clement to attempt the negotiation of a peaceful surrender, ended up stripped down to nothing but his breeches in the street outside his ransacked palace. Vowed nuns were sold for a coin apiece. The looters spared the bankers, particularly the Germans, who could arrange loans for prisoners to ransom themselves. Even amid the chaos of a sack, transfers and exchanges of money were still a necessity.

After three days of unhinged violence, the remaining imperial commanders began to reassert token control over their men. Thousands were dead; estimates range from four thousand to forty thousand, with the true number likely somewhere in the middle. Many more had been wounded. Sexual violence had touched practically every household in the city, even those of the Roman elite.

"Hell itself was a more beautiful sight to behold," wrote one commentator. All the riches of Christendom were now in the hands of a powerful rabble of filthy, famished, still-unsated mercenaries. From his hiding place in Sant'Angelo, Pope Clement could only watch and lament his fall: no longer one of the most powerful men in Christendom, and soon to become a captive puppet of the emperor.[3]

How did this relentless deluge of horrors come to pass? What compelled thousands of soldiers to ransack churches, take and torture prisoners, loot homes and palaces, and commit rape, murder, and a hundred other crimes on a staggering scale, in order to bring about the downfall of the holiest and richest city in their world?

The Sack of Rome was a seemingly unimaginable event, a complete inversion of reality, the world turned upside down. Rome was the heart of western Christendom, the center of the

European universe both culturally and religiously. Money flowed into the papal coffers from every corner of the continent. The tithes collected in the humble timber chapels of Scandinavia and the soaring Gothic cathedrals of France all eventually made their way to Rome. Now the pope had been brought low, his riches appropriated by humble soldiers, his city stripped of all its exalted grandeur, which was strewn helter-skelter with the dead.

It was the culmination of a tidal wave of upheaval, driven by the convergence of a multitude of profoundly disruptive processes. Exploratory voyages had made that Portuguese ambassador the representative of a wealthy king, and the revenues of the New World allowed Emperor Charles V to raise his army. The expansion of state capacity made warfare, itself transformed by the proliferation of money and gunpowder, vastly more devastating in potential, scale, and duration. The printing press upended the world of information, and not coincidentally spread the same Lutheran ideas that had inflamed so many German soldiers.

In just four decades—the blink of an eye, relatively speaking—Europe erupted. Around 1490, four decades before the Sack of Rome, Europe was a backwater. Paris, London, Barcelona, and Venice were all impressive enough locales by European standards, but an alien visitor looking for the high points of human achievement in that age would have much preferred to travel to Istanbul or Beijing; a contrarian might have chosen the charms of Tenochtitlan, Delhi, Cairo, or Samarkand.

Europe, meanwhile, sat apart, an outpost on the fringes of Eurasia. It was an economic and political periphery, an also-ran compared to the vibrant, expanding Ottoman Empire or the well-established Ming dynasty in China. No sane bettor would have placed their money on Europe as the genesis of globally vast colonial empires, much less the home of industrialization and the utter transformation of world economies several hundred years down the line. Yet by the dawn of the twentieth century, Europe and its direct descendant, the United States, dominated world affairs in a way that no other region had before. By 1527, as the imperial soldiers looted and pillaged their way through Rome, that future had started to take shape.[4]

The Great Divergence

This phenomenon, known as the Great Divergence, transformed western Europe from outpost to the absolute center of the world order. Starting with the Netherlands and Britain—the so-called Little Divergence that preceded the Great—Europe first slowly and painfully and then very suddenly leapfrogged over its most aggressive competitors in technological achievement, political power, and economic output. The growth and impact of Europe's rise make up the dominant historical processes of the last half millennium. Any understanding of our world that does not take these processes into studied consideration is incomplete: The legacies of colonialism and European domination are visible in every aspect of twenty-first-century life, from patterns of trade and economic development to sports and entertainment.

Nobody looking at the world in 1490 would have thought that future likely. Consider Europe at that time: Christopher Columbus was an experienced sailor, but his years-long efforts to launch a voyage west into the Atlantic had come to naught. Martin Luther was seven years old, and the prospect of a fundamental rupture in Christendom was inconceivable. Professional scribes produced as many handwritten copies of books as the printing presses that had started to crop up across western Europe. Gunpowder had redefined the siege and rendered the thin-walled castles that had been favored for centuries increasingly anachronistic, but armored men-at-arms on horseback still dominated the battlefield. In size, the army King Charles VIII of France marched into Italy in 1494 would not have been out of place in the campaigns of the Hundred Years' War a century prior.

The four decades preceding the Sack of Rome saw a dramatic rise in scale and intensity. The wars grew longer and more destructive; 1527, the year of the sack, was the thirty-third year of almost continuous warfare afflicting the Italian Peninsula and Europe beyond. The armies grew bigger, more sophisticated, and drastically more expensive. In response, the states employing them developed more complex and effective tools for marshaling resources. The first tentative voyages into the Atlantic—a few small ships cruising down the coast of West Africa in search of gold, ivory, and people to enslave—mutated into entire fleets bound for the Indian Ocean and armies bent on conquest in the recently encountered Americas. The printing press pioneered by Johannes Gutenberg seventy-five years before became ubiquitous, churning out enormous quantities of all kinds of material, but particularly religious propaganda.

By 1527, the path that led to the Great Divergence had become imaginable. Even if it was only a faint outline a long way down the road, the shape of that future world was coming into focus.

Why Europe? And *when* Europe? These two questions have occupied generations of history, political science, sociology, and economics scholars. The real transformation only came with the Industrial Revolution, some say, at the dawn of the nineteenth century; prior to that, China and Europe were neck-and-neck by every meaningful metric. Others argue that the exploitation of coal, which was readily available in western Europe, and rapacious pillaging overseas fueled the rapid growth of Europe at the expense of the rest of the world.

Others point further back to the seventeenth and eighteenth centuries, attributing Europe's explosive rise to factors like military technology and European states' economic ability to wage war. Other explanations include cultures of institutional, political, and technical innovation unique to western Europe, especially Britain and the Netherlands. For still other observers, the beginnings of the Great Divergence are to be found deep in the Middle Ages or even before, in amorphous European cultural characteristics, proto-capitalist stirrings, or the distribution of resources. A more convincing explanation in the "deep divergence" school of thought emphasizes a multipolar state system not found anywhere else in the world: a fragmented political landscape that created near-constant conflict within Europe, a continuous background hum of competition that set the tone for every other development in this period.[5]

All of these explanations and arguments have something to recommend them. Living standards and wages in Britain and comparably developed parts of India and China did not truly diverge until the dawn of the Industrial Revolution. But conversely, industrialization did not appear one day out of a clear blue sky; there had to be deeper roots to these developments, and the question is how deep into history those roots go.[6]

This book offers one answer to those two questions, or rather a slightly different way of framing and understanding them. Rather than focusing on a single variable, like a particular innovation or resource, it points to a particularly eventful period: the four decades between 1490 and 1530. In this brief span, less than a single human's lifetime, western Europe's future metamorphosis from backwater to superpower became possible thanks to a series of convulsive transformations.

It was not one single process or variable that caused these intense bouts of disruption, but the meeting of several. Voyages of exploration, expanding states, gunpowder warfare, the proliferation of the printing press, the expansion of trade and finance, and their cumulative consequences—religious upheaval, widespread violence, and global expansion—collided, interacting with one another in complex and unpredictable ways. This was an explosive mixture of developments, each of which was deeply consequential in its own right. The brief, intense period of their combination and impact dramatically altered the course of world history, laying the groundwork for a future that bears a remarkable resemblance to our own.

Economic Institutions

What brought these disparate trends—things as varied as the spread of printing presses and the use of mercenary armies—together was a particular set of attitudes toward credit, debt, loans, and investment. These attitudes governed how Europeans employed *capital*, their assets. We can think of them as *economic institutions*.

"Institution" here refers, on the most basic level, to a shared understanding of the rules of a particular game. More broadly, an institution extends beyond the rules to the systems, beliefs, norms, and organizations that drive people to behave in a particular way. Institutions get people to obey the rules of the game, to perpetuate them, and to tweak them in ways beneficial to those who use them. Institutions can be good or bad, helpful or detrimental, depending on the circumstances. The expectation that political loyalty will be rewarded with patronage—an institutional framework if ever there was one—might produce both durable ties and feckless corruption. How people behave in markets, what assumptions they bring to the transactions they make, how business and family dynamics interact: Institutions shape all of these things.[7]

Western Europe was not an especially wealthy place by broader Eurasian standards at the beginning of this period. Populations had fallen by as much as half from their peak in the early fourteenth century thanks to the combined calamities of the Black Death (mid-fourteenth century, with the continued recurrence of plague afterward) and a colder, less predictable climate. Bullion was in short supply. Destructive conflicts ravaged the continent for decades at a time, the Hundred Years' War between England and France being just one example. Internal strife racked practically every major kingdom in the second half of the fifteenth century. All of these factors contributed to a deep economic malaise that had lasted more than a hundred years.[8]

By the dawn of the sixteenth century, things had begun to turn around, but only just. Populations, the basis of all premodern economic growth, were beginning to rise across much of the continent. Trade was expanding once again. Still, none of this amounted to anything like an economic advantage, much less an indicator of future global dominance.

What Europe did have at this precise point in time was a set of economic institutions that were well suited to furthering each of those major processes that defined the coming era: exploration, state growth, gunpowder warfare, the printing press, and the consequences that went along with them. All of these things were expensive, capital-intensive processes and technologies. They depended on substantial amounts of money for initial financing, and even more to sustain them.

A ship or an entire fleet sailing off into the Atlantic required large up-front investments in the vessels, supplies, and labor to crew them. States of this period lacked the capacity to squeeze their subjects for all the cash necessary to fund their aspirations, so they needed loans and advances dependent on future revenues. The major purpose of those loans was to pay for gunpowder warfare on an increasingly enormous scale. War was a business, one with major up-front costs borne predominantly by private contractors who depended on credit to pay for recruitment and supplies. A printing press was a humble venture compared to a military campaign or a voyage to India, but it too necessitated a major outlay of capital for the type, press, paper, and expertise to operate it before a single penny of revenue appeared.

The same mechanisms and assumptions held sway everywhere, be it a prosperous Venetian merchant investing in a printing venture, an English trader buying a consignment of wool with only a token down payment, a Tyrolean nobleman mortgaging his lands to pay the signing bonuses of mercenary pikemen, a consortium of Spanish nobles and speculators pooling cash to pay an ambitious Genoese adventurer for a voyage into the unknown, or a king borrowing eye-watering sums of money from Augsburg bankers to buy his election as Holy Roman Emperor. Creditors gave out money in the expectation that they would get it back, either with return on the investment or with interest, depending on the type of transaction.

While this might sound obvious on its face, it actually requires a series of interlocking assumptions about the nature of money and credit, and an enormous amount of faith both in transactional parties and the broader framework that could sustain the terms of the deal. Trust between creditor and debtor or investor, trust between the parties and the authorities, both formal and informal, that could enforce a formal contract or an informal agreement: This trust in the reliability of the outcome was what allowed Europeans to pour increasing amounts of capital into these expensive processes. This was not the same as believing in guaranteed profits; loans by their nature imply risk, and speculative investments in new technologies and ventures can always fail. But in this case, enough people trusted in these shared assumptions, believed they would work, that they kept the spigot of capital flowing.

The economic institutions so central to this period were not the same as our present-day understandings. Credit was largely personal, relying far more heavily on reputation than on impersonal or mathematical measures of creditworthiness. Ties of kinship, marriage, ethnicity, and common origin, to name only a few, determined an individual's access to credit. Formal institutions and public methods of enforcement were deeply entwined with a far more intimate and private measure of obligation, of which money was only one part; it was as much a moral judgment about the worth of an individual, a firm, or even an entire community. The reverse was also true, in that monetary solvency spoke to moral and social worth.[9]

Why Then?

These were not entirely novel innovations in Europe at the close of the fifteenth century; in fact, the more commercially advanced regions and cities—places like the great trading centers of northern Italy and the Low Countries—had employed a sophisticated understanding of credit and investment for centuries, built on precisely these foundations. Nor were Europeans the only people in the world to pool their capital, utilize complex organizational forms for doing business, or extend loans for a variety of purposes. All of these things had existed for centuries, even if they appeared, disappeared, and then popped up once again over the millennia. From Rome to China, from the first century BC to the end of the Middle Ages, people found ways to do business and direct capital in productive ways. In that sense, fifteenth-century Europeans were hardly unique.[10]

But several things *were* different. First, these economic institutions were practically everywhere in western Europe. Multiple well-traveled axes of communication, mobility, and trade bound the region together. Goods, people, and ideas—including economic institutions shaping the availability and use of credit—could and did travel along these extensive networks.

Whether these institutions actually diffused, moving from place to place, or conditions were simply similar enough to drive the invention of similar solutions to the same problem is hard to say. Terminology and details varied substantially from place to place and sector to sector. Some regions had larger quantities of low-value coinage in circulation than others, which meant less use of everyday credit between common folk for their daily needs. These differences extended up the social spectrum: The Medici bankers of Florence organized their firm, and thus its capital, quite differently than did the Hanseatic traders of the Baltic or the Fugger merchant-capitalists of Augsburg. A coterie of Genoese financiers lending money to the queen of Castile, using her crown jewels as a guarantee, were not operating on the same scale as a German nobleman raising a modest company of pikemen on credit.

But all of them—from humble peasants buying ale and bread to the bankers underwriting state finance—understood the principles involved in extending loans and investments. Their most fundamental assumptions about security, collateral, risk, and reward aligned. The institutional framework functioned similarly all over western Europe because it had been traveling these routes across regions and up and down the social scale, under the radar, for centuries.[11]

Second, there were good reasons why those institutions had diffused (or been invented separately) across Europe. The later fourteenth and the fifteenth century, the key period of their development prior to their explosion at the beginning of the sixteenth, saw a major shortage of coinage. Mints closed, money changers went out of business, and goods went unsold, simply for lack of coin.

This was not a brief interlude; the "Great Bullion Famine" was an acute period in the middle of the fifteenth century, but the shortage lasted for decades. Silver was the medium through which most European business was transacted, and it was particularly scarce thanks to the exhaustion of mines and the massive negative trade balance Europe ran with the East. Its exports—cloth, mainly—were far less valuable than its imports. Bullion, gold and silver, was the only thing that could purchase the spices, silks, and other luxuries that European elites demanded. In the short run, the lack of coinage sharply contracted access to credit, particularly at the higher levels of the economy. Without coin, nobody could be sure their investment would bear fruit, or that their loan would be repaid. As a result, a deep depression gripped the economy throughout the middle of the century.

In the long run, however, business managed to continue. The way Europeans thought of money and credit evolved in response to the shortage. People found ways of working with little to no coin, as they had already been doing to some extent for centuries and grew more comfortable doing. When more coin did become available in the later fifteenth century, those institutions did not disappear; instead, they multiplied the effect of the newly abundant silver and gold, creating still more credit to flow through the economies of western Europe.[12]

Third, timing mattered. It was not so much that these institutions were superior to how the Indian merchants of Gujarat pooled capital or how Chinese farmers in Fujian valued their land, for example, but that they were particularly well suited to that particular moment. They effectively directed funds into a whole range of capital-intensive processes. Each of those processes had existed for some time, but the amount of capital pumped into them grew by orders of magnitude in a very short period of time. Money followed money when investors thought there were profits to be made. When state finance proved to be lucrative for lenders, rulers could borrow more, which forced other rulers to do the same. When a voyage down the coast of West Africa brought back gold and enslaved people, other financiers, seeing that opportunity was there for the taking, poured money into still more ambitious ventures. When the printing press found a road to profitability, more funds found their way into that industry.

The Crunch

The forty-year period on which this book focuses, from 1490 to 1530, saw greater and greater influxes of capital through this framework of economic institutions. Any one of these processes was a major development in its own right: Scholars have spent decades, centuries even, writing and arguing about them. There are good reasons for this. The emergence of the printing press, for example, can best be understood as a full-blown revolution in information distribution. The cobbling together of a truly global world that for the first time in human history included the Americas was not a minor blip. All of these processes collided in the short decades on either side of 1500. That was not a coincidence; the availability of capital had supercharged all of them.

Each process was intensely disruptive. The quick-as-lightning spread of Martin Luther's ideas, carrying the Reformation to the fringes of Europe within a few years, owed much to the new popularity of the printing press. War was ubiquitous: No fewer than thirty-two large-scale massacres of Italian civilians, some of which involved many thousands of victims, took place between the beginning of the Italian Wars in 1494 and the year 1528, just after the Sack of Rome. And Italy was only one theater of conflict—the New World empires of the Aztec and Inca fell within a generation of Columbus's departure in 1492, pouring the treasures of the Americas into European circulation and murdering vast numbers of people in the process.[13]

Any one of these developments was enough to upend the established order of the world, and they were all happening simultaneously, within a very concentrated period. They were not separate phenomena, but mutually reinforcing processes driven by the same underlying mechanisms. These processes then collided with a series of contingent, unforeseen events—accidents of birth and death, the timing of a decision, and so on—to produce an unprecedented global reaction.

That reaction was an age of transition, a time of extraordinary shifts in European life and society with far-reaching implications for the future of the world. We can call it a *critical juncture*, a decades-long crisis in which those various shifts converged to fundamentally alter the subsequent course of events. This critical juncture created *path dependence*: The future in which Europe came to dominate the world, while still a long way off, became imaginable only after this period of intense change. Increasing returns accompanied the enormous increase in scale that defined this forty-year period. Of course, there were plenty of critical junctures in the following three centuries that would eventually lead to the Industrial Revolution, but all of them depended on this first, foundational series of contemporaneous shifts.[14]

That is why this forty-year period matters in the grand scheme of history. But it is only half of the story. The other half is what a bewildering, unsettling, and eventful era this was to live through. Real people felt the Atlantic wind howling in their faces, heard the raucous chaos of a bustling port, and smelled the odor of burning gunpowder amid the madness of the battlefield. They fought, suffered, loved, bought, sold, plowed, spun, succeeded, and failed as the world around them changed irrevocably.

Momentous, world-altering events such as these can seem

impersonal if not woven into the fabric of everyday life. To that end, I've selected nine individuals to serve as windows into this story, real people who embodied the major themes of capital, state, warfare, and print in their daily lives, who both actively drove and passively experienced them. Some, such as Christopher Columbus, Queen Isabella of Castile, and the Ottoman sultan Suleiman the Magnificent, are well-known figures. Others, like the one-armed German nobleman Götz von Berlichingen or the hard-nosed English wool trader John Heritage, are less so. All of them help us better understand this era—what was at stake, what was lost, and what was gained.

It is easy to cast these changes as positive ones, as momentous climaxes in a larger heroic narrative. After all, they led directly to the Industrial Revolution and therefore our own, present world. It is always tempting to believe that we live in the best of all possible worlds, or at least a pretty good one, but grounding these shifts in the lives of real people, great and small, makes it clear that they were not necessarily—or even mostly—beneficial, at least not for the moment. Voyages of exploration led to mass enslavement, genocidal conquests, and the pillaging of entire continents. Rising states squeezed their subjects for taxes to pay for longer and more destructive wars, which in turn immiserated countless others. Printing fomented an information revolution, but the Reformation it helped create led to generations of vicious religious conflict and untold numbers of deaths as a result. Even if we accept that some degree of creative destruction is necessary for innovation and progress, it is destruction nonetheless.

Those costs cannot be forgotten. Balance sheets include both assets and liabilities. So too should the reckoning of this essential period of world history, which laid the groundwork in so many ways, both positive and negative, for where we find ourselves at present.

CHAPTER 1

———◦◊◦———

Christopher Columbus and Exploration

March 4, 1493

A knife-edged gust sliced through the rigging of the tiny ship. Wind from the south-southeast filled its triangular sail, driving the battered hull onward through the heaving waves of the eastern Atlantic. Early March was no time to be out on the open ocean, especially not at the end of the harshest and most dangerous winter sailors could remember. Ship after ship had gone down in the raging seas around the Iberian Peninsula. But after weeks of battling that fierce wind, the *Niña* was finally on the cusp of home.

A bustling port lay just ahead, tantalizingly close. The exhausted, sunken eyes of the ship's captain drank in the sight of the approaching city from the aft deck. He was perhaps forty years old or thereabouts. Decades spent exposed to the burning sun and salt spray of countless seas, from the burning equatorial coastline of West Africa to the icy environs of Iceland and the North Atlantic, had lined and creased his face into leathery folds. The man's name depended on precisely where he found himself at the moment: Cristoforo Colombo or Christoffa Corombo in his native Genoa, Cristóbal Colón in Spain and Portugal. In the Latin favored by the educated, he was known as Christophorus Columbus.

Seven long, challenging months had passed since Columbus set out with three ships from the tiny port of Palos, on the coast of Spanish Andalusia. They had first traveled south along the coast of Africa to the Canary Islands, through waters Columbus knew quite well. He had made the trip south at least once before, which meant he was familiar with the winds and currents of the area. And these sea lanes were becoming increasingly well traveled as Spanish and Portuguese ships brought back precious—and human—cargo from the Canaries and the great rivers of West Africa.

This familiarity was the source of Columbus's breakthrough revelation, one born of substantial practical navigational skill: To go west across the Atlantic, it was necessary to find westerly winds. Those winds, which Columbus was sure would take him on a shortcut to the riches of Asia, blew most reliably around the Canaries.

Working off of this fragile theory, Columbus and his crew went beyond the limits of European seafaring knowledge and sailed west into the unknown. Six weeks later, on October 12, 1492, they sighted land. They made landfall somewhere in the Bahamas or Turks and Caicos Islands of the Caribbean, where for the next three months Columbus cruised along the shores of this New World, marking the coastline of Cuba and Hispaniola before turning east for home across the Atlantic, confident that he had indeed reached the coast of Asia.

He was dead wrong, of course, but that voyage had nonetheless changed the course of history. Within decades, Old World diseases would ravage New World populations. Spanish conquistadors would topple the empires of the Inca and the Mexica. Treasure would flow into the coffers of Spanish kings, funding imperial projects on four continents.

All of that lay in the unknowable future as the *Niña* limped into Restelo's harbor, just outside Lisbon proper. A storm had separated it from the other remaining ship, the *Pinta*, a month before near the Azores. Still another terrible storm, one so vicious that it had "seemed to lift the caravel in the air," according to Columbus's diary, had forced the *Niña* into port here. Here happened to be the mouth of the river Tagus, the gateway to Portuguese Lisbon, instead of a city belonging to the Spanish monarchs Isabella and Ferdinand. Even more than Seville or Barcelona, however, the Portuguese port lay at the heart of a Europe that was rapidly expanding outwards.[1]

Whoever their current employers happened to be, Columbus and his crew were the quintessential representatives of the ever-growing world Lisbon represented. As with their Portuguese compatriots, it was not a feeling of visionary adventurism that drove the Genoese sailor out into the treacherous winds and complex currents of the Atlantic; rather, it was an insatiable hunger for profit that put him on the path to eternal infamy.

It was merchant-investors working in tandem with state-building monarchs who made the voyages of Columbus and his compatriots possible. Ships like the *Niña* did not appear out of thin air. Neither did the wages of their expert crews, or the expensive cannon that lined their decks. All of that cost money, which came from an alliance of financiers and royal interests. Only merchant-investors had the ready capital to fund these voyages, and only royal authorities could offer the umbrella of state authority for the protection and guaranteed monopoly rights that financiers required.

This era, a period two centuries in the making, marked the

first true beginning of a global world in human history. The story of that shift is less famous explorers gazing heroically into the unknown and more the scratching of quill pens in account ledgers, conversations between powerful royal officials and serious Italian financiers, and letters of credit and commercial contracts. The 1490s saw a massive influx of new investment, transforming tentative voyages into global business overnight.

The Roots of Atlantic Expansion

The briny reek of the sea, melding with the late medieval city stench of human and animal ordure, washed over the new arrivals as they pulled into port. Church bells tolling mingled with the hammering and sawing of timber in the port's busy shipyards competed for space on the wind with the cries of vendors hawking malagueta peppers and fresh-caught fish. Specialist German metallurgists, experts in the casting of cannon barrels, shivered in the late winter wind next to enslaved Africans taken from the Guinea coast and Florentine moneymen with ink-stained fingers. All had been pulled to Lisbon, voluntarily or otherwise, by the gravity of profit-oriented financial networks.

For more than 150 years, the city had served as the primary point of departure for expeditions traveling south for lands either little-known or unknown. Slowly but surely, ships crewed by Catalan, Genoese, and Portuguese mariners had crept their way down Morocco's prosperous coastline. Some twelve hundred miles southwest of Iberia lay the Canary Islands. The Romans had known about them, but their medieval successors were unaware of their existence. To the Genoese-led expedition that found them in the 1330s and the Europe that shortly learned of the discovery, they were something new and exciting. This revelation kicked off a flood of new undertakings, most of them operating out of the island of Majorca and directed south along the coast of Africa and into the unknown. Expert Catalan mapmakers and skilled Mediterranean sailors carefully plotted new routes, marked dangerous shoals, and charted winds and currents. After a caesura in the middle of the fourteenth century, business picked back up again soon after 1400, when the first successful attempt to conquer the Canaries came by way of a French expedition operating under the license of the king of Castile.[2]

The Portuguese were the most active explorers of the fifteenth century. Prince Henry "the Navigator" (1394–1460) has since received an undue amount of attention in popular narratives about the Age of Discovery. Henry was not a forward-thinking figure pulling a backwards Europe into global proto-modernity. In the fifteenth-century reality, Portuguese interest in Atlantic ventures long preceded Henry's time in the limelight. Portuguese sailors and ships were already a common sight in the teeming ports of western and northern Europe. Nevertheless, Henry's extensive activities in the realm of Atlantic exploration were in fact representative of the broader trends that formed the basis for the world of maritime activity that would produce Columbus a few decades later.

One thing stands out about this milieu: a distinct orientation toward profit-seeking, combined with a willingness to inflict violence. Strong religious sentiments, namely the concept of crusading, and the ideals of knightly chivalry wove themselves into a tapestry of lucrative bloodshed. Early Atlantic adventurers like those operating under the auspices of Prince Henry, and later Columbus, were hardly bold, altruistic explorers seeking out new knowledge in distant and uncharted waters. They were operating within a world of violence and commercial enterprise, where religious war and profit-hunting went hand in hand.

This was one of the defining features of the Atlantic adventuring world that eventually gave rise to Columbus: Prince Henry saw himself as a chivalrous knight, fighting Muslims with a crusader's zeal. At the same time, he was a keen investor with every finger in a different and potentially profitable pie. His intense interest in Atlantic maritime ventures fit neatly with his lust for profit. Henry's personal household—a wide-ranging organization of subordinates bound to the prince by personal ties, not his immediate family—was a beehive of this kind of intertwined activity. The household lay at the center of a web of profit-oriented investment that reached outward to merchants, ship owners, financiers, and nobles.[3]

Piracy, nominally directed at Muslim targets, was one such profitable activity. It was a violent outlet for the knights of Henry's household and the Portuguese nobility more broadly, while also proving quite lucrative. This business, known as "corsairing," was a constant source of low-level warfare in the western Mediterranean. Corsairs were not picky about their targets: Christian vessels were fair game if it could be argued that they were trading with Muslims.

That distinction could prove quite flexible. In 1426, for example, a ship Prince Henry owned, captained by a certain Fray Gonçalo Velho, tried to attack a very Christian merchantman. Gonçalo Velho was himself not only Christian but a member of a military-religious organization called the Order of Christ. Velho's attack failed, and he and his crew were captured and hauled into the port of Valencia. Velho and Prince Henry got off with an angry, chastising letter from the king of Aragon. This easy willingness to engage in any sort of high-seas violence if it promised profit crops up again and again in early Atlantic maritime history. It was an essential component of this volatile world.[4]

In the same vein, language of chivalry and crusading honed in encounters with Muslims served to justify the attempt to take the Canary Islands: A heavily armed expedition led by members of Henry's household would "convert" the pagan Canarians to Christianity. "In Henryspeak," writes his biographer Peter Russell, "conversion and enslavement were interchangeable terms." The ability to simultaneously treat newly encountered non-Christians as both objects of religious conversion and potential profit centers would have a long and tragic afterlife in the emerging Atlantic world, appearing again in Columbus's early assessment of the natives of the New World seventy years later.[5]

As Henry's sponsored efforts to conquer the Canaries were failing miserably, his corsairing activities continued, and other voyages operating under his banner were making their way south along the West African coast. The seemingly endless Saharan coast of northwest Africa was a formidable barrier. The occasional clusters of houses and craggy inlets in southern Morocco disappeared into nothingness. Waves of Saharan dunes extended all the way to the coastline. Strong, unpredictable gusts of fiery wind threatened to pull tiny caravels into rocky outcroppings and jagged reefs, ripping hulls open from stem to stern and leaving men for dead a thousand miles from home.

Further voyages in 1435 and 1436, directly sponsored by Henry and led by members of his household, had the dual mission of seeking profit and mapping this desolate coastline. There was little immediate profit in these journeys aside from enslaved people purchased from Muslim middlemen. What kept them going was the ever-present hope for gold.

Europeans of this time had a vague but basically correct understanding that gold came from farther south in Africa: vague, because they had no idea what Africa looked like, and basically correct, because the gold that reached Europe did overwhelmingly come across the Sahara from West Africa. Gold was valuable in any era, but it was particularly so in the first half of the

fifteenth century. Europe had been in the midst of a prolonged
bullion famine, with distinct shortages in both silver and gold, for
some time. The exhaustion of European mines and a consistently
high trade deficit with the East had created a drastic shortfall in
precious metals.[6]

Western Europe was a backwater in the long-distance trade
networks that connected it to Africa, the Indian Ocean, and East
Asia via the exchange routes that passed through Central Asia
and the Middle East. It had no precious metals or valuable spices
for export; its mass-produced cloth goods were not in demand on
the other side of the world; London and Paris were not teeming
with merchants from Calicut and Samarkand. This, more than
anything else, was why European caravels were heading out into
uncharted (for them) waters and not the equally—if not more—
capable Chinese junks or Indian dhows.

The search for gold, and immediate wealth, was one of the
driving forces behind the southward explorations of the Portuguese under Henry's aegis. As they inched down the coastline,
the Portuguese were entering a sophisticated and complex commercial world that was already deeply tied to the Mediterranean,
particularly the Muslim states of the Maghreb and Egypt. Local
traders protected their access to the valuable metal, one of a variety of goods—including cloth, iron, copper, and cowrie shells—
traded along routes that spanned from Mali to Morocco to Cairo
and beyond. Enslaved people were prominent among them and
had been for centuries, and the Portuguese quickly realized that
human beings, not gold, were the most immediately available
commodity.[7]

The profits from these early years of the slave trade sustained
consistent investment throughout the 1440s and beyond, when
Henry received a commercial monopoly on trading south of
Cape Bojador, a famous headland on the Saharan coast. A raiding

expedition to capture and enslave Africans led by a member of
Henry's household ran across the mouth of the Senegal River.
Further expeditions in the 1450s, farmed out to mostly Venetian
and Genoese merchant-adventurers, continued to head south,
reaching as far as present-day Guinea-Bissau.[8]

Henry's great press over the succeeding centuries is largely
the result of a nearly hagiographic chronicle he commissioned
in the 1450s: "O thou prince, little less than divine! I beseech
thy sacred virtues to bear with all patience the shortcomings of
my too daring pen, that would attempt so lofty a subject as is the
recounting of thy virtuous deeds, worthy of so much glory," reads
the author's invocation, which sets the general tone of the piece.
Ironically, the scope and ambition of Portuguese voyages grew
most notably in the wake of Henry's death in 1460.[9]

Fernão Gomes and the
Merchant-Investors of the Early Atlantic

In 1469, the royal monopoly Henry had held was leased to a well-
connected Lisbon merchant named Fernão Gomes. Gomes ruth-
lessly exploited this monopoly. His combination of political ties
and access to capital set the tone for this early Atlantic world.

Despite his importance at a key stage in early Atlantic expansion, Gomes is something of a shadowy figure. Few records
relating to his trade survive. Those that do are fragmentary.
Nevertheless, he speaks directly to the profit orientation of the
Atlantic world that produced Columbus and how the financial
networks of the late fifteenth century funded and incentivized
profit-seeking voyages.

Gomes was Portuguese, with close ties to the household of
King Afonso V. The African trade was not a free market; Gomes
was a minor nobleman, a gentleman-merchant, explicitly using

his royal connections to buy a monopoly, which represented a source of ready cash to a constantly cash-strapped king. He paid only 200,000 reis for this, roughly the price of twenty-five slaves, and despite tax breaks was often behind on those payments; even so, the Portuguese crown leased him another monopoly—this one on the trade in malagueta peppers—in 1473 for another relative pittance. Gomes's connections also went beyond the royal household. Within the diverse and wealthy mercantile community of Lisbon, Gomes was prominent. He was married to the daughter of an important Flemish expatriate merchant named Martin Lem (or Leme) and seems to have had financial ties throughout Lisbon's merchant community.[10]

Like Gomes, some of those Lisbon merchants and financiers were Portuguese. Others came from elsewhere, like Gomes's Flemish father-in-law. The major Italian cities all had outposts there: Florentines, Venetians, and Genoese were all represented. Each of these clans of merchant expatriates did business among themselves, as a unit tightly bound by family and civic loyalties, and retained their connections to their distant home cities. But they also did business with each other, pooling capital from their extended networks to use in a variety of profit-seeking ventures. Their assumptions about credit, investment, and risk were similar enough that there was no real barrier to cooperation, and all parties trusted in the institutional frameworks that allowed them to operate. The Fleming Lem, Gomes's father-in-law, had sought a monopoly on the cork trade in 1456, working in tandem with a Portuguese merchant and a number of Genoese.[11]

These resident merchants were mostly sedentary financiers, not merchant-adventurers. They had money to invest, and did so regularly, always with an eye toward maximizing their profits. They pooled their capital and cooperated on increasingly large-scale projects. Gomes's voyages to West Africa were a prime example: As many as twenty ships set out from Lisbon's harbor at a time to trade for ivory, gold, and slaves. Others continued farther down the coast, mapping as they went, always searching for new commercial opportunities in accordance with their contract. Gomes's ships reached deep into the Gulf of Guinea and then south past the equator, adding more than two thousand miles of detailed navigational knowledge. Over the six years he held the monopoly, from 1469 to 1475, ships under contract with Gomes accumulated new knowledge at a far faster rate than they ever had under Henry the Navigator.

Voyages of this kind were incredibly expensive propositions. Outfitting one ship for a months-long, six-thousand-mile round-trip voyage from Lisbon to the Gulf of Guinea, let alone an entire fleet, cost a king's ransom. Financial networks with deep international ties were a necessary prerequisite for this kind of activity. And backers expected profits. Gomes and his associates in Lisbon were hardly exceptional in this regard; the same mercantile and financial webs existed in every major maritime center of the western Mediterranean and the Atlantic, from London to Seville.

Italian and specifically Genoese expatriates were particularly prominent in these networks of financiers. They were the cornerstones of the partnerships that provided the capital for Gomes's and many other ventures, including that of Columbus. Genoa itself, located in the peninsular armpit where Italy meets the bulk of continental Europe in the west, was one of the major mercantile and financial hubs of the Mediterranean. Genoese ships traveled the connected seas, showing up everywhere from the edge of the Black Sea steppe to the Levant, London, and Bruges. Wealth flowed into the city from the twelfth century onward, the product of an increasingly lucrative long-distance trade powered by a complex set of financial tools and institutions. Ironclad commercial contracts, bills of exchange, and insurance agreements all helped to create a decentralized network of savvy and wealthy mercantile Genoese across Europe.[12]

But where Venice built an overseas and eventually an Italian empire, Florence dominated its Tuscan hinterland, and Milan acquired territorial hegemony in northern Italy, Genoa was not much of a political force by the second half of the fifteenth century. Its internal politics were too anarchic and violent, its oligarchs too competitive and disagreeable. Genoa's last great war with Venice, between 1378 and 1381, had seen the near conquest of the latter; within fifteen years, however, Venice recovered its maritime dominance while Genoa handed itself over to the French monarchs to acquire some semblance of political stability. The powerful Visconti dukes of Milan took over after that, and Genoa's colonial possessions fell to a variety of competing powers.[13]

Even while Genoa failed as a major Mediterranean political player, the Genoese themselves became even more important within the region's commercial and financial networks. They had already fanned out widely in both the eastern and western Mediterranean, forming both self-ruled colonies and resident communities inside other polities. Every major city in the western Mediterranean, from Tunis to Lisbon, had its resident Genoese merchants. The Genoese settled in Iberia took up residence in Castile, Aragon, and Portugal, and were particularly prominent in the Andalusian port city of Seville. They were chameleons who intermarried with the native elite and took pains to blend in. Early Atlantic voyages needed financiers, and these expatriate Genoese were moneymen par excellence. Aside from the Venetians, who were largely focused on the eastern Mediterranean rather than the west and the Atlantic, nobody in Europe had a deeper understanding of maritime trade and how to pay for it.

Their financial activities were one of the keys that would unlock the Age of Exploration.[14]

The Rise of Christopher Columbus

Risk-taking merchants and financiers were not Genoa's only export; the city's deep, protected harbor also produced some of the most technically skilled sailors and navigators of the age. One of those men was born in the city sometime in the early 1450s, the son and grandson of poor weavers in Genoa's thriving cloth industry. His name was Cristoforo Colombo, and he would spend the rest of his eventful life fleeing from his origins.

Columbus was defined by a sense of burning ambition at every stage of his life. Like every son of Genoa, Columbus knew that the sea offered a well-worn path to wealth and advancement. He was deeply ashamed of his humble background and actively obscured it whenever possible, creating the space for contrarian or conspiracy-minded modern commentators to cast him as Castilian, Portuguese, or Jewish. He was none of those things, only someone determined to leave his origins far behind.

Columbus's overwhelming drive for success often bled over into self-aggrandizement. He could be insufferable, boastful, and boorish, with precious little awareness of his many faults and weaknesses. More worrisome still was a tendency to violently overcompensate when he actually *was* aware of them, something that would play out tragically during his time as governor-general of the new Spanish territories in the Caribbean.

At the same time, however, Columbus was a highly skilled sailor and possessed at least some measure of real charisma. He had raw mental gifts: His friend and chronicler Andrés Bernáldez described him as a man of "great intellect but little education." Columbus's ambition could express itself in arrogant and ill-planned soliloquies about his greatness—he treated the king of Portugal to a particularly needling one upon his return in 1493—but also in the tireless pursuit of his goals, whatever those happened to be.[15]

Precisely when he took to the life of a Mediterranean sailor is, like so much else about Columbus's early life, unclear. His later habit of creating a glorious record of past accomplishments for himself obscures much about this period. One of the rare Genoese documents that refers to him states that he was still working in the wool business with his father to some extent in 1472, but he may have gone to sea for the first time before that, as a teenager in the 1460s. By the mid-1470s, he seems to have become a full-time sailor, and a well-traveled one at that. It is not easy to reconstruct the exact pattern or chronology of his journeys, especially given his tendency to lie and exaggerate. Over the next decade, however, they seem to have taken him to the farthest limits of the Mediterranean and the Atlantic.

He endured the heaving, driving seas of the northern Atlantic on trips to England and Ireland, and perhaps even beyond them to Iceland. A course due west took him to the Azores, recently discovered islands that were becoming sources of great wealth as a center of sugar production. The trade in alum, a salt necessary for the big business of the textile industry, brought him to the Aegean island of Chios in the distant east. He felt the harsh, biting desert winds coming off the Sahara on a trip south to the sweltering Gulf of Guinea, then the very limit of the known world.

By the middle of the 1480s, the Genoese sailor had acquired a breadth of experience that very few of his contemporaries could match. No single one of Columbus's voyages was extraordinary for a Genoese sailor: Genoese ships and foreign ships crewed by expert sailors from the city regularly plied the busy Atlantic sea lanes leading to northern Europe, the Atlantic islands, and south to West Africa. But for one man to go to all of those places, from Iceland to Chios to Guinea, was unparalleled. Even allowing some space for his customary self-regard, Columbus's assessment of himself stands: "Every sea so far traversed have I sailed," he wrote later, and God "endowed me abundantly in seamanship." In the course of these journeys, he accumulated a formidable practical knowledge of Atlantic currents and winds. He also learned how these long-distance voyages—routine, but fiendishly complicated in both financing and logistics—were paid for and organized.[16]

At some point, likely in the late 1470s, Columbus moved to Portugal permanently. From his new home in Lisbon, the Genoese sailor stood on the cutting edge of an expanding world, and one that was becoming increasingly complicated.

In 1475, the Portuguese crown took back its trading monopoly from the Lisbon merchant Fernão Gomes. It is almost certain that the reason for this was the outbreak of civil war within Iberia, specifically over the plum prize of the throne of Castile, one of the peninsula's major kingdoms. We will return to this subject in more detail in the next chapter, but for now suffice it to say that Queen Isabella's accession to the throne was far from seamless. King Afonso V of Portugal was married to his niece Juana, another potential claimant to the Castilian crown. War broke out between the two sides in 1475, with Isabella emerging victorious with the help of her husband, Ferdinand, the soon-to-be king of Aragon.[17]

Isabella's victory (and Afonso V's defeat) kick-started the process of Spanish state-building, but it also had major effects on the early Atlantic that Columbus inhabited. The Portuguese had never enjoyed a total monopoly on African trade; French, Flemish, and especially Castilian operators had repeatedly challenged their hegemony, most successfully in the Canary Islands.

The Portuguese had no problem with these speculative voyages so long as they paid the required licensing fees. The war over the Castilian throne turned this entire Atlantic rim into a full-blown war zone. Between 1475 and 1478, Castilian ships made slaving and trading journeys to West Africa and occupied several of the Cape Verde Islands. On the whole, however, the war at sea went the way of the Portuguese. A major naval battle just off the coast of Guinea in 1478 was a total Portuguese victory. The settlement of the 1479 Treaty of Alcáçovas ceded the Canaries to Castile and the other Atlantic islands to Portugal. West African trade would belong to the Portuguese, and so would anything beyond what was presently known.[18]

Two notable facets of the maritime aspects of this conflict deserve attention. The first is the extent of royal involvement of both the Castilians and the Portuguese. The kings of Portugal had previously been happy to take their cut of profits from licensed voyages or monopoly payments. Afonso V, however, saw control of African trade as an essential royal project and source of revenue that needed to be protected. Conversely, the crown of Castile was less involved than the Portuguese. It wanted its financial cut—20 percent—from licensed expeditions during the war, and it wanted all of the Atlantic islands: the Azores, Madeira, the Canaries, and the Cape Verdes. While Isabella only acquired the Canaries, this desire still marked a greater direct interest in Atlantic ventures than before.

The second aspect is scale. The Castilian fleet the Portuguese defeated in 1478 consisted of thirty-five vessels, all of which were loaded down with valuable ivory, gold, and human cargo at the time. Those thirty-five ships represented a massive financial stake on the part of the investors, of whom the Castilian crown was just one, and the return on investment would have been shockingly high had the ships made it home. First Gomes, then the Portuguese crown, and now the Castilians were seeing just how much money there was to be made from these ventures. Thanks to those profits, Columbus was the direct beneficiary of this conflict.[19]

Columbus's Plan

Columbus rode the wave of increasing interest in these kinds of voyages well into the 1480s. He traveled into the sharp winds east to Madeira in 1478 as the agent for a substantial Genoese sugar-buying consortium, the Centurione. This immensely lucrative (and growing) sugar business also explains his contemporaneous trips to the Azores and the Canaries. Columbus went further still, too: He felt the oppressive, humid heat of the Guinea coast on a journey to the brand-new Portuguese trading base of São Jorge da Mina sometime between 1482 and 1484, presumably trading in ivory, gold, and enslaved people. Year by year, the volume of this traffic increased, as did the returns to the merchant-financiers and the Portuguese crown. As the Atlantic opened and the money flowed, Columbus forged his way from irrelevance to power. He married an impoverished Portuguese noblewoman, Filipa Moniz Perestrelo, and with her had a son, Diego, who would become the focus of his dynastic ambitions.

By the middle of the 1480s, Columbus was beginning to formulate the plan for which he would eventually become famous. Experience had made him an expert on the Atlantic. Practical, hard-won knowledge went a long way, and to that base Columbus began to add a more theoretical supply of geography and cartography. The new technology of printing was fundamental to his education, and its spread made it possible for an autodidact without much in the way of formal schooling to acquire more elite learning. The works he read over and over were all printed, rather than the prior standard handwritten manuscripts; copies made their way to Columbus's little library from Louvain, Antwerp, Seville, and Venice.

Geography, both practical and theoretical, was a much-discussed and written-about topic in Columbus's early Atlantic world. As we shall see shortly, King João II of Portugal maintained a coterie of learned advisors around him at all times. The ancient geographical texts of men like Ptolemy were necessary to possess a fundamental understanding of the subject, and Columbus was plenty familiar with them. He also read more recent works, especially the early fifteenth-century *Imago Mundi* of the French cardinal Pierre d'Ailly. He read voraciously and actively, annotating his texts like a proper student. His edition of Marco Polo features some 366 notes on everything from the spices of Java and the pearls of Japan to the Mongol khan's facility for training hunting eagles. Columbus's readings were not especially critical, but they gave him a stock of learned information to buttress his practical skills.[20]

The aforementioned cardinal Pierre d'Ailly was the author who had by far the greatest impact on Columbus's education. He was also directly responsible for Columbus's catastrophically mistaken belief that the planet was much smaller than it actually is. This foundational "insight" was fortified by the then-current musings of Florentine cosmographer Paolo dal Pozzo Toscanelli, who went a step further by arguing not only for a smaller globe, but a narrower Atlantic. Columbus was familiar with Toscanelli, namely with a letter Toscanelli had sent to the king of Portugal in 1474 outlining his views. It is important to note that despite his particularly uncritical readings, Columbus was not the only one who believed this. Some of the most important geographers and cartographers of the age were just as wrong. None, however, fought as hard for that mistaken cause as he did.[21]

At some point in the 1480s, Columbus began lobbying to voyage west into the Atlantic. The story he told later was one of uninterrupted and unbroken confidence, a detailed plan hatched fully formed from his brilliant mind. Naturally, this was far from the truth. The target of his voyage may have been the Indies, as he later claimed, but there were other, equally plausible destinations: the Antipodes, the long-hypothesized but unknown continent that many thought existed opposite Eurasia; or more Atlantic islands like Madeira or the Azores, whose exploitation had already proven lucrative for the Portuguese crown and the Genoese sugar merchants for whom Columbus had been an agent.

But for his plan to move forward, Columbus needed a royal license. The Iberian monarchs—João II of Portugal and the dual monarchy of Isabella and Ferdinand in Castile and Aragon—were the most promising means of achieving it.

The Portuguese Atlantic

The year of Columbus's first approach to King João II was likely 1484. This was a propitious time to be pitching a long-distance, exploratory voyage to the Portuguese monarch: João II was a classic state-builder in the late medieval mold who explicitly set out to strengthen the power and financial security of central institutions in Portugal. This is a process to which we will return in depth in the next chapter. What is notable here is how for João II, the state-building process manifested itself in a specific royal interest in and control over overseas commerce and voyages of exploration. Where his predecessors had simply wanted a cut of the proceeds, João II wanted to direct all commercial activity in Africa through the royal household. The foundation of the trading port at São Jorge da Mina on the Gold Coast, which Columbus presumably visited on his trip to the Gulf of Guinea, had been an explicitly royal project.[22]

While profits rolled in from African ventures, João furthered the southerly exploratory voyages that the merchant Gomes had begun down the coastline. Two—or more likely three—expeditions under the command of Diogo Cão between 1482 and 1486 pushed past the equator, to and then up the Congo River, and south to the coasts of what are now Angola and Namibia. The profitability of the ongoing trade setup in Africa was an easy justification for further explorations; if gold, ivory, and people to enslave were present in such quantities in Guinea, what might they find farther south?[23]

Trading opportunities were one reason for funding expensive exploratory voyages, but there were other components at play as well. Another was the ongoing war against the western outposts of the Islamic world in North Africa. Legend held for centuries that a Christian king of great wealth and power, Prester John, lurked somewhere on the other side of Muslim territories. If they could link up with this mythical monarch, perhaps Islam could be defeated once and for all, and the Holy Land might return to Christian ownership. This spoke to a vein of messianic destiny running through the Portuguese royal family, particularly João's successor, Manuel I. The second reason was more straightforwardly commercial: The Indies were the source of exceptionally valuable trade goods. Spices were always in high demand, and every competent merchant knew that the Muslim states of Egypt and the Ottoman Empire blocked direct access to these goods and charged enormous fees as middlemen. Getting around them and straight to the source presented a commercial opportunity of incalculable value.[24]

Heading south to find the end of Africa would eventually take the voyagers to the Indies, but Columbus had another option: If he was right that the Atlantic was narrow and the world was small, a westward voyage would be not only viable but preferable.

There was no need to brave the long and punishing southward journey before nearing the source of those spices. The Indies were lurking just over the horizon, in the direction of the setting sun.

This, as best we can tell, was Columbus's pitch to João II. The Portuguese king did not bite. There were two reasons for this. First, João's team of navigational and geographic experts found his project implausible. Second, João found Columbus himself presumptuous and off-putting, particularly his exorbitant demands for rewards. João preferred to use members of his household for these kinds of voyages, like Diogo Cão, but he was also not averse to handing out contracts. In fact, he licensed a Flemish navigator named Ferdinand van Olmen to undertake a westward voyage very similar to Columbus's proposed project several years later, though he did not fund him. On balance, it seems most likely that the success of Cão's voyages combined with João's dislike of Columbus scuttled any hopes of Portuguese backing for the Genoese adventurer. At any rate, João soon launched another, even more ambitious effort than what Columbus had proposed. Under the command of Bartholomeu Dias, this expedition succeeded in rounding the Cape of Good Hope and entering the southernmost reaches of the Indian Ocean in 1487 and 1488. The riches of the East were within reach.[25]

Finding Patronage

Columbus had other options, though. The Catholic monarchs of Spain, Isabella of Castile and Ferdinand of Aragon, were similarly in the market looking to finance overseas ventures. They had given licenses to numerous expeditions during the civil war of 1475–79, and even in the late 1480s were backing the final attempts to conquer the Canary Islands. Columbus made himself at home at court and set about building support for himself and his project. This was a slow process beset by frustrations, but Columbus never doubted that he would prevail. His bullheadedness eventually gave him access to both patronage and capital, the two most essential components that would put him on the sea lanes to the discovery of the Americas. In the end, it was political and financial backing—not his exhaustive and well-respected geographic knowledge—that made his voyage a reality.[26]

The story of Columbus's project can be told, and has been many times, as a series of heroic scenes: Columbus's humiliating rejection at the hands of João II's panel of experts; his audiences with the Catholic monarchs of Spain, the humble Genoese weaver's son rising to the occasion to convince some of the greatest and bluest-blooded personages in Europe of his personal brilliance and the rightness of his cause; those forward-thinking royals, perceiving the possibilities and backing a venture that would change the shape of the world forever; his dejection at Isabella's final dismissal in the exotic, newly conquered Moorish city of Granada, departing the city for France or Genoa, only to be overtaken on the road outside the city by a royal messenger who told him the queen had changed her mind.

Those tableaux are far more narratively pleasing but less accurate than the reality of a dogged, motor-mouthed social climber pulling every political and financial string he could find over a period of six or seven years, while rulers busy with far more important ventures spared a few moments here and there to hear the pitch.

Columbus's time at court was a gradual process of inserting himself into overlapping networks of officials, important nobles, and financiers who already had interests in numerous Atlantic ventures. Some of those interests were rooted in messianic or apocalyptic trends looking for the ultimate defeat of Islam and the reclamation of Jerusalem. The forcible conversion of pagans

went along with this. Others, more of them, were simply looking for new venues for the pursuit of honor and chivalry. We
should not discount the importance of these lines of thinking;
Columbus himself believed in them wholeheartedly, and he knew
well their ability to persuade others. The last interest group was
purely commercial: merchant-investors of various stripes looking
for return on their capital. These were not mutually exclusive, as
we shall see, nor were they limited to the court of Ferdinand and
Isabella. In fact, they cooperated more or less seamlessly to push
forward the overall project of Atlantic expansion in both Portugal
and Spain.

It took the combined efforts of several groups, among which
all of the above interests were represented, to put Columbus over
the top and out to sea with the *Niña*, *Pinta*, and *Santa Maria* in
1492. He grew close to the court of Isabella and Ferdinand's heir,
their somewhat dull and less-than-impressive son Don Juan,
Prince of Asturias. This gave Columbus a series of back channels
to the royal court, strings he could pull to build support for his
venture. The most important of these connections was to Fray
Diego Deza, then the prince's tutor and later a bishop, head of
the Spanish Inquisition, and archbishop of Seville. The prince's
court was full of such rising stars, nobles and ecclesiastics alike,
who would go on to occupy powerful and influential positions.
Columbus's own burning ambition to achieve some degree of
noble status had only strengthened over the years—he was determined to ride those coattails as far as they could take him.

Another group was centered around the small seaport of Palos,
also in Andalusia. Palos has been a backwater for most of its history, overshadowed by nearby Seville, but for a brief moment in
the last quarter of the fifteenth century it was a key hub in the
emerging Atlantic. Ships and sailors from this small port had been
deeply involved in the ill-fated Castilian trading, slaving, and

corsairing expeditions during the War of the Castilian Succession between 1475 and 1479. Despite their lack of success in those ventures, Palos was home to a vast wealth of seafaring expertise. For this reason, it was the home port for Columbus's first, fateful voyage.

The final key group to back Columbus was the consortium of financiers and nobles who had overseen the final conquest of the Canary Islands in 1480. This was a clique that already possessed a substantial stake in Atlantic ventures, with Castilian financial official Alonso de Quintanilla at its center. Quintanilla had brought together a syndicate that included two Genoese merchants, Francesco Pinelli and Francesco da Rivarolo, the Florentine Gianotto Berardi, and the Andalusian Duke of Medina Sidonia. All operated in or near Seville, the jumping-off point for the Canary adventures. This was where the money was, and all were experienced investors. The Genoese formed a tight-knit and wealthy group, well connected to each other, to other Genoese merchants scattered throughout the Mediterranean, and to the royal court. Berardi had worked as a local agent for the Seville branch of the Medici Bank in addition to his own entrepreneurial activities, importing human cargo from West Africa to Lisbon and then reselling them. Quintanilla had found this group and brought them together for the Canary conquest. He would do the same, with much the same group, for Columbus.

Another key contributor, one unconnected to the previous Canary venture, was the Aragonese treasury official and financial wizard Luis de Santángel. In the final accounting, it was Santángel who brought all the different sources of funding together to pay for Columbus's expedition.[27]

The amount of money required—2 million maravedis, roughly the annual income of a mid-level provincial aristocrat—was substantial, but not mind-blowing. For comparison, Santángel had loaned the Spanish crown 10 million maravedis in 1491 to cover a variety of expenses. The ongoing military campaign against the Moors in Granada had required a loan roughly sixteen times that size. It certainly did not require Queen Isabella to pawn her precious jewels for ready cash, as the old story goes. Even in the context of maritime expeditions, the outlay was minor compared to the twenty-ship fleets of the Lisbon merchant Fernão Gomes, or the Castilian expeditions to West Africa during the late 1470s. Still, sums of that scale did not magically appear out of thin air. The Catholic monarchs were tied up with other financially draining projects, namely the final conquest of Granada. They could not simply snap their fingers and make the money appear, even if that had been the nature of their involvement with Columbus's expedition, which was not the case.[28]

How the funding came together provides a window onto an entire world of mercantile investment and the attitudes that underpinned it. Columbus was to front a quarter, 500,000 maravedis. He obviously did not have the cash on hand, so Quintanilla's syndicate in Seville provided it. Another quarter of the capital came from Palos, which also provided two ships for the voyage. The fishermen and merchants of Palos had been dodging their taxes for some time, and the two tiny caravels—the *Pinta* and the *Niña*—represented a payment in kind. Ferdinand and Isabella were to provide half the total, 1 million maravedis, plus Columbus's wages of 140,000 maravedis. The Crown did not have this kind of liquid capital sitting around, so Luis de Santángel turned to the very same network of Genoese moneymen in Seville, who backed Quintanilla for a short-term loan. Francesco Pinelli was the key figure there. To pay back that loan, Santángel authorized in the region of Extremadura a campaign of indulgence sales. These involved a payment in return for a remission of the buyer's sins, which was confirmed by a printed document. The proceeds of these sales, minus the printer's fee, went to the Crown, and from there to the Genoese financiers. It was a nifty little piece of work by Santángel, and Columbus was the beneficiary of these existing relationships and networks of state and mercantile financing.[29]

Columbus was not some doe-eyed naïf when it came to this aspect of planning, his nose too buried in books and maps and idealistic dreams to comprehend the monetary realities of his plan. He was a Genoese sailor born to a world of merchant ventures paid for by exactly this kind of investment cartel. His entire adult life had taken place in an Atlantic context where voyages like this were the norm. He had participated in many of them, including the Centurione sugar venture to Madeira and the other Atlantic isles, along with the trip to the Guinea coast. In fact, it is tempting to see that background as the precise reason why investors would be willing to stake their money on him. He understood how much capital would be necessary and what the return on that investment would look like for the various backers. Columbus understood the rules of this particular game.

The ultimate fate of Columbus's expedition was decided not so much by Columbus himself, but by a series of less exalted protagonists: the septuagenarian Quintanilla, the master of political wheeling and dealing, who bridged the gap between the royal court and the merchant-investors of Seville; Santángel, the financial genius who found creative ways of generating revenue to pay back investors' short-term loans; and numerous sober Italian moneymen with their fingers in a wide variety of lucrative pies. In the end, the success of Columbus's expedition came down to pens scratching figures in account books and shouted orders to clerks in cramped countinghouses. Commercial contracts and loan papers, handwritten bills of credit and indulgence letters rolling off printing presses by the thousands, conversations between powerful and wealthy people in the back rooms of palaces and richly appointed merchants' houses: These were the things that made Columbus's voyage possible.

Columbus's Voyages

Columbus's first voyage was a relatively brief affair. Seven months passed between his departure from Palos and his arrival in Lisbon, a walk in the park compared to the brutally demanding journeys of the Portuguese explorers Diogo Cão and Bartholomeu Dias in the 1480s. But what happened upon Columbus's arrival was as important as the journey itself: He crowed about his discoveries to King João II, who was miffed enough to nearly detain him and refused to let him return to his home port at Palos. It is not difficult to imagine how the intensely self-satisfied and not especially self-aware Columbus would have presented his discoveries, which he was convinced were around the rim of the Indian Ocean in the east. Far more important was the letter Columbus wrote and dispatched to Spain. He had first composed it while at sea, on February 15, and added a postscript upon arriving in Lisbon on March 4, 1493.

It was this letter, which he sent to both Isabella and Ferdinand and the arch-financier Luis de Santángel, that made Columbus and his discoveries famous, launching the myth that still resonates today. The letter quickly circulated and was printed numerous times, forever shaping the perception of both Columbus himself and the lands to which he had traveled: "And so it is that our Redeemer has granted to our most illustrious King and Queen, and to their famous kingdoms the achievement of so lofty a matter, at which all Christendom must rejoice and celebrate great festivities and give solemn thanks to the Holy Trinity, with many solemn prayers, for the exaltation that shall be derived from the conversion of so many peoples to our holy faith and, secondly, for the material benefits which will bring refreshment and profit."[30]

There could hardly be a better encapsulation of the forces and dynamics that drove the emerging exploration of the Atlantic. Royals took the credit, and vaguely plausible ideas about Christian conversion justified the expeditions. Lurking on the edges while driving both the goals and the mechanics of these expeditions was the expectation of return on investment. In fact, the initial contracts that had been drawn up between Columbus and the Crown dealt only with trade rights and control of territory, not a mission of religious conversion.[31]

Seeing the modest quantities of gold and other valuable goods that had returned with Columbus, money poured in for a follow-up expedition: seventeen ships, which were outfitted over the summer and departed for the Americas soon thereafter.

It was on this voyage that Columbus first floated the idea of enslaving people at a massive scale as a way of making this new expedition pay out, just as the Portuguese had done in West Africa. The brutal tactics Columbus and his subordinates employed on this voyage, including the mass exploitation of the native population, set the tone for all future Spanish endeavors in the Americas.

The Portuguese Break Through to India

By Columbus's third voyage in 1498, the Portuguese were finally sailing past the discoveries of Cão and Dias a decade prior. Whatever Columbus had found was obviously not the Indies, and for the Portuguese, the immense profits of the real India were just around the corner. It is not entirely clear why they waited so long to follow up on Dias's rounding of Africa in 1488; the most plausible theories revolve around King João II's many other pressing concerns, namely those of succession, tensions with Castile and

Aragon, and his rocky relationship with the Portuguese nobility. Some in Portugal resented the increasing strength of the monarchy and sought to curb it. Overseas expansion, the profits from which funded the Crown's expansive ambitions, was a point of disagreement and conflict about that larger issue.[32]

At the same time, King João II's existing interest in Africa was immensely profitable. The Portuguese crown brought in 8,000 ounces of gold per year between 1487 and 1489, enough to mint nearly 64,000 Venetian ducats' worth of gold currency. That was already a substantial amount, which rose further to 22,500 ounces (roughly 180,000 ducats' worth) between 1494 and 1496. Those amounts did not count the massive revenues from other sources, such as the 1.1 million reis the Florentine merchant Marchionni paid for a monopoly on trading in Benin in 1487. That 1.1 million reis was five times what Fernão Gomes had paid in 1469 for his monopoly on African trade. The numbers themselves are less important than the picture they paint of the drastic increase in Portuguese activity in these years.[33]

João II died in 1495. Without a direct heir, he was succeeded by his cousin, Manuel I. More than any other Portuguese monarch of this period, Manuel found appealing the apocalyptic, messianic idea of outflanking Islam and defeating it once and for all. Voyages to the Indies would open up a new front in this war and perhaps find allies, like the hitherto hypothetical Christian king Prester John. To Manuel and his immediate circle, these ideas were hardly flights of fancy—they were a powerful reason to return to long-range exploration after 1495. However, the Portuguese nobility put up strong resistance to such a risky venture, and one whose proceeds would presumably strengthen the royal party at their expense.[34]

The result of this infighting and bickering was a small expedition, comprising four ships and between 148 and 170 men, led by a compromise candidate named Vasco da Gama, a man with ties to both the powerful noble faction and Manuel's household. An expedition of this modest size was the most that could be managed given the ongoing conflict within the ranks of the Portuguese elite. Those four ships were full of men with experience in Atlantic voyaging and trading. The pilot of one ship, for example, had served on Fernão Gomes's voyages in the early 1470s. As was the norm for these ventures, it was partially financed by Italian mercantile interests. The same Marchionni who had bought a monopoly on trading in Benin in 1487 paid outright for one of the caravels, the *Berrio*. Whatever Manuel and his advisors were thinking about outflanking Islam, commercial incentives played a major role in funding and equipping the expedition.

On July 8, 1497, da Gama's tiny fleet set out from Lisbon and the mouth of the Tagus. It was gone for more than two years, finally limping home in September 1499 after a round-trip journey of more than twenty thousand miles. What da Gama and his compatriots found on the course of this epic passage was every bit as earth-shattering as Columbus's expeditions, and substantially more so in the short term. Da Gama had opened a direct route to India, an entry point into the richest trading system in the world.

The Indian Ocean trade networks formed a rough triangle linking the East African coast in the west, India in the middle, and the Malay Peninsula in the east. From there, its tendrils reached even farther into the Gulf of Thailand, the South China Sea, the Red Sea, and deep into the interior of Africa and Asia. Cloves, cinnamon, ginger, pepper, gold, pearls, silk: The Indian Ocean provided luxury goods in enormous quantities, all of which were in exceptionally high demand in a relatively impoverished Europe. That impoverishment was notable in the poor quality of trade goods da Gama tried to exchange for luxuries in

Calicut: wool cloth, a dozen coats, six hats, a bale of sugar, six basins, two barrels of rancid butter, two of honey, and some coral. It was the rough equivalent of walking into an Apple Store with a bag of russet potatoes and a pocketful of pennies. Nevertheless, da Gama managed to acquire enough spices to make for a profitable voyage: According to one estimate, it repaid the initial investment sixty times over.[35]

Marchionni had backed this venture and presumably saw a handsome return on his speculative investment. Other investors immediately jumped in, which helps to explain why the expedition that followed da Gama's was so much larger. It departed Lisbon in March 1500, just six months after da Gama had returned, and included thirteen ships and more than fifteen hundred men. Marchionni's syndicate financed one of the largest and best-equipped vessels on this voyage, which returned home in 1501 groaning under the weight of pepper, cinnamon, and other spices. This syndicate immediately backed another venture that same year, this one an entirely private expedition of four ships led by João de Nova. It too returned home loaded down with spices, and once again produced a sizable profit for the investors.[36]

The Portuguese crown sent out fleets of ever-increasing size on an annual basis like clockwork. Marchionni continued to invest in these voyages, and so did others: The extremely wealthy and well-connected Lisbon merchant woman Catarina Dias de Aguiar was a heavy investor in multiple India fleets, including that of 1503. So were various members of the Portuguese high nobility. Marriages and long-term commercial associations bound the merchant-investors and nobility together, particularly in Lisbon. The landed wealth of the nobility easily translated into investment capital for overseas voyages, and it did so regularly as the sixteenth century dawned. Further voyages took in financing from even more distant sources. Everybody wanted in on the action: The Fugger family of Augsburg, Europe's wealthiest and most powerful bankers, were heavily involved in the 1505 voyage. Additional consortia of German merchant-investors also provided large sums that same year.

Despite the wealth of money made from such ventures, commerce was only part of the rationale behind these clockwork expeditions. Manuel I had not forgotten the long-term goal of completely defeating Islam. The nobles who led and participated in these voyages were more interested in corsairing—piracy sanctified with a sprinkle of holy war—against the predominantly Muslim merchants and trading cities of the Indian Ocean than they were in peaceful commerce. In one particularly brutal incident that set the tone for future engagements, da Gama set fire to a helpless Muslim merchant ship he captured at sea: "With great cruelty and without any pity the admiral [da Gama] burned the ship and all who were in it," wrote an eyewitness. The reek of roasting flesh and ash were an ominous sign of Portuguese arrival. By 1511, Portuguese ships had engaged in barbaric acts from the Red Sea in the west to Malacca in the east. Beheadings, mutilations, hangings, and the omnipresent booming of cannon marked the Portuguese entry into this trading world from Mozambique in Africa to Ormuz on the Persian Gulf.[37]

The ships paid for by associations of merchant-investors were just as effective at committing shocking acts of violence as they were at finding profit in the spice trade. That purely commercial voyage sent by Marchionni and the other investors in 1502 still found time for a spot of corsairing and raiding. This had been just as big a part of the profit-seeking strategies of early Portuguese exploration down the African coast as trade in the time of Henry the Navigator, and it carried on here uninterrupted.

The End of Columbus

While the Portuguese were soon buried in the wealth of the Indies, the same was not true for Columbus, who quickly found himself in over his head, as did the Catholic monarchs. Whatever his substantial talents as a navigator and self-promoter, they did not extend to leadership or decision-making under pressure.

Columbus's governance of the West Indies showcased a disastrous mixture of cruelty, delusion, and panic. An expedition into the heart of Hispaniola in 1495 left thousands of the island's natives dead. Many more were captured to be taken back to Spain and sold into slavery. The idea of human beings as walking profit and labor centers already had a long history in the emerging Atlantic world. It had an even longer history in Genoa itself, one of the few places where slavery was standard practice in late medieval Europe. Columbus had been raised in Genoa and the Atlantic, and given this background, it was not a leap for him to discuss the possibilities of slaving as an economic model: In a 1498 letter to Ferdinand and Isabella, for example, he judged that perhaps four thousand people could be sold in Seville, netting 20 million maravedis. "And although at present they die in shipment," he wrote, "this will not always be the case, for the Negroes and the Canary Islanders reacted in the same way at first."

This easy recourse to slavery as a means of generating returns in an otherwise unprofitable venture would lay a tragic foundation for the future. Even after he was removed from his governorship in disgrace, Columbus's viciousness and incompetence had already woven themselves into the Spanish colonial project as a whole.[38]

Columbus's second and third voyages, in 1498 and 1502–4, searched with increasing desperation for the Asian mainland even as his health deteriorated, his body racked by a variety of painful ailments acquired over his last exhausting years. He had already lost his perpetual claim to govern his discoveries, and the Catholic monarchs had long since stripped him of his monopoly. The wealth of the West Indies could only be tapped in the form of enslaved people and meager gold mines rather than the incalculable riches of the Indies. His greatest claim, that he had found a new route to the East, was clearly wrong. In 1506, he died in disgrace, stripped of most of the honors and riches he had for so long hoped to acquire.

His heirs—a legitimate son, Diego, and an illegitimate one, Fernando—fared better. Titles, lands, and income flowed to them in a way that would have pleased their father. They even spent many years in lawsuits (the *pleitos colombinos*) against the Crown, hoping to recover yet more of what Columbus had initially been promised by monarchs who never expected him to find much of anything. The fact that they occasionally emerged successful from these lawsuits speaks to the strength of the climate for investment, if property rights could be challenged even against the Crown.

For much of the early sixteenth century, the Spanish crown sent out governors and royal officials, but it was mostly concerned with collecting its revenue and licenses. This remained true even as Hernán Cortés, Francisco Pizarro, and the other conquistadors brought huge swathes of the Americas under nominal Spanish control. The Portuguese crown was, as it had always been, much more directly involved.

It is easy to tell the story of Atlantic expansion and exploration as one of royal initiative, where the actions of figures like Vasco da Gama, Columbus, and their successors become stand-ins for royal actions. This certainly makes the narrative more digestible. For the Spanish, however, it is completely misleading. The voyages were almost entirely privately financed, and the vast majority of the profits were pulled into the purses of the investors, often

Genoese. In the case of the Portuguese, it more accurately reflects the reality of how Atlantic expansion functioned in the closing years of the fifteenth century and the dawn of the sixteenth. Even there, however, private capital played a major role: Portuguese kings were happy to include privately financed ships in their fleets from the beginning. In 1515, the Crown gave up trying to sell spices on its own account in Lisbon and transferred the whole operation to a private contractor in Antwerp, the key financial hub of the Low Countries and a place that would have a long afterlife as a node in global finance.[39]

European expansion into the Atlantic and Indian Oceans was neither a matter of forceful state initiatives nor of visionary entrepreneurs exploiting free markets. The participants, both royal households and merchant-investors alike, would not have recognized the distinction. The two were aggressively entangled at every stage of this process, as merchant-investors looked for monopolies to exploit, favorable returns on their capital, and the protective umbrella of violent force to guard and extend their ability to do business. Cash-starved royal households were always looking for revenues to finance increasingly ambitious projects. Whatever their commitment to the ideals of crusading, religious conversion, or full-blown apocalyptic messianism, the gnawing hunger for funds drove significant royal action in this period. In fact, large enough revenues enabled state-builders to pursue their more ideologically oriented projects, whatever the cost.

The application of the power of the royal household—itself not the same as "public" authority in the way we understand it today—to overseas ventures, and sucking the revenues those provided into royal coffers, fit together perfectly with the incentives of capital-providing financiers. Investors wanted monopolies, and royal resources and force could create them. This was not "state capitalism," a forward-thinking development in the history of capitalism as a whole, nor were the Portuguese monarchs Don Quixote, tilting at ideological windmills without regard for economic reality. This was hardheaded, intertwined Realpolitik and Crown business with long medieval precedents. It was not necessarily aimed at maximizing profits in a purely rational economic sense, but at maximizing the gains—broadly understood—to the Crown.[40]

In the 1490s and beyond, this process was supercharged by drastically greater investments and revenues than ever before. Kings, royal officials, and merchant-investors were not interested in free markets or competitive trade; they were after profit, however it appeared in their countinghouses and account books, and monopolies were not just acceptable but even preferable. They got that profit in staggering measures. Others paid the price for those profits with their freedom, as with the tens of thousands of people shipped from Morocco, the Canaries, West Africa, and the New World and sold into slavery. More paid with their lives, including the Muslims whom glory-hungry Portuguese *fidalgos* cut, shot, and blasted with cannon in the Indian Ocean. The natives of the New World were soon to die in far greater numbers from both direct action and disease: According to one estimate, some two hundred thousand people died under Spanish rule on the four largest Caribbean islands alone between 1493 and 1518. That was just a prologue for far worse to come.[41]

The quest for profit was not sentimental about these things. If spices, gold, and other precious objects could be obtained by peaceful trade, that was perfectly acceptable. If slavery was the sole means of generating revenue, or if the returns happened to be especially high, moral qualms would hardly stop the process. If corsairing was convenient and lucrative, and left piles of dead, that too was acceptable. If it required tens of thousands of indigenous lives to pull a meager return out of new colonies in the

Caribbean, those who might have stopped it chose not to do so. The human costs of this first wild burst of globalization were not collateral damage, but were in fact central to the success and profitability of the project as a whole.

As the *Niña* hove into the harbor of Lisbon in March 1493, carried by those dangerous, cutting late winter winds, most of that still lay in the future. Yet the hustle and bustle of Lisbon—the gold cruzados of pure West African gold clinking in Genoese financiers' countinghouses, the roar of the furnaces where master founders cast cannon, the clatter of hammers and saws in shipyards—spoke volumes to the process that was already under way.

Exploration and expansion into first the Atlantic and then the Indian Ocean were deeply intertwined with the other processes that defined this era, and they converged with financiers' hunger for profit and willingness to pour money into speculative investments like high-risk voyages of exploration. All of these things came together at the same time in the 1490s. Printing gave Columbus access to the books that shaped his deeply flawed worldview, it rapidly disseminated word of what he "discovered," and it had even provided the stacks of indulgence letters that allowed Luis de Santángel to pay for the expedition. Cannon played a central role in Portuguese colonial ventures in the Indian Ocean. Columbus had them, too. Networks of financiers, some of them Italian, others Flemish, and still others native to the Iberian Peninsula, provided the capital to pay for all of these expensive projects. The state-building designs of the Spanish and Portuguese monarchs, with their thirst for revenue and hunger to increase their capabilities, gave the whole thing license and drive. Common attitudes toward capital, investment, and credit, a shared belief in the viability of institutions that framed and supported them, made the billowing sails, holds packed full of gold, spices, and enslaved people, possible.

——— ◦◊◦ ———

CHAPTER 2

Isabella of Castile and the Rise of the State

April 1466

The woman was on her knees, praying as she had been since just before dawn: praying, praying, and praying still more for deliverance from her awful fate. Her hooded eyes, set deeply in a long face framed by straight brown hair, were tightly closed. Her thin lips moved soundlessly. She was young, barely past her fifteenth birthday. The wan afternoon light streaming in through the narrow, arrow-slit windows barely illuminated the dimness within, joining flickering candlelight in casting the room's lone occupant in darkness.

She shifted uncomfortably on her aching knees and licked her dry, parched lips. The arid cold of April in the heart of Castile drifted into the silent chapel, its thick stone walls muffling the sounds from the bustling castle that surrounded it, and left her shivering.

A powerful man, one of the most important nobles in Castile, was on his way to the city of Madrid. Pedro Girón intended to marry the young woman, and he was bringing three thousand men with him to ensure that the wedding happened as planned.

The young woman had not been consulted in the matter.

But she was no pawn. Her name was Ysabel—Isabella—and she was a princess of Castile, third in line to the throne, and half sister of King Enrique IV. Not coincidentally, Enrique had arranged for her marriage to Girón in return for his support in a particularly nasty and ongoing civil war. Isabella had no intention of serving as the unwilling mortar cementing an alliance that in no way furthered her own political interests, marrying a Castilian nobleman aligned with her feckless half brother Enrique. She knew what her future could be, up to and including sitting on the throne of Castile in her own right. Isabella had no army in Madrid, but that did not mean she was without weapons. To her, prayer was as dangerous as any corps of mercenary knights. *May God strike Girón dead*, she pleaded. Either Girón, or her. Either way, she would not marry him.

The afternoon light faded. As total darkness fell on the chapel, plunging the cloth-draped altar and its depictions of the Virgin into deepening shadow, Isabella rose from her aching knees. Breathing in the cool, desiccated air of the Castilian *meseta*, she offered one more prayer, hoping God had heard it.

Several weeks later, a messenger arrived, his horse thundering into the courtyard of the castle. Girón was dead, he said. The nobleman had died on the road shortly after leaving his stronghold. Isabella had prayed, and God had listened.[1]

For Isabella, princess and later queen of Castile, prayer was a statement of her agency and provided "a victory wrested from fortune by patience and fortitude." She grew to adulthood surrounded by men who intended to use her for their own political purposes. In the end, she bent them all—Enrique IV, her eventual husband Ferdinand of Aragon, popes, and innumerable lesser figures alike—to her will. In an age of immensely capable and ruthless rulers who built increasingly powerful states everywhere, from England and France to Castile and Hungary, the most talented and accomplished among them was this one unlikely queen.[2]

Over the course of Isabella's thirty-year reign (1474–1504), she united the two largest kingdoms of the Iberian Peninsula in a union that presaged modern Spain. Her armies completed the centuries-long *Reconquista*, erasing the last Muslim polity of Spain—the Emirate of Granada—from the map. In the process, she built the state apparatus capable of supporting ever more expensive and destructive warfare. The infamous and devastating Spanish Inquisition got its start under Isabella's watchful eye, extending the reach of Church and state ever further into the private lives of its subjects. Her royal officials, with her approval, sent Christopher Columbus off into the Atlantic with momentous and calamitous consequences. Her children married into the highest reaches of European royalty, namely the Habsburgs, creating a series of dynastic connections that set the agenda for the high politics of the new century. Finally, under her and Ferdinand's leadership, the great conflict of the sixteenth century—the endless wars between the Spanish and imperial Habsburgs and the Valois of France—took root.

This was a time of transformative change in the structures of political life in Spain and beyond. Isabella's talent, drive, and ruthlessness played a key role in creating that change.

The Rise of the State

Isabella encapsulates all the key political trends of a crucial era. Supported by a growing coterie of competent and highly educated officials, rulers across Europe sought to carve out greater power for themselves. Royal justice, driven by increasingly expansive interpretations of the law, brought rulers into arenas of life they had only rarely touched before. These men wanted to make war, just as they had throughout the Middle Ages, but now they could mobilize much greater resources for the task. Armies became larger and more professional, peopled with mercenaries—whose skills could be purchased on the open market—and stocked with pricey cannon. All of this made war far more expensive to wage, which forced states to find new and creative ways to pay for it. State finance became vastly more complex as those competent and highly educated officials scrambled to find new sources of tax revenue and credit arrangements to pay for a siege here and a key campaign there.

This is the old and venerable story of "the rise of the state." In its most extreme form, it is a triumphal narrative: Forward-thinking monarchs and their army of civil servants remake the bloated, ineffective carcass of feudal government into an efficient proto-modern bureaucratic machine. These new states prefigure the towering, absolute monarchies of the early modern period, and the nation-states of the present day.[3]

The slow, steady march of progress began here, with vision-ary rulers and a coherent upward trajectory toward something recognizably modern. But this makes the process seem far more rational, linear, and intentional than it actually was. The rulers of this period did not set out to create proto-modern govern-ment; they had far different and much more immediate goals in mind.

But something—many things—did fundamentally change around the end of the fifteenth century. Rulers like Isabella might not have been following a blueprint that inevitably led to the mod-ern state, but there is no question that royal power expanded dur-ing this time. Rulers consciously sought out the tools to increase their resources and capabilities, and they largely succeeded. Their own considerable talents and a favorable set of contemporaneous developments made it all possible.

So what, precisely, was expanding at this time? The kingdoms of western Europe at the end of the fifteenth century were not the administrative, fiscal-military states of the eighteenth or the bureaucratic nation-states of the nineteenth and beyond; rather, they were jumbles of territories that had happened to come into the possession of a ruling dynasty over the course of centuries of steady accumulation.

More precisely, rulers held a collection of particular *claims to rights* over specific territories. The king of France did not own the Kingdom of France; instead, he had a claim to rule the kingdom. Others might have claims of greater or lesser value, acknowledged by many or few. Beyond that, those claims—to taxation, the exercise of justice, a monopoly over salt sales or customs duties—could vary greatly from territory to territory. The claim that made the king of France ruler of the Duchy of Burgundy had no bearing on his rights in the Duchy of Aquitaine or the County of Artois, for example. Claims were acquired and embodied in the person of the ruler, who could collect and bequeath them as he saw fit. Local nobles and representative bodies, usually called *estates*, could and did fight over these claims with their rulers, trying their best to carve out privileges and exceptions for themselves. A strong ruler could maximize the value of his claims, but a weak one would struggle to exercise even the most basic rights to revenue and authority.

The mature political landscape of Europe in the thirteenth and fourteenth centuries was a finely woven, three-dimensional tapestry of competing claims to rights. Constant friction and conflict defined the system, as nobles, monastic institutions, episcopal sees, chartered towns, and kings all tried to get their due. Their claims overlapped, clashed, and ground up against each other. Did the revenues of a particularly prized estate belong to a prominent noble family, or to the king? Who had the right to collect a duty on salt, the local lord or the bishop? Did the legal courts belong to a lord or to the royal bureaucracy? These were the key battles that drove medieval politics.

The "regnal polity," in the precise but somewhat tortured words of the historian John Watts, was the big winner of late medieval politics in these many ongoing disputes. A regnal polity was typically but not necessarily a kingdom, and its ruler was typically but not necessarily a king. The apparatus of government gathered around the person succeeded in enforcing claims to justice, revenues, and the mostly exclusive use of force.[4]

Regnal polities—kingdoms like England, France, Castile, Aragon, and so on—were not the only players in the European political landscape, and they were not destined to emerge as the default mode of political organization. Their successful competitors fell into two major categories. City-states were prominent in several regions, and they might own a substantial piece of territory: Venice had an entire overseas empire, for example, but Strasbourg in the Rhineland controlled only its immediate environs. In fact, city-states—often run by economically literate merchant elites— were especially likely to utilize the most advanced techniques of government and taxation, far more than kingdoms beholden to rural noblemen. Venice punched well above its weight in wars against the Ottoman Empire and other great powers despite a comparatively small core territory, the population of which paled in comparison to France or even Aragon. Town-leagues dominated other regions. The Hanseatic League controlled the lucrative trade of the Baltic from its collection of urban centers like Lübeck, Hamburg, Gdansk, and Riga. The Swiss Confederation, centered on Bern, Zürich, and Schwyz, had recently come to prominence by crushing the ambitions of the Burgundian duke

Charles the Bold, adding territory and destroying some of the most advanced armies of the day.[5]

In fact, all forms of late medieval government, not just kingdoms, shared common developments and characteristics. They got more intensive and complex in their financial dealings and their personnel grew in number and competence. It was not a given that city-states and town-leagues would be overtaken by their royal competitors in this period.

Yet regnal polities did win in the end, and this period was the fundamental turning point. Consolidation, both internal and external, drove the entire process. Internally, rulers consolidated their authority at the expense of the other claimants within the borders of their territories. Rulers wielded more power and had access to greater resources, even if they utilized them less efficiently than did city-states. Externally, the rulers of these kingdoms consolidated with each other. Larger states swallowed smaller ones, occasionally through bloody conquest, but more commonly through marriage.

Regnal polities were ruled by members of blue-blooded dynasties. These were fundamentally *dynastic* states: The whole only existed as the sum of the claims of the ruler, who passed their claims to rulership from generation to generation. The easiest way for a ruler to acquire more claims was via marriage. This had been the case throughout the Middle Ages, but the process drastically accelerated at the end of the fifteenth century. Larger and larger territories passed into fewer and fewer hands. It was not just that these dynastic states consolidated internally and grew more efficient and complex; they also literally grew larger, often very quickly, as rulers made strategic marriages to heirs or heiresses and picked up new claims to territorial rule. City-states and town-leagues struggled to consolidate and expand on anything like this scale.

Isabella and Dynastic Consolidation

No ruler of this period had a more direct hand in the process of dynastic consolidation than Isabella. While Girón's attempt to marry her fell through, there was nothing stopping Enrique IV from trying again. But Isabella was determined to control her own fate. Marriage was her greatest problem, but it was also the potential solution to the conundrum in which she found herself in 1468.

That conundrum had come into being three years prior, a short distance down the road from Madrid, in the town of Ávila. In the shadow of the city's massive fortifications, towering walls studded with crenellations snaking around the hilly country, some of Castile's leading nobles and clergymen delivered speeches excoriating Enrique IV and his unfortunate rule. The king was too fond of Muslims, they said. He was a weak, effeminate homosexual, unfit to rule, and not even the father of his three-year-old daughter, Juana, who therefore could not be the heir to Castile. The rebel nobles produced Alfonso, Isabella's younger brother, an energetic and vengeful boy whose ancestry, unlike little Juana's, was unassailable. The plotters hurled a wooden effigy of Enrique IV to the ground and declared Alfonso king, putting a dramatic cap on an event known as "the Farce of Ávila."

When Alfonso died three years later, however, Isabella became the de facto alternative center of power. It was a role for which she seemed an unlikely candidate. Enrique IV had placed her and her mother in the town of Arévalo when she was a child and denied her all the revenues to which she was entitled as daughter of the late king. Isabella liked to portray her childhood as a difficult test, one that she endured and that had prepared and qualified her for political leadership. While a bit out of the way, Arévalo hardly qualified as exile from the political mainstream, but Isabella's spin on the story reveals much about her self-image and her sense of what made a leader appeal to her audience.[6]

Even at seventeen, she had a feel for the rules of the game of politics. Moreover, she was the legitimate daughter of the previous king, and Enrique's legal heir if the young Princess Juana's parentage was in question, which it certainly was in both literal and political terms. This was the case Isabella made: Several weeks after Alfonso's death, she referred to herself in a letter as "by Grace of God Princess and legitimate hereditary successor to these kingdoms of Castile and León."[7]

This was a definitive statement of lineage and intent, and a clear example of Isabella's style: direct, confident, and rooted in the belief that God had a plan for her. To maintain and exploit her promising new position, she needed allies. Marriage, and quickly, was the best solution.

Isabella had a number of suitors vying for her hand. As the best candidate for Castile's rule after Enrique's death, the leading claimant for the throne of Castile, she appealed to every ambitious nobleman or royal with a taste for power: Her husband might share in, or even dominate, the rule of one of western Europe's major kingdoms.

That was an attractive proposition, and potential matches emerged from every castle, estate, and palace in that part of the continent. A number of leading Castilian nobles made themselves available, but none had what Isabella was looking for. King Enrique IV and some of Isabella's advisors supported Afonso, king of Portugal, but the princess herself had no interest. The seventeen-year-old Richard, Duke of Gloucester, brother of King Edward IV of England, was a strong candidate: He had already established himself as a bold and skilled soldier long before he became the future Richard III, nephew-murderer and Shakespearean villain. But the ongoing political instability in England associated with the Wars of the Roses dulled his sparkle, and England was far away. Richard's eventual path took him to usurpation, death in battle, and infamy instead of the corridors of Spanish power.

Another option was Charles, Duke of Guienne and Berry, brother of King Louis XI of France and current heir to the kingdom. Unlike Richard, Duke of Gloucester, Charles was an unimpressive fellow. His main accomplishment at this point in his life was having been used as a pawn by his brother's enemies in a bloody civil conflict known as the War of the Public Good (in French, *La guerre du Bien public*, more on which below). While he held substantial lands that could constitute an independent power base, Charles was ill-equipped to use them in a way that Isabella would have found useful. No matter how exalted his bloodlines and relatives, the French duke was out.

Isabella had already made her choice. The young man she had in mind was the seventeen-year-old Ferdinand, king of Sicily and heir to the throne of Aragon. Along with Portugal and Castile, Aragon was one of the major kingdoms of the Iberian Peninsula, dominating its Mediterranean coast. It was centered on the cities of Zaragoza and Valencia, with Barcelona as a potent and semi-independent force within the kingdom. Its kings had long held overseas interests as well, including Sardinia, Sicily, and occasionally the Kingdom of Naples. By marrying Ferdinand, Isabella would combine the claims to Spain's two largest and most important kingdoms into a single dynastic line, along with a number of more distant claims.

This was the essence of dynastic consolidation. Castile was itself an amalgam of two older kingdoms, Castile and León. The crown of Aragon, to which Ferdinand was heir, was likewise the combination of several territories: Aragon itself, the County of Barcelona, the city of Valencia, and its various Mediterranean extensions. Each of these territories had its own history and usually its own institutions, customs, representative bodies, and laws. Only the ruler who held the claims united them, and they might each have vastly differing rules about inheritance and what precisely the ruler had the right to do within them. Castile and Aragon were not unique in this respect; every major kingdom within Europe at this time was a composite, to a greater (the Holy Roman Empire) or lesser (England) degree. This was a recurrent problem for every ruler in the region and a source of constant strain, internal conflict, and civil war.[8]

Ferdinand of Aragon

Isabella was surely aware of what her proposed marriage with Ferdinand represented: the combination of Spain's two greatest kingdoms in a single union. Such a union had never occurred before. Ferdinand's father, Juan II, the wily old king of Aragon, was determined to put his son in position to rule the entire Iberian Peninsula at Isabella's side. Enrique IV was equally determined to prevent this outcome. He was set on the Portuguese match, and he even told a group of Portuguese envoys to use force to restrain Isabella if she attempted to go through with the Aragonese marriage. Isabella's marriage to Ferdinand surely meant the effective end of Enrique's rule and the dispossession of his daughter, Juana.

Unfortunately for Enrique, Isabella understood public sentiment. The princess wrote to her brother, "I, alone and deprived of my just and proper liberty and the exercise of free will that in marital negotiations after the grace of God is the principle requisite, secretly made inquiry of the *grandes*, prelates, and *caballeros*, your subjects, concerning their opinion." If it were not clear enough whom the powerful people of Castile preferred—their palms greased by generous donations from the king of Aragon— children playing in the streets shouted "Banner of Aragón!" to broadcast their preference for an Aragonese match over the Portuguese. Patiently, expertly, the eighteen-year-old Isabella had maneuvered Enrique across the board and into a corner.[9]

But she was still in danger. With his bride surrounded by potential enemies, Ferdinand would not wait. He and a few companions set off into the countryside disguised as merchants, traveling across several hundred miles of potentially hostile territory to Valladolid. Enrique's men were out looking for him, and Ferdinand might be taken captive or even killed. Yet great rewards entailed great risks, and Ferdinand was willing to take them if the potential gain was the union of his Aragon and Castile. He rode into Valladolid in the dead of night to meet Isabella, and the two were immediately smitten.

When Ferdinand arrived in Valladolid to meet his would-be bride for the first time, Isabella saw a strong and fit seventeen-year-old of medium height. Straight brown hair framed a round face that featured an easy, frequent smile. Charismatic magnetism shone from that face, attracting men to his side and women to his bed, a fact that would later—quite understandably—enrage Isabella. Since childhood, Ferdinand had been raised to rule, to embody the chivalric and kingly virtues so valued by the political elite of his age. He jousted well and with enthusiasm and was no stranger to war even as a teenager: He had ridden into his first battle at the age of twelve. Over time, he would grow into a practiced and exceptionally ruthless—even amoral—politician, qualities that the equally gifted Isabella appreciated. The year before their meeting, Ferdinand had presided over his mother's funeral and given a tearful speech to the city authorities of Valencia so convincing that it ended the factional strife within the city. Even in youth, Ferdinand had a knack for the dramatic moment, and this is precisely what endeared him to his new bride.

The prince's lonely ride through the Spanish countryside to

stake his claim on Isabella was not just a romantic gesture, though it was the foundation of their genuine lifelong love affair. Late medieval rulership was more than coldhearted Realpolitik and teleological state-building. Kings and would-be kings were great nobles, members of a social group with its own distinct rules and norms of behavior. Service to a lady was part of the same complex of behaviors that included the ability to listen to counsel, generosity, and, above all, personal bravery, the precise markers of the ideal chivalric king. Making the dangerous journey to Valladolid to meet his bride was savvy public relations, and exactly the kind of thing that marked Ferdinand out as an adept future ruler.

For Isabella, the whole process of choosing a husband had been fraught with potential pitfalls. She had risked a variety of bad outcomes, ranging from imprisonment or worse at the hands of Enrique IV to picking the wrong husband to botching the timing. Yet she had walked the tightrope, choosing not only the ideal match but doing so at precisely the right moment. On October 12, 1469, she wrote to her brother the king, "By my letters and messengers I now notify Your Highness of my determined will concerning my marriage." This was no request for approval. Isabella had made up her mind, and she and Ferdinand wed two days later.[10]

Isabella and Ferdinand's union—and by extension the unification of Castile and Aragon—is a perfect example of how structural forces and the accidents of the moment combined in an explosive mixture. No matter how much consolidation was already happening, the marriage of these two hormone-fueled teenagers was dependent on the idiosyncratic political context of Castile in the late 1460s and the need for alliances in a time of civil war. Even more than that, it was the result of the personal qualities of the actors involved, namely Isabella and Ferdinand themselves. Both of them, but particularly Isabella, saw their options with striking clarity and played their political roles to perfection. Their talents meshed with and pushed forward structural trends of their period to produce the world-altering results we see in the rise of the state.

The Waxing and Waning of Royal Power

The ambitious rulers of late medieval kingdoms, like Isabella of Castile, did not operate in an ideological vacuum, pursuing an objective, sterile set of state interests. Instead, there existed a feedback loop between the cold realities of power and a political culture that prized particular characteristics in its rulers. In the overarching context of a deeply Christian society, subjects expected their kings to deliver royal justice and make war. Rulers who failed to do so were no rulers at all, and only tenuously clung to the throne. Those two things—justice and war—were also the means by which ambitious rulers could extend their authority and the power of the state.

This was hardly a new phenomenon at the end of the fifteenth century. For several hundred years, the state-building rulers of the Middle Ages had pursued these two paths with greater and lesser degrees of success.[11] Royal power waxed and waned in different places at different times amid a general trend of gradual upward growth. It reached a high-water mark in England under Edward III in the middle of the fourteenth century, when the Plantagenet king dominated his French adversaries at the peak of the Hundred Years' War. It reached its nadir in France following the disaster of the Battle of Agincourt in 1415. Subsequently, France's territory was divided into three parts, the king's ongoing bouts of madness left him locked in the palace, covered in feces and unable to rule for years on end, and there was little agreement on who even wielded true royal authority.

The low points came for Castile and Aragon in the 1460s, in Isabella's and Ferdinand's early years. This was an age of civil war and internal strife within western Europe as a whole, not just the Iberian Peninsula. Political instability had already consumed England for the better part of a generation, and the Wars of the Roses were still ongoing. The high nobility of France revolted against King Louis XI of France, resulting in an open civil war, the War of the Public Good, which dramatically destabilized France in the middle of the decade. The details varied from kingdom to kingdom, but all of these revolts shared a central concern: violent disagreement over the proper role and behavior of the king and the powers of royal government, varying from extreme weakness to tyrannical overreach. What rights did the king of France have in the Duke of Burgundy's lands? If the king of England was mentally ill and unable to rule, which high noble ought to wield royal power, and on what basis of legitimacy?

To complicate matters, foreign rulers regularly intervened in these conflicts, supporting rival parties to whom they were tied by dynastic marriages. The boundaries of kingdoms were porous, and nothing stopped key political actors in one kingdom from maintaining relationships with high nobles or kings in another. In fact, the political elite felt it was their God-given right to engage in such politicking. As a result, these were less separate civil wars than an ongoing web of violent, continent-wide political entanglements that stretched from the *meseta* of central Spain to the Scottish border. They were structural rather than personal, baked into the DNA of late medieval politics, a widespread reaction to the general trend of increasing royal power as the Middle Ages progressed.[12]

Isabella and Ferdinand grew to political maturity amid this kind of internal strife. Aragon dealt with a ten-year civil war centered around the independent-minded county of Catalonia. At

various points, the Catalan peasantry rebelled; the county's representative body, the Corts, offered the county's rule to Enrique
IV of Castile; and Louis XI allied himself with King Juan II of
Aragon—Ferdinand's father—against the Catalans, and then later
with the Catalans against Juan II in the hope of seizing a few
pieces of Aragonese territory.

Enrique, Isabella, and Ferdinand reached a fragile detente
based on an agreement that Isabella would succeed Enrique on the
throne at his death. When Enrique finally died in 1474, however,
this settlement immediately fell apart. On one side stood Isabella
and Ferdinand; on the other, Enrique's twelve-year-old potentially illegitimate daughter, Juana. Factions of Castilian nobles
lined up behind both sides. One factor complicated things further: the marriage of Juana to the fifty-year-old King Afonso V of
Portugal. This was technically a civil war, but Afonso's involvement made it something more, a product of that web of strife that
bound kingdoms together. The War of the Castilian Succession
lasted four long years, with Isabella and Ferdinand emerging victorious in 1479.

The War of the Castilian Succession was a chaotic and brutal
environment for Isabella and Ferdinand to learn the ropes of rulership. The preceding years of conflict had instructed them in the
necessity of forging collaborative ties with the nobility and the
towns—another key constituency—while still finding avenues to
exercise their authority whenever possible. Isabella especially was
heir to a recent tradition of strong royal prerogatives—claims to
rights to taxation, land, and justice—exercised under her father,
but which had lapsed during Enrique's chaotic reign. As she
came into her own, those royal prerogatives reemerged with a
vengeance.[13]

This was true of the generation of rulers that came of age all
across Europe at this time: The wave of civil wars and political

instability effectively settled centuries-old disputes about the limits of royal power in favor of the rulers, and taught the royalty who emerged victorious precisely how to go about expanding their capabilities.

Within Castile, royal power belonged to Isabella, not Ferdinand. This was clear from the moment their wedding contract was signed but it became much more obvious after she ascended the throne. Ferdinand ruled "as legitimate husband of Our Lady the Queen," meaning that he was king consort—not a Castilian ruler in his own right.[14] Isabella mollified her husband by promising to obey him, as any dutiful wife in the late fifteenth century was expected to do, but the realities of power-sharing were clear. As long as Isabella lived, she intended to rule as half of a partnership, not as a figurehead for her scheming husband.

There was consistent friction between the two of them, as expected in any power-sharing arrangement, and particularly one complicated by Ferdinand's consistent infidelity, but their broader goals usually aligned in productive ways. Their priorities quickly emerged in the aftermath of the War of the Castilian Succession. They assembled the Cortes, the representative body of Castile, and reinforced royal control over the institution with the aim of centralizing power and administration. One result was the compiling of Castilian law by jurists closely allied to royal interests. The specific reforms pointed toward greater reliance on royal decrees, the introduction of new tribunals directly responsible to the rulers, and reorganizing the chancery that dealt with legal matters. Most important, they reclaimed large amounts of what had once been royal land and revoked royal privileges—especially funds—granted to generations of Castilian noblemen for their support. All of this fell under the category of royal justice, one of the two traditional routes to expanding royal power throughout the later Middle Ages across Europe.[15]

But as effective as royal justice could be in the extension of royal power, nothing helped a ruler centralize his or her authority like the exigencies of armed conflict against another ruler. Kings were expected to wage war. It was a fundamental part of the ideology of kingship as it developed in the Middle Ages, part of what linked the king to his subjects, regardless of their status. War necessitated close contact between the king and the key nobles who served in his armies, pulling them ever further into the orbit of royal authority. War was expensive at every point in the Middle Ages, and became drastically more so in the fifteenth century as costly cannon and specialist mercenaries grew increasingly essential to victory.

The ruler's private resources, known as the royal domain, were nowhere near sufficient to pay for years of sustained war. This meant finding other ways of paying for it: in a word, taxation. Taxation required consensus between royal government and power brokers, whether representative bodies, town officials, or the nobility. This further linked the kingdom's constituent parts to central government. As with royal justice, it required a bureaucracy of learned officials who were loyal to the Crown to administer it, which gave the state further capacity to expand its powers. War made the state, in the famous words of the sociologist Charles Tilly, and the state made war.[16]

For Isabella and Ferdinand, war against the Emirate of Granada—the last Muslim polity left in Spain—beckoned with a welcoming hand.

The *Reconquista* and Granada

The *Reconquista*, the attempt to expel Muslim states from Spain, had been under way for more than seven centuries by the time Isabella and Ferdinand turned their attention toward Granada.

Muslims had first entered the Iberian Peninsula in 711, and within only a few years overran the Visigothic Kingdom that had dominated the region since the beginning of the sixth century. The last piece of Spain left to Christian rulers was a motley collection of mountainous and unattractive territories in the far north. From these humble beginnings in the shadow of the much larger, wealthier, and more complex societies of Muslim Spain, the *Reconquista* began. By the ninth century, Christian writers in these tiny kingdoms had developed the germ of the idea that Spain belonged to them by right, and that the Muslims must be expelled.[17]

It is easy to portray the entirety of the Middle Ages in Spain as one long and unceasing conflict between Christians and Muslims, but that was not the reality. Christian kings were perfectly happy to fight each other in addition to the rulers of the Muslim statelets, called *taifas*, that emerged after the end of the unified Caliphate of Córdoba in the eleventh century. Conversely, the petty kings (*Mulūk al-Tawā'if*) who ruled the Muslim *taifas* were perfectly happy to ally with or pay tribute to a Christian king. In this chaotic environment, faith was no guarantee of political allegiance. Territorial expansion and unsentimental Realpolitik went hand in hand with a genuine commitment to religious war.

The injection of the crusading ideals that had swept through Christendom after 1095 complicated matters further. Popes offered salvation in return for fighting the infidel in specific campaigns, not just in the Holy Land, but also Muslims in Spain and pagans in the Baltic. This was a powerful incentive that drew soldiers from all over Europe to the Iberian Peninsula. The special crusading taxes to which the pope had access, and which he could offer to Spanish rulers, were a different but equally compelling incentive. Kings were not only expected to wage war, they *wanted* to do so. It was part of the duty of medieval rulership. And if they could get paid to do it while burnishing their eternal souls and expanding their territory, so much the better. Over the course of the twelfth and thirteenth centuries, piece after piece of Muslim-held territory fell to the kings of Castile, Aragon, and Portugal. When Seville and Córdoba fell to the Castilian king Ferdinand III in 1247–48, it seemed as if the end of Muslim Spain was just around the corner. Only the tiny Emirate of Granada and the Rock of Gibraltar remained. With three increasingly wealthy and expanding Christian kingdoms arrayed against this tiny remnant, it was only a matter of time.

That time, however, happened to last just over two centuries. Gibraltar finally fell to Castile in 1462, and it was the only significant inroad in that period.[18] The feckless Enrique IV, Isabella's half brother, had made a great show of promising to bring the war to Granada during the early years of his reign after his accession in 1454. His unwillingness to carry the goal through to completion was a large part of what made him so unpopular. The key political actors of Castile had bought in, both figuratively and literally. Large armies were assembled, packed with the kingdom's greatest nobles and paid for by generous grants of taxation from the Cortes and the towns. But instead of finishing off the tiny emirate, Enrique dithered. He halfheartedly besieged strongpoints and raided Muslim territory, then handed out the lucrative proceeds of these campaigns to his closest supporters rather than the kingdom's important power brokers.

This was an offense on two fronts: first, to the role of the king as warmaker in chief; and second, much more seriously, to the whole project of *Reconquista*. It was bad enough for a king of England to fail to wage war on France. It was far worse for an avowed Christian king in the Iberian Peninsula to shirk his duty to face the enemies of the faith. By the middle of the fifteenth century, rulers of Castile were steeped in a tradition that saw Spain as religiously and culturally distinct. This was a messianic tradition that portrayed Spain as God's chosen place and its rulers as chosen by God to bring the world toward the end of time and the return of Jesus. History was divinely shaped, as historian Peggy Liss points out, and Spanish rulers had a key role to play in both the past and the future. This was the duty that Enrique abandoned by avoiding all-out war with Granada, and which Isabella and Ferdinand intended to fully embrace upon their accession. Waging war against the enemies of the faith was what a righteous ruler was supposed to do.[19]

For Isabella and Ferdinand, war against Granada carried a multitude of benefits. First, in the interest of hardheaded Realpolitik, it would bind the fractious nobles of Castile and Aragon to their rulers in a shared project after decades of dissension. More than any other arena, war was where the interests of the kingdom's key power groups aligned with those of the monarchs. War would also put the nobles in close and continuous proximity to the rulers. This mattered a great deal. For the political elite, rulership was personal, not institutional. A magnanimous gesture, a word of recognition in front of one's peers, public interaction at feasts and celebrations: These were the things that tied nobles and rulers together. Rulers were also great nobles, and great nobles were supposed to be capable warriors. That was a role Ferdinand could and did fill with aplomb. War was where nobles made their names and their fortunes, and successful campaigns meant spoils for Isabella and Ferdinand to distribute to their loyal followers. For her part, Isabella skillfully played the lady of chivalric romance, the object of devotion for whom valiant knights would fight and die. She understood the cultural script at hand, and precisely how it motivated the male nobles whose swords and private armies she would need in order to conquer Granada.

On paper, the Nasrid dynasty of Granada did not seem like a

particularly formidable opponent. The emirate was a tiny slice of southern Iberia centered on the city of Granada and the prosperous seaport of Málaga. Some three hundred thousand people lived there, a tiny number compared to the five million of Castile and the one million of Aragon. In previous conflicts over the centuries, powerful Muslim rulers in Morocco had crossed the Strait of Gibraltar to bail out their coreligionists in Spain whenever the Christians made territorial gains. No such help was available now.

Enthusiasm ran high in both Castile and Aragon. Despite a truce with Granada in 1478, war was clearly on the minds of Isabella and Ferdinand, and had been for years. In fact, the promise of war had been explicitly written into their marriage agreement. The two "always had in mind the great thought of conquering the kingdom of Granada and of casting out from all the Spains the rule of the Moor and the name of Muhammad," wrote the chronicler Pulgar. Repeated civil wars had been justified because they prepared Castile for its inevitable war with Granada.[20] As the War of the Castilian Succession drew to a close and Isabella and Ferdinand consolidated rulership over their twin kingdoms—Ferdinand formally took the crown of Aragon in 1479—they prepared for war. Royal agents reclaimed the substantial properties and revenues that had been granted out to beneficiaries over the preceding decades, opening up still more funds. The militias of Castile's cities and towns, a key foundation of royal power, readied themselves to march.

When the conflict began, it did so unexpectedly, with a surprise Granadan attack on the frontier fortress of Zahara at the very end of 1481. The Castilians struck back in the opening months of 1482, seizing the city of Alhama as Isabella and Ferdinand headed south to the war zone and there assembled their forces. Urban militias, knights who held land grants in return for military service, nobles and their private armies, and highly trained mercenaries whose services the rulers bought on the open market all assembled at the rulers' call. They based themselves in Medina del Campo, the key trading and financial hub of Andalusia. This was precisely the right place from which to direct, and pay for, the coming conflict.

This was not just a geopolitical rivalry between two states or a simple land grab; it was religious war, and the participants understood it as such. The Church collected large amounts of taxes that were formally designated (but rarely used) for financing crusades. Heated negotiations between pope, king, and queen kept those funds in Spain instead of sending them on to Rome. Still more back-and-forth discussions convinced the pope to produce a crusading bull. The "gates of paradise would be opened to eternal glory with the holy apostles and glorious martyrs," wrote Pope Sixtus IV, promising full remission of sins to all who participated in the campaign in any capacity.[21] The war with Granada was one of the last true crusades, heir to nearly four centuries of holy warfare between Christian and Muslim, not just in Spain but across the entire Mediterranean world.

A visitor who arrived in Medina del Campo at the outset of this new war could glimpse both the high medieval past of crusading and the future of warfare. Cannons and barrels of gunpowder to fill them rolled into Medina del Campo in large numbers. So did feared Swiss mercenaries, who had made a name for themselves over the previous decade and would dominate battlefields across Europe in the coming century. This may have been the last crusade, but in essential ways it also presaged the vicious and destructive conflicts that opened the sixteenth century.

The Queen's War

While the war in Granada seemed like an easy victory on paper, in practice it proved to be a brutal, grinding affair. The emirate was tiny compared to Castile and Aragon, but it was protected by the jagged, snowcapped peaks of the Sierra Nevada. The approaches to its major cities bristled with fortresses and walled towns, and the routes leading in passed through canyons, defiles, and an array of treacherous terrain. It was the perfect battleground for hit-and-run raids and ambushes. The overconfident Castilians and their formidable queen soon found this out the hard way.

The campaigns of 1482 provided a lesson in terms of the requirements of cutting-edge warfare. Ferdinand abjectly failed to take the fortress of Loja. His soldiers were poorly disciplined and unprepared and had nowhere near the artillery or provisions required for an extended siege. The next year was no better. The Marquess of Cádiz and the master of Santiago, an order of religious knights like the famous Templars or the Hospitallers, planned a raid in force directed at the mountains near Málaga. The mounted knights soon found themselves penned in the narrow ravines and approaches to Málaga. On the hills and ridges above them, the Granadans pelted the raiders with arrows and stones. Shivering in the March chill, trapped in the maze of canyons, thousands of Castilians died. More were captured. Only a few managed to escape back to safety, surviving on whatever they could find in the arid mountains and nearly dying of thirst. The rout at al-Sharqiyya was a disaster, a frontier raid turned into a bloody and humiliating debacle, and it showed that the Granadans would not roll over in the face of a putatively rising state.[22]

From then on, the Castilians proceeded more cautiously. Larger and more disciplined forces took a systematic approach, besieging fortresses with cannon and stone-throwing engines and pillaging the countryside to choke off the flow of resources to the enemy. Swiss mercenaries, French engineers, and German cannon founders went south to bring the Castilians up to speed on the most current techniques of war. Weavers from Burgos and smiths from Seville left behind their tools to take up arms. The hot Andalusian sun roasted knights in their steel armor as they rode along dust-caked roads. Trains of pack animals clopped along the mountainous tracks that led through the Sierra Nevada, loaded down with grain, gunpowder, crossbow bolts, and all the other necessities of war. Year after year, castle by castle, town by town, the tide of war turned in Isabella and Ferdinand's favor.

Understanding the requirements of this new style of warfare was one thing, but paying for it was another, and the cost was staggering. Thousands of soldiers marched into Granada practically every year between 1482 and 1491, and the armies only grew as the war went on: Six thousand knights and twelve thousand infantry on one expedition in 1484 grew to ten thousand knights and forty thousand infantry on the final approach to Granada in 1491. These were some of the largest armies of the Middle Ages, dwarfing the forces Henry V of England brought to the Battle of Agincourt. Each of those Castilian soldiers had to be fed and supplied on months-long campaigns in unfriendly and difficult terrain. The number of pack animals required to carry supplies for all those soldiers was mind-boggling: thirty thousand horses, mules, and oxen for the eighteen thousand soldiers in 1484, for example, and proportionally more as the Castilian armies expanded.[23] To make matters even more complicated, French incursions into the northern territories of Aragon meant that Ferdinand had to fight there as well. War on two fronts was even more complex and demanding than war on one. Isabella and Ferdinand would have to find ways to manage and pay for all of it.

State Finance

War had always been costly. Richard the Lionheart mortgaged most of England, from royal lands to offices, to pay for the Third

Crusade. Whenever the English or French got the upper hand in the Hundred Years' War, they could usually thank improvements in their kingdom's fiscal system. But war had never been quite so ruinously expensive as it became in the fifteenth century. The final English defeat in the Hundred Years' War came as much from financial exhaustion as from King Henry VI's political incompetence. The Wars of the Roses that soon followed grew directly out of the enormous debts the previous war had left behind.[24] Charles the Bold, Duke of Burgundy and one of the most outstanding military innovators of the period, managed to bankrupt some of the richest territories in Europe—Flanders, Picardy, Brabant, and Burgundy itself—with a standing army and constant warring. Charles's fiscal failings led directly to the duke eating the business end of a Swiss halberd outside the city of Nancy in 1477, finishing both his ambitions and his dynasty.[25]

Lest they end up like Charles the Bold or Henry VI—cleft in two by a halberd or imprisoned and bludgeoned to death by a usurper—Isabella and Ferdinand needed to find ways to pay for their war habit. To meet their insatiable needs for capital, the rulers turned to a vast array of funding sources. We have already seen the fevered negotiations with the pope that tapped the firehose of Church taxes. Over the course of the war, this turned out to be a vast amount of money: more than 600,000 Aragonese florins, or 159 million maravedis. It was still nowhere near enough. This was a crusade, though, and even noncombatants could glean a taste of salvation by donating to the cause year after year. Silver-tongued preachers spread out across Castile and Aragon to drum up funds, and this flow of cash yielded another 450 million maravedis.[26] These were absurd sums—Columbus's voyage in 1492 cost only 2 million maravedis in total—and they were still nowhere close to sufficient.

Isabella, Ferdinand, and their clutch of sharp financial advisors tapped every available source of revenue. As much as possible, the war was made to pay for itself: The entire population of Málaga was held for ransom after the city's capture in 1487. Those who could not pay—the vast majority of the population—were sold into slavery to defray the costs of the campaign. The Crown took a neat sales tax on these sales of human beings, as well as a large lump sum of gold for the ransom of some 450 Jewish citizens who had lived in the city.[27] Raiding for profit had funded frontier warfare for centuries, and the scale increased as the number of soldiers rose over the course of the war. Taxation in the form of grants from the Cortes, Castile's representative body, covered some of the remainder. So did taxes from the Hermanadades, religious/military organizations spread throughout Castile, and an array of sales taxes and customs duties.[28]

But it still wasn't enough, and the only way to make up the difference was through loans. Lending to princes and kings was inherently risky business, and the chance of social and political advancement more than the rational hope for return on investment drove firms to lend money to rulers. Nothing prevented a ruler from forgoing his obligations or dying on the job. Kings did not necessarily hold themselves accountable for their predecessors' debts. More than one major banking house had gone under after gambling on a dynasty. The largest commercial firms of the Middle Ages, the Bardi and Peruzzi of Florence, went belly-up after King Edward III of England defaulted in the early days of the Hundred Years' War. Edward III survived and thrived, but the Bardi and Peruzzi did not. The Medici Bank was the most important financial institution of the fifteenth century, and the losses its Bruges branch incurred lending to Charles the Bold before his death helped drown the firm as a whole.[29]

Quite often, firms did not have a choice in the matter. Forced loans from wealthy merchants or entire communities were one avenue for rulers to exploit, and they did so all over Europe. Isabella and Ferdinand collected large sums in this manner—in Spain they were called *emprésitos*—only some of which they ever intended to pay back. Still more money came through straightforward borrowing from anyone who would lend to them, including the nobility, urban communities, bishops, cartels of merchants, and Genoese merchant-investors, some of whom went on to involve themselves in Columbus's voyage soon after.

Royal finances during this long, grinding, expensive war resembled a series of spinning tops. Consider the 1489 campaign to take Baza, one of the key fortress-cities guarding the northern approaches to Granada. The preparations for the campaign involved forced loans from urban communities, bishops, and nobles; a special tax on individual head of cattle; a subsidy from the clergy as a whole in addition to a tithe; and the revenues from the sale of bulls of crusade, the salvation-granting devices mentioned earlier. As the campaign went on and the costs mounted, the need for funds increased. Luis de Santángel, future financial organizer of Columbus's expedition, arranged international loans. But those funds would not arrive in time to meet the ongoing needs of the campaign for wages and supplies, however, so Santángel advanced his own funds for immediate cash. More loans from Francesco Pinelli (known as Francisco Pinelo to the Castilians), one of the Genoese merchant-bankers, and others covered the difference. Finally, faced with additional costs toward the end of the campaign, Isabella pawned her jewels as security for still more loans.[30]

The Baza campaign ended when Isabella herself arrived, a magnificent and commanding presence surrounded by her household, and the city surrendered soon after. Yet this was only a single campaign in a single year. Stretched over the course of a decade, the conflict strained royal finances well past the breaking point. War on this scale required much more sophisticated fiscal arrangements, better administration, and sharp financial advisors like Luis de Santángel and Alonso de Quintanilla, both of whom helped finance Columbus's expedition. As convoluted as those mechanisms seemed, they were nothing next to the complexities of running a decade-long war.

One of the solutions Isabella, Ferdinand, and their advisors employed to fund the war would have a long and productive future: a long-term public debt, in which buyers purchased annuities and received regular interest payments from royal revenues. If this sounds familiar, that is because it remains the basic structure of public debt today. Isabella and Ferdinand made their combined kingdoms the first territorial state in Europe to adopt this model of financing, and others followed suit over the course of the sixteenth century.

Long-term public debt was not a new idea. Venice carried one as early as 1262, and so did many other city-states, including Genoa, Florence, Hamburg, and Cologne. Barcelona, an autonomous city within Aragon (though not a city-state proper), also had a long-term public debt beginning in 1360. This was an effective and well-known method of financing, but not one that had been available to rulers of large states prior to Isabella and Ferdinand in 1489. Why? One reason was that kings were not reliable borrowers, at least not when compared to compact city-states ruled by merchant oligarchies who had a strong occupational familiarity with debt and credit.[31]

Starting in 1489, however, amid the financial stress of the Baza campaign, Isabella and Ferdinand were able to tap the enormous potential of this new revenue source. It gave them great flexibility and deep pockets, precisely the kind of resources rising rulers needed to carry on wars of ever-increasing scale and duration. Long-term public debt, administered by savvy and well-educated officials, was one key component of the rising states that would dominate the coming century.[32]

The End of Granada and Looking Inward

Thin lines spread outward from the queen's eyes, the surrounding skin sallow and paper-thin. The beginnings of a double chin peeked out from below her rounded face. Her eyes had always been hooded, and the exhaustion of decades of exertion pushed them deeper into her skull. The years had not been kind to Isabella, but her eyes still burned bright, and her thin mouth turned upward into the barest hint of a smile. This—January 2, 1492—was her moment of triumph. Adorned in a golden crown and rich silks, she sat astride a magnificent, impatient horse that pawed at the ground outside the gates of Granada. She was surrounded by retainers and tens of thousands of soldiers drawn up into disciplined ranks.

The gates opened, and fifty armored men on horseback rode out. In the lead was Abu 'Abd Allah, known as Boabdil, the last emir of Granada, mounted on a humble mule. The queen's gaze fell on the emir and then on her husband, Ferdinand, to whom the emir bowed and doffed his cap. That was enough of a gesture of submission for the king of Aragon. The group trotted back toward Isabella. Abu 'Abd Allah offered to kiss her hands in recognition of his defeat, but Isabella refused. Still, she said, he ought to behave himself in the future. As always, the queen left no doubt as to who held the power in this monarchy. The keys to the city, passed from the emir to Ferdinand to his wife, hung heavy in her hand.[33]

After nearly a decade, the war in Granada finally came to an end as 1492 dawned. That was a fateful year for Isabella and Ferdinand, both an end and a beginning: the end of the *Reconquista*, and the launch of Columbus's long-shot voyage into the Atlantic. It also featured the culmination of more than a decade's investment in religious orthodoxy, as the Spanish Inquisition—with the firm agreement and aid of Isabella and Ferdinand—succeeded in converting or expelling hundreds of thousands of Spain's Jews. This was the dark side of the rise of the state, as if a decade of ceaseless religious war and fiscal exactions were not already enough. The tools that rulers created and embraced at the end of the Middle Ages went beyond war and justice and allowed them to reach deeper into the lives of their subjects than ever before.

The Spanish Inquisition was a state project. This had not been the case for the many medieval inquisitions between the twelfth and fifteenth centuries, which were without exception directed by and responsible to the papacy. By contrast, the Spanish Inquisition, while staffed by clerics, was beholden to Isabella and Ferdinand, not Pope Sixtus IV and his successors in Rome. The Inquisition's main object was religious uniformity and orthodoxy within Spain: an inherently political project, one that accorded perfectly with Isabella and Ferdinand's larger goal of unification and royal control. The Inquisition could be and often was used against recalcitrant factions and individuals within Castile and Aragon, wielded like a cudgel against those whom Isabella and Ferdinand deemed enemies.

The Inquisition, however, very quickly spun out of control. Even Pope Sixtus IV, who had approved its beginning in Castile and expansion in Aragon, protested its excesses. Hundreds of supposedly hidden Jews, false converts who still worshipped in the old ways in secret, were burned at the stake. Interrogation and torture awaited thousands more. Even the "reconciled" still suffered grievous penalties. The Inquisition confiscated vast tracts of property and staggering amounts of money, much of which found its way into the pockets of both the secular and the Church officials who approved the persecutions, with Isabella and Ferdinand taking their own cut. Throughout the 1480s and into the 1490s, the Inquisition operated effectively beyond royal control, though always with their approval. While the final expulsion of the Jews in the spring and summer of 1492 came as a surprise to Isabella and Ferdinand, they did not oppose it.

All of these actions, from confiscation and torture to public executions, were part and parcel of Isabella and Ferdinand's broader program, and a fundamental part of their future successes. They—Isabella, especially—saw themselves as the heirs to centuries of Spanish political and religious exceptionalism. Crusading went hand in hand with the belief that Jews who had converted to Christianity—the main targets of the Inquisition—should be closely surveilled, and when found wanting, forcefully punished. The fact that the vast majority of the *conversos* were innocent of any wrongdoing, even those who were tortured and executed, was beside the point. There was a strong messianic element to Isabella and Ferdinand's rulership, the fulfillment of an apocalyptic Christian destiny. The vast increase in administrative, fiscal, and military capacity—the essence of the rise of the state—was less a coldly rational expression of forward-looking modernity than a product of their attempt to fulfill goals that reached back centuries into the past.[34]

Dynastic Entanglements

The same financiers and efficient fiscal mechanisms that had powered the conquest of Granada sent Christopher Columbus sailing off into the Atlantic in the summer of 1492. As he did so, Spain was witnessing the dawn of a new age. Crusading was a prestigious activity for any medieval ruler, and Isabella and Ferdinand had triumphed in an openly religious war. Churches across

Europe echoed with prayerful celebrations of their victory. They had remade their state with administrative reforms and built a firm fiscal foundation. The writ of royal justice flowed throughout Castile. The ill-disciplined and lacking Castilian soldiers of the early days of the Granada campaign had been forged into the precursors of a professional standing army. A decade of war had bound the nobles and towns of Castile and Aragon ever more closely to their rulers. At the same time, the Catholic monarchs had reformed the Church within their territories, weeding out unfit clergy and essentially appointing themselves arbiters of the faith within their lands. The fearsome Inquisition, another arm of state power, enforced religious and cultural uniformity. An increasingly united Spain, led by Isabella and Ferdinand, now stood at the forefront of European powers.

Rising dynastic prestige meant two things: first, more opportunities for connections to other dynasties through marriage; and second, the opportunity to enforce some of the less convincing claims to rights a ruler might count in his or her portfolio. A ruler's great-grandfather might have been duke of this or king of that, a fairly meaningless title in itself, but a standing army, fiscal capacity, and dynastic aggression could turn a throwaway claim into the basis for a continent-spanning war. Isabella and Ferdinand played both of those cards over the course of the 1490s, binding themselves to the other key dynasties of Europe and setting up claims to vast swathes of territory. In the process, they entangled themselves with the broader politics of the continent and launched the dynamics that would dominate the entire sixteenth century and beyond.

The first sign of this emerging order, the order Isabella and Ferdinand were creating, came in 1494, the year King Charles VIII of France invaded Italy. His Valois dynasty had long supported a claim to the Kingdom of Naples, and the demise of its ruler that year gave the hotheaded young Charles an opportunity to exploit it. Accompanied by his standing army, Swiss mercenaries, and one of the largest trains of cannon ever assembled in Europe, Charles sliced through the meager Italian resistance. In the process, however, he made enemies, namely Ferdinand of Aragon, who had his own claim on the Kingdom of Naples.

Buttressed by the support of the infamous Rodrigo Borgia, the newly elected Aragonese pope, Ferdinand entered the war against Charles. This was the beginning of the Italian Wars, which would last for the next sixty-five years and pit the Valois of France against their European rivals in a vast and never-ending contest for continental domination. The wars grew and the states rose in a self-reinforcing cycle of violence and expansion.

The states got larger, too. The initial rival of Valois France was Ferdinand of Aragon, armed with the resources of Spain, itself a composite state made up of Aragon and Castile and their constituent parts. Yet the process of dynastic consolidation was only just beginning. Isabella and Ferdinand had a number of children, all of whom married into other dynasties: Two daughters became queens of Portugal; Katherine of Aragon famously married not one but two English princes; and most importantly, their eldest daughter, Juana, married Philip the Handsome, a prince of the Habsburg dynasty. More salient, Philip the Handsome was the heir to the vast Habsburg domains in the Low Countries and Austria, and the likeliest future candidate for Holy Roman Emperor.

Isabella's health, waning in the aftermath of so many pregnancies, illnesses, and the loss of two of her children, took a turn for the worse in 1503. Castile and Aragon had by then been at war for more than two decades. Ferdinand was currently fighting the French in the northern reaches of Catalonia, and their armies had recently taken Naples. The stress and strain had worn on her for years and she developed a high fever that came and went, as well as an unshakable internal pain. Her condition fluctuated over the course of 1503, but even the bad spells did not keep her from her work: signing documents, sending endless streams of letters, and handling the business of ruling the kingdom while Ferdinand was at war. Above all, Isabella was trying to prepare her daughter and heir, Juana, for the rigors of ruling Castile.

Isabella distrusted Philip the Handsome, an acquisitive dynast with grand designs for his new wife's future kingdom. Juana lacked her mother's force of personality, her instincts for playing the game, and her ruthlessness. The princess was something of a tragic figure, emotional and depressed, but also unfairly tarred by both her faithless husband and her Machiavellian father, Ferdinand, as unfit for rule. Philip fully intended to rule Castile through her, while Ferdinand had no intention of giving up Castile's resources in the middle of a multifront war.

Isabella's condition worsened throughout 1504. Her fevers returned with a vengeance. Her signatures no longer appeared on any but the most important documents, and then not even those. The last thing was her will, which affirmed that Juana would succeed: "Conforming with what I ought to do and am obliged to do by law, I order and establish and institute her as my universal heir," Isabella wrote, though her lack of enthusiasm for the plan was obvious. At the end—November 26, 1504, at the age of fifty-three—she received the sacraments and died as she had planned, with Ferdinand by her side.[35]

Juana succeeded to the throne, though Castile did not have to deal with Philip the Handsome for long. He died in 1506, and the brewing conflict between him and Ferdinand over the rule of the kingdom never came to a head. Ferdinand succeeded in sidelining Juana until her and Philip's son, Charles, came of age. When he did, Charles became the most powerful ruler of the sixteenth century, the culmination of the process of dynastic consolidation.

He inherited Castile from Isabella, Aragon from Ferdinand, the vast and wealthy Low Countries from his long-deceased grandmother Mary of Burgundy, and the Habsburg domains of Austria from his other grandfather, Maximilian. As if all of that were not enough, Charles, like Maximilian, was also elected Holy Roman Emperor.

Fewer and fewer rulers held more and more claims to rights. Those rulers' lands grew more administratively and fiscally complex. Wars lengthened, became more destructive and more costly. What had been a conflict between Ferdinand and Charles VIII over Naples became a conflagration that stretched from Italy to the Low Countries and the Pyrenees to the Rhineland in just over a generation. All over Europe, states were rising, none more so than Isabella's Spain. Her ruthlessness and talent towered over the era, setting its political, ideological, and financial bases. Her personal gifts and personality helped drive a wave of structural change both within and without her own kingdom. Literally and figuratively, her blood planted the conflicts, triumphs, and disasters of the coming century.

CHAPTER 3

———— ৵৹ ————

Jakob Fugger and Banking

February 1508

ate winter snow softened the jagged Alpine ridges rising
around the narrow valley. A road snaked its way down
through a cleft in the peaks, back and forth across the face of the
hills, winding in and out of stands of evergreens. Drops of water
fell from the icicles hanging from their branches, a steady *drip-drip-drip* as the temperature rose to just above freezing.

The clomp of hooves and soldiers' boots on flagstones drowned
out the dripping of the icicles and the gentle swishing of tree
branches in the winter wind as a column of men marched south
down the road. They shivered against the cold, their breath escaping in puffs of steam in the mountain air. Long pikes more than
twice as tall as their bearers and big-barreled arquebuses weighed
heavy on the shoulders of the marching infantry, their legs pumping in flashy breeches, an array of colorful crimson, yellow, blue,
and black.

These were mercenaries, German *Landsknechte* headed south
across the Alps to join the army of the Holy Roman Emperor,
Maximilian I. Despite the season, the soldiers were not alone

on the road. Wagons loaded down with copper trundled south, headed for Venice and its rich markets. Others went north, caravans overflowing with silks and spices. Couriers bearing vital documents, the lifeblood of the nascent banking industry— letters, notes of credit, and bills of exchange—flogged their tired horses up toward the Brenner Pass.

One man in particular had his fingers in all of this traffic. He was not present on the road himself, though he knew it well, despite not having passed this way for some years. The coins jingling in the soldiers' purses had been drawn on a letter of credit his firm had provided, on the basis of a loan made to Emperor Maximilian. The coins were made from silver, silver that had come from mines the man leased. The wagons rumbling south down the road carried his copper, bound for warehouses he owned in Venice. The wagons full of luxuries headed up the road, bound for lucrative northern markets, appeared as investments in account books housed in the firm's Venice office. Some of the couriers pushing their tired horses up into the wintry Alps carried his vital letters of credit and bills of exchange.

His name was Jakob Fugger. At this moment, he was safe and sound, warm and dry, in his palatial home in the city of Augsburg some two hundred miles away. He had traveled widely in his youth, spending many months on the trade routes spiraling outward from Augsburg, but those days were long past. Now envoys from the most powerful nobles in Europe came to pay him his due, and his reach extended everywhere. Mines in Tyrol and Hungary, money transfers for the Church, investments in Portuguese trading voyages to India, bets on currency exchange rates on the Antwerp money market: These were only a few of the activities that made the firm of "Ulrich Fugger and Brothers of Augsburg," of whom Jakob was the youngest and most active representative, one of the richest in Europe.

In the years leading up to his death in 1525 at the age of sixty-seven, Jakob Fugger would build this firm—later styled "Jakob Fugger and His Brothers' Sons"—into the most important finance and investment firm in Europe. Through a long-standing connection to the Habsburg dynasty, Jakob and his agents financed the elections of emperors and wars of vastly increasing scale and violence. In the sheer extent of his activity and its centrality to the process of state growth and the transformation of war, as well as his lone-wolf intensity, Jakob Fugger stood alone at the peak of European business. At his death, reports of his wealth made him the richest man who ever lived.

He stares out at the viewer from Albrecht Dürer's famous portrait with icy, calm self-assurance and just a hint of a smirk. A well-justified belief that he was smarter and more driven than his competition hovers beneath a humble surface. Above all, he was proud of his wealth and the work that had gone into acquiring it. He believed he had earned the millions of florins in his account books and had done so fairly. "Many in the world are hostile to me," he wrote. "They say I am rich. I am rich by God's grace without injury to any man." Others disagreed, claiming those same actions made him greedy and un-Christian. The armies he financed slaughtered Italian townspeople by the hundreds and thousands. The relentless, remorseless quest for profit squeezed the miners working Jakob's silver and copper mines so hard that they openly rebelled. Martin Luther wanted to curb him like a disobedient horse; one of Fugger's many convoluted financial schemes lay behind the sale of indulgences that so offended Luther that he wrote the *Ninety-Five Theses* and launched his career as a reformer.[1]

Jakob Fugger's stunning wealth was the result not only of his own considerable talents, but of a particular moment of transformative structural change in the world of banking, finance, and the broader European economy. While he was an extraordinarily successful and ruthless figure, his firm was one of many south German operations that exploded into prominence in the decades around 1500. The diversified portfolio of the firm, ranging from deposit banking and money transfers to industrial investment, was typical. The Habsburg dynasts' hunger for funds led them to many other lenders, the Fuggers included.

During Fugger's age, the center of economic gravity shifted from the Mediterranean fringe to northern Europe. The tools of finance—loans, currency exchange, accounting, and money transfers—became increasingly central. They left behind the medieval trading cities of Italy and south Germany and wound themselves into the fabric of the economy as a whole: in mine-shafts sunk deep into the mountains of Tyrol and Slovakia, in parish churches in rural northern Germany, and on the decks of merchant ships bound for India. Key sectors, such as mining and war, grew more and more capital-intensive. Capital was gasoline, poured onto the smoldering embers of royal ambitions and technological change. Firms like Fugger's provided that capital, stoked the fire, and grew impossibly rich in the process.

Medieval Banking and Usury

As Jakob Fugger's account books recorded increasingly larger sums of florins, gulden, and ducats in the opening decades of the sixteenth century, the practice of banking—the core of Fugger's business—had deep roots. Its beginnings lay in the Commercial Revolution of the High Middle Ages, centuries before Fugger's birth.

The sophisticated economy of the Roman Empire featured dense networks of interregional trade and full monetization, which meant lots of coinage and people thinking of the value of goods and services in monetary terms. This created a variety of banking practices, including loans for both consumption and investment. In the centuries following the empire's dissolution, however, the economy drastically contracted in scale and complexity. Banking is only necessary in a fully monetized economy with strong flows of information and high levels of medium- and long-distance trade. All of that disappeared in the early Middle Ages.[2] After the year 1000, however, activity once again expanded. The population grew, agricultural productivity rose, and trade moved beyond high-value luxuries like silks and spices to cheaper bulk goods, particularly cloth. Italian merchants were notably active, heading east to Constantinople, the Levant, Egypt, and north over the Alps to Champagne and the Low Countries. Slowly but surely, cities like Venice, Genoa, Siena, Florence, and Lucca became centers of international trade; small transactions and isolated sojourns became yearly trips to organized markets. The fairs of Champagne grew famous as clearinghouses for the continent's trade.[3]

By the middle of the twelfth century, Italian long-distance trade had given birth to a new era of banking. Such trade had specific needs: for currency exchange, because twelfth-century Europe had dozens of different monetary systems; for money transfers, since carting loads of coin from Genoa to Champagne was an open invitation for robbery at the hands of petty lordlings and their gangs of knights; and for investment capital to finance these increasingly large-scale expeditions. Banking had begun there with lowly entrepreneurs dealing in amounts small enough to take their cash reserves home in a chest every night. By the end of the thirteenth century, however, banking had matured into a major industry. Three classes of bankers had emerged, ranging from pawnbrokers—generally regarded as the scum of the earth— to money changers, who also took interest-bearing deposits, to the merchant-banking elite. While the first two categories were indispensable to the daily operation of trade and credit, it was the latter—merchant-bankers—who dominated medieval banking.[4]

The individuals and firms that occupied the top rungs of the medieval banking hierarchy always held diversified interests. The Medici Bank of Florence, the source of the famous family's wealth and power and the key financial institution of the fifteenth century, took on whatever activity carried the promise of return on investment: financial services for the papal court in Rome, the spice trade in Venice, luxury items for the court of the Duke of Milan, and cloth production in Florence itself, in addition to the usual interest-bearing deposits, money transfers, currency exchanges, and loans.[5] Capital—its productive use and growth—was key, not any particular line of business. This was also the case for Jakob Fugger and his family.

However, loans—the provision of credit—proved to be the heart of banking. In our modern era of credit, where we employ everything from straightforward student and auto loans to hyper-sophisticated tranches, this sounds straightforward. But the provision of credit carried serious complications in the business environment of the Middle Ages. The Church had strong feelings and guidelines on usury, which it defined in precise terms: Whatever exceeds the principal is usury (*Quidquid sorti accedit, usura est*). Nobody lends money without the expectation of return on investment, so what looks like a general ban on interest would seem to present a major barrier. In practice, however, usury was taken to mean a *certain* gain exacted by virtue of a loan. Bankers took this prohibition seriously, and worried with appropriate fervor about the state of their souls. More than a few wills of prosperous medieval investors set aside money for pious donations to clean up any residual usurious sins that might have snuck through. "He who commits usury goes to hell," wrote a fourteenth-century Italian, "he who doesn't, faces penury."[6]

This meant that standard loans as we understand them, with their set interest rates and payment periods, were prohibited. Still, bankers provided credit. How? If the loan involved a currency exchange, or went toward a speculative investment, the fact that it carried some risk made it theologically acceptable. Interest could be passed off as a gift unrelated to the core transaction or a share in investment profit, or through a slight tinkering with exchange rates on a currency transfer. The usury prohibition was serious business—no banker who cared about his position in his community wanted to be the target of a haranguing Franciscan's street-corner sermon on greed and usury—and it shaped the tools bankers employed in their trade in meaningful ways.[7]

By the last quarter of the fifteenth century, while the Fugger family was emerging at the top of the Augsburg heap, financiers throughout Europe understood and utilized these particular tools, such as bills of exchange. Dense financial networks spiraled outward from the major centers of commerce and finance: London, the Low Countries, the trading cities of the Hanse along the Baltic, the Rhineland, Catalonia, and Italy. Bills of exchange, which changed currency and concealed interest rates on loans, traveled easily between Florence and Bruges, Lyon and Milan, Venice and Strasbourg. A letter of credit issued in Lucca could be cashed at a banking establishment on Lombard Street in London, where the money could be used to buy wool from a consortium of English merchants. Banking had firm institutional foundations and agreed-upon ways of doing business, means of collective regulation, and a sense of trust and contractual integrity. It was the most highly developed form of the basic concepts of credit, and the economic institutions that underpinned them, all across Europe.

From 1200 to 1500, banking proper remained an Italian specialty, carried out by Florentines like the Medici, Genoese, Lucchese, and Sienese. But as the sixteenth century dawned, the center of financial gravity shifted quite suddenly and sharply north of the Alps. There, the cities of south Germany emerged as entrepots of international trade and finance, and Augsburg and the Fuggers found themselves at the heart of this new state of affairs.

The Rise of the South Germans

South Germany—roughly the region stretching from the Rhineland in the west to Munich in the east, bounded by Austria in the south and Frankfurt in the north—was not exactly the star of the medieval European economy at the turn of the sixteenth century. But it was no backwater, either. It was urban by medieval standards, stocked with populous locales like Augsburg, Nuremberg, and Ulm, though not as many large, dense cities as the Low Countries, northern Italy, or even the Rhineland. It had a thriving cloth industry, but not one that rivaled Flanders, Picardy, or Tuscany.

What south Germany really had was the good fortune of being in the right place at the right time. It lay in the heart of Europe, the crossroads of several of the key trade routes that united the continent, precisely when regional trade spiked and markets all across the continent were integrating. The vast, wealthy cities of northern Italy, like Milan and Venice, were just a hop across the Alps. The Rhineland, another vital north–south artery, was next door. The east–west route linking that region to the plains of Hungary and Poland ran directly through south Germany. There was easy access to the increasingly productive mines of Austria and Hungary. Essentially, south Germany offered natural geographic connections to the most important trade routes and markets in this part of the world.

It is one of the great paradoxes of medieval history that the Black Death, which killed somewhere between 40 and 60 percent of Europe's population—around fifty million people in total— also drastically raised living standards for those who survived. Scarce resources were concentrated in fewer hands, and attitudes about consumption shifted toward the more conspicuous and public. The steep increase in demand for fine cloth garments was one of the most visible symbols of a rise in living standards, and all across Europe, cloth production rose dramatically. South Germany was perfectly placed to cater to this growth industry. The region specialized in a durable cotton/wool combination called fustian, and fustian required infrastructure: the importation of raw cotton from Italy, the provision of credit to the manufacturers, and the distribution of the finished product to markets across Europe. The merchants of south Germany's thriving cities were perfectly placed to meet both needs. They popped up in Venice, Milan, Strasbourg, Cologne, Antwerp, London, and as far afield as Lisbon, selling high-quality cloth and establishing dense commercial networks that spanned the continent.[8]

The dramatic northward shift of banking and the rise of the Fuggers ultimately comes back to this fustian boom. Once established, medieval commercial networks tended to be remarkably durable and flexible. As long as there were trusted people in place who knew how local markets worked and what routes to take, the exact thing being transported—even money itself—could move along those same paths, using the same intermediaries. This had been true of the Florentines in the fourteenth and fifteenth centuries, and it would prove so again with the south Germans in the later fifteenth and sixteenth centuries.[9]

The Fuggers of Augsburg were the direct product of this

environment. The progenitor of the family was a weaver named Hans Fugger, who moved to Augsburg from a nearby village in 1367. The cloth industry was good to Hans, and at some point after arriving in the city he moved out from behind his loom to attend to the more lucrative aspects of the business. Details are scanty, but we can surmise that they included trade and financing. By his death in 1396, Hans had carved out a place for himself among Augsburg's wealthy elite, rising far beyond the station of a simple weaver.[10]

The family business continued under Hans's capable wife, Elisabeth, and their two sons, Andreas and Jakob. The two brothers worked together at first, presumably engaging in long-distance trade, but eventually split into separate firms. Andreas and his descendants, known as the Fuggers "vom Reh"—"of the roe deer," so named for the deer on their coat of arms—built a large and successful trade and financing business before it crashed in the 1490s. The descendants of this elder Jakob Fugger became the Fuggers "von der Lilie"—"of the lilies"—including the more famous Jakob Fugger the Rich.

Fifteenth-century Augsburg hummed with the tunes of big business. Almost nowhere on the continent had more to offer for those looking to make a fortune in buying, selling, trading, and manufacturing. Its elite was fundamentally mercantile, a collection of wealthy traders, financiers, and large-scale artisans who dominated both the city's economy and its politics. They were a tightly connected and exclusive bunch: united by marriages and a labyrinthine series of investments, driven apart by political and commercial competition. The Fuggers were neck-deep in this world, and established themselves as one of its leading families in the three generations that passed between Hans Fugger and the famous Jakob the Rich. Hans married the daughter of the master of the weaver's guild, and his son Jakob married the daughter of a wealthy goldsmith. Both of these women were excellent businesspeople in their own right, and each drastically increased the family fortunes after their husbands' deaths.[11]

Liquid capital flowed through these family and business networks at the apex of Augsburg society in ever-increasing quantities, like a river turning the wheel of a watermill. Every marriage between members of the city's elite was a new commercial bond, another opportunity to find money for profitable investment, and those investments were both varied and widespread. The long-distance cloth trade, the foundation of south Germany's new-found wealth, was just the beginning.

The Fugger Family

Jakob Fugger the Elder, the son of Hans Fugger and the founder of the Fuggers von der Lilie, had a number of children. This was an asset in the world of south German merchant clans: Sons were sent out to manage branch offices in other cities, and daughters could make advantageous marriages with other members of the merchant elite. Everything was an opportunity to further the family's prospects for wealth and honor, values that were fully intertwined. Three sons were particularly important to the prospects of Jakob the Elder's family line: Ulrich, Georg, and Jakob the Younger, whom we know as Jakob the Rich.

While Jakob the Rich is the most famous of the Fuggers, treating him as an outlier fundamentally distorts the reality of the business and social environment of the time. Hans Fugger had been wealthy, and Jakob the Elder was among Augsburg's richest citizens before his death. Jakob the Rich did not become so from humble circumstances or unlikely origins. He was not a bolt of lightning from the blue, but a product of a world already in motion. Family was everything: an anchor, a foundation, and, in material terms, the basis of an extended network that provided both reliable business associates and access to that most precious of resources, liquid capital.

When Jakob the Elder died in 1469, his business continued in the hands of his family. His wife, Barbara Bäsinger, was intimately involved in the running of the firm and remained so for decades. The family's taxable wealth, legally in Barbara's hands after her husband's death, doubled between 1472 and 1486. All seven of their sons had some role in the business; six of them were directly involved in working for the firm, including three who died young, and the fourth, a cleric named Marx Fugger who died in Rome in 1478, pushed some minor financial transactions for the Church in the family's direction. This was already a thriving, diversified, and geographically extensive firm by the time Jakob—born late, in 1459—came of age.

There is an old story that Jakob, like his elder brother Marx, was destined to be a cleric, since his family procured a clerical benefice for him in childhood. As this story goes, Jakob had to be pulled away from the Church and into the grimy world of business, a tug-of-war for his soul in which money won out over spirituality. This was not the case. In reality, his father had purchased a benefice for him—essentially, the rights to revenue from a parish, in this case located in the village of Herrieden, some sixty miles north of Augsburg. Sometimes the owner of a benefice actually performed the clerical duties associated with his parish; more often, he paid another cleric to do the job while pocketing the income himself. A benefice was simply one more smart investment for an upwardly mobile merchant family, a possible preparation for a clerical life should that prove viable for one of its many sons.[12] Jakob Fugger seems to have spent only a few months in Herrieden, and formally gave up his benefice in 1479.

The pursuit of money had called to Jakob long before he

resigned his benefice. One of his brothers, Peter, died in Nuremberg in 1473 while working for the business. Two other brothers, Hans and Andreas, died young while doing commercial apprenticeships in Venice some time before that. With their deaths, Jakob's participation in the family firm moved from a possibility—one modified by the teenager's ownership of the benefice—to a necessity. By 1473, the same year his brother Peter died, Jakob had traveled to Venice to take up his own commercial apprenticeship.

Venice and the Commercial Geography of the Late Middle Ages

This route from the emerging commercial powerhouse of south Germany to the center of the late medieval trading world in northern Italy defined both Jakob Fugger's career and the transformation of the European economy. From Augsburg the road ran to Innsbruck, the center of the Tyrol, then south over the Alps, into the Veneto, and on to the marshy splendor of Venice itself.

Jakob Fugger was no older than fourteen when he made this journey. No diary or letter tells us how he felt about it, or about his brothers' deaths. He set off south through the plains and low hills of the Lech Valley, following the river as it wound through rich farmland dotted with the occasional patch of forest. The spires of parish churches marked out the dense collection of villages crowded around the road. Peasants went out to work their fields and tend livestock, producing enough surplus to feed thriving cities like Augsburg, Ingolstadt, Munich, Ulm, Memmingen, Nuremberg, and others farther afield. Grain traveled north by road and along the river Lech. Cloth too traveled from the countryside to the cities, produced by a putting-out system where urban merchants—the Fuggers presumably among them—bought the raw wool and cotton and handed it over to peasants to weave, then collected the finished product and sold it on to buyers all over Europe. Perhaps the teenaged Jakob Fugger traveled south with just such a shipment; if not, he certainly saw them on the road, draft animals straining against their loads. The bulk cloth trade was the foundation of south Germany's wealth, and even an adolescent apprentice merchant understood that.

The flat plain of the Lech Valley dissolved into the crags of the Wetterstein Mountains as the road continued south. High ridges and jagged peaks rose up on every side where the road turned east and met the narrow Inn Valley. Innsbruck, the center of the Tyrol, one of the components of the Archduchy of Austria, lay at its heart. This was the home of one branch of the Habsburgs, soon to be one of the up-and-coming noble dynasties of Europe and key to the Fuggers' later fortunes. Farther east, up the Inn Valley at Schwaz, a complex of silver mines churned out a wealth of precious metal that only whetted the insatiable appetite of Archduke Sigismund. As a teenager, Jakob might not have been aware of the full implications of the mining boom. As an adult, he certainly was: Mining would soon become one of the firm's major interests.

The Brenner Pass, one of the major routes across the Alps, is just twenty miles to the south of Innsbruck. Wagons and heavily laden pack animals competed for space on the narrow road: Cloth and metal went south, while luxury silks, spices, and raw cotton went north. Other passes to the west carried still more traffic, including steel plate armor from Milan, other varieties of cloth, and wool. As he summited the pass, Jakob felt the chilly bite of the thin Alpine air. This was his first southward journey, but it would not be his last.

Jakob and his companions went south through meadows dotted with grazing sheep and blooming flowers and felt the cool shade as they passed through evergreen forests. After a few days' journey, the craggy ridges and peaks softened into rolling hills, and then the vast flat expanse of the Po Valley finally opened up before them. People were thick on the ground in densely urbanized northern Italy. Vicenza and Padua had populations in the thousands, each of them larger than Jakob's native Augsburg, and smaller cities, towns, and villages filled the landscape that lay between.

The thick black earth of the Po Valley was some of the most fertile in Europe, but not enough to feed every mouth in northern Italy. It took endless ships full of grain from the vast fields of the peninsula's southern reaches—Sicily and Naples—to meet the demand, and occasionally farther afield as well. This was an enormous business that required a constant stream of fat-bellied merchantmen plying the Adriatic and Tyrrhenian Seas, the provision of short-term credit to provide capital investments for the voyages, and the transfer of large amounts of cash via bankers. Europe's other great urban area, the Low Countries, mirrored this trade but with grain coming from Poland via the Hanse merchants of the Baltic.

Crossing the Po Valley, Jakob saw wagons groaning under the weight of sacks of grain. They competed for space on the road with dust-stained couriers carrying commercial papers and contracts, pilgrims headed for the holy sites of Rome who burned with religious zeal, and scarred mercenaries toting well-used weapons. Barges full of cereals slowly edged down the valley's many canals and rivers. Heading east toward the Adriatic, the solid, fertile ground dissolved into the marshy morass surrounding the lagoon of Venice. There, like a beacon amid the swamp, was the crown jewel of medieval Europe's greatest commercial region. This was Jakob's destination, the place where his brothers had died, and where he would learn the ropes of banking and commerce from masters of the trade.

Venice was the keystone of the trading networks in this part of the world. From it, vital routes spiraled outward in every direction. The harbor inside the lagoon serviced northern Italy and the Adriatic coast directly, bringing in timber for shipbuilding from Dalmatia and grain from southern Italy to feed the hungry mouths of this whole region. Luxury spices and silks traveled here from Alexandria, shipped via the Nile, across the Red Sea, and over the Indian Ocean before that. The cotton that the south German merchants brought north passed through here, as did some of the finished fustian searching for productive markets. Italian capital, funneled through the Medici of Florence and numerous other banks, found productive investment opportunities here. Crusade taxes and proceeds from sales of indulgences—literally buying salvation—passed through the Venetian money market on their way from the Church's far-flung outposts in Hungary, Poland, and Scandinavia to Rome. The Fondaco dei Tedeschi, the bustling house of the German merchants at the foot of the Rialto Bridge, was Jakob's classroom in his education as a businessman. From there, just on the Rialto, he could see the money changers and bankers. The bustling wharves and warehouses packed full of goods were a short stroll away.[13]

Nowhere else in Europe were the tools of commerce so finely honed and developed. In later life, Jakob Fugger was famous for his encyclopedic knowledge of bookkeeping. It is likely that Venice during the 1470s exposed him to the most cutting-edge examples of that art and science. Accounting mattered: The more accurately it reflected assets and liabilities, the better the manager could gauge where the firm stood, where the money was going, and, most importantly, how much it could afford to risk. The bigger the firm and the more complex its dealings, the more important accounting became.

Jakob Fugger's firm would grow to an unprecedented scale,

and its books were always in impeccable order. Decades after Jakob's time in Venice, a young Augsburg native named Matthäus Schwarz spent years seeking the finest training in accounting, making pilgrimages to Milan, Genoa, and Venice and soaking up everything he could learn. Upon his return to Augsburg, he went to work for Jakob Fugger, who put Schwarz's accounting knowledge to the test in a demanding oral examination. Schwarz realized at that moment, he later wrote, that all his extensive training was "little more than nothing" compared to Jakob Fugger's vast experience with and instincts for financial accounting. He could have simply stayed in Augsburg and learned from the master.

The whole of the medieval trading world was visible from Venice's docks: English wool, Indian spices, and Florentine bills of exchange. The teenaged Jakob gleaned everything he could from this open-air school. He was fond enough of Venice that he retained the Italian form of his name, Jacobo, well into his later years; here too he probably picked up the habit of wearing a gold beret, the hat so fetchingly perched atop his head in Dürer's famous portrait. Jakob's personality was defined by a deep vein of cold, ruthless rationality, but these faint glimmers of sentiment offered the slightest hint at something else.[14]

State Finance

In the early 1480s, as Jakob reached adulthood, new opportunities began to present themselves for the family firm. Business was booming in the capable hands of Ulrich; Georg; their mother, Barbara; and Jakob, who added his own talents to those of his brothers and the family's formidable matriarch.

State finance and mining were largely responsible for the staggering growth that followed over the subsequent decades. These two sectors sucked up enormous amounts of capital in orders of magnitude greater than before. More than anything else, this clear change in scale is what marks Jakob Fugger and his contemporaries as a real shift from their predecessors. They accumulated more capital, invested it in larger ventures, and reaped a great deal more profit from their activities.

In the 1480s, Archduke Sigismund, a cousin of the Holy Roman Emperor, Frederick III, ruled Tyrol. Sigismund was well into his fifties by that point and had enjoyed a long and not particularly distinguished career as a political wheeler-and-dealer. His major accomplishments had been trading one set of lands for another, mortgaging still others for cash, and participating in the alliance that eventually brought low his erstwhile ally, Duke Charles the Bold of Burgundy. This was all routine for an ambitious dynast of the period, as were the mixed results of his efforts. Not everybody, or even every Habsburg, was a winner. Yet Sigismund had something his contemporaries did not: the silver mines of Tyrol, made productive by expensive new techniques. A mining boom had hit the region, and production skyrocketed.

Archduke Sigismund retained strong customary rights over the mines' output and used their newfound wealth to further his ever-expanding (and continuously unsuccessful) political ambitions. Still, there was never enough money on hand to cover everything he wanted to do. Sigismund was hardly unique in this regard; we have already seen how Isabella and Ferdinand required constant injections of liquid cash to fund their wars. The major difference between them was the success rate of their respective ventures.

The solution to Archduke Sigismund's financial plight was, naturally, loans. Luckily for Sigismund, the thriving commercial cities of south Germany were right next door to Tyrol, and their equally thriving merchant elites had plenty of on-hand capital to lend. These businessmen, however, were nobody's fools. They were unlikely to make large investments in an archduke, no matter how well connected his dynasty, without something to guarantee their loans. This is how state finance and mining came to be closely intertwined for south German entrepreneurs of this age, including the Fuggers. After all, what better security on a loan could there be than pure silver?

Ulrich, Georg, and Jakob Fugger made their first loan to Archduke Sigismund in 1485. The grand total: just 3,000 florins, which paled in comparison to the 10,000 Sigismund owed to another trading firm and the 60,000 he had incurred to the director of Tyrol's financial administration. The Fuggers charged no interest on this relatively small sum, avoiding the usury prohibition entirely, and instead took their payment directly in silver: 1,000 marks, some 618 pounds' worth of precious metal. The relationship quickly deepened when Sigismund went to war with the Republic of Venice in 1487. Wars, as we know, require money, and Sigismund was already strapped for cash. A loan of 14,500 florins followed in the fall of 1487, then one for another 8,000 in the spring of 1488. A whopping 150,000 florins topped off the batch in the summer of that same year. In return, the Fuggers received the entire output of the archduke's silver mines at Schwaz.

The transactions involved here were labyrinthine. Technically, the Fuggers were buying the silver at a fixed price—eight florins per mark—and then paying the smelter five florins per mark for his work. The difference, three florins per mark, went to pay back the archduke's loan. Two hundred marks of silver per week went to the archduke's mint in the town of Hall to produce fine silver coinage, but the rest was the Fuggers' to sell on the open market. The difference between the fixed purchase price and the silver's real market value was the source of the Fuggers' profit on the transaction.

By the end of 1489, Sigismund owed the Fuggers the astronomical sum of 268,000 florins. The brothers could not possibly
have had all that on hand, meaning that they must have secured
outside capital investment from somewhere. The likeliest sources
came from the Fuggers' extended network within Augsburg:
from their wives' dowries, from their in-laws, from cousins, and
from peers at the elite drinking club that defined Augsburg's high
society. Each of those investments was yet another obligation that
had to be repaid. It is also possible that they themselves borrowed
some portion of the capital they loaned out, calculating that their
profit margins would make up for the interest they paid.[15]

Ensuring profitability was a demanding enterprise in and of
itself, requiring precise accounting to make the books balance,
a series of complex calculations—X amount of silver at Y likely
price for a loan of Z amount—and a deep knowledge of the European metal markets to make those calculations reasonably accurate. Matthäus Schwarz, Jakob Fugger's bookkeeper, summarized
the difference between his and his master's methods and those of
their competitors: "These little men write down their dealings in
poorly kept scrap-books, or on slips of paper, stick them on the
wall and make their reckonings on the window-sill." That would
not do for the brothers Fugger. Their precision determined the
success of their entire enterprise.[16]

Archduke Sigismund's debts eventually pushed him out of
his lands and into ignoble retirement. His replacement was his
Habsburg cousin Maximilian, the son and soon-to-be successor of Frederick III as Holy Roman Emperor. As an energetic,
bull-necked eighteen-year-old in 1477, Maximilian had made a
huge gamble, riding hundreds of miles through rival rulers' territory to make the romantic gesture that secured his marriage to
Mary, heiress of Burgundy. That charismatic and flamboyant act
made him co-ruler over the wealthy Low Countries in addition

to his motley collection of hereditary lands in the Holy Roman Empire. Mary's early death made that task even more difficult, leaving Maximilian the insecure and disliked regent for his young son, Philip, whom we have already met. This lucrative inheritance came at the cost of war with France, and Maximilian only retained his lands with personal bravery on the battlefield and with immense expenditures. The Fuggers vom Reh, the other line of the family, were one among many groups of bankers who made loans and transferred money to Flanders to pay Maximilian's soldiers in the late 1480s. In fact, the city of Leuven (now in Belgium) was supposed to guarantee one of Maximilian's loans to the Fuggers vom Reh. Leuven's refusal to do so directly caused this branch of the Fuggers' devastating bankruptcy.[17]

Maximilian spent his life plotting to expand his lands and secure still more for his children. He was successful, but at an enormous financial cost. By 1490, when he took over as archduke, his profligacy was already noteworthy, and it would become legendary by the end of his life. "At times when he wished to set forth to war," wrote an Augsburg merchant a couple of decades later, "his servants were so poor that they together with the emperor could not pay their reckoning at the inn."[18]

But an empty treasury was never enough to halt Maximilian's ambitions. He had an innovative, restless mind, one that never stayed fixed on the same plan for very long. One minute he was supporting pretenders to the English throne; the next, he was funding some of the first printed political propaganda; then he was plotting to outmaneuver the king of France and marry the heiress of the Duchy of Brittany; the next month, he turned his attention toward seizing territory from the Republic of Venice.[19] There was always a new scheme, another military campaign, a fresh diplomatic initiative, and all of it cost money that Maximilian did not have on hand.

Ulrich Fugger and Brothers of Augsburg were quite happy
to lend money to Maximilian, continuing the relationship they
had begun with his Habsburg cousin and predecessor, Sigismund. This begs the question of why they were willing to do
business with such a blatant spendthrift, whose limitless ambition so obviously exceeded his means. The answer was simple:
security. Unlike their now-bankrupt cousins, the Fuggers vom
Reh, Ulrich, Georg, and Jakob took their guarantees in the form
of precious metal, just as they had with Sigismund. Vast quantities of silver financed increasingly large loans, and the Fuggers
made immense profits as a result. One optimistic estimate suggests 400,000 florins in profit between 1485 and 1494, which is
likely too high, but only by a matter of degrees.[20]

Others lacked the Fuggers' precision and hardheaded sense for
business. In 1494, the Fuggers retained a claim on 40,000 florins'
worth of silver from Maximilian's mines as payment for previous advances. Maximilian had already pledged that silver as security for a substantial new loan from a consortium of Nuremberg
merchants. The Fuggers pressed their claim and got their silver,
Maximilian kept the money, and the Nuremberg merchants were
left out in the cold. Financing a rising state could result in either
of two outcomes: disaster, or untold wealth. The brothers Fugger
found the precise route to navigate between the disastrous outcomes of default and princely displeasure. All the great plans of
this era's state-building monarchs were built on access to credit.
Some creditors made out better than others.[21]

Mining

The silver mines of Tyrol, and the loans the Fuggers and others
secured on them, gave Maximilian the resources to pursue some
(but never all) of his capacious dreams. The silver mines on which

Maximilian's financial edifice rested were a recent development at the end of the fifteenth century, made possible by the feasibility of extremely expensive methods of extracting and refining the metal. Mining became incredibly capital-intensive, and the correspondingly large profits it produced enabled another capital-intensive process: state formation. The two developments were intertwined, and the Fuggers had a hand in shaping both.

Mining was hardly a new industry at the end of the fifteenth century. Copper could be found in tandem with silver as part of the same ore, and massive veins laced the hills and mountains of central Europe, which were riddled with centuries-old mine shafts. Even the ore-refining process that exploded in popularity around this time was not new. Liquation, or the *Saigerprozess*, involved adding lead to the copper-silver ore and repeatedly heating it until the silver bonded to the lead and drained away, leaving behind increasingly pure silver as a result. While probably known for centuries, this method was neither particularly popular nor cost-effective.[22]

Two things had to change to make large-scale liquation viable in the second half of the fifteenth century. First, the price of silver rose thanks to shortfalls in production from the more accessible European sources, which made it profitable to tap seams of ore containing relatively more copper and less silver. These seams were deeper in the ground, which meant the shafts had to be drained with pumps and special tunnels, which cost money. Also costly were the smelting furnaces and workshops, which had to be built bigger for workers to separate smaller quantities of silver from larger amounts of copper. Second, south German merchants like the Fuggers had the capital available to sink into these mine shafts and the relevant machinery. Everything involved in these operations was expensive, and they required large numbers of both skilled and unskilled workers, all of whom had to be paid. None of these mining operations would have been possible without investors willing to risk their money on them. Luckily, the aggressive, capital-flush merchant elite of cities like Augsburg, Nuremberg, Ulm, and Frankfurt fit that bill perfectly.[23]

An unslakable thirst for silver drove the initial expansion of the mining industry. The metal was the basis for the everyday coinage of the continent in addition to being precious in its own right, and its inherent value made it worthwhile to tap even difficult sources. Silver, however, was just the beginning. The same process that separated pure silver from copper, and the same kinds of facilities, could easily produce pure copper as well. Casting bronze cannon and other weapons for the ceaseless rounds of wars dominating the time required copper, and demand rose dramatically.

Capital—cold, hard cash—is what takes a technologically feasible process and scales it to meet consumer demand. This fact is every bit as true today for things like game-changing technology firms like Facebook or Uber as it was at the end of the fifteenth century for mining. South German merchants, just like the venture capitalists of today, saw opportunity in the earth and seized it. None did so more effectively than the Fuggers.

Jakob and his brothers, however, never jumped into a new field without doing their due diligence first. They had observed the financial dealings of Archduke Sigismund and Maximilian after him for years before they ever loaned either of them a single florin. The brothers spent their entire lives in proximity to the expanding mining industry of Tyrol, closely monitoring the cost of both silver and its production, before taking the metal as security. Their move into copper and mine ownership was no different. They first got a sense for the market by acting as Maximilian's agents, reselling some of his copper in Venice in 1492, then bought up some Tyrolean copper on their own account in May 1494. In the meantime, the firm purchased shares in mines near Salzburg, moving steadily from distribution to ownership.

This was all careful preparation for their next move. On November 15, 1494, an agent of the Fuggers' firm signed a contract with a businessman and mining engineer named Hans Thurzo and his son, Georg. Thurzo was a native of Kraków and had recently leased an extensive silver and copper mining complex in Neusohl, in what is now Slovakia. He was a mining expert with extensive experience in the industry and deep contacts with the Hungarian political elite, but he needed financing. The contract the brothers' agent placed in front of him would provide it.

The scale and complexity of this new operation was mind-boggling. It required careful political handling: The mines technically belonged to the king of Hungary, who had recently come to a dynastic agreement with Maximilian. The bishop of Pécs claimed the mines himself, and it took pressure from Maximilian and 700 ducats' worth of gifts from the Fuggers to get him to sign over his leases to Hans Thurzo. Every new lease and piece of construction required the approval of the king of Hungary, a relationship that had to be carefully massaged. Providing credit to the Hungarian royals helped with that, as did the 10,000 florins' worth of presents the Fuggers gave to various powerful ecclesiastics and Hungarian officials between 1494 and 1500. The brothers calculated, quite rightly, that any potential loss would be offset by the massive mining profits.[24]

That was just the political side. Profitable mines required expensive machinery, vast smelting works, and hammer mills, and the Fuggers paid for larger and larger installations at Neusohl and elsewhere. Lead was an important part of the *Saigerprozess*, so the Fuggers had to acquire their own lead mine and buy more of the essential raw material on the open market. Outside their relationship with Thurzo, the brothers acquired still more mines and built additional smelting works elsewhere. The total investment in their Hungarian mining trade topped a million florins by 1504, more than 100,000 florins per year.

Once mined and smelted, the copper and silver had to be taken to market. Much of it went to Venice, especially early on, but soon there was far too much production for any single market to handle. A Europe-wide distribution network of staggering scale was the only viable solution. New roads, financed by the Fuggers, carried the refined metal. Ongoing relationships with the petty lords, bishops, and the princes who owned the lands through which the goods would travel kept the materiel safe in transit and minimized pesky tolls and delays. Agents in the key points of the network, including Wrocław, Kraków, Ofen (now Budapest), and Leipzig, coordinated shipments. Carters carried the goods to Gdansk, Stettin, and Lübeck on the Baltic, where longshoremen loaded it onto ships bound for Antwerp, the emerging financial hub and key port of northwestern Europe. Money moved from place to place in vast quantities, paying the employees in each location and transferring the remaining funds back to the home office. Streams of information about prices, the state of current accounts, and subordinates' performances flowed from every place in the network back to the center in Augsburg. The whole Hungarian copper enterprise was organized as a separate contractual entity from the Fugger firm proper; the main firm technically bought the copper and silver and then sold it on, which added another layer of bookkeeping complexity to the operation.[25]

The profits associated with these efforts were astronomical. The Neusohl mines alone accounted for nearly 40 percent of Europe's copper output, leaving aside the already lucrative silver, and the Fuggers played a dominant role in the Alpine copper trade, which made up another 40 percent of European copper production. It took forty-one ships to carry the Fuggers' Hungarian copper from Gdansk to Antwerp in 1503. Those ships accounted for just one of several points of origin, and for only a small portion of their total copper stock.[26] By 1504, Ulrich Fugger and Brothers of Augsburg was already one of the wealthiest firms in Europe.

Diversified Interests

As the Fuggers' business expanded and grew more complex, the brothers remade their firm with a series of new contracts. These agreements laid out in specific terms that the three brothers were now equal partners, how much of their invested capital was to remain with the firm, and how payments to heirs were to be made in the event of the death of one of the brothers. This replaced the traditional arrangements, more reliant on custom, that had existed for most of the firm's existence. The Fuggers were not alone in this. Contracts of this kind—precise, focused on the main partners rather than extended family, and excluding feckless or greedy heirs—were becoming the norm among south German merchants. The brothers renewed this agreement after its initial six-year term expired, and then let it run afterward without a formal renewal. Ulrich died in 1506, Georg in 1510, leaving Jakob alone atop one of the largest firms in Europe.

Only then did the business become Jakob Fugger and His Brothers' Sons, a lone-wolf operation with Jakob exercising dictatorial control over both his few surviving family members and a complex network of diversified interests: "I have determined to carry on and manage the business myself, and to take industriously in hand my two brothers' sons," stated the new firm's articles of association. "Furthermore shall my above-mentioned four nephews collectively... recognize and look upon me as the head of this my business, together which such trade as I give them to do and accomplish." Jakob was in charge. Of that there was no question.[27]

Jakob, soon to be bestowed his immortal nickname of "the Rich," tends to get most or all of the credit for the success of his firm; he is the star of the show, the Richest Man Who Ever Lived. But while Jakob was an exceptional businessman—much of the impetus for the firm's development of mining and state finance was his doing—his brothers were hardly slouches in their time. Both had defined roles, and there is no indication that they botched or ignored their responsibilities, obliging their genius younger brother to bail them out. Georg was often resident in Nuremberg, where he coordinated the firm's activity in one of its major markets and transshipment points. Ulrich handled things in Augsburg, including the delicate relationships with other members of the city's merchant elite that were so essential for raising capital and finding reliable agents and employees. Jakob's extensive travel on behalf of the firm—to Venice, to Vienna in 1494 to cement the new Hungarian trade, through the Tyrol, and to Frankfurt, among others—was only possible because of his brothers' activities. The firm, like practically all south German merchant affairs, had been a group effort. Jakob's iron-fisted rule between 1510 and 1525 was the exception, not the norm.[28]

Jakob's viselike grip on the firm's operations after 1510 was also unusual in comparison to its contemporaries and competitors; the Welsers of Augsburg, the second-largest firm of the period, had no fewer than eighteen partners, and probably more. Yet the wild growth in that period, and the firm's exceptionally diversified interests, were precisely the norm. The Fuggers were not the only south German merchants, or even Augsburg natives, dealing in Tyrolean silver or Hungarian copper. They were also not the only ones making loans to the insatiable Maximilian. The Fuggers still dealt in bulk cloth, which had been the foundation of their business, and the luxuries purchased on the teeming Rialto of Venice. They dabbled in the new Portuguese trade with India by investing in the 1504 fleet. Other firms had different points of emphasis: The Welsers and Höchstetters (also of Augsburg) invested much more heavily in Portuguese voyages and the spice trade, which were only ever minor lines of business—though profitable ones—for Jakob and his brothers.[29]

All of the south German firms, regardless of the name in the window or their precise emphases, employed the tools of banking and finance. The Höchstetters took deposits from anybody who would offer them, ranging from servants to princes, and paid interest on those deposits. The Fuggers were more discerning about their investors and focused their efforts on Augsburg's merchant elite and their considerable network of extended family and marriage relations. They also took money from political allies and other wealthy financiers, including Cardinal Melchior von Meckau, an ambitious ecclesiastic and administrator for the Tyrolean administration. His unexpected death in 1509 actually left the Fuggers in dire straits, since the 150,000 florins he had on deposit represented most of the firm's working capital at the time. As with any other bank, the Fuggers paid out interest. They were merchants and investors first. Banking was simply a means to an end, a way of raising the necessary capital to fund their other endeavors.[30]

The real utility of banking went far beyond deposits and interest. Bills of exchange, letters of credit, and money transfers in all of their varied forms were central to the practice of banking. The Fuggers and their ilk continued along those same lines. They were innovators, not in the tools at their disposal, but in scale and density of use. Where the famous Medici had dealt in tens of thousands of florins' worth of bills of exchange only a few decades earlier, the Fuggers and their contemporaries worked with hundreds of thousands. It is not a coincidence that Antwerp emerged as the new center of the European financial world in the early sixteenth century, replacing Bruges, which the Italians had favored for centuries. The scale of their business was drastically larger, and that scale served as a gravitational field bending the orbit of the wider commercial world around it.[31]

Because of the convoluted nature of their varied business interests, firms like the Fuggers were constantly moving eye-watering sums of money from place to place and exchanging one currency for another. A loan to Maximilian was not a single transaction but a whole series of them. The creditors assembled the capital from funds on hand and new investments or secondary loans, each of which was its own transfer; in 1515, for example, Jakob had to borrow heavily from "good friends" to make a massive loan to the emperor.[32] The Fuggers then transferred the money to the destination (or destinations) via one or more bills of exchange. Upon receipt, the Fuggers' local agents might need to engage a money changer to get the necessary quantities of hard cash, which was yet another layer of transactions. State finance was just one piece of the Fuggers' business, and it required multiple transfers of funds and a detailed command of all the banker's financial tools.

Compared to state finance, the Fuggers' business with the Church was minor. The Church relied on the tools of banking to run its myriad financial dealings. Every newly elected bishop owed the pope a duty called the *servitia*. The pope claimed a portion of every benefice, the income from a parish like the one Jakob the Rich had held in his youth. Each diocese collected crusade taxes, which might or might not be used for crusading. Some regions owed a special tax called Peter's Pence. Last, but not least in terms of long-term importance, the popes claimed a portion of the proceeds from sales of indulgences, the spiritual get-out-of-jail-free cards that cleansed the buyer's sins and pulled beloved relatives out of Purgatory. These amounts of money were not necessarily large in themselves—a few thousand florins here and there—but they were numerous, and the ecclesiastics making these transfers were good friends for any important firm to maintain.

The Fuggers handled financial transfers for the Church as early as 1476, probably thanks to the efforts of their soon-to-be-deceased brother Marx Fugger, who was a cleric stationed in Rome on behalf of the family firm. These transactions continued as necessary for decades afterward, including advances on a crusade subsidy for the Kingdom of Hungary against the Turks in 1501. On many occasions, they handled indulgence payments for popes Julius II and Leo X, the latter of whom financed the building of St. Peter's Basilica in Rome. The most famous of these dealings occurred in 1516, when the Fuggers loaned a substantial sum to a would-be bishop to buy his office. A sale of indulgences paid back the loan, and the Fuggers transferred the proceeds to Rome. This was everyday business for the Fuggers, but the sales drive had serious unintended consequences: The exploitative marketing campaign employed to sell the indulgences so bothered Martin Luther that he was compelled to write his *Ninety-Five Theses*, lighting the fuse of the Protestant Reformation.

Ironically, when the imperial authorities summoned Luther to Augsburg in 1518 to account for his dangerous words, the reformer made his passionate case for self-defense in Jakob Fugger's lavish home.[33]

The Habsburg Future

Tyrolean silver was the key to unlocking state finance on a new scale, which in turn created further opportunities for capital investment in mining, the profits of which could be tapped for still more loans. This was a classic capitalist feedback loop, and it was the foundation of the Fuggers' business. It also drew them deeper and deeper into Maximilian's endless, expensive, and only rarely successful schemes.

Maximilian's debts had ballooned to the point of absurdity in the first two decades of the sixteenth century, mostly due to his burgeoning interest in Italy. In theory, Holy Roman Emperors—the office into which Maximilian had followed his father—enjoyed a vast array of rights to legal jurisdiction, revenues, and control over much of the peninsula. Those rights slipped away after the middle of the fourteenth century as emperors turned their attention toward Germany. The Italians grew richer, better able to defend themselves, and more secure in their cultural and political independence. Yet a powerful and engaged emperor could always try to reclaim those lapsed rights, and the endlessly, tiresomely ambitious Maximilian had pushed just such an attempt to his financial limits.

Following King Charles VIII's descent into Italy in 1494, and the wars that ensued between his France and Ferdinand and Isabella's Spain, Maximilian saw his opportunity. In 1508, he joined a coalition against the Republic of Venice, looking to seize disputed land along their Alpine border. Maximilian remained engaged in off-and-on wars in Italy and the Low Countries for the rest of his life. At first, he was fighting the Venetians as part of an alliance with the French, the Spanish, and the pope; before long, he was fighting against France. The results were mixed, as they so often were for Maximilian: His soldiers' initial forays into

Venetian territory in 1508 ended in crushing defeat and humiliation. The emperor led a larger army south himself in 1509, but failed to take Padua, and was only saved by the grace of French intervention. Maximilian then switched sides, turned on the French, allied with the English and Ferdinand of Aragon, and won a major victory in the Low Countries in 1513. It was precisely the kind of duplicitous, too-clever-by-half warring and politicking with which Maximilian had occupied his entire life. The Italian Wars and associated conflicts saw a drastic increase in the scale and cost of war, and Maximilian had to find the money to pay for all of it somewhere.[34]

Once again, the Fuggers found themselves at a critical point, filling Maximilian's coffers and enabling the ongoing conflict. Maximilian used future mining output as security to borrow 300,000 florins from the Fuggers in October 1508. This loan paid for his failed Padua expedition of the following year. Other creditors, like the Florentine Frescobaldi, even borrowed from the Fuggers to facilitate still more loans to Maximilian and transfers on his behalf. The amounts grew and grew, paying for further wars, luxurious entertainments, and various schemes. "We must necessarily entertain our royal brothers and their children, as well as the high personages whom they bring with them, using royal regalia, silver plate, and other tokens of honor," Maximilian wrote in 1515. "As you yourselves may imagine, we require for this a considerable sum of money." It is impossible to imagine a more fitting epitaph for the spendthrift emperor.[35]

By 1518, nearing the end of his life, Maximilian was flat broke. Jakob Fugger loaned him the comparatively minuscule sums of 1,000 and 2,000 florins at a time simply to meet household expenses and pay for food.[36] His debts to the Fuggers were so vast that Jakob could not have separated his firm from Maximilian even if he had wanted to, and Jakob Fugger did not, in fact, want to. Despite the travails and difficulties of doing business with Maximilian, the relationship had proven incredibly profitable over the past three decades. The mining business, the linchpin of Jakob's wealth, relied on the political relationship that the repeated loans helped cultivate.

Maximilian's heir, a nineteen-year-old named Charles, looked like a much safer investment. The grandson of Isabella of Castile and Ferdinand of Aragon, Charles had already taken over his grandparents' combined kingdoms following Ferdinand's death in 1516. He controlled the Low Countries in his own right as the great-grandson of Charles the Bold, the long-dead Duke of Burgundy. Most important, when Maximilian died, the young Charles would also have the best possible claim as his grandfather's successor as Holy Roman Emperor.

The position of Holy Roman Emperor, however, was an elected one. Seven key lords of the empire had votes in 1519: the archbishops of Mainz, Cologne, and Trier; the king of Bohemia; the elector of the Palatinate, a collection of fragmented territories around the Rhine; the Margrave of Brandenburg, whose territory centered on Berlin; and the elector of Saxony. And Charles was not the only candidate. King Francis I of France and Henry VIII of England were both contenders, and the aggressive Francis had already received guarantees from two electors.

Maximilian knew that he and Charles would have to buy the necessary votes. The old emperor was out of money, but Charles was not. The young king had tremendous resources in both Spain and the Low Countries to serve as security on any loans. Only one man could be counted on to provide that much money. Maximilian began negotiating with Jakob Fugger in earnest and secured his agreement at the end of 1518. Come January 1519, as he lay dying, the old emperor could rest assured that all his years of plotting and failure and ruinous debt and ambition had placed his grandson in position to become the most powerful ruler of the sixteenth century.

Jakob Fugger was the agent of that coronation. He agreed to put forward the staggering sum of 543,585 florins, roughly two-thirds of the total cost, in support of Charles. In the end, Jakob covered the entire 850,000 florins himself, cashing bills of exchange from the Welsers of Augsburg and a trio of Italian firms for the last third. Charles—now Charles V, king of the Romans, and soon to become a crowned emperor—had a throne, and perhaps more important, a creditor.[37]

The End of Jakob Fugger

This was the action that transformed Jakob Fugger from merchant to kingmaker and secured his reputation for all time. "It is well known that Your Imperial Majesty could not have gained the Roman Crown save with mine aid," Jakob wrote to Charles V a few years later, "and I can prove the same by the writings of Your Majesty's agents given by their own hands."[38]

Whatever his debts, Charles V was not much more concerned with repaying loans than his grandfather had been. Still, that did not much affect the health of Jakob Fugger's firm. The revolving door of loans and payments continued. Hundreds of thousands of florins slowly trickled into the Fugger account books and more went out to pay Charles's soldiers and the innumerable expenses accrued by an ambitious, restless, and powerful emperor.

But time had passed since the days of Jakob's youth, and he was growing old and sick. He turned sixty-six years old in 1525 and kept his relentless work habits, only reluctantly entrusting his nephews with roles in the firm. As Christmas approached, his health deteriorated, and still he kept working. Archduke Ferdinand of Austria—Charles V's brother—was in Augsburg for a conclave with important local nobles. The archduke's aides talked Fugger into one last loan, for old times' sake, even as he lay on his deathbed. Two days before his death, in his last act as head of the firm, Jakob denied a loan request from Duke Albrecht of Prussia. Albrecht was a recently converted Lutheran, and Jakob Fugger—a staunch supporter of the traditional Church—did not do business with heretics.[39]

Dawn was hours away in the early morning of December 30, 1525, and no sound disturbed the streets of Augsburg. A thin stream of candlelight flickered through the glass windows of Jakob Fugger's magnificent house onto the street beyond, bobbing up and down as a priest strode through the dark and deathly quiet home. Only a nurse attended the dying man, who had been comatose now for nearly two days, when the priest arrived to administer last rites. Fugger's wife was elsewhere, perhaps with the man she married soon after his death. His only child, an illegitimate daughter, was with her mother and the man she had married. His nephews—his close partners and associates for the past decade and a half—had business elsewhere or did not care to be present.

When Jakob Fugger died, at around 4 a.m., the city slept. Nobody recorded the details of the funeral in the coming days, and there is little indication of mourning. Jakob Fugger's pen recorded instructions, commands, and figures, never sentimentality. It would not have been fitting for him to die surrounded by friends and loving family. Those were not the kinds of relationships he cultivated. The impact of his life made itself felt in different ways: in the charitable foundations he left behind in Augsburg, the wealth he had brought to his native city, the art that adorned his home, and the overstuffed account books he bequeathed to his nephew and chosen successor, Anton. Between 1511 and his death in 1525, Jakob had increased the firm's assets nearly ten times over. He began life as the youngest son of a prosperous merchant and ended it as one of the richest people who ever lived.[40]

Following his uncle's death, Anton Fugger turned the firm into the court banker to the richest and most powerful monarchs in the world, their rule stretching from Peru to Hungary, in a period of war and sudden change. Yet Anton, for all his own talents, was simply building on foundations laid down by his uncle. The shift in scale from a few thousand florins in loans to Archduke Sigismund to Charles V owing hundreds of thousands was the one that mattered, the defining shift of a period of global transformation. Jakob Fugger's capital flowed into mining, state-building, war, the suppression of peasants' rebellions, and voyages of exploration and global trade. His money lay at the root of all these developments.

As silence descended within the Fugger house, facing the old Roman road that ran through Augsburg, Jakob's money created a deafening racket elsewhere in Europe. Pumps slurped up water deep inside mine shafts. Trip-hammers pounded onto bits of ore to break them up. Superheated furnaces whooshed and melted down the ore. Oxen bellowed and mules brayed, protesting against their too-heavy loads. Coins tumbled into purses and chests, clink after satisfying clink. Pens scratched entries in account books, debits and credits in neatly organized columns. Even in death, Jakob Fugger's books always balanced.

———— ⚭ ————

CHAPTER 4

Götz von Berlichingen and the Military Revolution

June 1504, Landshut, Bavaria

The rotten-egg stench of burnt gunpowder permeated the humid summer air, clashing with the earthy aroma of congealed sweat on unwashed bodies and the ordure of horses. The beasts neighed and nickered, but the clang of steel on steel, the sharp crack of arquebuses, the twang of crossbow strings loosing their bolts, and the booming roar of cannon drowned them out. Above the din, men's cries carried all the way to the town of Landshut and the castle walls rising in the distance beyond. Summer sunlight glinted off the polished steel plates of men-at-arms on horseback as they drove their lances down into the droves of enemy foot soldiers sheltering in a shallow ditch. Long pikes jabbed upward and arquebus muzzles exploded in flame and drifting clouds of white smoke in response.

Driven back by the fierce defense, the men-at-arms spurred their horses and retreated while the clash continued in the open field. One of them raised the flat visor of his helmet and pushed it onto the back of his head. Sweat plastered thinning strands of blond hair to a high forehead and dripped down a bulbous nose. Only a few lines marked a face just reaching its midtwenties, but a lifetime of violence had long since rearranged its features with scars and that crooked, misshapen nose. Dents and scratches old and new marred his steel breastplate and helmet. A battered, well-used sword hung at his right side.

Having wiped the sweat of exertion from his eyes, he swung his visor back down and reentered the fight alongside the other men-at-arms, who thrusted with their lances as they tried to get over and around the ditch. The roar of cannon pierced the clangs and cries of the battle; lance held tightly in hand and close to his body, the soldier was readying himself from shoulder to fist for another thrust when a blast sounded across the battlefield, followed by a sudden, hideous crunch. The young man-at-arms felt a sudden pain in his right forearm and looked down through the narrow slit of his visor. His lance lay on the ground near his horse's hooves, but he did not recall dropping it.

It took a moment to register that only a thin ribbon of mangled flesh was keeping his hand attached to what remained of his arm. The enemy cannonball had driven the pommel and crossbar of the sword deep into the meat of his forearm through the tiny gap between his steel gauntlet and the metal plates of his vambrace, nearly severing the limb.

The image seared itself into his brain. Many years in the future, long after blindness had taken his sight, Götz von Berlichingen had no trouble recalling every detail of that moment: the precise way in which the scales of his armor plate were bent around the edges, how the crossbar had lodged in his flesh, the way his hand dangled at an obscene angle from mere tissue.[1]

Years of training, battle experience, and the onset of shock kept Berlichingen calm in the saddle as he turned his horse and galloped away from the skirmish. If the injury itself did not kill him, infection certainly would. But perhaps as a testament to his particular combination of relentless pugnacity and devilish luck, Berlichingen did not die. Following a protracted recovery, he replaced his mangled right hand with an iron prosthetic, determined to continue his life of scrapping, pillaging, feuding, and war for years to come.

Holy Roman Emperors would declare Götz of the Iron Hand—as he soon came to be known—both an outlaw and a valuable mercenary. A noble by birth, he would fight alongside peasants in one of the largest social revolts in European history. Johann Wolfgang von Goethe would find his memoir two centuries after his death and turn him into the hero of a famous play.

As a member of the lower nobility, Berlichingen was defined by both war and his broader role in society. Nobles fought for material rewards and for status. Yet as the sixteenth century dawned, gunpowder, rising states, and enormous influxes of capital were fundamentally changing the art of war. For people like Berlichingen, this Military Revolution was a world-upending sequence of events. What was a knight to do if any upstart artisan with an arquebus could blast through his fine, expensive armor and win the day? The freedom to defend one's honor and status with private violence was a key facet of a knight's identity; what freedom did he have if emperors and princes went around exerting their increasing authority and making war their public business?

Most nobles made their peace with this new state of affairs. The day of the armored knight dominating the battlefield may have come to an end, if it ever actually existed, but a knight with land and resources could still make war his profession. After all, this was the great age of well-paid mercenary armies. All across Europe, knights and nobles transformed themselves from feudal warriors to military entrepreneurs. Credit and contracts, the bread and butter of European commercial society, were no less a part of the business of war than they were of banking, mining, or the wool trade.

The region of southern Germany that Götz von Berlichingen called home was a key epicenter of the business of war throughout this period. His extended family, friends, acquaintances, and rivals—knights and nobles all—dove headfirst into this world of military entrepreneurship. Berlichingen, however, did not embrace that path. He insisted on fighting his private wars and feuds, robbing merchants and quarreling with bishops and other knights, and repeatedly getting into trouble with authorities. His antics would result in his living fifteen years under house arrest. And in the end, the growing war machine of the sixteenth century managed to pull in even this most hardheaded of soldiers. The old ways and the new met, clashed, and the new eventually emerged victorious.

Military Revolutions

Götz von Berlichingen's life saw a deep, rapid, and fundamental transformation of warfare. Massed firepower rendered the armored knight obsolete; armies grew; and strategies and tactics that relied on these larger armies became infinitely more complex and ambitious. War took a greater and greater toll on society: More crops were burned, more villagers were slaughtered in senseless raids, more young men lay dead on battlefields, more wealth was squeezed to pay for the mounting costs, culminating in the decades-long calamity that was the Thirty Years' War between 1618 and 1648. That conflict turned the entirety of central Europe into a burnt-over war zone, killing roughly 15 percent of the population in the region and becoming proportionately the most destructive conflict in European history. That was where the transformations of Berlichingen's lifetime inevitably led. Gunpowder, the new fortifications built to withstand cannon after the fifteenth century, and the intertwined issues of the size of armies and the increasing scope of war combined to produce a rising chorus of tragedy.[2]

These developments may have been less revolutionary than they seem, since all of them grew directly out of developments made between 1300 and 1500. War in the Middle Ages had not been stagnant. In fact, the stereotyped ideal of a feudal king calling on his vassals—armored knights all—to render him limited military service in return for land had long since been outmoded. All of the English armies of the Hundred Years' War (1337–1453) were paid. Volleys of arrows from their longbowmen had ended the battlefield reign of aristocratic knights long before the first arquebus came out of a foundry. Cannon first appeared on battlefields in the middle of the fourteenth century, and by the middle of the fifteenth they had set the tone for siege warfare. King Charles VII's artillery train shredded the final English army to bring the war to French soil in 1453. That same year, the Ottoman sultan Mehmet's cannon blasted holes in Constantinople's formerly impregnable thousand-year-old walls. France finished its long war with England by employing a professional standing army built around companies of armored lancers and archers. The dukes of Burgundy followed suit, as did many of the Italian city-states around this time. As the new century opened, most of the technologies and mechanisms of raising armies that would dominate the 1500s were already in place, and had been for some time.[3]

The opening decades of the sixteenth century, however, brought a series of dramatic shifts. The preexisting technological shifts and logistical structures coalesced into a distinct method of waging war that revolved around pikes, handguns, artillery, and fortifications. Infantry did not immediately eclipse the armored man-at-arms on horseback, but the balance of numbers—and tactical importance—did appreciably move toward foot soldiers. All of this drove a massive, rapid increase in the scale, intensity, and cost of war. And Götz von Berlichingen had a front-row seat.

The Italian Wars, the defining conflict of the coming century, erupted in 1494 when King Charles VIII of France crossed the Alps. The twenty-three-year-old king, hungry for land and glory, marched south with an army full of professional lancers, Swiss mercenary pikemen, and the largest artillery train Italy had ever seen. He rampaged his way to the throne of the Kingdom of Naples, forever changing European power politics in the process. The following year, King Ferdinand of Aragon entered the war, adding a rising Spain to the conflict. Then Holy Roman Emperor Maximilian opted to get involved, hoping to win some ripe territorial prizes for himself. The Republic of Venice added itself to a coalition opposed to Charles's expansive Italian ambitions. Both sides tried to entice King Henry VII of England to join them.

The stage was set for a vast, interlocking, almost constant state of conflict that would last for decades. It began with Charles VIII and his designs on Naples but soon morphed into a dynastic and geopolitical conflagration that engulfed Europe entirely. From the moors of Northumberland to the rocky coast of Granada, from the peaks of the Pyrenees to the vast flats of the Hungarian Plain, army after army set forth to fight battles, lay sieges, and immiserate those villagers and townspeople who had the misfortune of lying in their path. Over the next sixty-five years (1494–1559), the longest period of general peace lasted just five years. Even outside the great-power conflicts of western Europe, wars large and small were easy to find: campaigns against the Ottomans in Hungary and the Mediterranean; the incessant raids by Barbary corsairs on the coasts of Italy and Spain; the smaller wars of princes, nobles, and cities against one another. The last of these was Berlichingen's particular specialty. While he was not a direct participant in the Italian Wars, his social world was full of people whose lives and business interests revolved around those enormous conflicts.

Incessant battlefield slaughter and grinding sieges created fertile ground for military entrepreneurship and innovation. The riches of kings, emperors, and princes flowed into the pockets of recruiting captains, mercenary soldiers, cannon founders, armorers, suppliers, and the bankers who transferred the funds. The actual amounts of money involved always fell short of what the contracts promised, but the sums were nonetheless considerable, requiring the tight squeezing of rulers' fiscal resources to even come close to making good. The armies grew larger and stuck around longer, and the off-seasons were fewer and further between. War had become a business like any other. This, more than any technological change, was the essence of the Military Revolution.[4]

Swimming Against the Tide

This era produced great captains who assembled thousands of mercenaries on contract for kings and emperors. Innovators experimented with new battlefield formations that maximized the possibilities of gunpowder handguns and cannon, while commanders developed grand strategies and visionary tactical plans for handling soldiers in clashes that dwarfed those of the previous century.

Götz von Berlichingen was not one of them. Even well into his stout, potbellied sixties, he remained a man-at-arms, riding off to war on horseback, wearing a full suit of steel plate and carrying a sword and lance. His wars were mostly small-scale feuds between cities and noblemen rather than the epic confrontations of dynastic states.

But Berlichingen was still a part of the Military Revolution. War for honor and profit was his occupation from childhood to retirement, and violence was a fundamental part of his identity. He continued to raise troops on contract in the service of lords, princes, and emperors. His family, friends, and rivals were all in the business of military contracting, some on a truly enormous scale. As has been true throughout history, war is less heroic battles and more a drudgery of marching, raiding, and skirmishing, all of which Berlichingen highlighted at length in his memoir. The sound of gunfire, that haunting melody of new warfare, often rang in his ears. There is no better symbol of the Military Revolution than Berlichingen's defining injury: A cannonball destroyed his strong right arm, the sword-swinging, lance-holding means of enforcing his knightly prowess.

Berlichingen's stubborn insistence on doing things his way was in direct contravention of the rising tide of state power that surrounded him. Feuding lay at the core of his occupation and self-image, and his dozens of petty wars feature prominently in his long-winded, self-congratulatory memoir; the practice was on its way out, however, and Berlichingen was a member of the last generation to make their living in that fashion. Princes and emperors squeezed the political and legal systems of their respective capacities for private war, eventually managing to pull men like Berlichingen into their military machines. Berlichingen's final campaigns were on contract, as a part of an army led by the Holy Roman Emperor Charles V. Even a maverick, independent killer like Berlichingen eventually succumbed to the trends of his age.

The Life of a Noble

Despite his distinctive iron hand and boastful memoir, Götz (short for Gottfried) von Berlichingen was a deeply ordinary member of his social class. Born around 1480 in what is now Baden-Württemberg, approximately eighty miles west of Nuremberg, he was the youngest of eight surviving children born to the minor nobleman Kilian von Berlichingen. With three older brothers, Gottfried had no chance of inheriting the family's eponymously named estate of Berlichingen. He would have to make his own way in the world, and that way was built on violence.

"I have verily heard from my blessed father and mother, and also from my brothers and sisters who were older than me, as well as from old servants and maidservants who were in service with them, that I was a wondrous young boy," his memoir begins, "and that I already showed and behaved in my childhood that many people realized and deduced that I would shape into a war-ring man (*kriegsman*) or horseman (*reuterßman*)."[5]

If we are to believe the author—and there is no reason to doubt him—war was his calling from an early age, and everyone around him knew it. His childhood involved riding, hunting, swordsmanship, working with the lance, and all the other regular activities that prepared him for a life of warfare. At fifteen, he became a page and groom to his cousin, Conrad von Berlichingen, a knight of some standing, and served him until he died several years later. Berlichingen's first war came at age eighteen, after Conrad's death, when he joined up as a page in the Holy Roman Emperor Maximilian's campaign to retake Burgundy from France in 1498. The campaign was a failure—Berlichingen remembered it mostly for the fact that his employer gave him a fine French coat as payment—but it was his first taste of real war. He saw armored lancers die of heatstroke, and he broke into castles and burned a village, experiences that he would repeat many times over the next six decades.

Violence was a profoundly fundamental part of Berlichingen's identity. During an intense altercation with a Polish servant—he had mussed up the Pole's finely coiffed hair—Berlichingen hit him over the head with a short sword. He was around eighteen at the time. That same year, he and a friend brawled with a trumpeter, an incident that left a long, deep gash on his head. This sort of thing was a constant feature of Berlichingen's life, and he tells many stories of this kind. That he felt these kinds of incidents were worth narrating—and one can only imagine how many he left out—highlights the fact that his instinctive reaction to any sort of challenge to his honor or status was violence.

This was typical for men of Berlichingen's social class. In fact, it was the essence of chivalry. The modern sense of the term, as a code of behavior for dashing, honorable knights, bears little resemblance to its medieval definition, the core of which was violence. Knights and nobles justified their existence as a social elite by fighting for acceptable causes; religious wars against Muslims or heretics were best, but a clever knight could turn any sort of conflict into a soul-burnishing positive. Knights were famously sensitive about their social standing, and an insult—from a Polish servant or a wayward trumpeter, for example—necessitated an aggressive response; otherwise, the offended party could hardly call himself a knight at all. Vengeance, anger, and drawn weapons were all basic parts of the knight's experience and emotional tool kit.[6]

In 1500, following a campaign against the rising Swiss Confederation and their fearsome pikemen, a twentysomething Berlichingen "donned armor for the first time" and from thenceforth considered himself a professional man-at-arms. In the parlance of the times, "knight" was a social rank; "man-at-arms" was a skill set and an occupation. It referred to a man who typically fought on horseback with lance and sword, clad from head to toe in expensive plate armor. Even around 1500, when Berlich- ingen took up this path for good, the man-at-arms was hardly outmoded on European battlefields. Nor was chivalry. It was not dying out, despite technological and logistical shifts in the prac- tice of war. In fact, chivalry had enmeshed itself into the mutat- ing ethos of a noble class that wanted to maintain its place in the world of war despite those ongoing changes.[7]

Honorable combat was all well and good, and Berlichin- gen's memoir is full of these encounters. He recounts charging a *Wagenburg*—a fortified ring of wagons bristling with artillery— and holding open a gap in the lines long enough for his com- patriots to get through despite being wounded and his horse dying under him. This kind of thing was the bread and butter of knightly life, but Berlichingen also casually mentions the looting and burning of a church, killing peasants in the course of a feud, serving with a band of robber-knights, and other incidents that would seem at odds with our idea of chivalry. Those are modern misconceptions, though. For men like Berlichingen, there was no such contradiction.[8]

Nor was there any contradiction between payment and hon- orable war; very much the opposite. This was a long way from the centuries-out-of-date idea of land for military service. Cash was a perfectly fine reward, as when Berlichingen and his brother Philip received 2,000 gulden—a hefty sum—from Margrave Friedrich of Brandenburg in return for their services as men-at-arms in one of his many wars. Money could purchase loyalty, as Friedrich well understood.

It was only a short jump from payment for military service to contracting the military service of others for pay. Showing up with a horse, armor, and weapons had for some time been insufficient to meet the rising military needs of princes, kings, and emperors, and the sharp uptick in war at the beginning of the sixteenth century supercharged what was already an ongoing process. Nobles like Berlichingen still saw war as their business, and military entrepreneurship—recruiting, organizing, and leading units of hired soldiers—offered a viable continuation of their social role.

This was Berlichingen's milieu. He was not a major military contractor himself early in life—he and one of his brothers made up two of the three men-at-arms in the first contract he mentions in his memoir—but he was surrounded by major players in that field.[9] He had a loose concept of kinship; by virtue of his six married siblings (the seventh, Kilian, was a Teutonic Knight and thus celibate), Berlichingen was related to practically every other nobleman within a hundred-mile radius. As with the Augsburg merchants, business and family went hand in hand. There was always a relative recruiting for a war, like his cousins Neidhard, Götz (a different Götz—it was a common name), and Sigmund von Thüngen, who hired him as a squad leader in a company of man-at-arms for the Landshut campaign in which he lost his forearm. Two of his brothers were fighting on the opposing side, as it happened, and Berlichingen would have preferred to fight with them. This was the reality of noble life at the dawn of the sixteenth century: It was just business.[10]

Contract Warfare

"Peace, peace," a man-at-arms shouted, struggling to make his voice heard over the din of armor and horse tack as dozens of riders pulled up their mounts. The men surrounded a pair of figures locked together and exchanging furious blows among the leaves and dirt of the forest floor. One of them wound up on top, drew back a solid iron hand, and repeatedly struck the other in the face, cracking his nose and sending blood and teeth flying. "Peace!" shouted the man-at-arms again, emphasizing his point with a loaded crossbow. His riders followed suit.

The man with the iron hand ceased his pummeling and looked up. "He was beating my captives," said Berlichingen, gesturing toward a pair of disheveled peasants leaning against a tree. "If you put your hands on me, I'll break them," he continued, but did not protest at traveling along with the group of riders when they went to an inn for a drink. Berlichingen was now technically a prisoner, but that was nothing to worry about or be ashamed of: It was something of an occupational hazard, and easily reversed. His captor and drinking buddy—"we drank and were merry," Berlichingen says—was an acquaintance by the name of Georg von Frundsberg (1473–1527), a noble and man-at-arms of some reputation. They had fought in the Landshut War and taken plunder together, and whether it was the drink, their shared experience of war, or their family connection (he called Berlichingen "brother-in-law"), the two parted on exceedingly friendly terms.[11]

It is not hard to understand why they got along so well, swilling beer and wine in a crowded inn and swapping stories of feuds, friends, and battles. They had a great deal in common on this occasion in 1504 or 1505, when they crossed paths at the brawl and reconvened at the inn: family, for one, and the same violently chivalric worldview. They came from the same part of Germany, within a few dozen miles of each other, and were nobles of roughly the same social rank. Above all, they shared an occupation. Both were soldiers-for-hire and had presumably been on different sides of whatever petty war had led them to that forest.

Even at this early date, however, they were on opposite ends of the business spectrum. Frundsberg showed up to capture Berlichingen with twenty or thirty men-at-arms; that was a small force for him at the time, and he was used to raising much bigger companies. By the end of his life, Frundsberg would become one of the largest-scale contractors and commanders in an age of drastically increasing military scale. His last contract, in 1527, accounted for the eye-popping total of sixteen thousand mercenary infantry. When he did not receive the money to pay them, they went on to sack Rome and imprison the pope himself.

Frundsberg was one of the key figures in the transformation of war in this period and an innovator in scale, but he was heir to a tradition of contract warfare with deep roots in the preceding centuries. That was the norm throughout Europe by the time Berlichingen and Georg von Frundsberg entered the business, a centuries-long evolution of military and commercial institutions toward a common form. The precise term for such an agreement varied from place to place. In England, the contract was an indenture; in France, a *lettre de revenue*; in Italy, a *condotta*; and in Germany, a *Bestallung*. The responsibilities of the contractor and the formality of the deal varied, as well. In Italy, the most deeply commercialized and contractually sophisticated part of Europe, a *condotta* was a precise and complex piece of business. While Germany was a commercially advanced region, a *Bestallung* was generally quite informal up until around 1500—it might not even take written form, but instead consist of a verbal or even implicit agreement. In England, captains tasked with recruiting soldiers usually received cash advances from their employer—usually the king or a great nobleman—which they then paid out. In Germany, more often hiring came at the recruiter's own expense and risk, turning the military entrepreneur into both a creditor and a soldier.

Two types of military contracting existed side by side. In the first, a captain recruited or acquired soldiers, formed a company, and then went looking for a contract. These could be short-term assemblages put together for a single campaign, like those in which Berlichingen often found himself as a young man: His Thüngen cousins, presumably subcontractors for the commander, pulled him into just such an ad hoc arrangement for the Bavarian war that took his arm. By contrast, the Great Companies of fourteenth-century Italy, like those of the famous mercenary John Hawkwood, were reasonably permanent. They stuck around year after year, drilling, training, and drawing wages while staying ready for the next campaign. Permanence had also been the norm for the ambitious Italian *condottieri* of the first half of the fifteenth century, like Muzio Attendolo Sforza and Braccio da Montone, whose soldiers followed them from employer to employer.

In the second major type of military contracting, an employer went looking for soldiers, or a person to find soldiers, rather than the other way around. This was the norm in France and England especially. English lords were particularly fond of "retaining," in which they made regular cash payments to men who in times of war signed onto formal indentures and hired others on their behalf. There was a rough German equivalent that turned the retaining middleman into a figure called a *Diener von Haus aus*. This form of retention produced the armies that fought the Wars of the Roses, as well as every other late medieval army in England. By 1500, this second form was either the norm all across Europe or becoming so: There were no permanent bodies of soldiers that were not directly contracted to an employing state.[12]

In effect, Europe's military systems had converged on a common arrangement around 1500. A captain, practically always a nobleman, received a contract from an employer (prince, king, or emperor) to recruit a set number of soldiers, and then went about fulfilling the order. The differences lay only in the nature of the recruiter's connection to his employer and either the provision or lack of an advance payment from employer to recruiter. The system relied on a large, sophisticated, contractually based, and geographically widespread market for mercenaries. War was private business, mostly subcontracted from rulers to entrepreneurs, rather than a public state function built on standing armies. The standing armies that did exist may have been the core of a ruler's military capabilities, as they were in France, but filling out an army for a serious campaign required the services of hired professionals.[13]

Berlichingen came into adulthood and set off on his first military campaigns surrounded by this environment of contractual combat and military entrepreneurship. When Georg von Frundsberg was not capturing Berlichingen in a forest, he was mostly off recruiting soldiers by the hundreds and thousands to fight the emperor Maximilian's many wars. Berlichingen's business, meanwhile, was on a smaller scale, but followed the same pattern: He recruited and led 150 men-at-arms for a feud in 1514 and 70 or 80 on behalf of his brother-in-law the following year. In any case, an extremely large force was nothing more than an aggregate of smaller ones, recruited by the dozen, 100, or 500, a main recruiter subcontracting to lesser captains. For both men, with their various scales of operation, credit was key to the arrangement. A nobleman's land and estates, and his reputation as a soldier, were surety for payment. Why would a mercenary man-at-arms, or a group of foot soldiers, take contract with Frundsberg or Berlichingen? Because they believed the two men were good for the money they had been promised. That was credit, both literal and figurative.[14]

Both men's chivalric upbringing made this environment easy to navigate. War was both honorable and suitable for a nobleman of their ilk and an often lucrative occupation that shared much in common with the mercantile activities common to their south German homeland. Everybody, whether a weaver or a banker or a soldier, understood contracts and the exchange of money for services. War was no different; it was better, in fact, because it still carried a whiff of the old nobility.

Berlichingen's memoir focuses far more on violence, its uses, and its benefits than the contractual basis for organized conflict, but that is not because he was oblivious to it; very much the opposite. Instead, it is because he was so steeped in the concept of military service for material gain that it was simply part of the background noise of his life. It was not necessary or interesting to talk about how he joined a company of mercenary knights, or the agreements, written or verbal, he used when assembling a company of a hundred men-at-arms for the Holy Roman Emperor Charles V. Everybody in Berlichingen's world already knew.

Landsknechte and Swiss

South Germany, along with being the epicenter of war-as-business, also served as a major artery for the international mercenary market. This was partly due to its commercial sophistication, the ubiquity of contracts, and an abundance of credit for both captains and princes, and partly due to the lack of a singularly powerful overlord with a monopoly on military force. Emperor Maximilian was a man of immense ambition, as discussed in previous chapters, but he could not have stopped his supposedly subordinate lords from fighting the Landshut War in which Berlichingen lost his hand even if he had wanted to. The Holy Roman Empire was decentralized and full of squabbling lords and cities who considered it their God-given right to fight each other for an estate, a town, or a trade route. This created consistent demand for mercenaries on the local and regional level. Where demand for a service exists, so does a market for that service, and nowhere in Europe did a more highly developed mercenary market exist than in south Germany. The two opposing sides of the Landshut War pulled from that regional market, recruiting both foot soldiers and local men-at-arms like Berlichingen.

There were several regional markets for mercenaries in Europe at the dawn of the sixteenth century. The many petty lords of Ireland hired axe-wielding Norse-Scotsmen called gallowglass to fight on their behalf. The fringes of the Balkans—modern Albania, Croatia, Greece, and Serbia—produced exceptional light cavalry, available to the highest bidder. Italy's market was particularly sophisticated at this time, the result of 150 years of extreme expenditure by the peninsula's deep-pocketed and fractious collection of small states. Venice, Milan, Florence, the pope, and the Kingdom of Naples all required the services of mercenaries, and the *condottieri* developed a distinct and effective fashion of waging war to meet that need.[15]

Condottieri featured prominently in the armies of the ongoing Italian Wars, particularly in leadership roles. Their professional, deeply experienced approach to war baked itself into the emerging military synthesis of the sixteenth century. Yet Italy could not provide enough—or enough of the right kind of—soldiers to meet the voracious demands of French kings and Holy Roman Emperors. Only the south German market, where there lived a particular kind of soldier—the kind Georg von Frundsberg specialized in recruiting and leading—could do that.

The so-called *Landsknechte* were foot-slogging pikemen, trained to fight shoulder-to-shoulder in dense formations. Their pikes—thirteen to eighteen feet in length, on average—could repel even the fiercest charges of heavily armored cavalry: No horse, no matter how heavily armored or well trained, would willingly crash headfirst into a sharp wall of spearheads. At the same time, their tightly packed square or rectangular formations gave pikemen the kind of momentum that allowed them to steamroll their way through opposing infantry during an advance. A square of *Landsknechte* packed closely together bristled with sharp points and moved with surprising speed and coordination, carrying a tremendous amount of weight. When a formation of pikemen rolled forward, it simply crushed any and all opposition.

However, there was a catch, or rather a series of catches. A pike was an unwieldy weapon even in ideal battlefield conditions. Using it effectively took training and practice, and all the more to employ it in a tight formation. Maintaining those condensed but still reasonably maneuverable formations was difficult under the best of circumstances. Doing so in the heat of battle amid the terrifying, earsplitting cacophony of crossbow bolts, arquebus shots, and relentless cannon fire presented an altogether more grueling challenge. When two pike formations collided, the sheer violence it produced was shocking even to those inured to combat. The Italians simply called it "bad war": men stabbing and shoving, wood splintering, sharp points penetrating vulnerable flesh, bodies being trampled to pulp underfoot. Unmotivated or poorly trained soldiers simply would not stand under those circumstances and would instead break and run from the fight. Discipline and professionalism were key, the kind of collectedness that came out of strong communal bonds. These men knew each other, came from the same communities, and had learned their craft over the course of years and decades. They had a distinct identity that marked them off as separate from outsiders. But that degree of discipline and professionalism, of course, cost money—lots of money.

These prerequisites and their associated costs illustrate why this distinctive method of waging war first appeared in the Old Swiss Confederacy. This mountainous territory bordered the Holy Roman Empire and the ancestral lands of the Habsburg dynasty, and its independent-minded inhabitants had no interest in submitting to either. Over the course of the fourteenth and fifteenth centuries, its rural and urban cantons (self-governing communes) united in an alliance for mutual aid and defense. The eight original cantons—Uri, Schwyz, Unterwalden, Glarus, Zug, Lucerne,

Berne, and Zürich—fended off attacks on their independence from the Habsburgs of Austria and later the Duke of Burgundy. Once established, they expanded outward in every direction, adding new cantons and establishing themselves as an unlikely but genuine power. This consistent and opportunistic military activity rested on a highly effective militia system, wherein each canton supplied trained, equipped soldiers for short-term campaigns. Discipline within the ranks came as the result of regular training with people who all knew each other. Farmers practiced archery with friends from the next plot over while shopkeepers swung halberds with their neighbors and artisans hefted pikes with cousins and brothers.

Aggression was the Swiss trademark: Go in, crush the opposition in a single decisive battle, and then return home. The intensity of their advance—the offensive steamroller—set them apart from other pike-using infantry in late medieval Europe, namely the Scots and the Flemings, who were more than capable of driving off charging cavalry but became sitting ducks for archers, artillery, or hand gunners. While the Swiss' face-first approach entailed casualties, they were resolved so long as the effort got them back to their fields and workshops sooner rather than later. For two hundred years, Austrian knights, Burgundian professionals, and Italian *condottieri* all tried their luck against the nigh-unassailable Swiss militiamen. More often than not, they paid with their lives.[16]

Until the 1470s, Swiss efficacy on the battlefield was a trade secret known mostly within the boundaries of west-central Europe. Then came the Burgundian Wars (1474–77), when Duke Charles the Bold—one of the foremost military innovators in Europe and an aggressive expansionist—faced an alliance of the Swiss, the Duke of Lorraine, and the tacit support of the king of France. In three devastating consecutive battles, with blocks of Swiss pikemen playing the winning role, Charles lost an army, his treasury, and ultimately his life.

Swiss military prowess was finally getting the press it deserved. Louis XI of France recruited six thousand Swiss soldiers for a campaign in 1481; in 1482, they fought for Isabella of Castile at the beginning of the war against Granada; by 1494, when Charles VIII of France invaded Italy and set off sixty-five years of continuous fighting, mercenary service was already a popular secondary career for tens of thousands of Swiss. The same structures of community organization that supported militia training for purely Swiss interests could easily be tapped to provide mercenaries on contracts negotiated with kings of France and dukes of Milan. The Swiss went to war often enough that a large pool of hardened, professional soldiers existed who could do the difficult job of maintaining the outer edges of the pike square and harness the energy of the mass of less experienced men in the middle. The combination of an effective organizational system and intense, long-term training with a uniquely effective military tactic made them the most sought-after mercenaries in Europe.[17]

Right next door to the expanding Swiss cantons, of course, was south Germany. Imitation being the sincerest form of flattery, key observers, like the future emperor Maximilian, noted the effectiveness of the Swiss with a combination of admiration and alarm. The result of those observations, from the late 1470s on, was the raising of German pike infantry. These were the *Landsknechte*, and their method of fighting was a direct copy of the Swiss model. Maximilian took them to the Low Countries to fight the invading French in 1479, even hefting a pike himself to show his solidarity with his new soldiers. To Maximilian, the *Landsknechte* were *liebe, ehrliche, fromme*—dear, true, pious—the honest and valued servants of a vigorous ruler.

After 1493, Maximilian, now emperor, had the first claim on the services of *Landsknechte*, but they were mercenaries to the core, with no real pretensions to loyalty: Any captain in possession of a contract from a prince or lord could hang his arms outside a tavern, put out the word, and take on any willing recruits. Soldiering was a respectable occupation, and consistent demand from conflicts both within and without south Germany created a thriving market. For an adventurous young man from a family of urban shopkeepers or middling farmers, mercenary service offered the promise of reasonable pay—twice that of a day laborer and a bit more than a journeyman artisan—and a hefty dose of social prestige. By imperial decree, *Landsknechte* were exempt from the sumptuary laws that restricted what non-nobles could wear. Bright colors and fancy hats, slashed pantaloons, eye-catching codpieces, jewelry, armor, weapons, all of them marked out *Landsknechte* as belonging to a distinct subgroup within society. *Landsknechte* swaggered wherever they went, and they had good reason to do so.[18] There was no shortage of soldiers.

The Swiss—their great rivals and uncomfortable neighbors—hated *Landsknechte* with a passion and rarely took prisoners when they met on the battlefield. But there were more *Landsknechte* than Swiss available for hire throughout Europe in the early sixteenth century, and they showed up everywhere from England to the Low Countries to Naples. Even more than the Swiss, whose mercenary work was a by-product of their militia system and the overflow of soldiers it produced, the *Landsknechte* were an almost pure product of the market. Both *Landsknechte* and Swiss troops cost huge amounts of money to hire and keep in the field, all the more because it only made sense to hire them in the thousands. Their daily wages piled up as campaigns dragged on month after month, and they were never shy about demanding what was owed to them. The Swiss routinely held up their employers for more cash, sometimes on the eve of battle, and the failure to pay *Landsknechte* had tragic consequences: The 1527 Sack of Rome, and all the carnage it entailed, was the direct result of such contractual shortcomings.

Götz von Berlichingen grew up in the heart of this world. Emperor Maximilian's final attempt to subordinate the Swiss cantons to Habsburg control was Berlichingen's first real campaign, the one in which he saw churches burning and never got to fight a real battle. That was probably for the best: If he had spitted himself on a Swiss pike in an ill-advised charge, like so many men-at-arms of this time did, we would not have his incredible memoir. It was a *Landsknecht* who helped him to safety outside Landshut when the cannonball hit his arm, and they repeatedly appear as background scenery in the story of Berlichingen's life. Every man-at-arms who survived to the Iron Hand's age knew the value and the danger of the humble pike and the man wielding it.[19]

Gunpowder

The increasing dominance of pikes on the battlefield, and the mercenary system that produced them in large numbers, was one key part of the military revolution. The rise of gunpowder weaponry was another. Together, the distinctive combination of pike and handguns would dominate battlefields until the middle of the seventeenth century. At the same time, cannon rendered the high, thin walls of medieval castles and towns obsolete, creating a rapid and pricey arms race in the construction of new fortifications.

Berlichingen saw all of this as it unfolded. A shot from a cannon destroyed his right arm, and by that point he had already charged headfirst into a fortified position bristling with booming artillery. He was perfectly happy to employ gunpowder hand gunners in his wars and feuds, understood how to deploy them in skirmishes and ambushes, and knew how it felt to stare down the loaded barrel of one. From the very beginning, gunpowder was a fundamental part of Berlichingen's experience of war. He still saw crossbows on a regular basis, but even common civilians were familiar with gunpowder weapons: One of Berlichingen's feuds involved a tailor hiring him to recover 100 florins that were supposed to have been paid out as a reward for winning a target-shooting match.[20]

The firearm Berlichingen saw most regularly was the famed arquebus. Early handguns had been plain metal tubes fired by touching a lit match to a powder charge: powerful enough to punch through armor, but inaccurate and dangerous to their users. The arquebus, which started to replace that earlier model after the middle of the fifteenth century, featured several major improvements: a trigger mechanism connected to a lock, which when pulled did the messy job of actually firing the weapon, and a stock with which to brace and aim the weapon. Barrels grew longer, averaging around forty inches, which made the weapon more accurate and substantially increased muzzle velocity. Best of all, arquebuses were relatively inexpensive and easy to produce. Any halfway skilled smith with access to iron and wood could make one.

As with pike infantry, south Germany was the epicenter of this innovation. Arquebuses grew out of a substantial need for portable, effective weapons to defend city walls in times of trouble, and south Germany, with its constant fighting and density of cities, had both the need and the incentive to drive the advancement of firearms technology. Even the term "arquebus" derives from the German *Hackenbüchse* through a couple of intermediate language loans, and Berlichingen's memoir is full of slang references to *Büchse* of one size or another.[21]

Even as Berlichingen saw the flame of discharging firearms and felt the gusts of air from their passing shots, the arquebus was redefining the contours of European battlefields. The Battle of Cerignola in 1503, the year before Berlichingen lost his hand to a cannonball, marked a turning point. The Spanish commander,

Gonzalo de Córdoba, an experienced veteran of the wars in Granada, used a combination of pike-armed *Landsknechte* and Spanish arquebusiers to repel an attacking French army composed of Swiss mercenaries and mounted men-at-arms. Safe behind a ditch and embankment, the German pikemen held off the charge while arquebuses raked the attackers with shot, creating a killing zone thirty to forty meters deep that no Swiss pikeman or French *gendarme* could safely cross. For the first time, the argument goes, firearms won an open battle. In reality, the ditch and embankment were just as important to Gonzalo's victory, but very few future battles would take place without firearms playing a major role. They shredded attacking *Landsknechte* at Ravenna in 1512, scythed through Swiss pikemen by the thousands at Marignano in 1515, and cut down the cream of the French nobility at Pavia in 1525, killing King Francis I's horse and leading directly to his capture.[22]

While arquebuses (and their larger successors, muskets) remade battlefields, artillery transformed sieges to an even greater degree. When King Charles VIII of France marched into Italy in 1494 with his army, the finest and most expensive in Europe, it was not the mercenary Swiss pikemen or professional men-at-arms who caught the eye of Italian observers; it was his enormous train of cannon. "They were planted against the walls of a town with such speed, the space between each shot was so little, and the balls flew so quick, and were impelled with such force, that as much execution was done in a few hours as formerly in Italy in the like number of days. . . . Such artillery rendered Charles's army very formidable to all Italy," wrote Florentine historian Francesco Guicciardini. This was an exaggeration on several counts when it came to the actual course of Charles's campaign, a handy story to explain a shocking and rapid Italian collapse, but there was a core of truth: Medieval fortifications were no longer viable when faced with large, well-manned cannon.

This had been true for some time. Charles VIII was not the first ruler to blast down castle or town walls with artillery. His grandfather, Charles VII, had ended the Hundred Years' War with the mere threat of bombarding English garrisons and occupied towns in Normandy, and cannon played a key role in the Ottoman conquest of Constantinople. It cost large sums of money to assemble a viable artillery train like Charles's, but by the 1490s they were effectively de rigueur. Yet the balance of effectiveness between offense and defense continued to seesaw, and that balance was about to tip back in favor of the defensive side.

Military architects and engineers were hardly ignorant of the challenge cannon presented to their craft; even before Charles VIII's invasion of Italy, advances in fortifications had already begun to make life more difficult for would-be besiegers. Rounded surfaces might deflect cannon fire, but the real solution lay in lower and thicker walls, angled bastions protruding from the line of the walls to provide flanking fire, and wide, deep ditches. In its complete form, contemporaries knew this type of fortification as the *trace italienne*. It was both necessary and incredibly expensive to build, but its value lay in its ability to stall an attacking army for an entire campaigning season or even longer. That in turn led to larger armies and still greater costs. That feedback loop between cannon, fortifications, and growing costs was the essence of the Military Revolution.[23]

Big Wars, Small Wars; Old Wars, New Wars

The iron fingers of Berlichingen's prosthetic hand drummed impatiently on the carved stone of the tower. Narrowed eyes set within a scarred, increasingly round face scanned the valleys that spread outward from the high point of his castle, looking for the telltale clouds of dust rising above the wooded hills that indicated approaching riders. A hundred men-at-arms, sturdy and experienced: that was what he needed for his next campaign, a force large enough to support him in a war on behalf of Duke Ulrich of Württemburg. He had put out the call to his cousins and brothers-in-law to find the right sort of fighter, and all he could do now was wait and hope.

Then, off to the west: a hint of rising dust. Berlichingen watched the blur resolve into individual riders approaching the walls of his fortress, which jutted upward from a crag of rock to overlook the small nearby town. He counted a dozen figures, including four men-at-arms, some familiar faces among them, and eight pages to arm them and care for their horses. Not enough, but a start. Descending from the tower, he could hear iron-shod hooves clattering on the cobblestones of the courtyard. This place, the Castle of Hornberg, was new to Berlichingen. He had recently bought it with money earned from his capture and ransom of the Duke of Hesse. Parts of the structure were centuries old. Over those centuries, these worn stones had seen this exact procession many times: men-at-arms, covered in the dust and grime of the road, arriving to fight in a private war for honor and profit. The lord of Hornberg raised his iron hand in greeting, smiled, and called for beer.

Götz von Berlichingen specialized in small wars. The fragmented political structures of the Holy Roman Empire created ample conflict between nobles and cities, prince-bishops and knights, organized leagues of towns and great lords. It was the nature of the system, and within that system there was a great deal of room for a violent, opportunistic man like Berlichingen to pursue a career as a soldier for hire. Material reward went hand in hand with the defense of his personal honor and status as a minor nobleman, and small wars were his path to gain in both respects.

In his memoir, Berlichingen recounts minor campaign after minor campaign: robbing Cologne merchants on the road from Frankfurt in pursuit of a feud against the former city; employing hand gunners in a riverboat ambush during a feud with the bishop of Bamberg; taking captive a group of traders for ransom; defending the small town of Möckmühl for the Duke of Württemburg against the Swabian League and getting captured for his trouble. In all these many scrapes, the numbers of men involved were consistently low. Berlichingen cobbled together thirty men-at-arms in his war for the duke and raised another thirty in one phase of his long fight against the city of Nuremberg. When imperial authorities ordered four hundred riders against him during that clash, those were insurmountable odds, even for an experienced and dedicated feuder like him.[24]

All of this—abducted knights, stabbings over dinner, bad blood from feud after feud—might seem impossibly distant from the great transformations of the Military Revolution happening at the same time. Mass slaughters at places like Ravenna and Pavia, expensive sieges of sparkling new fortresses, and ballooning armies of tens of thousands of pikemen and hand gunners understandably command all the attention. Next to them, Berlichingen and his paltry few men-at-arms, his centuries-old castle, and his myriad feuds seem like a dead end, a throwback to a bygone age of private, small-scale war.[25]

But a Military Revolution that does not account for the vast majority of military activity is not much of a revolution at all. Most conflicts of this period were skirmishes, raids, local wars, and petty feuds, not titanic battlefield clashes that rewrote the course of political and military history. Even the most pivotal battles took place within larger campaigns that featured slogging sieges, foraging, skirmishing, and raiding. Local rivalries and enmities, and the requisite violence of both, played out in the context of much larger political upheavals.

There was simply no real division between small wars and big ones, or between old methods of war and new ones. Berlichingen was no fool—he had seen cannon in action on many occasions—but living in a castle clearly still appealed to him, and so long as it was not facing a major artillery train, a castle still had utility as a defensive structure. Moreover, men-at-arms, those armored tanks on horseback and the direct descendants of the medieval knight, played a prominent role on battlefields well into the middle of the sixteenth century. It would never have occurred to Berlichingen that these riders—men he called upon to fight in his small wars—were obsolete. Men-at-arms in full suits of armor, charging with lances in hand, fought alongside artillery, pikemen, and hand gunners in even the most cutting-edge armies of this period. And when it came to roughing up merchants, raiding villages, and fighting in feuds, there was simply no substitute for a hulking, armored monster on horseback.

The connection between old and new, large and small, was even more obvious: The same people participated in conflicts of all shapes and sizes, honing their trade and learning the ropes in local and regional wars before marching hundreds of miles to fight in larger clashes, then returning home to perpetuate the cycle.

When Berlichingen was imprisoned for several years after his capture at Möckmühl in 1522, who intervened to release him? None other than Georg von Frundsberg, by then the most prominent recruiter and leader of *Landsknechte* in south Germany and a key associate of the new Holy Roman Emperor, Charles V. Marching off to Flanders and Italy from time to time with large armies he had raised on contract did not stop him from being involved in local politics with his wayward friend, Berlichingen. In fact, Frundsberg went directly from fighting in the Württemburg war in which von Berlichingen was captured to raising *Landsknechte* for a campaign in Picardy, in northern France. His intervention on Berlichingen's behalf occurred during a brief gap between those campaigns. By this point, the scale of Frundsberg's soldier trade was enormous, raising hundreds and thousands of troops for individual campaigns. In 1526, he mortgaged everything he owned to front the costs for sixteen thousand *Landsknechte*, the force that eventually went on to sack Rome when Charles V failed to pay their wages.[26]

Frundsberg, to name just one of the many people who followed this same path, did not distinguish between large and small wars, nor between what future observers would consider key conflicts and those that could be labeled irrelevant in hindsight. He used the same tools in all of them, from pikes to handguns to artillery to men-at-arms, and employed the same contract-based recruiting methods for all. The rank-and-file *Landsknechte*, hand gunners, and men-at-arms were no different, bouncing from campaign to campaign as their needs, social and familial connections, and opportunities allowed. Large and small wars both sucked up funds in huge quantities, paying soldiers' wages and incentivizing new developments and innovations. Professionals had every reason to keep fighting, and new recruits received plenty of inducements. The sheer volume of conflict kept the wheels of war turning.

Götz of the Iron Hand was not a renowned commander or a prominent military contractor. Most of his wars were small, essentially legal disputes carried out by violent means rather than the great conflicts of kings and emperors. Yet the Military Revolution was the result of an ongoing dialogue between conflicts small and large. Constant fighting gave rise to markets of professional soldiers who honed their skills and military technologies through consistent practice. The real transformations of war in this era were the direct result of men like Götz von Berlichingen: people with the ways and means to make war their business.

The Last Campaign: Saint-Dizier, 1544

Sweat soaked Berlichingen's handkerchief as he mopped his brow, seeking temporary relief from the humid, oppressive August heat of eastern France. There was a great deal more to mop now than there had been in his youth. His blond hair had long since beat a retreat from his forehead. It was 1544, and he would turn sixty-four years old in a matter of months. It seemed a lifetime ago that he had ridden into battle outside Landshut, and it had been: forty years in total. More sweat poured from his armpits, running over the curves of the barrel-like torso concealed under the layers of plate armor that protected it. *The Devil's own heat*, he thought, imagining a crude woodcut of flames featuring a demon devouring the pope, which he had seen in a printed pamphlet years prior. He was getting too old for this.

The scent of gunpowder invaded Berlichingen's nostrils with all the force of a rampaging army. It hung in the stifling air, great white clouds of smoke drifting slowly on the scant breeze. A row of cannon—heavy ones, siege guns—belched still more of the sulfurous reek and smoke. He squinted and saw the shots crash into a low, squat wall some distance away, leaving a crumble of ruined stone and dust behind. The fortifications that protected the city of Saint-Dizier were brand-new, unmarred by the ravages of time and combat, at least until now. They looked strange compared to the walls of a castle, Berlichingen mused: low, thick, with angled, protruding bastions to provide flanking fire along the wall and platforms for artillery. It was a far cry from the kind of private fortress that could protect—or at least had protected—a feuding knight from his rivals. His Hornberg Castle had served well enough at that for years, at least until the authorities had imprisoned him there for more than a decade: too many feuds, too many enemies, and the small matter of his participation in the largest peasants' rebellion anyone could remember. Berlichingen had claimed that the rebel peasants forced him into a position of command, a convenient excuse, and he was lucky to have escaped execution in the bloody aftermath.[27]

But now he was out. It was good to feel the weight of his armor, heft a sword in his good left hand, hear the crude banter of the camp, and taste the gunpowder on the wind. Two years before, Holy Roman Emperor Charles V had asked him to raise a hundred men-at-arms for an outing against the dastardly Turks. He had leapt at the chance for escape. Even if many of his men-at-arms had died along the way to Hungary, from disease rather than a Janissary's arrow or the blade of a *sipahi* cavalryman, it was better than sitting at home. And once he was out, he stayed out, setting off on this campaign with the emperor into France with another company of men-at-arms. But armored men on armored horses were not much use in an extended siege. They had already picked the countryside clean, though not to the satisfaction of an experienced looter and feuder of Berlichingen's caliber: "If I would be called Emperor Charles, so it bethinks me, I would take that way and leave behind me a souvenir, and burn in such a way that they would have to say for the next 100 years that Emperor Charles had been there, and the affair would also turn more quickly to a peace," he wrote later.[28]

An ache in Berlichingen's back, a slipped disk from a fall many years before, brought his attention back to the here and now. A German cry went up and down the line. The guns stopped firing, the gates of Saint-Dizier opened, and a party of horsemen rode out to parley. Berlichingen grimaced, this time from a twinge in his right hand, the phantom pain of a hand lost and gone these past forty years. He looked down at the iron prosthetic, reminding himself of what he had lost and gained, and smiled.

CHAPTER 5

——— ⚭ ———

Aldus Manutius and Printing

September 1508, Venice

As the first rays of morning light struggled to penetrate the mass of brick and stone buildings crowding the canals, Venice was bustling. Everybody had somewhere they needed to be. Market stalls required their stocks of fresh produce. Merchants had deals to strike and contracts to sign. Bankers had accounts to review, sums to calculate, and bills of exchange to negotiate. Venice was a city of business, and business started early.

The hubbub failed to disturb one passerby, his shoes tramping on the planks of a rickety wooden bridge above the canal. *Festina lente*, "Make haste slowly," was his motto, and that was exactly how he walked: quick, precise steps, the gait of a man who knew his way around Venice's labyrinth of alleys and squares. A stack of aging leather-bound manuscripts occupied both his arms and his attention. One significant problem in particular plagued his acute, well-trained mind: how to translate the manuscripts' centuries-old handwriting into high-quality, mass-produced print.

Shouts rose up from the canal, boatmen yelling at each other animatedly as they plied the waters. One long, slender craft laden with fruit and vegetables had nearly collided with another bearing a pair of patrician merchants. Curses flew back and forth. Wild, angry gesticulations utilizing the poles that propelled the boats through the narrow channels threatened others floating past, leading to a flurry of recriminations. Ducking around the hollering boatmen and their flailing poles, the man with the manuscripts narrowly missed being drenched by the contents of a chamber pot flung from a second-story window.

His name was Aldo Manuzio—Aldus Manutius to his scholarly brethren, customers, and posterity—and he was the finest printer in all of Europe. Bibliophiles and professional scholars across the continent eagerly sought out his products, coveting the dolphin-and-anchor logo of the Aldine Press as a sign of the highest standard in both textual accuracy and beautiful typesetting.

Aldus was nearing his sixtieth birthday. His posture was slightly hunched from the regular strain of carrying books, and his eyes squinted from nearsightedness, but his mind was as sharp as ever. His thoughts flitted back and forth from classical Latin to ancient Greek—his favorite—to the Venetian dialect with every step, through narrow alleys and over brackish canals, mulling over particularly appealing phrases and calculating the rhythm of poetic meter in a choice verse. His mind wanted to live in the beauty of language, not the mundanities of the printing business.

Unconsciously, Aldus slowed his pace before realizing he was nearing his combined home and print shop. No doubt his father-in-law and business partner, a tightfisted miser named Andrea Torresani, was waiting for him with a list of complaints and directives. *To the Devil with him*, Aldus thought, and then chastised himself. Torresani may have been unpopular, but he was rarely wrong in his calculations of a product's potential success, however much Aldus might wish otherwise.

The aging printer saw the bell tower of the Church of

Sant'Agostino up ahead as he emerged onto a small square, one of many such open spaces located throughout Venice. Relics of a landscape long since past, when the city had been a scattered collection of tiny patches of land within the lagoon, each square had its own collection of houses, workshops, and a parish church facing the open *campo* in the middle. A thousand years of relentless work—of dredging and sinking wooden pilings and filling in rubble—had created new land and closed the gaps between the original islands. Venice was a palimpsest of forgotten geographies, tangled concentrations of alleyways recalling dried-up channels and rows of houses marking what had once been the edge of dry land.

Aldus spied the door of his plain, two-story house and sighed. It would be bustling inside, he knew: compositors setting type, ink splattering, the clatter of the press, his children laughing and crying. If he strained his ears, he might be able to hear Torresani muttering about too-high wages, or the scratching pen of Erasmus of Rotterdam, who was temporarily residing in Aldus's home and would soon be known as the greatest living writer in Europe. Holding the manuscripts in one shaking hand, Aldus sighed one last time, opened the door, and waded headfirst into the chaos.

Print shops were abundant in Aldus's Venice and throughout Europe. Johannes Gutenberg first set type to paper in Mainz when Aldus was still an infant; over the course of Aldus's life, the new technology spread like wildfire across the continent. Not only did printing revolutionize the book publishing trade, but it kick-started a massive overhaul in communications, transforming everything from intellectualism to religious belief in the relative blink of an eye. Indeed, none of the enormous shifts of the sixteenth century—from the upheavals of the Reformation to global exploration to the approaching Scientific Revolution—could have happened without the emergence of the printing press.[1]

Printing itself was a cutthroat industry. Most early printers,

Gutenberg included, wound up bankrupt or worse. Decades of experimentation produced numerous dead ends and false starts as the new technology searched for a product that readers would buy and a model that made sense. Far too often, printers flooded the market with more books than it could possibly absorb. But investors kept pouring money into print shops everywhere from Westminster to Prague, and slowly but surely, printing established itself as a viable business.

Aldus Manutius was a scholar at heart. A schoolmaster in his younger years, today he is famous for his beautiful italic typeface, for making the ancient Greek classics widely available in print for the first time, and for rubbing elbows with literary luminaries like Erasmus. Collectors today are willing to pay top dollar for his gorgeous productions, and his insatiable thirst for knowledge embodies the spirit of Renaissance humanism. Yet Aldus's ability to make those intellectual contributions relied on a hardheaded, capitalistic business sense, both his own and that of his partners. That is the broader story of printing in the sixteenth century: how hunger for profit drove the usage of transformative technology and launched one of the first ages of information.

Gutenberg and the Book

By the time the Mainz artisan Johannes Gutenberg first hit on the idea of combining movable type and a simple screw press in the late 1440s, European book production had already shifted from monasteries to private bookshops. Squinting monks crammed into *scriptoria*, copying out Bibles and the odd classical text as part of their holy manual labor, had not yet disappeared; however, scribal workshops—many in university cities like Paris—were springing up to meet the steadily rising demand for books sweeping through late medieval Europe.

Aristocrats filled out their libraries with richly decorated and illuminated romances and devotional works. Children needed grammars and other basic texts for their schoolwork. Universities, which were churning out graduate after graduate in theology and especially law, required tremendous volumes of specialized texts. The notaries and professionals of cities like Florence, Augsburg, Bruges, London, and Venice, for whom reading and writing were professional skills and a way of moving up in the world, all had a taste for books. So did the literate bureaucrats staffing the chanceries of monarchs like Isabella of Castile. Readers in the middle of the fifteenth century—of whom there were more than had previously ever existed, though still far fewer than in the following centuries— wanted more books, and they wanted them at a lower cost. The invention of the printing press was a way of meeting this demand.[2]

Johannes Gutenberg was already an experienced entrepreneur by the time he turned his attention toward book production around 1448. Then nearing his fiftieth birthday, Gutenberg received a decent education and might even have spent some time at the University of Erfurt before embarking on a career as a master craftsman. While living in Strasbourg, he taught goldsmithing or coinmaking while pursuing further investment in a large-scale casting process for mirrors. An impressive collection of relics was set to go on display in the nearby city of Aachen, and it was generally believed that a mirror catching the reflection of these holy objects would retain some of their spiritual force. Gutenberg and his associates gathered investment capital and produced a large number of these mirrors to sell to relic-viewing pilgrims; unfortunately, Gutenberg had the year wrong, and produced the mirrors too early. That eye for opportunity combined with problems in execution would bedevil him in later years, but the incident speaks strongly to the artisan's experience both with crafting processes and the business environment. Both were key to the emergence of printing.[3]

It may have been at Strasbourg that Gutenberg first experimented with presses and movable type, but secretive, recriminatory lawsuits between business partners and the ephemeral nature of early printed pages has obliterated any sure evidence of it. What is certain is that on October 17, 1448, Gutenberg—an entrepreneur with more than a decade's familiarity in securing investments for capital-intensive artisanal processes—was back in Mainz, securing a loan of 150 gulden at 5 percent interest from one Arnold Gelthus, a cousin. Gutenberg followed that by borrowing an additional 800 gulden from Mainz merchant and money-lender Johann Fust.

What Gutenberg had in mind was indeed visionary. He put his coinmaking and goldsmithing expertise to use, cutting thousands of individual pieces of metal type, each of which represented a letter or abbreviation. This task required serious skill and ingenuity, not to mention patience and capital reserves, since it would take months of uninterrupted work to create the necessary type long before anything profitable could come of the venture. Once cut and cast, the type could be arranged into words and sentences in the press itself, forming a single page of a printed text. The press itself was simple, derived from similar mechanisms used for winemaking: A lever drove a metal plate downward, but instead of crushing grapes, it pressed a piece of paper onto the inked metal type. This process was repeated as many times as necessary, with typesetters rearranging the blocks for every subsequent page, over and over. With enough repetitions, the printer ended up with dozens, hundreds, even thousands of identical copies of each page, and thus copies of an entire book.

Everything about this process was labor-intensive and expensive, from cutting the type to procuring ready stocks of paper to running the presses for weeks or months on end; but all of that paled in comparison to the challenge of copying an entire manuscript by hand. A scribe would spend weeks or months on such a task—perhaps even years for a large text like the Bible—and could only produce a single copy at a time. By contrast, printing, despite its enormous up-front costs and technical demands, had massive advantages.

The first product of Gutenberg's press, probably the proof of concept that convinced Fust to loan him additional funds, was not his famous Bible. Instead, it was the hundreds or thousands of copies of a schoolbook: the *Ars minor* of Aelius Donatus. It was not a prestige text, and its owners did not cherish their copies. Today, only fragments of Gutenberg's preliminary work remain, barely identifiable as the first products of an invention that would change the world.

The Bible, by contrast, was a much riskier venture: a big, expensive book for which most readers had little use on a day-to-day basis. This first major project was a prestige text, and the Gutenberg Bible hewed as closely as possible to the luxury manuscripts popular around that time. Each page was comprised of two columns, adorned with forty-two lines of closely set, elegant gothic text. Most of the original 180 copies were printed on high-quality paper, but 40 were set on vellum, a far more expensive option. Buyers could add their own illuminations, further increasing the cost of an already pricey text.

The Gutenberg Bible was a perfect illustration of both the possibilities and the pitfalls of early printing. That one book required the casting and setting of 100,000 individual pieces of type and then printing 1,282 pages 180 times, totaling 230,760 runs through the presses. This entailed twelve printers working with six compositors to run six presses continuously for 330 working days. From beginning to end—casting the type to binding the finished products and delivering them to buyers—more than two years must have passed. Despite its exceptional cost, the entire first printing of the Gutenberg Bible sold out immediately: 20 gulden for a paper copy, roughly the annual wages of a master craftsman, and 50 for vellum. A scribe might need three years to produce a manuscript Bible; Gutenberg had 180 of them, all of impeccable quality.

But this process required enormous amounts of ready cash for both materials and labor. Fust, Gutenberg's financier, had provided at least two injections of capital; when the Bibles were finished and sent off to their buyers, he wanted his investments repaid. Unfortunately, Gutenberg—who had either been stiffed by his buyers or had unwisely reinvested the profits in new projects—did not have the money.

Regardless of the cause, Fust was in no mood to wait. He sued Gutenberg and won, and the legal judgment handed over the printer's only asset: the contents of Gutenberg's print shop. Within a year of completing his great project, the inventor of the printing press had been cut out of the business. The gap between investment and return was one of the earliest fundamental issues with printing, one that required decades of experimentation and a great many failures to fully grasp, much less solve.[4]

Venice and the Spread of Printing

After ridding himself of the unreliable Gutenberg, Fust found a new partner in scribe and Gutenberg assistant Peter Schöffer, who had testified against his former employer in the lawsuit that cost him his business. They proved to be a formidable pair: For the next decade, Fust and Schöffer collaborated closely, churning out psalters, legal texts, and mundane items like letters of indulgence for the Church.

Their monopoly was exceptionally short-lived, however. As early as 1460, another press appeared in the city of Bamberg, utilizing the same crude type Gutenberg had used for the projects that preceded his Bible. By the end of that decade, presses were churning out books in the trading cities of Strasbourg, Cologne, Leipzig, Basel, and Augsburg, while Schöffer himself was distributing his books through a bookshop in Paris. (His partnership with Fust had ended when Fust died of the plague in 1466.)

A press emerged in the French capital in 1470, and one came to Nuremberg that same year. Rome got its own press in 1467, followed by Ferrara, Florence, Milan, Bologna, and Naples in 1471, and several more Italian cities over the course of the next year. The urbanized and wealthy Low Countries got their own presses in Bruges, Antwerp, and Louvain soon after. A printer set up shop in Westminster, just outside London, in 1476. The pattern was clear: Commercial centers, with their access to investment capital to fund the presses and established distribution networks to sell product, were emerging as the new epicenters of the industry.[5]

No commercial center had more to offer than Venice, where a press first appeared in 1469. Perched among a marshy swamp, constructed on tiny patches of built-up land and protected from the Adriatic Sea by a series of sandbars called *lidi*, Venice at first seemed an unlikely location for one of Europe's richest trading cities. Over the past millennium, however, Venice had transformed itself from a collection of fishermen and salt-panners eking out a living on the fringes of the Roman economy to the hinge of the medieval world. It was the meeting point of every major trade route of the age, joining Alexandria to Augsburg, Milan to Constantinople, and Tunis to Bruges. Staples and luxuries alike came through Venice's port, including grain, timber, silks, and spices, stopping over on their way to a hundred different destinations. The trade routes changed over the centuries, shifting away from Constantinople and the lost crusader states of the Holy Land toward Alexandria and the Red Sea, but Venice's position at their confluence did not.

These trade routes were Venice's veins and arteries, the liquid capital flowing through them its lifeblood. A reliable legal system enforced ironclad contracts for everyone from commercial princes to foreign traders to laborers carrying out repairs. The city's government, dominated by a mostly closed aristocracy of wealthy merchants, did everything in its considerable power to protect and further its commercial interests. State-funded warships, oar-driven galleys constructed in the city's famous Arsenal and packed with fighting men, protected Venice's merchants abroad in the Mediterranean, while Venetian administrators ruled over an archipelago of vital naval bases and port cities that dotted the eastern Mediterranean Sea.

The aristocratic infighting and social revolts that periodically plagued other Italian city-states and urban Europe at large rarely upset the basic stability of the Venetian state. The Medici of Florence maintained a branch of their famous bank in the city, dabbling in everything from currency exchange to long-distance trade. Jakob Fugger came south over the Alps to hone his considerable financial skills during his apprenticeship near the famous Rialto Bridge. Venice was a safe, profitable place to do business. Capital was secure there, and if properly tended, it might bloom.[6]

Venice was a natural home for the emerging print industry. And given the city's deep and enduring connections to Germany, it came as no surprise that the first printer in the city was a German by the name of John of Speyer, who worked in tandem with his brother Windelin. John, however, died soon after arriving in Venice, and the printing monopoly the Venetian authorities had granted him fell by the wayside. A Frenchman, Nicolas Jenson, was the lucky beneficiary of that vacuum.

Jenson was a shadowy figure. One story, which would circulate virulently a century later among French bibliophiles, held that he had been a die cutter at the Paris mint, and King Charles VII of France had chosen him personally for a secret mission to Mainz to learn the secrets of printing from Herr Gutenberg himself. By the time Jenson returned to France in 1461, the story goes, Charles VII was dead and his son Louis XI was in charge; Louis despised his father and his father's officials, and therefore was not interested in what Jenson had to offer. Spurned, Jenson showed up in Venice a

few years later and went to work, quickly becoming the most prominent printer in the city. Another version of the story, circulated
by Jenson himself, claimed that he, not Gutenberg, had actually
invented printing. Jenson was certainly French, a skilled craftsman
absolutely, and he may indeed have worked at the royal mint in
Paris. The rest was likely great public relations for an unscrupulous
businessman plying his trade in a young, competitive field.[7]

The Frenchman, like all early printers in Venice and points
beyond, was not producing books for a mass market. Reading was
not nearly widespread enough among the general public for that
to be a possibility, and books, even printed ones, were expensive
commodities. The pool of potential customers, then, was limited. Venice, with its ready funds for investment and abundance of
skilled labor, held a particular friendliness toward capital-intensive
business operations, thereby creating a cutthroat environment for
printers. By 1473, there were a dozen presses active in the city.
The resulting glut of texts, especially of the ancient Latin authors
so beloved by the fashionable scholars who dominated the ranks
of regular readers, ruined all but the best-funded and most skilled
printers in the city. Cycles of boom and bust defined early printing in places like Venice, even as they made more books available
to more readers than had ever been previously possible.[8]

Aldus Manutius and Scholarship

Snippets of animated conversation followed by laughter floated
through the halls of the villa, bouncing off the plastered walls
and echoing down smooth stone floors. Cool wine splashed into
elegant silver cups and drained into eager gullets, fueling still
more chatter. A half dozen men were locked in deep discussion,
faces flushed from drink. No outsider could have followed the
course of their exchange as it bounced back and forth from Greek

to Latin to Italian, full of references to precise philosophical and linguistic terms and alternatively praising and slandering obscure academics for their scholarly contributions, or lack thereof.

The small group had frequently exchanged letters and knew each other far better in writing than in person. All were scholars, or fancied themselves as such, ranging in age from their early twenties to middle age. They were excited to be here near the town of Mirandola; the villa where they were staying belonged to the family of the young and precociously intelligent Giovanni Pico della Mirandola, who had organized this gathering. There also was the fiery Greek scholar Manuel Andramyttenus, an acquaintance of some of the age's most promising young literary talents. Others were nobles with scholarly pretensions and interests, collectors of ancient manuscripts, and dabblers in Attic Greek.

The least distinguished of the bunch, with his shoulder-length hair framing a face punctuated by a long nose and crinkling, intelligent eyes, his worn, patched robes still stained with the dust of travel, was Aldo Manuzio. A wandering scholar who had just taken up residence at Carpi, a few miles down the road from Mirandola, Manuzio was serving as professional tutor to the young lords of his new home.

Their talks went on long into the night, fueled by Pico's fine wines and a stack of precious manuscripts. They debated Homer and Plato, argued about Cicero's style, and came together in their critique of a shoddy Venetian printed edition of Martial's poetry. Pico was the most forceful and creative of the bunch; others were sharper on the fine points of classical texts, but Manuzio was a peacemaker, always looking for common ground and quiet agreement. All shared a deep and abiding love of the classical past and the belief that studying and assimilating its wisdom improved the present world. When they parted the next day, wondering if they would ever be fortunate enough to meet again, that belief stayed with them.

While hardly the most distinguished scholar of his era, Aldus Manutius was nonetheless acquainted with practically all of them. Dense networks of scholars kept alive by letters, precious ancient manuscripts sent from one person to the next, new ideas passing from hand to hand were the bread and butter of the intellectual Renaissance. Aldus was like a spider at the center of the scholarly web, and meetings like this gave physical form to connections that otherwise existed only in writing. Giovanni Pico della Mirandola, the linchpin of this gathering, later became one of the era's most inventive philosophical thinkers. The young men Aldus instructed in Carpi, especially the city's future prince, Alberto Pio, went on to patronize serious scholarly activities. Greeks like Andramyttenus popularized the study of a language that had been largely lost in the West for centuries, and that brought to the fore radical ideas about philosophy and the nature of reality. Aldus's path was different, but no less transformative.

That path took Aldus to Venice, and to the business of printing. Nearly all the early printers, from Gutenberg to Jenson, were artisans. Aldus, by contrast, was a scholar and an educator at heart, and would remain so his entire life. Aldus's Italy was awash in intellectual ferment, full of towering intellects with wide and eager followings engaged in cutting-edge research and experimentation founded on the Latin classics. Aldus was not nearly so illustrious around 1480, when he took up residence in Carpi and became tutor to the young princes. He was "a sober and gentle character, approaching the age of thirty and with a good background of Latin scholarship," wrote biographer Martin Lowry of him around this time, "a professional man of letters, clinging to the fringe of the academic world and taking the opportunities that came his way."[9]

Given his lack of sterling credentials and impact on his field, contemporaries did not record much about Aldus's early life. He was born near Rome around 1450 and received his education in the city, where he heard lectures from a colorful cast of itinerant scholars who wandered from patron to patron and city to city looking for fame and fortune. At some point, probably in the 1470s, he relocated to Ferrara and supplemented his Latin studies with Greek. When the rulers of Carpi went looking for a tutor for their two young sons, Aldus must have seemed like a natural choice. The fashionable intellectual circles in the Romagna region knew him well: He had all the requisite skills in both Latin and Greek, including composition. Toward the end of the 1480s, after the better part of a decade spent teaching Alberto and Leonello Pio, Aldus penned some verses in Latin for the edification of his young charges. Study hard, he told them, and follow the examples of Julius Caesar and Alexander the Great. It was all standard, run-of-the-mill subject matter for the genre.

The verses Aldus wrote and subsequently printed for Alberto and Leonello Pio and addressed to their mother, Catherina, are utterly conventional but perfectly competent by the exacting technical standards of Latin poetry. In that sense, they offer a measure of insight into Aldus's personality, which otherwise does not shine through from the available source material. He was not particularly focused on making a serious mark as a scholar and avoided controversy like the plague. This was something of an oddity, considering the intellectual circles in which he moved: When two of Aldus's acquaintances at the University of Padua—both renowned scholars—exchanged academic insults throughout the 1480s, Aldus took no side and stayed on good terms with both. Public recognition through controversy often meant support from a wealthy patron, and patronage meant a good living. For Giovanni Pico della Mirandola, he of the fine villa and good wine, the ultimate goal was nothing less than a complete, and radical, philosophical system. Aldus supported his friend Giovanni and stayed in regular contact with him for years. Giovanni's work drew the ire of secular and religious authorities across Italy and got him into considerable trouble, even within the relaxed environment prevailing in Florence. The brilliant young man was eventually poisoned in 1494, cut down at the peak of his intellectual powers. Aldus, by contrast, had no interest in burning that brightly, or rocking any well-established intellectual or legal boats.

Stranger still, a life of comfortable patronage—a nice piece of property, access to books, the company of like-minded intellectuals—seems not to have appealed to Aldus. His pupil Alberto Pio made such an offer when he reached adulthood, and Aldus flatly refused. This was the consummate, perhaps even stereotypical, teacher: meticulous, fussy, conventional in his tastes and views, deeply committed to his chosen subject matter, and, above all, utterly devoted to the work of education. Strong ideas about the right ways to teach essential linguistic skills, namely Latin, occupied much of his mental energy. He loved language in all its forms, rhythms, and complexities. Communicating that love to others would dominate the rest of his life.[10]

We do not know exactly what pulled Aldus away from Carpi and his young students. Perhaps the ability to reach a larger audience was what eventually drew the schoolmaster to the rough, grimy business of printing, and to Venice, sometime around 1490. It certainly was not a rift with Alberto Pio, who remained devoted to his former schoolmaster throughout his own long, eventful life. All we can say for certain is that in 1490, Aldus planned to continue his educational activities through the medium of the press.

The New Learning

Practically all the early printers were entrepreneurial craftsmen drawn from the upwardly mobile ranks of the guildsmen who dominated Europe's towns and cities. Goldsmiths, mint-masters,

The Money-Changer and His Wife, by Quentin Matsys, 1514. The couple are dressed as prosperous burghers of Flanders, rather than nobility. The man weighs coins and jewels, an activity that would have been common in any office or countinghouse of the period, while his wife looks through the pages of a devotional text. *(Wikimedia Commons)*

View of Innsbruck, c. 1495, by Albrecht Dürer. Innsbruck was the most important city of Tyrol, in the Alps, and the gateway to the Brenner Pass, which sits just under twenty miles away to the south. It was a key stopping point between southern Germany and the vast commercial possibilities of northern Italy. *(Wikimedia Commons)*

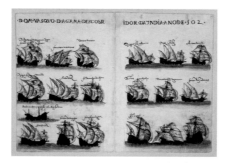

The Portuguese India fleet of 1502, from the *Livro de Lisuarte de Abreu*. Note the mixture of types of vessels, including both caravels, ships with triangular sails well suited for coastal exploration; and carracks (*naus* in Portuguese), square-rigged vessels developed for transoceanic voyages. *(Wikimedia Commons)*

Wedding portrait of Isabella of Castile and Ferdinand of Aragon, c. 1469, artist unknown. When considering late medieval and early modern dynastic
politics, it is essential to remember that many of the players were no older than
teenagers; the two soon-to-be monarchs depicted here, whose marriage
shaped the future course of millions of lives, were eighteen and seventeen
years of age, respectively. *(Wikimedia Commons)*

Isabella of Castile, c. 1490. This might be how the queen looked around the time of the conquest of Granada, the last Moorish stronghold in Catholic Spain. *(Wikimedia Commons)*

Jakob Fugger, c. 1520, portrait by Albrecht Dürer. Dürer was one of the most celebrated artists and gifted portraitists of the era, and he captured in this painting some of the ruthless banker's personality: The hat and the coat are expensive but not flashy in the context of the time, and Fugger's face displays a slightly bemused, knowing expression. *(Wikimedia Commons)*

Portrait of Götz von Berlichingen, taken from the manuscript of his memoir, c. 1567. It is unclear whether the artist actually knew Götz—the manuscript dates from shortly after his death—but the well-groomed hair and beard, bullish neck, and armor all speak beyond the man himself to the archetype of the feuding nobleman and mercenary warrior. *(Wikimedia Commons)*

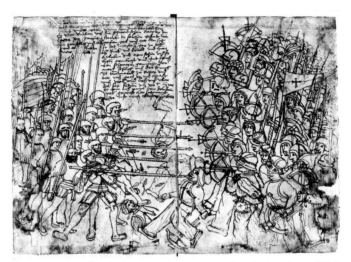

Battle at Old Älvsborg Castle, Västergötland, Sweden, 1502, by Paul Dolnstein. Dolnstein was an engineer who sought additional employment as a *Landsknecht,* or German pikeman, on various campaigns, including this small 1502 war in Sweden. Dolnstein, a firsthand observer of this battle, shows the *Landsknechte* on the left and the Swedish rebels on the right. *(Wikimedia Commons)*

"Bad War," by Hans Holbein the Younger. Holbein depicts the meeting of two blocks of infantry, one of Swiss and one of *Landsknechte*. The men are armed with pikes, long spears thirteen to eighteen feet in length, and such clashes were impossibly violent and chaotic, which is why contemporaries often simply called them "bad war." *(Wikimedia Commons)*

ΑΡΙΣΤΟΤΈΛΟΥΣ ΗΘΙΚΩΝΕΎΔΗΜΊΩΝ,
ΤΟ Α΄.

A page from Aldus Manutius's edition of Aristotle, 1495-98. Manutius had several competitors in the market for Greek-language works, but none were as successful. He was regarded as the finest printer in all of Europe, and his Aldine Press, with its dolphin-and-anchor logo, set the standard for both textual accuracy and beautiful typography. *(Wikimedia Commons)*

Martin Luther, c. 1520, engraving by Lucas Cranach the Elder. Note the tonsure or shaved scalp and lean, almost gaunt profile: This was Luther as a young firebrand at the height of his powers, still a member of the Augustinian Order though he was soon to be excommunicated. *(Wikimedia Commons)*

Hans Luther, c. 1527, by Lucas Cranach the Elder. The face of Luther's father speaks volumes to the financialized, brutal world of the mining industry, which shaped his son's character in indelible ways. *(Wikimedia Commons)*

The Wittenberg Castle Church (*Schlosskirche Wittenberg*), after a 1509 engraving by Lucas Cranach the Elder. This was where, in 1517, Luther is said to have posted his *Ninety-Five Theses*, an attack on the sale of indulgences, or spiritual get-out-of-jail-free cards, that launched the Protestant Reformation. *(Wikimedia Commons)*

Suleiman the Magnificent, c. 1530, either by the Venetian portraitist Titian or a member of his school. The prominent, aquiline nose, mustache, and turban were all distinctive characteristics noted by the sultan's contemporaries. Suleiman ruled the Ottoman Empire at its peak, a superpower spanning three continents. *(Wikimedia Commons)*

The Siege of Rhodes, 1522; artists unknown. This Ottoman depiction of the siege, created in the late 1550s, is part of an official history of Suleiman's reign known as the *Süleymanname*, with 65 images accompanied by Persian-language verses. The surrender of the island fortress gave Suleiman control of the eastern Mediterranean. *(Wikimedia Commons)*

Maximilian I, c. 1519, by Albrecht Dürer. Maximilian was nearing the end of his life when Dürer painted him for the last time—the sketch on which the painting was based was made in 1518—and years of politicking and war had taken their toll on the old man. The ambitious Holy Roman Emperor had spent most of his life plotting to expand his lands, usually with mixed results. *(Wikimedia Commons)*

Charles V, c. 1515, by Barend van Orley. The son of Maximilian was not an especially handsome man, by either the standards of his time or our own, and the jutting Habsburg jaw shows up prominently in this portrait of the teenaged soon-to-be king and emperor. Charles's dominions spanned much of modern-day Germany, Austria, and Italy and included Spain and its colonies in North America. *(Wikimedia Commons)*

the sons of prosperous weavers, middling merchants: These occupations largely provided the pool of talent, those familiar with craft processes and how to finance them at scale, who drove the expansion of the printing industry from Gutenberg all the way to Aldus. Aldus, however, was a scholar and educator, a learned man steeped in the intellectual climate of the Renaissance.

"Renaissance" is a tricky term, and generations of historians have rightfully questioned its value when applied either to an era, to cultural tendencies, or to a series of intellectual movements. The notion of an all-encompassing Renaissance that produced the modern individual, modern secularism, and modern states, and generally seeded the ground for the world to come, has largely disappeared. What is left is the reality of a wealthy, increasingly literate, urban civilization in Italy that produced a vibrant cultural interest in the ancient classics. This movement, which thought of itself as a *renovatio* ("renewal"), or rebirth of lost glories from the Roman (and later Greek) past, blossomed between 1300 and 1500. Beginning with Dante and Petrarch in the fourteenth century and then spreading to ever-wider circles of professional scholars, government officials, and interested amateurs, scholarship focused on the ancient classics had come to dominate education by Aldus's time.[11]

Broadly speaking, we can call this educational paradigm and its focus "humanism." This term is anachronistic—it was coined by a German scholar in 1808 or 1809—but it derives from the *studia humanitatis*, the group of subjects that an *humanista*, a master of grammar, rhetoric, history, and philosophy, might teach to students. At the core of this curriculum and the intellectual movement that produced it was the belief in the unimpeachable wisdom and eloquence of the towering giants of antiquity. Livy, Virgil, Ovid, Suetonius, and especially Cicero offered direct access to the glorious perfection of a bygone age, one that stood in stark contrast to the fallen and decayed world in which the humanists thought they lived. By returning to the study of these past masters, and emulating their language and moral concerns, humanists could bring about a better world.[12]

That was the idea, to the extent that humanists articulated a broader set of aims. For the most part, they dove into the intense study and emulation of classical texts because they liked doing it, because they were surrounded by other people who liked doing it, and because it was useful to them. Some of the greatest early humanists were deeply involved in government, particularly in republican Florence, and saw deep parallels between the active life of a citizen in their time and place and that of ancient Rome. The urban, profit-oriented businessmen of Italy—merchants, bankers, and industrial entrepreneurs—doubled as the peninsula's political elite, forming a unique oligarchy known as the *popolo grosso*.

Elsewhere in Europe, rural noblemen dominated political life, relegating wealthy urbanites to a secondary role in a kingdom's affairs, at best. Not so in Italy: In the sophisticated, labyrinthine political world of the Italian city-states, eloquence and persuasiveness could be a potent weapon, a reflection of the wielder's *virtù*, his capacity for reason, moderation, and self-control. The intense study of classical authors, who putatively shared the same conception of *virtù*, improved that ability.[13]

As the fifteenth century went on, humanism as an educational practice emerged and proliferated. The close reading of the classics would inculcate true *virtù* and the practical skills necessary to serve in government, or to lead one. This marked a distinct overall shift from the standard medieval curriculum, which for centuries had employed a rigid, hierarchical approach to learning. Most humanists were simple enthusiasts, or people who sought the shine of the most advanced and fashionable education for their children, rather than headline-grabbing scholars like Aldus's friend Pico della Mirandola.

The humanists despised and brutally critiqued this medieval norm, the combination of rote grammar and the *ars dictaminis*, and offered something better: "For those with noble minds and those who must involve themselves in public affairs and the community, it is useful to study history and moral philosophy," wrote the early humanist Pier Paolo Vergerio. "From moral philosophy we learn what it is appropriate to do, while from history we extract the examples to follow.... With eloquence, instead, one learns to speak gracefully, with gravity, in order to win over the hearts of the multitude."[14]

This paradigm shift created a booming market in new education, and by 1450, a well-heeled youngster could pick up a fine Ciceronian Latin stylebook and some instruction in history, moral philosophy, and rhetoric from a humanist scholar in just about any city in Italy. Aldus Manutius, born in a small town near Rome and hardly a scion of the *popolo grosso*, did not have access to such a wonderful curriculum in his youth. He received a standard medieval education in grammar, and only later sought out the kind of classical instruction that was becoming de rigueur in his time. Wandering experts offered lectures on the latest trends in Latin and Greek, and while universities were often slow to adopt the new learning, that tendency did not last forever.

A variety of paths drew students to the study of classical antiquity: youthful education at the feet of gentle schoolmasters like Aldus; late-night exchanges between enthusiasts like the one at Pico's villa; full-blown public debates between rivals hungry for the admiration of their peers; and finally, the ready availability of the raw materials, the classical texts that inspired such devotion and wonder among their readers.

We cannot be sure what pulled Aldus to Venice and to printing. The scholar offers only vague hints in the introductions to the various editions that rolled off his presses. But it is hard to escape the tentative conclusion that he saw printing as something positive and transformative, a means of bringing the wisdom of ancient literature to the masses. Education, from Aldus's perspective, led naturally to the mass production of books. "I have decided to spend all my life in the service of my fellow-men," he wrote in the introduction to his Greek grammar. "God is my witness, I desire nothing more than to do something for them, as my past life shows, wherever it has been spent, and I hope my future self will show that still more."[15]

The Dirty Business of Printing

In the introduction to one of his first printed texts, Aldus summed up the thorny business of printing: "Though I could lead a quiet and peaceful life, I have chosen one full of toil and trouble."[16] From an early time, the scholar understood the difficulties of his new profession. When he traded the predictable calm of a classroom for the riotous, chaotic clatter of a print shop, Aldus was not just entering a new field; he was making his way into an exceptionally competitive, cutthroat industry, an unforgiving battlefield on which printers sought every possible advantage and often went bust as a consequence of making even the slightest error.

Aldus arrived in Venice around 1490, presumably with an eye toward pursuing a career in printing, but it would be years before he produced a single page. Getting a new operation off the ground took both time and money. The former he had, perhaps thanks to some generous and unmentioned support from his old student Alberto Pio, but the latter would take some doing. That was likely why Aldus went to Venice rather than Florence: The latter city was the more renowned center of scholarship, particularly for Greek, but the city on the lagoon was a much safer bet for securing funding for a new printing enterprise.

Venice was full of wealthy entrepreneurs, but why would any sharp, tightfisted investor hand his hard-earned cash over to a middle-aged scholar? Aldus had no reputation for producing original works of staggering genius. He was not an intellectual superstar, and those enthusiasts inclined toward humanism were not filling lecture halls across Italy to hear him speak on the latest developments in Greek scholarship. Aldus was rather a humble educator of middling reputation, comfortable and competent, albeit someone who came with an impressive list of contacts among more exalted intellectual ranks. Unlike the artisans who dominated early printing, Aldus had no background in capital-intensive manufacturing ventures. He was not a natural candidate for any investor to trust with a large amount of capital in a risky industry.

Despite those serious shortcomings, Aldus nevertheless succeeded in securing funding. It took some time, and it is safe to assume that he continued to work as a teacher upon arriving in Venice. He was also working on another, equally substantial project concurrently: a new Latin grammar entitled *Institutiones Grammaticae Latinae*, for which he found a printer in March 1493. The printer—an experienced, stingy provincial from Asola named Andrea Torresani—would play a key role in Aldus's life for the next two decades as his business partner and, eventually, his father-in-law.

As far as we can tell, Torresani was a thoroughly unpleasant man: overbearing, overcautious, and cheap. The great Erasmus, who spent time with both Aldus and Torresani during his stay in Venice in 1508, would produce a vicious pen portrait of the businessman a couple of decades later. He was a penny-pinching miser whose only concern was profit, Erasmus wrote, content to serve sour, watered-down wine, scrawny chicken, shellfish dug out of the latrine, and bread made from dough leavened with clay. Since Torresani was too concerned with profit to keep an eye on his sons, his progeny spent their days drinking, gambling, and enjoying the company of prostitutes while poor Aldus and the workmen groaned under the weight of their ceaseless labor at the press. Erasmus's pen was sharp as a rule, and his scathing words came as a response to charges of ungrateful gluttony during his time in Aldus's household, but there is nothing in his portrait that is fundamentally at odds with any other description of Torresani. As far as the evidence goes, his acquaintances did not much care for the man.[17]

But there is no denying that Torresani knew his craft. He got his start in printing as an apprentice to the old Frenchman Nicholas Jenson in the mid-1470s, bought his master's type fonts when Jenson retired at the end of the decade, and then continued in business up until his first dealings with Aldus in the early 1490s. During that time, Torresani explored every aspect of the trade. He financed short-term partnerships with other printers; he acted as a bookselling agent for Paduan printers; and he printed works of his own, like Aldus's grammar. In all of those dealings, Torresani was the portrait of a sober, conservative businessman, leaning hard into established markets and conventional tastes for legal texts and the Latin classics. Between his business acumen and personal background, he embodied the essence of successful printing, the spiritual successor of the hardheaded Johann Fust at the dawn of the industry.

Aldus did have two advantages, each of which offered a potential line of business to explore: his deep knowledge of ancient Greek, and his contacts with those on the cutting edge of this new and increasingly popular branch of scholarship. Following the success of his Latin grammar book, a safe text with a guaranteed readership, Aldus could offer Torresani something quite different from his usual fare. The market was already flooded with the Latin classics, but books in ancient Greek were few and far between; only a dozen or so had been printed in the language, mostly due to the belief that nobody was clamoring for more. If Greek really was the next big thing, the coming frontier of scholarship—as Aldus and most scholars in the know believed in the early 1490s—then he could offer Torresani the chance to corner the market before anybody else could get a foothold.

Printing Greek drastically amplified the challenges that already faced a new printing endeavor, and this, combined with the belief that the market for Greek works was thin, was why so few others had tried in the half century since Gutenberg's first experiments. The venture would require the cutting and casting of new dies, a laborious and expensive endeavor, made more so in this case by the fact that even a city as large and cosmopolitan as Venice was not exactly crawling with skilled metalworkers who had an expert's command of the Greek language. Aldus would have to pick a typeface from the manuscript "hands" or styles popular at the time, then supervise the cutting and casting of thousands of individual pieces of type. It would be years before a single page came off the presses. More important, it would cost tremendous amounts of money.

The cost was high enough that Torresani wanted to share the risk with a partner, and he found one in Pierfrancesco Barbarigo. The Barbarigos were one of Venice's oldest and most distinguished families, equal parts rich and powerful, who reached the height of their fame and fortune in the decade prior to Aldus's arrival in the city. First one Barbarigo and then another was elected doge, ruler of Venice. Pierfrancesco was son of the first and nephew of the second, which made him both wealthy and exceptionally well connected. From the beginning, the printing venture that eventually became known as the Aldine Press had firm financial and political foundations. This was no poor, well-meaning teacher lost in a scholarly dream, producing texts for the benefit of humanity with no concern for their profitability, but a well-capitalized business concern backed by an experienced entrepreneur and one of the richest and most advantageously connected men in a commercial powerhouse of a city.[18]

The Aldine Press

Aldus needed every bit of backing his partners could offer. Between 1469 and 1490, when he arrived in Venice, more than a hundred printing companies had tried to break into the business in the city. Twenty-three were still active in the 1490s, and only ten of those survived into the sixteenth century. The average life span of a Venetian press was eighteen months, and the vast majority produced only a single edition of a single book before going belly-up. Aldus was proposing to not only enter this cutthroat industry, but to do so with a business strategy focused around an entirely unproven, untested product.[19]

Barbarigo, a passive investor, poured a few thousand ducats into the venture; Torresani offered money and technical acumen, and Aldus provided the intellectual muscle. This was a strong combination of skills, and the consortium produced a steady stream of texts that flew off the presses and into the hands of readers. What they produced suggests a planned program rooted in good business sense. The first pages to come off the press in March 1495 belonged to an extremely basic Greek grammar book, the work of a Constantinopolitan exile named Constantine Lascaris, plus another two Greek grammars and a dictionary. The early years of the press also saw the publication of a collection of poetry from Theocritus and Hesiod, along with the comedies of Aristophanes.

These were all essentially educational texts, the raw materials for building an ancient Greek reading public from the ground up. Teachers could use the grammars to instruct their pupils in the fundamentals, and then follow with the short poems of Theocritus and Hesiod and the conversational Attic Greek of Aristophanes. At the same time, the press produced the collected works of Aristotle in five enormous volumes over the course of three years. Aristotle was the best known and most respected writer of ancient Greek, and Aldus produced the first full-scale compendium of his works to appear in print. Even texts that seem rather obscure today, like the pharmacological works of Dioscurides and Nicander, fit neatly into an academic controversy of the late 1490s.[20]

The plan that drove Torresani's and Aldus's operations is obvious in hindsight: Print instructional materials to capitalize on the growing interest in Greek instruction, thereby building out the reading market for Greek-language works, and then produce the most sought-after texts for that market. This was easier said than done, but by all accounts, Aldus and Torresani succeeded. Their works were pricier than their competitors', ranging from two to four times as expensive for the same title, but they nevertheless sold well. Erasmus, then building his reputation as a writer, complained in a letter of being unable to get his hands on a copy of the Greek grammar of Friar Urbano Valeriani. Aldus's overarching desire to educate seamlessly blended with the dictates of the market.[21]

But the industry was brutal. Aldus was not the only printer to set his sights on owning the Greek-language market, and he had serious competition. There was the Florentine printer Lorenzo de Alopa, for example, who produced beautiful type and had easy access to the excellent Greek manuscript collections of his own city. De Alopa went out of business in 1496, but there were still competitors in Venice, ranging from pleasant cooperators like the Cretan scribe Zacharias Callierges to the bullishly confrontational Gabriel of Brasichella. But luck was on Aldus's side: None of his competitors survived the general economic downturn at the very end of the decade, leaving him the sole printer of Greek in Venice, and the most prominent in Italy.

Cornering the Greek market was not enough to keep the press afloat, however, and Aldus soon had to expand the scope of his operation. Despite focusing on Greek works for the first several years, Aldus had happily printed a few Latin and Italian texts as well, including short commissioned works that either brought in ready cash or patronage from important Venetians. Now, as the business became even less forgiving, the established market in Latin texts looked like a safe, conservative way of guaranteeing large, profitable sales. Works by the bestsellers of the early print age, including Virgil, Ovid, Juvenal, Martial, Cicero, Catullus, and many others, joined the continued production of Greek texts like Philostratus, Thucydides, Sophocles, and Herodotus.

Aldus's Latin works were just as desirable as his outstanding Greek texts. He developed a beautiful italic typeface, "those small types, the most beautiful in the world," according to Erasmus. He also printed in a small, portable octavo format, which was both less expensive than his larger productions and better suited for large print runs. In an octavo, sixteen pages of text were printed on a sheet of paper, which was then folded three times to produce eight leaves; compare that to a quarto, with eight pages folded twice, or a folio, with four pages folded once, and it is clear just how much paper and size an octavo would save. Even if the book itself were not sold for a lower price than its competitors—some of Aldus's were, but most were not—the cost of producing the editions was lower, thereby increasing the printer's profit margins.[22]

With the Greek and Latin classics, Aldus and Torresani carved out a substantial chunk of the market for their press, and they continued to respond to the whims of consumer tastes as new cycles of rapid growth and equally rapid decline overturned their business. When Erasmus visited Venice in 1508, he lived with Aldus while completing a new work, the *Adagia*, which rolled off the presses and into the ranks of the sixteenth century's bestsellers. Yet a difficult period during which Venice was engulfed in expensive and disastrous wars led to several interruptions in production, including the apparent death of the Aldine Press between 1509 and 1512. The press managed one final burst of activity, with an emphasis on Latin and Greek texts along with a selection of famous works in Italian, before Aldus died and the press shuttered again in 1515.

Doing Business in the Book Market

The end of the fifteenth century and the beginning of the sixteenth was a transformative period in the history of books, when print firmly overtook manuscripts and established itself as the medium of the future. In that time, printed books had been available for a generation of readers, both responding to and shaping their tastes. Nearly five decades of cutthroat competition had changed how printers understood and catered to those readers. And as tastes slowly changed, so did the books printers produced. Theological and devotional tracts dominated at first, including Bibles and Bible commentaries, lives of saints, books of hours, hymnbooks, and sermons. According to one estimate, this diverse category of texts, popular among both laypeople and the clergy, accounted for nearly 45 percent of all printed book production before 1500. Literature, broadly defined, accounted for another 36 percent, while law and science made up the rest.[23]

Aldus's overall output, with its emphasis on Greek and then the Latin classics, was not typical of successful printers of the age. He rarely printed devotional literature; an edition of the Italian letters of Catherine of Siena was a notable exception, and possibly even an act of atonement for his sins. Editions of classical authors, Aldus's bread and butter, accounted for only 5 percent of all books printed during the fifteenth century. In other ways, however, Aldus was reflective of broader trends. His Latin octavos focused on the most popular authors, like Cicero, Virgil, and Ovid. He regularly produced Greek and Latin grammars for schoolmasters, one of the most reliable markets for printed materials. As demand changed, he moved away from Greek toward Latin and then the vernacular Italian, with editions of Dante and Petrarch. Prior to his association with Aldus, the pragmatic Torresani had produced legal texts for university instructors and students, one of the most reliable if demanding markets for printed texts. While innovative in some respects, including format, typeface, and the publication of ancient Greek texts, Aldus was generally quite conservative in what he chose to print. So were the vast majority of printers.[24]

This conservatism was a response to the two fundamental problems plaguing early printing. First, practically all of the costs came up front. New types were a one-time investment, but a massive one: Aldus spent thousands of ducats on his Greek and fine italic typefaces, roughly the amount of the Fuggers' initial loans to Archduke Sigismund of Tyrol. Götz von Berlichingen could have hired a troop of men-at-arms for a substantial campaign for the cost of the type alone. On top of the type, the printer had to pay for thousands of pieces of high-quality paper for every edition. Then came the costs of labor, which were roughly equivalent to the amount spent on paper: In 1508, Aldus employed around fifteen people, probably running five presses at a time with three skilled laborers per press. All told, it cost Aldus somewhere north of 200 ducats per month to keep his shop in continuous operation, roughly the annual income from a well-off nobleman's landed estates. But while costs were continuous and had to be paid from the very beginning, the revenue came later. The printer would not see a single coin until the edition was complete and in the hands of the buyers, and perhaps not even then.[25]

The second problem of early printing—and indeed printing today—was estimating the size and location of the market for a given work. Were there five hundred buyers for a new edition of Cicero's letters to Atticus, or three thousand? How many people really wanted a complete set of Aristotle's works? And where might those buyers be found? These sound like basic issues to a post-industrial world of mass manufacturing and global distribution networks, but practically all book production prior to the invention of the printing press had been bespoke: If a customer wanted a copy of a manuscript, they went to a scribe and ordered one. Scribes did not need to guess the size of the audience for a work or seek out buyers. Printers did, which explains why they were so reluctant to try new titles, and also why Aldus's decision to move forward with Greek-language productions on a large scale was such a bold move. Nobody really knew whether there was enough demand to support printing enough copies to make the venture worthwhile.

To make matters more complicated, there were nowhere near enough readers in a single city—even one as wealthy, populous, and sophisticated as Venice—to support print runs of the size required to keep an operation like Aldus's in business. He was likely the most prolific printer in Europe between 1499 and 1504, and probably again after 1512. This meant that he, like practically every other printer of the age, had to seek out customers on a sprawling scale. To sell out his typical first print runs of one thousand to three thousand copies, Aldus would need to move beyond the Venetian patricians and Paduan scholars in his immediate vicinity. Augsburg merchants, Oxford academics, Frankfurt book dealers, Lyon bibliophiles, Hungarian mining magnates: To make his endeavor worthwhile, all of them would need to become acquainted with the products of the Aldine Press.[26]

The central problem was the sparsity of a general reading public. The rural villages of peasant farmers that made up most of the European population were not exactly overflowing with highly literate people with disposable income to spend on printed books. Potential consumers tended to cluster in large cities where merchants, clerics, students, and the otherwise educated usually resided. Every successful printer maintained distribution networks connecting these clusters of readers, relying on precisely the same mechanisms of financial transfers, credit, and trust that underpinned European commerce as a whole. The Nuremberg printer Anton Koberger, a direct contemporary of Aldus, had agents working on his behalf all across the continent: Venice, Florence, Milan, Bologna, Lyon, Paris, Augsburg, Munich, Ingolstadt, Vienna, Danzig, Posen, Breslau, Kraków, and Lübeck. All of these intermediaries operated on credit, recording copies received and then remitting payment back to Koberger. For his part, Aldus maintained relationships with important scholars everywhere in Europe, from England to Switzerland to Germany. These scholarly connections doubled as a distribution network, absorbing a substantial portion of any print run.[27]

Since it revolved around far-flung networks and the chancy transmission of information about demand and pricing, business was often untenable. Printers constantly asked for news of what consumers were interested in, how many copies were available, and who was printing what, but this was no guarantee of success. An infinite number of all-too-common problems could sink even the best-capitalized and sharpest-run presses, not all of which were within the publisher's control. A printer could put out a book for which there was no demand at all; he might correctly gauge that there was some demand for a title, but overestimate it and produce too many copies; he might print an edition unaware that a rival had just flooded the market with five hundred copies of the same title; he might pick a bad manuscript copy of his chosen text as a source, one full of misspellings and slips of the pen, or hire an editor who did not pick up on errors in composition. Discerning consumers were unlikely to purchase a bad-quality text.

Even if everything else went right, an accident might damage or destroy the books in transport, the printer's agents in distant cities might pocket the profits, or unforeseen circumstances could disrupt the distribution networks that got the books from the press to the buyers. Venice's involvement in the War of the League of Cambrai, from 1508 to 1516, was disastrous for Aldus's business: He shut his doors completely from 1509 to 1512, Venice's low ebb, when constant conflict ravaged northern Italy and made it nearly impossible to distribute the thousands of books necessary to keep the press afloat. The exigencies of high politics could drive even Europe's most prolific printer to take a hiatus, and he was one of the fortunate ones. Others went out of business permanently.

Information Revolution

"*Studeo*," said Aldus, his narrowed eyes fixed on the sheet of hand-written paper in front of him. It was a reflexive, exasperated Latin utterance designed to shut out the clamor of the print shop that surrounded him. Ink balls thudded onto individual dies as presses scraped and clattered. Paper chafed and crinkled. Compositors and pullers and inkers chattered among themselves. The wails and laughter of children and the thuds of tiny running feet on floor-boards came down through the ceiling. Several pens scratched as Aldus made emendations to the text in front of him and an overworked editor named Seraphinus rewrote sections of a draft before handing it off to the compositors.

The last pen moved incessantly over the paper, held in the hand of a sharp-nosed fortysomething in a shabby gown sitting at a cramped corner desk. The wandering scholar already possessed a healthy reputation for wit, skill, and a wide variety of intellec-tual gifts, and he had come to Aldus's shop to spread his works as far as the finest press in Europe could take them. Erasmus of Rotterdam would be famous soon, and Aldus Manutius, he knew, could speed that process along.

Proverbs were Erasmus's concern of the day, the well-known

sayings sprinkled throughout the vast literature of classical antiquity. They flowed from Erasmus's pen onto the paper in front of
him, accompanied by witty, learned commentary on their meaning and application. When a sheet was full, Erasmus took it to
Seraphinus for edits, then back to Erasmus for more, and finally
to Aldus, who read, revised, and then passed along the final text
to the compositor to set the type and print.

Aldus tolerated no interruptions. "*Studeo*," he said, over and over
again, the lines around his eyes wrinkling deeply in concentration.
Erasmus, in the perfect Ciceronian Latin both men spoke, asked
why he took such pains with the material. "*Studeo*," came the reply.

It was an ambiguous word, full of shades of meaning, the kind a
grammarian like Aldus relished like a gluttonous connoisseur confronted with a sprawling feast. On the one hand, it simply meant
"I'm working," thereby cutting off any potential delay to the process with a single utterance. On the other, however, it implied that
Aldus was learning, studying, drinking in the wisdom Erasmus was
pouring onto pages that would soon be read all over the continent.
Aldus was otherwise engulfed by the clamor of his family, fifteen
employees, a working print shop, and a demanding father-in-law
and business partner. But at least in a single, oft-repeated word, the
fleeting, remembered joys of cutting-edge scholarship could still
sneak through the cracks of everyday life.[28]

"At the end of his life, Aldus was a crushed and disillusioned
man, tragically unable to see the successes that are so obvious
to us today," writes his biographer Martin Lowry. The dramatic
spread of Greek in early modern Europe was Aldus's doing, and
his readable italic script and portable editions helped simplify the
act of reading for the masses. But despite his having built a product and a legacy that would live on for centuries, the stresses of
the industry eventually took their toll.

Indeed, the new technology broke most of the people who

tried to turn it into a profitable business. Some printers managed to survive by repeatedly playing the hits, cautiously expanding into new markets, and leveraging their political connections for monopolies and exclusive privileges, as Aldus did whenever possible. Most, however, did not. Bankruptcy and failure were the most common outcomes for would-be printers, draining the pockets of financiers in the relentless hunt for profits.

More than ten million books, comprised of forty thousand different editions, rolled off the presses between 1450 and 1500. Another fifty million—some hundred thousand editions—followed in the first half of the sixteenth century. Even that first number, ten million, was probably more books than had been produced in the entire millennium prior to the invention of the printing press. Print was a genuine agent of change, disseminating everything from the ancient classics to basic grammar to new languages to the wit of Erasmus to an increasingly vibrant and hungry reading public. Printing created news, as we understand it, and propaganda, as more ephemeral products joined the editions of Cicero and sermons. The coming scientific revolution of Copernicus and Galileo relied on the mass availability of print.[29]

And even then, the most consequential work to come out of the printing industry emerged not in the great commercial centers of Venice or Augsburg but in a small, out-of-the-way university town in eastern Germany. It was Wittenberg, the home of an obscure Augustinian monk named Martin Luther, that would transform print into the key weapon of an enormous religious upheaval that would split the continent at the seams.

———— ❧ ————

CHAPTER 6

John Heritage and Everyday Capitalism

April 17, 1512, Moreton-in-Marsh, England

The weathered gate creaked on its hinges as it shut, the sound merging with the relentless bleating of the hundreds of sheep packed into the adjacent pasture and the occasional bark from a pair of shaggy sheepdogs. Two men chattered good-naturedly back and forth on either side of the gate. The farmer's daughter was getting married later in the year, after the harvest. Would the wool merchant attend the festivities? Of course; any social gathering was a chance to mingle with the wool producers of this particular corner of Gloucestershire, to pay off ongoing debts and cement relationships with the producers who provided him with a few sacks of wool every year. His competitors would certainly be there, settling their own debts and making the rounds. John Heritage—wool merchant and entrepreneur of Moreton-in-Marsh—could not afford to pass up such an opportunity.

Heritage smiled, thinking of strong ale, a good meal, and productive bargains waiting to be struck. Then his conversation with the farmer turned to the current business, his words taking on a harder edge. The merchant, meanwhile, trained a practiced eye on the nearby flock busily cropping at the pasturage: good quality for the most part, he thought, but not the best the Cotswolds could produce. He offered ten shillings per tod—the twenty-eight-pound unit of measurement of wool in which it was sold. Ten was fair, he thought, but the farmer wanted eleven: That was what a competitor was offering, he said. Fine, Heritage replied, but if the quality was not up to par, he would expect a steep discount upon delivery. The farmer wanted half up front: He had a wedding to pay for, after all. Heritage agreed, but only if the farmer was amenable to a repayment schedule that stretched all the way past Christmas, maybe even to Lent. This farmer was a reliable producer with a sterling reputation, and Heritage could be sure his credit would not be abused.

Back and forth they went, haggling and arguing with the deftness and patience of people who had performed this dance dozens of times, until finally Heritage counted out a few well-worn silver coins from his purse and handed them over the creaking gate. *Two pounds six shillings*, he thought, making a mental note of the amount.

Heritage hauled himself up onto his horse's saddle and bade the farmer farewell, then set off down a narrow lane made muddy by a brief rainstorm the previous night. Only the chirping of birds and the distant bleating of sheep disturbed his train of thought, mentally repeating the amounts of the three different transactions he had made that morning so he wouldn't forget them. The bleating grew louder as the road sank. Sheep grazed amid raised embankments and ruined walls that marked what had once been a prosperous little village, the spire of its abandoned church rising toward the clouds currently hanging low in a steel-gray spring sky. Fields of grain had long since given way to empty pastures, livestock replacing the people killed by outbreak after outbreak of the plague.

The abandoned village receded as Heritage's horse placidly

covered the last few miles to Moreton-in-Marsh. He dismounted in the courtyard of his home, situated on the village's outskirts, shaking flecks of mud from his cloak and handing off his horse's reins to a waiting servant. He repeated the amounts of money to himself one more time, then walked under the low-hanging timber lintel into his home. In his study, a leather-bound book waited for him on a shelf. Its pages contained the lifeblood of Heritage's business.

The merchant retrieved the account book and opened to a blank page. On it, he wrote the name of the farmer and left a blank space for the total amount of wool to be received, then scratched in "*payd yn ernys* £2 6s," followed by another large blank space to fill in the rest. He did the same for the other two deals he had made that busy morning. Over the course of the year, he would fill in the remaining spaces with bits of money paid at various times, totals given out, and the amount of wool collected. In this way, he could keep track of the general shape of his complex and reasonably profitable trading business.

Notes made, Heritage closed his account book and placed it back on the shelf. He poured himself a cup of ale from a pottery jug his wife, Joan, had left out for him. Wool trading was thirsty work, and there was always more to be done.

John Heritage was not an especially extraordinary person. He was a prosperous trader and farmer with a variety of business ventures in his small corner of Gloucestershire, most of them centered around the production and sale of wool. For more than two decades, Heritage made the spring rounds of his neighborhood, striking deals with various farmers, each of whom owned a few hundred sheep. He returned to collect in the fall, hiring carts to haul the wool eighty miles to London for sale to the major merchants who dominated the foreign-trade sector of the economy. Even in his little corner of the Cotswolds, Heritage had competitors in the wool trade, some outselling him by twice as much every year and rising into the ranks of the merchant grandees. In the grand scheme of commercial activity in England at the time, he was a bit player.

But people like him were ubiquitous figures in an increasingly commercialized society. They were the indispensable middlemen who bound the countryside, where the vast majority of the population lived and worked, to the urban centers of trade that connected each individual part of Europe to the greater whole. Moreover, Heritage's account book has survived, an invaluable and exceptionally rare document that gives us real insight into how he did business over the course of more than two decades. We can understand Heritage and his world in minute detail.

Heritage aggressively sought out new opportunities in everything from land and wool to imported luxuries. His skill at managing his affairs comes through clearly in his account book, as does the sense of constant competition with his rivals. But none of that is remarkable; what is striking about John Heritage is how common people like him were at this specific time and place in history. No less than Jakob Fugger and his ilk, Heritage was a profit-oriented businessman who kept meticulous accounts and possessed a sophisticated understanding of how to use credit. He was a capitalist, or at least a proto-capitalist, who could be quite ruthless in securing an advantage. The ubiquity of people like him points to the deep penetration of commercial activity, and commercial values, in a Europe on the cusp of enormous change. It was in fact overflowing with people like John Heritage, prepared to exploit the challenges and possibilities of the era.[1]

The Late Medieval Countryside and the End of Feudalism

At first glance, cities like Venice and Augsburg might seem like the beating heart of the European economy around 1500. Major urban centers were in fact the places where capital, goods, and innovation all bubbled to the visible surface. Yet the vast majority of people lived in the countryside, not cities. Even in the most urbanized regions, like northern Italy and the Low Countries, far more people resided in rural than in urban areas. Nor were country-dwelling peasants unsophisticated yokels; all of the economic growth and change that powered this era came from the toil and ingenuity of these common folk, people who produced the raw materials that enabled both urban life and the large-scale exchange that remade the European economy around this time. John Heritage and people like him were the key links between urban and rural life in this dynamic and evolving economic order.

The Black Death—the wave of mass death caused by the bacterium *Yersinia pestis*—defined the late medieval countryside. In the years around 1350, the first wave of the plague killed tens of millions of people in Europe, effectively halving the population wherever it struck. This was not a one-off calamity; the plague returned repeatedly to decimate subsequent generations. As if these reoccurring, massive shocks of disease were not enough, the climate worsened substantially over the course of the fourteenth and fifteenth centuries, ushering in a colder, wetter period now known as the "Little Ice Age." Mortality rose across age groups, dropping life expectancy from roughly twenty-five years to twenty, and fertility could not keep up with the losses. Simply put, there were far fewer people in the countryside toward the end of the fifteenth century than there had been two hundred years before. The deserted village John Heritage had passed on his ride to Moreton-in-Marsh was one of many (twenty-nine, by one count, in that small corner of the world), its crumbling walls and sunken lanes a tangible legacy of the plague and its aftermath.[2]

The impact of the population shrinking so much, so quickly, and remaining at dangerously low numbers over the ensuing decades had dramatic effects on the economy and society. Our classic portrait of medieval Europe hinges on the feudal order, in which peasants—unfree serfs—were tied to the land and bound in compulsory, life-long service to their lord. That kind of arrangement thrived when masses of impoverished serfs huddled in drafty huts, making their meager living by tending the lord's plots of grain for starvation wages. Practically every scrap of available land—much of it marginal and unproductive—had to be used to grow grain. Calculated by calories produced per acre, grain was the crop that could feed the greatest number of people. With land scarce and food expensive, the serfs were stuck: They could not leave or marry without their lord's permission, and they had scant leverage to demand better conditions from their noble superiors. Thanks to favorable climate conditions, the High Middle Ages—the period from about 1100 to 1300—had caused a massive spike in population and economic growth.

That growth came at the cost of immiserating the peasantry and locking in this exploitative social order.[3] The Black Death, however, made that medieval social order untenable. The economy immediately and seriously contracted in the wake of the initial outbreak, with GDP falling by 26 percent in Spain, 35–40 percent in Italy, and about 35 percent in England. The outbreaks of plague that followed, compounded by a colder, wetter, and more unpredictable climate, meant that there were far fewer people living in 1425 than there had been a century before. Such was the case in England up until John Heritage's day and well after.[4]

This had significant and numerous implications. Fewer people meant fewer workers, and thus a greater demand for labor. If a peasant's work was drastically more valuable in a tighter labor market, why bother to show up to plow the lord's fields or clear his ditches? If wages for workers in a nearby town were spiking thanks to another culling of plague, why allow yourself to be tied forever to a less-than-promising bit of land in the countryside? At the same time, the high demand for staple goods like grain, which had incentivized lords to use the serfs' forced labor to work their personal lands (demesne holdings) while renting out the rest to their tenants, went away. Under these conditions, it was easier for lords to lease out their land to those formerly unfree tenants and collect cash rents instead.

While the economy as a whole went into a serious recession over the course of the fifteenth century, this new reality of lower population, abundant land, and weakened lords had real benefits for peasants in the countryside. Land was cheap and plentiful. Wages were higher. Food cost less and diets improved, as people took in a greater variety of vegetables and more meat compared to their grain-heavy eating habits prior to the Black Death. An ambitious peasant could slip the shackles of serfdom and accumulate considerable land and wealth on his rise up the social ladder. Lords possessed less leverage with which to demand services from their social inferiors. With less demand for grain, localities and regions could specialize in different goods, which a heavily monetized and commercialized economy would then distribute throughout increasingly busy trade routes. These developments were not universal; they varied from region to region and even locality to locality. But they were general trends observable across much of western Europe, from England to the Rhineland, in the aftermath of the Black Death. And they provided the context in which John Heritage grew up and thrived.[5]

John Heritage and His Family

Heritage's family were the prototypical social climbers of the post-plague world. They held a sizable parcel of land, which they had owned for generations, in the parish of Burton Dassett in southeast Warwickshire. John's grandfather (also named John) had come up far enough in the world to join the fraternity of the Holy Cross in Stratford-upon-Avon in 1466, some four years before the younger John's birth. Fraternities like that of the Holy Cross were both religious and social organizations; they collectively employed one or more priests to say prayers for the souls of the members, paid for regular ceremonies, and held an annual feast. These fraternities served as valuable networking opportunities for savvy, business-minded artisans and merchants in the region, whose ranks included the Heritage family.

The annual dues for the fraternity of the Holy Cross were not cheap, which meant that John the Elder and his son Roger, who joined at the same time, were at the very least prosperous. When Roger died in 1495, the family was doing quite well: According to his will, in addition to his family plots, Roger leased two hundred acres of arable land and even more pasturage from the lords of the manor of Burton Dassett, producing grain, wool, dairy, produce, and livestock. He owned 860 sheep and 40 cattle and employed six servants to run the entire operation. After paying £20 in annual rent, he might make £10 in profit. That was a fine living for a country yeoman, an active class of entrepreneurial rural businessmen who took advantage of beneficial conditions in the post-plague landscape to rise out of the mass of the peasantry.[6]

Our John Heritage—Roger's son and John's grandson—came into the world around 1470. This made him roughly twenty-five years of age when his father died, leaving him to take care of Roger's substantial property and his eight children, four boys and four girls, of whom John was the eldest. It fell to him to care for this large brood. We don't know precisely how John felt about his father, or about his new responsibilities. The sources we do have are purely administrative—wills and account books, incomplete and unsatisfactory documents. No diaries or chronicles that might contain emotive information about family relations survive.

For whatever reason, Roger did not seem to have had much confidence in his children, at least apart from John. In his will, he warned his executors not to hand over the specified bequests to his children if they were "wasters" or "of evil will or disposition." His daughters would not be allowed to marry someone unacceptable, or they would lose their inheritance. None of this gives us any reason to think Roger was anything other than a stern patriarch, ruling over his extended household with an iron fist.[7]

Looking after his father's estate and all his siblings' futures was a major task for the young John Heritage. Roger's affairs had been complicated. He both owned and leased land and traded in myriad goods. The old patriarch had maintained business contacts across a range of larger towns, all within twenty miles of home; he owed money to an innkeeper in Buckinghamshire forty miles away, and he had interests in London—the commercial and political heart of England—eighty miles southeast of Burton Dassett.

But Roger had failed to leave his son ready cash to distribute to meet the will's obligations. As his siblings came of age and needed their dowries and bequests to start their independent lives, John had to find the individual amounts of money the will had specified. That meant taking a proactive hand in management to ensure a steady flow of income while simultaneously looking after the family's interests at large. His sisters needed husbands and his brothers needed wives—and occupations. They all needed to prepare for an uncertain, precarious future.[8]

Enclosure and Capitalism

John Heritage looked out over the family land. He knew every lump and bump of its fifty acres, every spot where a large rock might catch the plow, the dead ground where a wayward ewe could hide, every tree that offered shade on a hot summer day.

He had spent all of his twenty-seven years in a thatched-roof farmhouse looking over that land. A few elderly sheep waiting to be butchered and skinned occupied a small enclosure near the farmhouse. The grain grew high in the late summer sun. This was a good, well-tended crop on productive land that had given the Heritage family life and prosperity for nearly two centuries.

But 1497's harvest would be the last. Soon, the grain would be gathered up and would not be replanted. Hired laborers working under Heritage's watchful eye would remove the small sheepfold and the barriers separating the Heritage land from the surrounding fields. The farmhouse was already empty; the family's belongings, remnants of generations of occupancy, were packed into a few hired carts. They would trundle the twenty miles down the road from Burton Dassett to the village of Moreton-in-Marsh, the childhood home of Heritage's wife, where the family would take up new residence.

John turned his gaze toward the rolling, gently sloped land surrounding the Heritage fields. It belonged to the lords of the manor of Burton Dassett, the Belknap family. His father, Roger, had leased a large portion of it for years. Hundreds of sheep and a few dozen sturdy cattle used it for pasturage. The family land and the leased pasture had been the core of the family business for all of John's life, and it had given Roger, his late wife, Elizabeth, and their eight children a good living.

That good living was not enough for John. Stress ate away at him. His brother Thomas, away at Oxford, wrote constantly asking for more money to pay his living expenses. His sisters, each on the verge of marriage, needed dowries to begin their new lives. But it was more than that. Roger had been an ambitious man in life, a social climber always looking for something better; the same fire burned even hotter in John. He had dreams of something bigger than Burton Dassett—dreams of bulging purses, a large, half-timbered house on a street crowded with prosperous frontages, a dozen servants hanging on his every instruction, expensive educations for his sons, and the admiration of his surly, ruthless in-laws, the Palmers. Profit was the path to getting all of that, and more.

Roger Heritage had not been the Belknaps' only leaseholder; some sixty other people, residents of the township of Burton, had rented fields and planted crops. For generations, sons had followed in the footsteps of their fathers, grandfathers, and still more distant ancestors, tilling the land and making their livelihoods in this large parish under the shadow of its prominent church steeple and windmill. No longer, thanks to John Heritage and his agreement with Edward Belknap, the new lord of the manor. All sixty people would be turned out, forced to find their way in the world away from their ancestral home. John Heritage would lease the whole manor from Belknap, encircling the formerly arable land with hedges and ditches and turning it into pasture for a large flock of sheep.

For Belknap, the advantages were obvious: He only had to deal with a single leaseholder rather than dozens, making a tidy profit with a minimum of worry. With wool prices rising and labor costs still sky-high, it was more profitable to use land for low-intensity pasturage than to engage in grain farming, which required a great deal of labor and yielded pitiful returns. For John Heritage, this was an opportunity to vault himself up the social ladder—if he hired the right people to manage his flocks and found the right buyers for the wool, he could become a commercial force practically overnight, if he could successfully oversee a much larger, riskier, and more complex enterprise than he or his unpleasant father had ever previously run.

Enclosing the fields and turning them into pasture was a rational, profit-oriented move for both Belknap and Heritage. And in doing so, Heritage—who presumably birthed the plan—revealed himself to be a genuine entrepreneur with both ambition and a deep ruthless streak. Ejecting sixty people, all of whom Heritage had likely known since birth, from lands they had held for generations, was a heartless but perfectly rational strategy. For Heritage, tearing apart the social fabric of Burton Dassett—the place he had spent his entire life—was a small price to pay for social advancement. This sums up the emerging capitalist logic of the period quite well, just as the downtrodden miners had scarcely troubled Jakob Fugger and the mistreatment of Caribbean natives had not much bothered Christopher Columbus.[9]

What John Heritage did to Burton Dassett has a long and contentious history. "Enclosure," as it was called, lies at the heart of a debate about how, precisely, a fully capitalist economy emerged in this period. In one version of this story, entrepreneurs like Heritage evicted a stable, landed peasantry off their land to make room for rational, capitalist management while simultaneously creating a landless rural proletariat—the muscle for a new agrarian capitalism. The story of John Heritage thus becomes a story of oppression, of lords and their accomplices conspiring to immiserate the peasantry.

This was true. The people of Burton Dassett, questioned about their eviction in an official inquest some twenty years later, were hardly thankful to John Heritage and Edward Belknap for their harsh introduction to capitalism. However, it is impossible to deny that pasture was a more efficient, profitable use of the land than arable farming had been. Most enclosures were in fact carried out by peasants, usually on land they leased or owned outright. Heritage was hardly a lord, and he was atypical of the kind of men who pursued enclosure for profit. And most enclosures happened on land that was lightly used, or in some cases completely abandoned. In this, Heritage's mass evictions, while hardheaded, were comparatively rare.[10]

Of course, that fact would hardly be of much comfort to the former residents of Burton Dassett. John Heritage and Edward Belknap made large amounts of money at their expense and hardship. It may have been why Heritage eventually left the area altogether and moved down the road to Moreton-in-Marsh: He had worn out his welcome among his former neighbors.

The Account Book

Given the savvy and occasionally ruthless ways in which he conducted the rest of his affairs over the ensuing decades, it seems unlikely that John Heritage lost much sleep over the evictions of the tenants at Burton Dassett. When we next catch a glimpse of him, several years have passed since his move from Burton Dassett to Moreton-in-Marsh. Using his in-laws' connections, the capital from his newly leased pasture, and all he had learned from his father, Heritage reinvented himself as a wool trader in addition to all his other activities.

A rare source tells us about Heritage's diverse business affairs. In 1501, the man found himself in London, likely plying his trade. While in the city, he purchased a paper book with ninety-six blank leaves. For the next twenty years, he recorded his wool dealings in this account book, jotting down names, locations, sums, weights of wool, and various other things he needed to remember.

That information was obviously useful to Heritage, but it is beyond precious to us as modern observers for one simple reason: This kind of record, from this type of person, almost never survives to the present day. Account books were common, but their survival over the course of many centuries is not. They simply were not useful enough to preserve, since the information they contained was specific to their users and the economic worlds those users inhabited. Wool trades, town artisans swapping their customers' debts, pawnbrokers' transactions: These were the bread and butter of medieval and early modern economic life, but they were rarely interesting enough for subsequent generations to save them.

Except for Heritage's account book, which by some stroke of luck ended up in the archives of Westminster Abbey. It was not labeled or remembered but sat there for centuries collecting dust. Finally, in the 1990s, a music historian named Roger Bowers came upon it entirely by chance. He had been searching for old sheet music, spare leaves of which were often used as filler to bind books. Bowers told a friend of his discovery, who then told historian Christopher Dyer, who had known Heritage's name from research into leases, wills, and other assorted documents in the area of Burton Dassett. Through this series of unlikely events, the account book came into the hands of a historian who could firmly place Heritage into both his extremely local and much broader worlds.[11]

Heritage's records give us access to a kind of economic activity that is difficult to see from other sources: the diversified dealings of a rural entrepreneur. The account book contains transactions systematically and consistently kept over the course of two decades, allowing us to track the scale and location of Heritage's wool dealings. He experienced ups and downs, dealt with different people, and tried out a variety of strategies over the years, some of them more successful than others. In all of these affairs, the account book tells us things about Heritage and his world that other sources—wills, land transactions, and the like—simply cannot.

Accounting was already a widespread and growing practice throughout Europe at the beginning of the sixteenth century, and keeping track of transactions in systematic fashion was not a new concept. In Italy, the most commercially sophisticated region of Europe, state-of-the-art double-entry bookkeeping was de rigueur after appearing nearly two centuries before. Jakob Fugger learned best practices in Venice during his apprenticeship in the 1470s and 1480s and regularly quizzed new hires about their accounting knowledge for decades afterward. It is not surprising that large firms like the Medici Bank, the Fuggers, and their many contemporaries needed tight management practices to keep hold of their far-flung enterprises. The Medici, for example, carried out detailed annual reviews of each local branch of their firm based on auditing the books.[12]

But Moreton-in-Marsh is a long way from Florence, Augsburg, or even London. John Heritage was not managing a firm with multiple branches and dozens or hundreds of employees sprawled across Europe's major commercial centers, dealing in tens of thousands of ducats' worth of business on an annual basis. Instead, he was an enterprising independent wool trader with only a few shepherds, household servants, and a clutch of temporary hirelings on the payroll. Despite that, his operation was still complex enough to benefit from systematic recordkeeping.

Cosimo de' Medici would have turned his nose up at the apparent disorganization of Heritage's account book and fired any manager who presented him with a record of this kind. It certainly would not have passed Jakob Fugger's stern muster. Rather than a sophisticated double-entry system, or even a continuous list of transactions, Heritage organized the account book as a series of individual memoranda to himself. In that sense, it was as much of a memory aid as an account book, a way of keeping track of the overall shape of his dealings and reminders of his various obligations rather than a perfect record of every debit and credit. Here is a typical example from the year 1505:

> Thomas Kyte 42 tod prec' the tod 11*s* and to geve 2 Tot £23 2*s* 0*d*
> Flesys yn. Payd yn ernys 40*s*. Payd at delyveryng 40*s*.
> Payd on Mychelmas evyn £6. Payd yn Blokley £3. Payd
> yn Crystmas Halydays 40*s*. Payd on Goodtyde Tewysday
> 42*s*. Payd be hys servand the 28 day of April £4.
> Payd yn Stowe 20*s*.

Heritage bought forty-two tods of wool, each weighing twenty-eight pounds, from a farmer (evidently one working on quite a large scale) named Thomas Kyte. He agreed to pay 11 shillings (*s*) per tod (*prec' the tod*) and paid out the amount in installments over the course of the following year: 40*s* in earnest money (*yn ernys*)—a down payment that was effectively a loan to the producer—when the deal was struck, 40*s* at delivery (*at delyveryng*), the large sum of £6 (at 20*s* per pound) on Michaelmas in late September, and another £3 at some unspecified date in the town of Blockley. Forty more shillings followed on Christmas, then another 42 on Shrove Tuesday at the beginning of Lent, here called *Goodtyde Tewysday*. Two more installments completed the transaction: £4 on April 28, and a final 20*s* at some unspecified later date in the town of Stowe. The total value of the transaction, recorded on the right side of the page at the top, was £23 2*s*.[13]

This one relationship between Heritage and Thomas Kyte, with its ongoing payment plan, was a lot to keep track of. Heritage made many deals like this every year: The bargain with Kyte was for a little over 8 percent of the total he purchased in 1505, and that was one of the larger and more complex deals he made that year. The single page of the account book on which that series of dealings appears included five transactions. At the bottom of each page, Heritage kept a running tally of the weight of wool purchased and the amount of money he had spent on it, along with a final total. He did the same at the end of each year, giving himself an annual shape of the business, if not a continuous record of his resources at any given moment.

The type of recordkeeping Heritage preferred was common at the time. Known as a charge/discharge system, it was the basic method in use with the royal exchequer and a variety of estates and manors throughout England and beyond. Charge/discharge was better suited as an auditing tool for estate managers and owners than for keeping track of a complex and diversified business, but the method suited Heritage's purposes well enough. The major advantage lay in familiarity—all around Heritage, estate managers and merchants utilized this exact system, or variations thereon. If legally challenged on the validity of a particular transaction, a common occurrence in a litigious and competitive environment, Heritage could present a well-understood accounting method as evidence. His humble, well-kept book had a good chance of standing up to scrutiny.

Sophisticated double-entry bookkeeping was not unknown in England: One precocious London merchant named Thomas Howell, who was involved in the trade with Spain, utilized it as early as 1517. Other merchants kept accounts with debits and credits on opposite sides of the ledger, though not true double-entry systems. All of these options were more systematic and accurate on a day-to-day, month-to-month basis than the simple approach Heritage favored. He might not even have been aware of the existence of more sophisticated accounting techniques, or if he was, have felt that they did not suit his particular needs.

At first glance, Heritage's account book is confusing, even chaotic. He used obscure symbols in his totals. His trading year straddled two separate calendar years, meaning that much of what he counted as "1511" occurred in 1512. Multiple entries are incomplete. But rather than denigrating Heritage for "grossly, obscurely and lewdly kept" accounts, as one contemporary put it, we should focus on what the account book actually did. The obscure symbols were common within the community of London wool traders. His trading year was the same utilized by his contemporaries. The account book had an internal logic and a system that made sense to Heritage, serving the strategic need of calculating the general progress and shape of his transactions over the course of the year. In what was a largely oral culture, the book and its seemingly haphazard organizational scheme served as a potent memory aid. Over time, Heritage included more and more information in his accounts, clearly learning from his past actions and mistakes about what he did and did not need to write down. On the whole, this method suited Heritage well enough to last for two decades of consistently profitable business.[14]

Ultimately, what matters about the account book is less the precise nature of the system contained within it than the impulses and mindset it expresses. Heritage was monitoring his business interests, carrying out adjustments and corrections, and making rational judgments on the basis of long-term profitability and quantified experience. Whether he was on the cutting edge of accounting techniques or not, it was the mindset of a true capitalist.

The Wool Trade

Heritage was an entrepreneur at heart, one driven by a combination of ambition and obligation: the obligation to take care of his possibly underwhelming siblings, the ambition to move up in the world. His wife's relations, the Palmers, were a prosperous bunch with a nasty reputation, and Heritage may have felt pressure to impress them. Regardless, he began by transforming his family's generational landholdings into one piece of a leased pasture on which he kept his own sheep and cattle. That was a large, profitable business, but it was not enough for the new husband and father, with children of his own to support. Even at the peak of his business, Heritage was a minor figure, but even so, the sheer scale and complexity of his activities tells us a great deal about the commercial context in which he was operating.

Wool production was a major piece of the English economy around 1500 and had been for centuries. Sheep grazed on fine English pasture produced high-quality wool, which was then exported to the Low Countries or even as far away as Italy for weaving into cloth. English wool was not the only kind on the market, and as the later Middle Ages progressed, fine Spanish Merino wool came to dominate Flemish cloth supply. This was not as serious a blow as it might seem, because domestic cloth production within England spiked precisely when exports plummeted. Still, as Heritage's enterprise attests, exports remained a major industry. The total hovered between five thousand and ten thousand sacks annually during the years covered by Heritage's account book. At his peak, which also happened to be the industry's low point in 1505–6, Heritage accounted for about 1 percent of England's total wool exports.[15]

The wool industry contained a variety of roles and scales of business. Some farmers kept only a few sheep, grazing them on pastureland held in common by a village community. Other producers were more specialized, keeping hundreds or thousands of head on large tracts of pastureland leased from a landowner. This was the category to which Heritage belonged in his capacity as a leaseholder in Burton Dassett, for example, ranging from north of a thousand sheep to more than two thousand over the decades. Above Heritage were the large estate owners, either lords or monastic institutions, that maintained flocks whose numbers could rise into the thousands. All of those sheep needed shepherds, who typically were either the farmers themselves or servants. At shearing time, vast amounts of labor went into collecting the fleeces and the fells (skins) from animals that had reached the end of their usefulness.

Once sheared and collected, the wool had to be processed, packed, and shipped off for export. That was where Heritage came in. He was one of a class of buyers called broggers who went up and down the countryside buying wool and bringing it to the big export merchants in London for sale. Those merchants belonged to a specialized, wealthy, and powerful group known as the Merchants of the Staple. They held a royal monopoly on export and sent their purchased wool to the port of Calais, on the continent, where it was subject to tolls before it could be passed on to its final buyers. This made Heritage the consummate middleman, the physical embodiment of the link between producers and big-time exporters, someone who had to deal with both the rural and urban aspects of the economy in equal measure.

This was a cutthroat business. Wool prices were already high and continued to rise throughout Heritage's career. The countryside around Moreton-in-Marsh was dotted with sheep, and every ambitious trader in the region with dreams of large profits wanted their wool. This put producers, who ranged from smallholders with a few dozen head to the big institutional estate managers with thousands, in the driver's seat when it came to negotiations. They had their pick of middlemen, driving a fiercely competitive seller's market.

Wool trading was not an easy path to riches. Large profits required a correspondingly high volume of trade, and every farmer with whom Heritage dealt had multiple potential buyers for their wool. Staying in business for as long as Heritage did would imply that he maintained a reputation for fairness and honesty, in addition to some ability to read the market and adjust his activities accordingly.

In line with this observation, Heritage found a specific niche: working with the small-time wool producers, farmers running flocks in the hundreds or low thousands, rather than trying to cultivate relationships with the nobles and religious institutions running the largest operations. This entailed working with more producers, humbler folks of lower social rank and means, to collect a viable amount of wool for sale to the London merchants. This substantially complicated Heritage's business. A single transaction with a wool producer could mean payment in eight different installments, as in the case of the purchase from Thomas Kyte in 1505, and he made fifteen or more of those every year. It was far simpler to buy from a few very large producers, but Heritage took the opposite path. Only early in his career, in 1501 and 1502, did he buy large quantities of wool from the landed gentry. He never did so again.

The most likely explanation for Heritage's decision was that the big producers wanted enormous sums of money up front. In 1501, for example, he had to pay the wealthy landowner William Greville the huge sum of £41 in earnest money. Compared to the 40 shillings he paid Thomas Kyte, the difference was astronomical. Other producers, perhaps those with family connections to wealthy merchants or landowners with liquid capital, would find it far easier to raise earnest money in those quantities. Heritage had neither and did not want the pressure of working with credit on that scale. He was almost certainly the one who eschewed working with large-scale farmers, rather than the other way around. We might surmise that he developed a particularly deep understanding of the local wool market and the strengths and weaknesses of its producers, and that he had well-developed skills in bargaining and negotiation that played to his knowledge of the local landscape. His apparent facility with basic accounting would also have been a substantial help, allowing him to keep reasonably close track of a larger number of transactions than less savvy competitors.[16]

This was not an easy way to make a living. Information about prices and quality was essential to his business, and Heritage must have spent most of his time riding around the countryside, chatting up farmers, shepherds, and petty merchants about the latest news. How were Kyte's flocks looking? How much did his nasty in-laws and competitors, the Palmers of Moreton, intend to pay per tod? Would farmer Peryn be in the town of Stowe soon, so Heritage could pay him those last 20 shillings on market day? Each entry in the account book, every record of a payment or sale, represented a meeting and a conversation. It stands to reason that Heritage was an affable sort of fellow, skilled at wheedling necessary information out of a wide array of contacts that he assiduously maintained in the course of his work.

Heritage's profits from this business were never of the magnitude to raise him from the ranks of yeomen to gentry. Wool trading was big business for intelligent, knowledgeable professionals, and Heritage had to work hard to remain on the profitable margins of the profession. In fact, he always made more from his direct ownership of sheep and the sale of their fleeces than he did from the tremendous amount of time and effort he spent buying and selling. Thanks to his account book, Heritage seems to have realized this, and consciously drew down the scale of his trade over the course of his career in order to focus on other aspects of his business.

Merchants and the Workings of a Commercial Society

Sweating under the late August sun, the carters hauled on their horses' reins and guided them down the rutted, sunken path. The travelers knew the route well. They artfully dodged wagons heading in the opposite direction and the occasional noble astride an expensive horse followed by his inescapable party of hangers-on. This was no mean feat with nearly two thousand pounds of wool weighing down each of the seven carts in the miniature convoy, a pair of tall bales called *sarplers* packed into the bed.

The traffic worsened as the wagons approached London. The carters exchanged words, some friendly, others less so, with the drivers of the other wagons bearing that year's wool to the city. It had taken them five grueling days to get here from Moreton-in-Marsh, back up the road in Gloucestershire. Others had come from farther still, all of them converging on the beating commercial heart of England. Now, as they neared the city, they were joined by the man who had hired them. John Heritage, dressed in his finest cloak and hat, a touch of gray showing at his temples and a satisfied smile on his well-lined face, fell in with his half dozen hired wagons and braced himself for a busy day.

Heritage's whole year had led to this: His wool, so painstakingly sought out, had been assessed and collected from his suppliers and was now being sold to the major buyers of London. The transactions were already set, at least in principle. Visits to London earlier in the year had led Heritage into a series of agreements with the rich merchants of the city. First up on his list were a pair of men named Thomas Spring and Thomas Pargetter, both of them Merchants of the Staple, the exclusive mercantile corporation that held a royal monopoly on wool exports to the continent. Other buyers belonged to the Mercers, another elite mercantile corporation comprised of well-heeled urban merchants. All of them bought from a range of sellers, including Heritage.

Smoke rose in the distance as the convoy approached the city. Heritage absentmindedly steered his horse along a road he had traveled dozens of times, collecting his thoughts and planning his day. He would call on Spring and Pargetter first to collect an additional portion of the payments they owed him, then meet one of the Mercers at the King's Beam—the official scales where wool was weighed—around noon. It would be a good year, 1509, he thought, spurring his horse onward and leaving the carts behind. The combined reek of London—the Thames, woodsmoke, thousands of unbathed bodies, and churned, muddy streets—threatened to knock him off his horse. The wool trader quickened his pace, breathing deeply. To him, the air smelled like money.[17]

Heritage was the quintessential middleman, uniting city and countryside into a single vibrant economic unit. Every year, he piled his fleeces, painstakingly collected from over a dozen suppliers, into hired carts and brought them the eighty miles from Moreton-in-Marsh to London. As we have seen, he was hardly alone in doing so: Burdened carts packed England's roads while the rivers, canals, and coastal shipping routes groaned with barges, boats, and tall ships. England was already a deeply commercialized society, bursting with people who were producing for and buying in markets rather than living hand-to-mouth. In that society, there was plenty of room for a diverse group of merchants to handle shipments from place to place and profit from the transactions.[18]

In a deeply commercialized society, however, merchants did not handle all, or even most, of the total volume of transactions. Commoners were perfectly capable of doing that themselves, traveling from the countryside to the nearest city or town to sell their surplus in markets and buy what they needed. In late medieval Exeter, for example, the effective range for that kind of low-level commerce was about six miles, the distance a peasant could reasonably expect to cover with his or her goods in a single day. The farther the goods had to travel, the greater the capital requirements; the greater the capital requirements, the richer the merchants; the richer the merchants, the more likely it became that a specialist would handle it.[19]

Heritage sat right in the middle of this merchant hierarchy. "Merchant" is a vague term that covers a variety of practices and occupations, including impoverished itinerant peddlers, general retailers, specialists in particular crafts, and exceptionally wealthy and diversified merchant-capitalists. At the top were the big-time urban merchants, men who belonged to corporate organizations

or guilds that owned official privileges and monopolies over certain goods: the Staplers with wool, the Mercers with fine textiles,
and the Grocers with spices.

These were extremely wealthy people who wielded serious
influence. Working through their guild organizations, which
were more like corporate lobbying groups than labor unions,
they collectively bargained with the political authorities. Their
money clinked into tax coffers and political figures' pockets alike,
buying them exclusive privileges and monopoly rights. Top merchants could have thousands of pounds in assets spread among
warehouses, urban and rural real estate, industrial investments,
valuable trade goods, and liquid capital. The Staplers, the rich or
at least well-off merchants who owned the wool export trade, fell
into this category. They were the group to whom Heritage sold
most of his stock, followed by the Mercers and other unidentifi-
able but necessarily wealthy merchant buyers.[20]

Most merchants, particularly the wealthiest ones, were urban.
Cities were centers of demand for goods and services, the kinds
of things smaller merchants could provide firsthand. Heritage, by
contrast, was a rural operator; his home was in the countryside,
as were his business interests, and he only traveled to London on
occasion to carry out transactions. Yet he, and many like him,
were the necessary link between a commercialized countryside
and the broader trade networks that made Europe an integrated
economic unit. The Staplers and the Mercers are easier to see in
the source material—they wielded more influence and had vastly
greater assets—but there was no European economy, the engine
that drove all the other processes of the era, without Heritage and
people like him.

The key fact is that Heritage was hardly unique within England, and England was hardly an outlier when it came to the
extent and depth of its commercialization. A similar account,

with similar people, could be written for many different regions at this same time. Take Castile as an example: Its international trade flowed through many small Basque and Cantabrian ports before flowing out to a network of inland market towns and cities via oxcart and mule train, all with the active involvement of a variety of merchants spread over the territory. The animals and products were different, but all over Europe, a commercialized countryside fed into local, regional, and then international trade routes. There were John Heritages everywhere.[21]

Credit and Money

Credit provided the fuel for Heritage's business, and European commerce in general. Heritage never paid his suppliers the full amount all at once—the London wool buyers with whom he transacted never paid him in full, either. "Earnest money," the down payments Heritage provided to his wool suppliers, were effectively loans; so was the earnest money he himself received from his London contacts, like the £60 he owed to a "Master Nychyls," presumably a merchant in the city. The result was a constant balancing act of money coming in and money going out over the course of the year. Heritage borrowed money to loan to his suppliers, got paid in installments, and paid it out in chunks, thereby weaving a complex and constantly evolving web of credit that bound together farmers, rural merchants, and urban capitalists.

But the fact remained, there was not enough cash in circulation to meet the full needs of a deeply, thoroughly commercialized market society. This was true everywhere in Europe, not just in John Heritage's England, but it was a typical case: There was only £900,000–£1 million in hard currency circulating around 1500, although by 1520 that amount would double. This came out to approximately 8 shillings of cash per person, a tiny amount considering annual incomes were somewhere north of £4 per person. To make matters more complicated, most of that hard currency was gold, far too valuable to use for the transactions that dominated the humbler corners of the commercial economy. It made no sense for a day laborer to buy ale or a pie for a few pence with a gold coin worth two weeks' wages.

Barter was one solution for this. Even a sophisticated merchant like Heritage still made use of it on a regular basis. He paid with sheep, other livestock, summer grazing for other people's livestock, grain, hay, even firewood. This made sense; in the absence of cash, simply exchange one good for another. But even barter transactions were calculated in monetary terms. Heritage and his contemporaries existed in an economy that, while it often lacked money, was nevertheless fully monetized.[22]

Everybody, from the humblest day laborer to the king himself, employed credit and did so on a regular basis. This created a dense web of exchange and obligation stretching throughout the continent: city to city, then out into the countryside. John Heritage's wool went mostly to the Low Countries via the English-held port of Calais, where artisans eventually turned it into fine cloth for reexport across the continent. Every stage of this process involved debt and credit, promises and transactions made that moved mostly theoretical money from account book to account book, with trust being the glue holding the entire commercial system together. Everybody owed somebody else.

The End and John Heritage

Raindrops pattered on the thatched roof, sluicing off in sheets to further muddy the farmyard. Concern weighed on John Heritage's aging face as he looked over the sums listed in his well-traveled account book, calculating payments both outgoing and received.

The numbers, he concluded, did not add up. He was nearing his fiftieth year in 1520. Gray had fully infiltrated his thinning hair. Lines surrounded his shrewd, calculating eyes. Twenty-five years of managing sheep, twenty of crisscrossing the countryside to buy wool, dozens of trips down the road to London, and the constant stress of managing his debts had taken their cumulative toll.

Perhaps it was time to try something different. His son, Thomas, was a skinner's apprentice in London and on his way toward a prosperous career as a member of the Skinners' Company. John had taught him well, and a future as a diversified merchant like his father was in the offing. Perhaps Joan would like to live in London, John thought; it might ease his wife's mind to move elsewhere following the recent death of their other son, Richard. He had been a troubled lad, fighting and causing problems in Moreton-in-Marsh, and he had been responsible for more than a few strands of that graying hair.

John had altered his business over the years in an attempt to keep up with the shifting demands of the economy. He had tried to make it big as a wool trader at first, then settled into his niche collecting from small-time farmers, all the while maintaining his own personal flock. When the price of wool rose, Heritage expanded his flocks, cutting back his activities as a trader. It was simply getting too competitive for him. His younger rival, William Willington, had engaged in an even more ruthless program of dispossessing tenants to enclosure pasture than Heritage had tried at Burton Dassett twenty-five years earlier, which gave Willington more capital to work with. Willington was lord of a manor and a member of the Staplers, and Heritage simply could not compete with that kind of access to capital. Willington could make more and bigger transactions and maintain far higher profit margins than Heritage, even in a time of rising wool prices.

All of which led Heritage to increasing his presence as a

farmer, dealing in other goods like tar and gunpowder, and even expanding into straightforward money-lending. He still made a comfortable living, though less than he had at the outset, but he was tired. London might revitalize him, he thought, and it would be good to see more of Thomas. Heritage slammed the account book shut with a final thud, straightened his hat, and walked out into the deluge, mounting his horse and setting off down the road to Moreton-in-Marsh.

John Heritage effectively disappears after 1520, when he made the last entries in his account book. By 1522 he was no longer living in Moreton-in-Marsh and owned a house outside Cripplegate, in London, in the early 1530s. We know nothing beyond that—not even when he died. There is some irony in the fact that his personal fortunes seem to have declined even as the English economy grew steadily more prosperous, and that others followed his lead in dispossessing their neighbors by enclosing their fields. We do know that his son prospered as a member of the Skinners' Company and as a trader, following in his father's footsteps with considerably more success. In that way, Heritage's legacy survived his end.[23]

As a diversified businessman, Heritage was a reflection of a deeply commercialized Europe, both its opportunities and its pitfalls. His hunger for profits drove him, no less than the Genoese financiers who had enabled Columbus, the investors of Aldus Manutius's Venice, or the military entrepreneurs of Götz von Berlichingen's south Germany. Heritage was deeply ordinary, and his simple profit- and market-oriented behavior shows us how fundamental that was to the European economy. A society that made John Heritage and others like him possible (and ubiquitous) was one willing to take risks and invest in everything from overseas voyages to gunpowder warfare to printing presses without much regard for who might suffer, or benefit, in the process.

CHAPTER 7

Martin Luther, the Printing Press, and Disrupting the Church

October 31, 1517, Wittenberg

The friar's rapid footfalls splashed through murky puddles and along the churned streets of Wittenberg, flecks of mud staining the trailing hem of his black habit. The October morning chill cut through the woolen cloth of his distinctive clothing, but the friar paid it no notice. His mind was elsewhere, hands fiddling with a length of rolled-up heavyweight paper. A university instructor with lectures to plan for his students later in the week and a preacher with a sermon to deliver to Wittenberg's faithful this coming Sunday, the friar had plenty of other matters to occupy him, but they failed to take as he made for the distant spire of the castle church. Instead, his thoughts were gripped by matters of theology. He was a doctor of the subject, qualified to dispute and debate in public, and that was where his attention currently lay.

One of his parishioners, an artist's apprentice and an eager listener to his sermons, greeted the friar respectfully as he passed. Brother Martin barely noticed, automatically inclining his head and briefly fixing the other man with a look from his piercing brown eyes. Too many Latin phrases were blaring in his head to respond in kind.

Precision was key when formulating propositions for public debate. The statements on the document he held were provocative and strongly worded, as was the point. Brother Martin was concerned for the souls in his care, and the practice of selling indulgences—those beloved spiritual get-out-of-jail-free cards—threatened their paths to salvation. He was, characteristically, angry, fingers pinching the paper in a reflexive tic of frustration. Anger was a personal flaw of which he was well aware, and one for which he routinely asked God's forgiveness.

Morning sunlight, thin in the October air, broke through the clouds. The friar felt its gentle heat bloom across his bald spot, which was surrounded by a fringe of hair in the tonsure required of Augustinian friars. He sweated despite the chill, beads of moisture dripping from his brow onto his gaunt cheekbones and down his sharp nose. When he spied the spire of the castle church just ahead, Brother Martin breathed a sigh of relief.

It was a new building, completed just a decade before, the centerpiece of Elector Frederick's sprawling Renaissance palace. Within a few years of its construction, some of the holiest relics in Christendom had found a new home in that church—a vial of the Virgin Mary's breast milk, a twig from the Burning Bush, piles of saintly bones stored in gold and silver reliquaries—totaling 18,970 individually catalogued objects, all of them with the power to cleanse a pious pilgrim's soul of his sins.

There was the door, papered over with layer after layer of printed text. Wittenberg town ordinances and papal pronouncements competed against decrees of the elector of Saxony and various calls for academic disputation for space. Martin Luther, dismayed, unfurled his *Ninety-Five Theses* and skimmed the rough, undecorated, slightly smudged text. The university printer Johann Rhau-Grunenberg was good enough for small printings of a minor work, but he was glacially slow, unimaginative, and far from able to meet Brother Martin's exacting standards. If he were to print a book, he would have to look elsewhere; for now, the *Ninety-Five Theses* were a simple call to academic disputation. They were not important enough to demand better quality, and he had only asked for a few copies. Now, where might he find a hammer and a nail?

Brother Martin found the necessary implements near the door, and with a few sure strokes, he drove nail into wood until the proclamation was secure. His work done, he turned and left the castle church behind. In cramped, slanting, inelegant type, no different from that of a half dozen other texts nailed to the door, his *Ninety-Five Theses* cried out for debate, beginning with one indelible phrase: "In the Name of our Lord Jesus Christ. Amen."

It was early still. Nobody was loitering nearby or at the door of the castle church to mark the occasion. Even if they had been, what was one more call for an academic disputation in an out-of-the-way university town? Professors and their pedantic arguments did not concern the powerful elector of Saxony overmuch, much less the pope in his seat of power a thousand miles away in Rome.

As Brother Martin walked back through Wittenberg to the university, perhaps his thoughts turned away from indulgences and his call for disputation toward his many other responsibilities. He had lectures to plan and a sermon to deliver on Sunday, and neither he nor anyone else was aware of the significance of what he had done. But the Augustinian monk's theses were the first shots fired amid a religious upheaval that would fundamentally transform the Christian world. This was the beginning of a Reformation that brought about the end of unity in Christendom and left the formerly universal Church one sect among many, irrevocably tearing asunder a community of believers united across hundreds of years and thousands of miles.

Over the next 130 years, hundreds of thousands of people would die in conflicts as Europe tore apart at the seams, riven by a potent mixture of genuine religious fervor and shortsighted political power grabs, all of it underpinned by a constant deluge of inflammatory material from the printing presses.

The long-standing desire for Church reform collided with the oddities of the moment and the unique talents of Luther himself in a volatile mixture of circumstances. Martin Luther—a passionate, intelligent, and exceptionally gifted communicator—was a lit match falling into the gunpowder barrel that was sixteenth-century Europe. The resulting explosion would remake the future of the continent.[1]

The *Ninety-Five Theses*

Later that same day, October 31, Brother Martin sent an excoriating letter and a copy of his theses to Bishop Albrecht of Mainz, regional sponsor of the campaign of indulgences that had so irritated the Augustinian monk and his direct superior within the Church hierarchy. "I have no longer been able to keep quiet about this matter," he wrote. While he couched his critiques in respectful, even obsequious language, Luther made his outrage blatant. "Works of piety and love are infinitely better than indulgences, and yet these are not preached with such ceremony or such zeal.... It is said that contrition is not necessary in those who purchase souls [out of Purgatory] or buy confessionalia."[2] This, to Luther, was simply wrong. In his response, he offered Albrecht an out—surely this had all been done without the bishop's knowledge or consent—but the criticism was not exactly subtle. Subtlety was never Luther's strong suit.

The letter first went to Magdeburg, where it was opened on November 17, and was then sent on to the bishop's palace at Aschaffenburg. There was no reason to think that a powerful ecclesiastic, especially a member of the prominent and princely Hohenzollern family, would take much—if any—notice of an obscure Wittenberg professor's complaint.

But Albrecht did take notice. He forwarded the *Theses* to theologians at the University of Mainz for their opinion, who recommended sending them along to Rome for examination. The wheels were in motion, and Church authorities would soon pass judgment on Luther's orthodoxy.

The questions Luther raised, which struck at the heart of major issues about salvation and authority, were not going to be settled by structured debate between university theologians. In addition to Albrecht of Mainz, Luther sent copies of the *Ninety-Five Theses* to several other recipients, including the bishop of Brandenburg, who wanted nothing to do with any controversy. Two of Luther's other acquaintances, however, were more receptive. A friend in Nuremberg had the *Theses* reprinted, and from there they spread like wildfire. Desiderius Erasmus, the most popular and widely read author in Europe, soon forwarded an elegant copy printed in Basel to his humanist friend Thomas More, the author of *Utopia*, who was living in England. Within months, Europe's leading intellectuals were discussing Brother Martin's case against indulgences.[3]

This early reception marked the beginning of the Reformation. The *Ninety-Five Theses*, which may have been translated into German in another edition printed in Nuremberg, had slipped the net of academic debate and entered the mainstream of educated European thought. They inspired the commissioner of the indulgence campaign, a Dominican named Johann Tetzel, to respond to Luther with his own printed materials. This warranted another response from Luther, his *Sermon on Indulgences and Grace*, written in the vernacular German and intended for a lay, nonacademic audience. This *Sermon* became another bestseller. Pamphlet after pamphlet flooded the booksellers' stalls of Germany and beyond. By 1520, Luther was the most read author in Europe.

The *Ninety-Five Theses* were an unlikely candidate for the eventual cause of a European conflagration. The author was an obscure theologian at a new university in an out-of-the-way corner of the Holy Roman Empire, far from the traditional homes of the mainstream scholarly community. The *Theses'* original language, Latin, was inaccessible to most of the reading public, much less the illiterate peasants who made up the bulk of Europe's population.

But *something* about the *Ninety-Five Theses* touched a nerve. The author may have been an academic, but he wrote clearly and forcefully. More important, Martin Luther was a well of talent and drive that had not yet been fully tapped. He had found himself in the right place, at the right time, with the right mixture of skills and attitudes to generate something truly extraordinary, the consequences of which would reverberate for centuries.

The Miner's Son

On July 2, 1505, a young student was riding between his home of Mansfeld and Erfurt, where he attended university. It was a gloomy day, clouds hanging over the hills that occasionally broke the monotony of the flat fields and pastures. The student was just four miles short of his destination when the storm that had been threatening to come down on him all day finally broke. Rain pelted him as thunder roared. Lightning flashed in every direction.

"Saint Anna," the young man wailed, calling on the patron

saint of miners for protection. With his next breath, he promised that if she spared him, he would enter a monastery straightaway. Miraculously, the thunder and lightning ceased, and the student had a new vow to keep.

He was a promising twenty-one-year-old, the eldest son of a prosperous, hardworking copper miner named Hans Luder. The youthful Martin had received a thorough education, culminating in a master of arts degree from the University of Erfurt. The path he and his father intended for him to take would soon lead to the study of law, which would either make the young man a valuable asset to his father's mining business or prepare him for a lucrative career in the expanding administrative apparatus of Elector Frederick of Saxony. An upwardly mobile marriage into the comfortable, entrepreneurial elite of Mansfeld would surely follow.

The storm changed all that. Forgoing all other plans, Martin set his sights on a life of austere piety in Erfurt's community of Augustinian monks. This was the path that eventually led him to the door of Wittenberg's castle church in October 1517.

But his early life shaped the future reformer in profound ways. His consistent image of God as a stern, overbearing judge surely drew something from his experiences growing up with his father, a tough but fair patriarch. Woe betide the favorite son who disappointed him.

In a portrait from late in life, painted by the celebrated Lucas Cranach, Hans Luder stares out at the viewer. His is a face pinched, lined, and a bit battered by the passage of time. It naturally twists toward a barely suppressed snarl, conveying a mixture of simmering anger, truculence, and raw intellect. Hans Luder had lived through decades of backbreaking work in a complex, rapidly changing industry. Brawls and dark tunnels, labyrinthine credit arrangements and resentful workers all had left their mark on that face. Cross this man, the portrait seems to say, and expect

consequences. Hans had a reputation as a hard man, once breaking up a drunken fight by pouring beer on the brawlers and then
beating them bloody with the empty jug. Mining was a brutal business, rife with noxious fumes, danger, competition, and
extreme financial risk. Miners stole from one another and argued
over the boundaries of their shafts. Their disagreements regularly
devolved into barroom knife fights. Surviving, much less pros-
pering, in such a rough-and-tumble environment required a stern
constitution and no small amount of luck.

As the Fuggers had proved, there was money to be made in
mining—potentially a great deal of it. Hans Luder tried, failed,
tried again, and succeeded just long enough to set young Martin
on his path to success.

But whatever his future course, young Martin grew up in the
combative world of the miner. He was used to invectives, insults,
and fists. As he aged, he simply transferred those experiences to
print and theological disputation instead of mining. It is not hard
to see the roots of Luther's willingness to send a critical, provocative letter to a powerful bishop in his father's obstinate, risk-
taking nature.[4]

Education, Hans knew, was the key to Martin's future. For the
father, the son's education was an investment—an expensive one
not provided to his many other children—in the family's future.
Legal entanglements were central to the mining business, with
plenty of opportunities for men to manage them, and Hans had
every intention of setting his gifted son in that career.

Young Martin first attended a local school in tiny Mansfeld,
where he learned the fundamentals of Latin grammar, logic, and
rhetoric. This was the foundation of his knowledge, though he
would later consider these early lessons to have been lamentably
ineffective and brutally enforced. He had wealthy maternal relatives in Eisenach, a small town of approximately four thousand;

there, he attended a parish school that further acquainted him with Latin and grammar. In 1501, at the age of eighteen, he departed yet again, this time for the University of Erfurt. It was then that his educational focus shifted to philosophy, the foundation of the medieval university's scholastic approach and something Luther later came to loathe with all his heart; it was sterile and unappealing to a curious, hardheaded young man. It took him four years to complete his baccalaureate and master of arts. His career as a law student in Erfurt lasted just a few weeks before the infamous thunderstorm set him on a different path.

This was as complete an education as an upwardly mobile miner's son could hope to achieve in this particular corner of eastern Germany, but young Martin was hardly alone in trying. The very ordinariness of his upbringing and schooling speaks to the time and place in which he lived—he was well-off but not rich, born to a family that had to work hard to live while still aware of those above and below them on the social hierarchy. Mansfeld and the other mining towns of the region were full of men like Hans Luder, entrepreneurs with minds for figures and hands that could withstand the heat of a smelter as easily as an unruly drunk; but Hans saw more and better opportunities for his son and did his level best to provide them.

Long before he pinned the *Ninety-Five Theses* to the church door and made his own irrevocable contributions to serious, disruptive change, Martin Luther was a product of this era's massive, financially driven shifts. Mining, a booming industry driven by new, capital-intensive technologies and widespread distribution networks—controlled by financiers like the Fuggers—made Hans Luder enough money to purchase his son an education. Martin never could have gotten that education without printed texts, which allowed him to study grammar, philosophy, and the law, and do so affordably—at least until he abandoned it. The printing industry, as we've seen, grew out of these same profit-driven financing mechanisms. Even as a young man unknown to the wider world, Martin Luther could not have existed without these key transformations.

But this was only a taste of changes to come. The constant risk, the sharp rises and devastating falls of that financialized world that had so carved his father's face profoundly shaped young Martin's sensibilities and understanding of the world. He despised capitalists throughout his life and mistrusted money in general, even though he understood the necessity of lending at interest. He once called profit-bearing shares in a mine *Spielgeld*, "play money," and refused to accept them. Most important, he developed a visceral hatred for the idea of buying one's way out of sin. Money was not, and could not be, a solution for the concerns of the soul. "The miner could call on the saints, especially St. Anna," writes his biographer Lyndal Roper. "But in the end, he faced God alone."[5]

Brother Martin and the Church

Whatever young Martin was when he knelt before the high altar of the Augustinian monastery of Erfurt in July 1505, where he took his vows as a novice, he certainly was not looking for an easy life. These observant Augustinians were known for their austerity and piety. Monks were expected to adhere tightly to their rule, which involved a great deal of silence, confession, and strict performance of their hours, the regimen of daily prayers that formed the backbone of monastic life. Manual labor, even cleaning the latrines, was every bit as much of the novice's life as prayer and contemplation. The Erfurt house supplemented its dedicated observance of the Augustinian Rule with close connections to the city's university, where Luther had until recently been a student. Many of the house's forty-five to sixty monks taught courses there.

This was far from the only religious option available to Luther; Erfurt, a city of perhaps twenty-four thousand inhabitants, had not only a second Augustinian house, but houses belonging to the Carthusians, Dominicans, and Franciscans. That he chose the observant Augustinians says a great deal about his personality. It was a prosperous foundation, endowed with income-generating properties to support the institution, but the Augustinians did not let themselves sink into the contemptible laxity for which so many devotees were castigated. Young Martin could simultaneously further his scholarly ambitions, keep his vow, and nourish his aching soul in a focused and exacting environment.[6]

By joining the Augustinians of Erfurt, Luther was entering one tiny corner of an expansive religious world. The universal Church touched every corner of western Europe and practically all aspects of life from politics to market behavior, but it was not a monolithic institution. Very much the opposite: Because it channeled and encompassed practically all spiritual life, the Church, by necessity, had to be a big tent.

It contained multitudes: poor, illiterate priests in isolated rural parishes with secret wives and broods of children, who rarely saw their uninterested parishioners; charismatic Dominican preachers capable of attracting crowds of thousands in towns and cities; places like the brand-new castle church of Wittenberg, built in Renaissance style and packed with holy relics in expensive gilded cases; towering Gothic cathedrals, already centuries old, dominating the skylines of the continent's prosperous urban centers and serving as headquarters for rich, powerful bishops who pulled political strings from London to Leipzig; leaky-roofed monasteries, housed by a few elderly monks in threadbare robes begging for donations to fix a tumbledown refectory; university theologians steeped in the brutally dense works of Thomas Aquinas and William of Ockham who spent their time teaching students and arguing about scholastic philosophy; devout laywomen, reading books of hours in the privacy of their prosperous homes; sword-swinging Hospitaller Knights, soldier-monks in armor and black habits, beheading Muslim sailors on the decks of galleys under a blue Mediterranean sky.

The Church was all of these things: corrupt and saintly, worldly and mystical, impossibly wealthy and desperately impoverished. Some monasteries struggled to tread water, while others owned thousands of head of livestock and managed estates that stretched for miles around opulent complexes of buildings. Some bishops were inherently political animals, scions of great and powerful families, like Albrecht of Mainz, while others were dedicated shepherds of their flocks' spiritual needs. Thinking of the Church as a singular thing, or a compact hierarchy stretching downward from the heights of St. Peter's, fundamentally misrepresents what it really was. The Church as it existed in this time is best understood as a sprawling, overlapping, and occasionally competing series of networks and institutions, some of them tightly controlled and others quite outside any measure of oversight. This Church was intertwined with everything from the political legitimacy of kings to caring for the poor to international finance.

Martin Luther's humble cell in his Augustinian monastery in Erfurt was one tiny, out-of-the-way corner of a religious landscape that spanned the length and breadth of Europe.

At the center of all this sat the pope. In 1505, when Luther entered the monastery, the papacy was not what it had been at its peak several hundred years before. The days of popes making credible claims to universal authority and facing down the most powerful rulers of medieval Europe were long since past.

The position was currently held by a fierce, ambitious man who ruled under the name of Julius II. Pope Julius was much more interested in war and expanding the papacy's temporal political power than in spirituality; he despised his predecessor, the notoriously corrupt Borgia pope Alexander VI, more for the two men's vicious, decades-long political rivalry than Borgia's active sex life or extreme nepotistic tendencies. Of course, Julius II was no less committed to advancing his family's interests through the institutional power of the Church.

An ignominious hundred-year exit from Rome, when popes resided in the Provençal city of Avignon, had not helped. The Western Schism of 1378 to 1417, when two and eventually three candidates claimed the papal tiara, was far more damaging. With the papacy in crisis, the conciliar movement tried to move authority within the Church from the pope to regular councils. The papacy managed to survive these challenges, returning to Rome and outlasting the conciliarists, but the Church's rulers never regained their full financial strength or the deep control they once held. In the process, papal legitimacy took a serious blow, and kings clawed back much of the control over the Church in their lands they had lost to the popes in prior centuries, especially revenues and powers of appointment to key posts.[7]

The response of the fifteenth-century popes, in whose footsteps Julius II and his successors followed, was to shift their focus to Italy. On top of his duties as the spiritual head of the Church, the pope controlled a portfolio of territories in central Italy; his court in Rome differed only in scale and opulence from those of the other Renaissance Italian princes. Money from all over Europe was flowing in, making Rome an indispensable provider of capital for banks that operated throughout the continent. The papal *curia*, the bureaucracy, became increasingly staffed with Italians; popes stacked the College of Cardinals with relatives and supporters. Nepotism became an art form, papal officeholding a source of spoils to distribute to extended family. The Medici, for example, slipped their own members into the top ranks of the papal hierarchy whenever possible.

For the first few years of his monastic life, Brother Martin couldn't have been overly concerned with the political machinations of popes living thousands of miles away. Rome was a distant thought, a place of impossible holiness more than a real political center full of bureaucrats and officials with worldly interests and failings. Soon, however, the truth would become inescapable.

Reform

Martin Luther quickly developed a reputation as a pious and gifted young man with genuine potential for advancement within the Augustinian Order. It was not surprising, therefore, when the novice Luther was chosen to travel to Rome to help plead the Erfurt house's case to the papal bureaucracy.

The case was a controversy over the reform of the order. Luther's house, and many others within Germany and beyond, belonged to the reformed branch, which preferred a more austere interpretation of the Augustinian Rule; however, this put them at odds with many other Augustinian houses, which were more relaxed in their performance of their monastic duties. Lest the Augustinians split entirely, Luther's spiritual mentor and direct superior—an influential theologian and church politician named Johann von Staupitz—brokered a deal to merge the reformed and nonreformed congregations, to the satisfaction of no one. Reformed monasteries like Luther's, where appeals were taken all the way to the pope, were particularly dissatisfied. This incident triggered Luther's trip to Rome, the longest journey he ever took.

This is a drastic oversimplification of a conflict that involved dozens of monastic institutions and thousands of monks across Italy and Germany, real principles of monastic devotion, the internal politics of the Augustinian hierarchy, and the ambitions of men like Johann von Staupitz. Conflict and disagreement were more features of the religious system than bugs.

The desire for reform was a fundamental part of how both clerics and laypeople experienced their religious lives. The history of the medieval Church is effectively the history of reform, of ongoing efforts—successful or otherwise—by a variety of actors, both within the Church and without, to fix the institution's many problems. Kings wanted to hold clerics accountable to secular law when they committed crimes, as they so often did; the problem of "criminous clerks" was constant and never resolved to anyone's satisfaction. Laypeople sought deeper engagement beyond the standard offerings, or they desired more suitable clergy—less inclined toward lechery, less fond of drink, or better educated—to service their spiritual needs. Occasionally this desire for change within the Church got them labeled as heretics to be investigated and, in some cases, burned at the stake. In other instances, it made them righteous reformers destined for sainthood. The conciliarists who tried to shift power from the pope to regularly assembled councils at the beginning of the fifteenth century did not want to destroy the Church—they wanted to save it from decades of schism and corruption.

As Martin Luther set off for Rome in November 1510, he and his companions were the heirs to and participants in an ongoing movement to improve the Church. Brother Martin was a creature of this deeply rooted desire to fix what ailed the Church. Opinions differed on precisely what that was: corruption and nepotism, too much or not enough papal authority, a lack of devotion or the wrong kind of devotion from the laity, and subpar clergy, among many other complaints. These strains of reform, which

Luther later took up with the *Ninety-Five Theses* and what followed, were signs of a vibrant and engaged religious culture. The Church was hardly in a state of terminal decline.[8]

Indulgences

When Luther arrived in Rome, exhausted after his long journey and not entirely fond of the Italians he met along the way, what he found there scandalized and resonated with him in equal measure. He marveled at the holy sites and fine churches but despised the priests who hurried through the Mass to squeeze more paid performances into their day. The corruption of the Roman clergy appalled him, particularly in later years as he thought back to what he had seen in his youth. Yet as he rose within the Augustinians of Erfurt, earned his doctorate, moved to Wittenberg, and began to teach theology while preaching sermons to parishioners, Brother Martin was a perfectly orthodox monk. Whatever he saw in Rome, it did not cause him to question the fundamental concept of papal supremacy.

While visiting the center of Christendom, Luther saw many things: crumbling classical relics like the Coliseum, vast open spaces populated with grazing cattle, an endless array of churches and holy processions, and a new basilica rising in the Vatican. Refurbishing the venerable Old St. Peter's had been on the papal to-do list for the better part of a century, but plans had recently become more ambitious. A simple remodel wasn't enough. In its renewed might, the papacy required an entirely new building, the most elaborate and richly appointed in Christendom. The foundation stone was laid in 1506, not long after Luther joined the Augustinians, but there was little progress in construction for some time. The problem, as it soon became clear, wasn't engineering the enormous dome; it was paying for it.

Brother Martin could not have known it when he first arrived in Rome, but the cost of a new St. Peter's would directly cause the crisis that made him famous.

In the *Ninety-Five Theses*, Luther's ire fell on indulgences, a remission of sins granted by the Church in return for a specific action—the purchase of a certificate, a donation for victims of Turkish piracy, alms for the poor, or a visit to a specific church or holy site. Because they provided funds for so many different programs, indulgences were central to the late medieval Church's funding model for a variety of different purposes. Indulgences were rooted in the doctrine of Purgatory, where even well-meaning, pious souls might have to spend time in limbo before ascending to heaven. An indulgence could free the soul of a beloved relative from Purgatory and transfer them directly to paradise. Luther himself took advantage of this provision while in Rome, kneeling to the Santa Scala for the benefit of his grandfather's soul.

But while indulgences mattered a great deal to the Church's ability to act as social guardian of the disadvantaged, Purgatory was a relatively new development, and while discussions of indulgences went back to the twelfth century, they had only become relevant in the few decades before Luther penned the *Theses*.

The proliferation of the printing press caused this new concern with the theology of indulgences. Through this medium, an indulgence campaign became a full-blown media event, a mass-produced remission of sins available to the general public for a price. It was this new fund-raising technique, rather than a fundamental shift in the underlying theology of indulgences, that made the concept stand out to Luther and his contemporaries as objectionable. There were deeper issues, which Luther raised at length in the *Ninety-Five Theses*, but they were less important than the fact that the printing press made indulgences cheap to produce and therefore a source of ready cash for the Church. Indulgences were simply everywhere, and no clergyman who cared about saving souls could avoid them.

By 1516, indulgence sales had become a major source of income for the Church. In Spain, they helped fund the war against Granada, providing more than a million ducats' worth of revenue over the course of a decade. Without them, the extended campaigns would have been impossible to sustain. A small campaign of sales in remote Extremadura even helped pay for Columbus's first expedition in 1492.

Indulgences were a tried-and-true funding method that proved viable across Europe. What faithful Christian, fearful for the state of their soul or fretting over a dearly departed relative now in Purgatory, could balk at dropping a few coins in return for some spiritual certainty? The benefits were twofold: Proceeds funded good works ranging from poorhouses to crusades, and the buyer received spiritual solace in a frightening world. The financial machine of the Church ground on.[9]

Leo, Albrecht, and Jakob

Attacking the crass marketing of indulgences as a consumer product, and even the deeper theological underpinnings of them, might not have made much of an impact had Luther not launched his brazen ideological assault on Bishop Albrecht of Mainz, Pope Leo X, and (indirectly) the Fugger family. Church doctrine and its theological underpinnings was one thing, a topic that a university professor like Luther was within his rights to discuss; intensely fraught political and financial relationships were a more serious matter, one that demanded attention.

Bishop Albrecht had not yet reached his twenty-eighth birthday when his underlings received Luther's letter in December 1517. He was a member of the Hohenzollern family, one of the most powerful in the Holy Roman Empire. His brother, Joachim, was prince-elector of Brandenburg, one of the seven men who elected the Holy Roman Emperor. Since Albrecht could not rule Brandenburg himself, he and his family looked to the Church for opportunities to expand their power and influence. In 1513, at the tender age of twenty-three, Albrecht became archbishop of Magdeburg (and administrator of the see of Halberstadt besides). Magdeburg was a wealthy see and Halberstadt was valuable, but both benefices paled in comparison to another see that became vacant the following year.

The archbishopric of Mainz was one of the greatest prizes in Europe. It was the largest see in Germany, and whoever held that seat was the primate, or leading bishop, of the entire region. The archbishop of Mainz was also a prince of the Holy Roman Empire, a territorial ruler with substantial lands and resources; more important still, the prince-archbishop was one of the seven electors of the empire. This would have been a position of immense power at any time, but at this particular moment it was even more valuable: The current Holy Roman Emperor Maximilian was almost sixty years old and nearing the end of his life. An election was just around the corner, and the candidates competing for the throne would pay handsomely in bribes for the elector's vote. Mainz would repay the cost of acquisition many times over.

That is, it would if Albrecht could add the see of Mainz to the archbishopric of Magdeburg. He was duly elected to office after promising to pay Mainz's debts and protect the city against the elector of Saxony. Albrecht still had two major hurdles to overcome: first, his youth—he was technically too young to hold the office—and, second, a papacy that increasingly frowned on the holding of multiple episcopates at the same time. Priests and bishops who held multiple benefices, as the revenues from these offices were known, were a powerful symbol of the corruption that clerical reformers and concerned laypeople attacked. Regardless, Pope Leo X was a pragmatic man. Perhaps the two sides could find a compromise.

That compromise, ultimately, was money. Albrecht would pay Leo for the papal dispensations necessary to render his acquisition acceptable. It was a large sum: 23,000 ducats, three to four times what Columbus's first voyage had cost. Albrecht did not have that kind of cash on hand, but the Fuggers of Augsburg did. And they were quite happy to lend the money to Albrecht and transfer it on to Rome.

But the question then became, how were the Fuggers to recoup their investment in the now prince-archbishop Albrecht of Mainz? A campaign of indulgence sales would fit the bill nicely. As luck would have it, there was already such a campaign in the works in 1515, intended to fund Leo's increasingly ambitious plans for the new St. Peter's Basilica in Rome. Albrecht would keep half the proceeds from indulgence sales in his sees of Magdeburg and Mainz in order to pay back the Fuggers, while the other half would pass on to Rome. The Fuggers would handle that transfer as well and exact another fee for their services in the process.

To meet its goals, the campaign would need to raise nearly 50,000 ducats. That was a significant amount of money, and accumulating it would require a skilled salesman to drum up enough popular interest to fork over the cash. A tall order, but not impossible. Luckily, Albrecht found such a man—a Dominican preacher named Johann Tetzel.

Tetzel knew the process inside and out. Even if the phrase Luther famously attributed to him—"As soon as the coin in the coffer rings, the soul from Purgatory springs"—was not strictly correct, it certainly captured the essence of Tetzel's approach to hawking indulgences. He was persuasive and ostentatious, a tireless traveler who could cover hundreds of miles over the course of his sales. In this, Tetzel differed very little from the popular itinerant preachers of the age, who performed sermons as a kind of public theater, packaged and delivered to draw a crowd. He was a top-notch salesman, and his product was salvation.[10]

By 1517, indulgence sales were a heavily structured business. Organizers like Tetzel contracted printers ahead of time to produce media advertising upcoming sermons as well as the indulgence certificates themselves, preprinted pieces of paper outlining the purchase and the remission of sins, awaiting only the name of the soul to be saved. They came in incredible quantities, sometimes running into the tens of thousands of copies, and even contained a space for the purchaser's name to be filled in by hand. An early campaign in 1490, in Austria, distributed fifty thousand indulgences. Printers loved them: Indulgence certificates and broadsheets were lucrative contracts to have. While large runs of books were inherently risky because of the substantial up-front costs and the reading public's mercurial tastes, indulgences were the kind of short-term jobbing work that kept printers in business in an otherwise tumultuous industry. The Church loved them, too: Indulgences were effectively a way of printing money while easing the concerns of the faithful about the fate of theirs and their dearly departed relatives' souls.

Naturally, Martin Luther hated everything about this process.

He was far from alone in considering all of this crass, unpalatable, and theologically dubious. It is telling that even without knowledge of his *Ninety-Five Theses*, his opponent-to-be Cardinal Cajetan was at the very same time formulating his own theological critique of indulgences in an attempt to scale back abuses of the practice. These elite clerical complaints dovetailed with popular cynicism about the Church's financial incentives. When an indulgence salesman visited the German city of Lübeck in 1503, for example, one observer remarked that the visitor's concern for saving souls hadn't stopped him from leaving with a few thousand florins for his trouble. Sentiments like this crop up time and again.[11]

Whatever the structural underpinnings of the Reformation, the specific crisis that arose and blossomed because of Luther's *Ninety-Five Theses* was intimately tied to recent critiques of indulgence and the identity of Albrecht of Mainz. Wide constituencies of both laypeople and clerics had serious and increasingly strident problems with indulgences, which fed directly into larger critiques of both Church doctrine and material corruption. When combined with the circumstances of the indulgence that Johannes Tetzel was shilling in 1517, namely its deep ties to some of the most powerful and well-connected people in Europe, it is not hard to see how a conflagration might erupt.

Printing, Luther, and Reformation

Without printing, the Reformation could not have existed. This is a common enough sentiment that it has entered the popular imagination: The new medium of mass communication, this line of reasoning goes, meant that the church could no longer control the message. It was only a matter of time before some reformer or reformers came along and used it to splinter Christendom. There is some truth here, but the emphasis on inevitability is deeply misplaced. So is its corollary: the sense that Luther himself was replaceable, or that any other reformer might have accomplished what he did if given the opportunity. The reality was far more complicated and unique to the combined circumstances that existed in 1517 and through the years that followed. Luther's obsessions and his talents interacted in complex ways with the medium of print and the other dynamics of the moment.

The university professor turned out to have a remarkable knack for writing clear, compelling, and entertaining German prose. Nobody could have predicted that a theologian who had previously worked almost entirely in Latin would also be an exceptionally gifted vernacular stylist, but this fortuitous turn of events became the foundation of the Reformation. Luther could turn a Latin phrase well enough to capture the attention of Europe's scholarly elite, and at the same time reach a vast general reading public. He and the equally important printers with whom he worked quickly seized on the possibilities. Luther and his fellow reformers were not just tapping into an existing technology; they were creating a brand-new reading public, an expansive and expanding market to which printers could cater and sell.[12]

When the *Ninety-Five Theses* appeared in Albrecht of Mainz's mail, print had already been around for a couple of generations; Luther had never known a world without it, nor had Albrecht. Practically every other major actor involved in the Reformation controversy had only ever lived in a world with print. Aldus Manutius's reach into the rarefied world of humanist book consumption was just one aspect of the industry's growth. Luther's childhood schoolbooks and later his university texts were both products of the printing press. University professors had small runs of text prepared at the ubiquitous print shops that clustered around institutions of higher learning; Luther's printing of the *Ninety-Five Theses* was well within standard practices. Pardoners advertised indulgence sales with printed broadsheets, and their products were mass-produced on paper or rich vellum. When Luther walked through Wittenberg, he saw plenty of handbills, flyers, pamphlets, sermons, and books. Printed products were simply everywhere in his world. Still, print's full potential had yet to be unleashed. That was where the Reformation, and Luther in particular, had a pivotal new role to play.

The *Ninety-Five Theses* made up a deeply technical theological text, written in Latin, the language of both the Church and scholars. The initial reaction to the *Theses*, naturally, took place in Latin. It was the language that clerics and the well-heeled international scholarly community, people like Erasmus and Thomas More, used for their discussions. Latin, however, was inaccessible to the vast majority of the common people, in Luther's Germany and elsewhere in Europe. As long as the uproar surrounding the *Ninety-Five Theses* stayed in Latin, any reform movement it sparked would remain confined to the educated elite. This had been the case for many prior reform movements: Whatever the masses of laypeople might have felt about the Church's shortcomings, Church reform was not an issue in which they had much say.

But if the debate around indulgences and their implications could slip the bonds of Latin and enter the vernacular languages that artisans, burghers, merchants, and country yeomen used for their day-to-day business, then Church reform might be able to find widespread traction.

There was only one major problem with that: On October 31, 1517, the day Luther hammered his theses to the door of the Wittenberg castle church, nobody—least of all Luther—knew that there was a vast audience that would be eager to pay cash for religious literature, from Bible translations to catechisms to inflammatory pamphlets.

The key to the rapid success of the Reformation was that printers, most of them based in German-speaking areas, quickly realized these buyers existed, learned what they wanted, and then published ample content to meet demand. Luther, for his part, turned out to have exactly the right combination of ideas and the technical writing skills to convey them to mass audiences in ways they wanted to read. His works sold incredibly well, and the fact that they sold—thereby ending up in the hands of people who read them—was the cornerstone of the Reformation's rapid spread and deep impact.

Punching Back

Luther's many thousands of readers did not unquestioningly consume his works and adopt his views as their own; from the very beginning, he faced serious opposition from those he attacked and threatened, namely within the Church. As they absorbed Luther's attacks, his targets fired back, likewise through printed works. Conflict, mediated by print and the dictates of the print market, was central to the spread of reforming ideas.

What began as a fairly straightforward attack on the abuse of indulgences quickly spiraled into something much larger, as Luther's opponents picked up on the radical implications of his ideas and pressed him to explain himself. Luther responded to their rhetorical needling with increasingly extreme and vitriolic statements. Printers with their eye for profit sensed potential in these exchanges. They were quite happy to flood the market with pamphlets and longer texts arguing about reform. More and more readers picked up on the back-and-forth debate. This created all the conditions—a highly invested reading public and market incentives to supply it with material—for a rising crescendo of written violence.

Unsurprisingly, the first printed resistance to Luther came from his primary opponent, Johann Tetzel, the skilled if not especially scrupulous Dominican preacher responsible for overseeing the indulgence campaign that had so irked Brother Martin. Eight hundred copies of Tetzel's work were printed and brought to Wittenberg, with instructions that they be distributed among students at the university. An angry crowd made sure that never happened—they seized every last copy and burned them, a grim foreshadowing of the increasingly vicious and dangerous path the Reformation would take in years to come.

Luther decided to up the stakes. He responded to Tetzel with a short, punchy vernacular text, his *Sermon on Indulgences and Grace*. This, unlike the *Ninety-Five Theses*, was explicitly intended for a German readership, not his fellow academics. Luther had made the conscious decision to take a theologians' debate and turn it into a matter for the public. The printers obliged: The *Sermon* appeared in four Leipzig editions, two each in Nuremberg, Augsburg, and Basel, and at least two in Wittenberg itself.

Tetzel, whatever his flaws, was nobody's fool. He recognized what Luther was doing and responded with a vernacular pamphlet of his own, *Rebuttal Against a Presumptuous Sermon of Twenty Erroneous Articles*. This was a clear, well-argued, mostly polite text, and it raised some key points: Luther was treading close to the condemned heresies of John Wyclif and Jan Hus, the latter of whom had been burned at the stake a century before for supposed heresies. Tetzel's text demonstrated that the vernacular was available and viable, but unfortunately for him and his supporters in the Church, printers did not agree. Luther got his hands on the *Rebuttal* immediately—"an unparalleled example of ignorance," he called it—and responded with yet another vernacular pamphlet, which appeared in at least nine German editions before the end of 1518. The unrelenting stream of printed abuse from Luther broke Tetzel's spirit. The Church hierarchy publicly and humiliatingly washed their hands of the charismatic, flamboyant indulgence salesman, and he died soon after.[13]

From there, events began to fly out of Luther's, or anyone else's, control. Albrecht passed Luther's writings on to authorities in Rome, where the respected theologian Prierias needed only a few days to determine that the *Ninety-Five Theses* were heretical. His judgment on the matter was printed as a pamphlet in Rome, and then reprinted in Augsburg and Leipzig. When Cardinal Cajetan arrived in Augsburg as the pope's legate to deal personally with Luther, the reformer's fate had already been decided. Cajetan had his own deep concerns about indulgences, enough that he had recently written a serious condemnation of the practice. In different circumstances, he and Luther might have hammered out an agreeable compromise, even a way forward for the Church. But the issue went beyond indulgences—this was about the Church's authority, and ultimately the supremacy of the pope over the Church as a whole. On this issue neither the Church nor Cajetan would give any ground. Luther would have to recant or be excommunicated.

This decision drew battle lines in the emerging conflict between Luther and his supporters and the Church. With the press as a new battleground and the printers aware that the reform debate moved product, the floodgates opened. New voices, like the formidable theologian Johann Eck and Luther's associate Andreas Karlstadt, began publishing their own views. Reconciliation was no longer an option.

Luther's Bestsellers

Luther followed the *Ninety-Five Theses* with a torrent of new material throughout 1518 and 1519. Forty-five works, twenty-five in Latin and twenty in German, covered everything from dense theology to instructions for pastoral care to controversial polemic. Even as Brother Martin worked himself into an exhausted frenzy, writing to the edge of a nervous breakdown, his books and pamphlets flooded the continental market. He paid little attention to the potential consequences the Church or secular authorities might impose on him. Any attack on Luther or his interpretations of Scripture, whatever its merits, compelled an immediate response, which soon found its way to the print shop and then to the public at large.

None of this would have mattered had Luther not so easily grasped the mechanics of the printing industry: what printers could produce and on what timeline; how editions of his works spread throughout Germany and beyond; what people wanted to read; and how much they were willing and able to pay for. He had found the sweet spot between printers' needs and readers' desires and tailored his output accordingly.

The numbers over these few years tell a pair of remarkable and intertwined stories, of Luther's rise and the simultaneous growth of the printing industry, as the printers of Germany and beyond figured out how to exploit his popularity to maximize their sales and reach. In 1517, Luther published three texts, printed a total of six times (six editions, in the parlance of the industry). In 1518, he produced 17 texts, which were printed at least 87 times. In 1519 he wrote 25 more texts, and printers reacted accordingly, publishing him in at least 170 new editions. A more recent estimate from this period puts the total number of separate printings closer to 291 overall. The year 1520 proved still more productive: 27 works in at least 275 separate printings, almost as many as the previous two years combined. We will never know exactly how many copies of Luther's works rolled off the presses, but a conservative estimate puts it at around 1,000 per edition. That would suggest at least half a million copies of his works entered circulation in only three years.

All of this happened with bewildering speed, irrevocably shifting the landscape of printing, reading, and religious reform. At the outset of 1518, Luther was an unknown university professor living in Wittenberg and writing in Latin for an overwhelmingly academic audience. By the end of 1519, he had become Europe's most published author and the most famous person in its

German-speaking regions. By the end of 1520, he was the most prolific living author since the invention of the printing press.

Many of these new publications, likely the majority of them, were brief. Twenty-one of the forty-five separate works Luther produced in 1518 and 1519 were pamphlets of eight pages or fewer. Since they were usually printed in quarto format, with four pages of text per side, each pamphlet required only one sheet of paper. An edition of a thousand copies was therefore an easy investment for any enterprising printer, perhaps two or three days of work at the most, with a guarantee that buyers would soon run through the stock. All Luther had to do in these early days was dispatch a letter with a single copy to a friend in one of Germany's printing centers—places like Augsburg, Leipzig, and Nuremberg—who would then find a printer ready and willing to produce an edition. Printers were sensitive to the dictates of their market and were constantly searching for new ways to profit. Luther's works were the perfect antidote to uncertainty and high up-front costs before any revenues could be realized from a given print run.[14]

Luther thus found a wide collection of new allies among the printing industry. Whether or not they themselves were invested in his ideas, his works sold, and that was what really mattered to them.

Melchior Lotter was a printer in Leipzig, and an accomplished and successful one at that. Early in 1518, he printed an edition of Johann Tetzel's response to Luther, and then two editions of the official Roman rebuttal to Luther's critique of indulgences. Just a few weeks later, however, he printed an edition of Luther's works, and even opened a branch office in Wittenberg the following year to service Luther's needs. Before long, he became one of Luther's close collaborators.

Lotter was not looking for controversy. He wasn't a true believer in the Reformation or its message. He simply saw in which direction the winds of profit were blowing. This insight, repeated over and over by printers across Germany and Europe beyond, was the key to the dissemination of Luther's ideas. If the Church's responses had sold in either Latin or German, printers would have produced them en masse. But consumer interest lay in the Evangelicals, as Luther and other reformers called themselves, and particularly in Luther himself.[15]

On top of his relationship with Lotter, Luther built a deep and mutually beneficial partnership with the celebrated artist Lucas Cranach, one of Wittenberg's most famous residents. Cranach, who was the court painter to Elector Frederick and one of the most productive, prosperous, and competent artists of the era, had interests and talents that went far beyond portraiture. He was a partner of Melchior Lotter in his Wittenberg printing expansion and himself an exceptionally savvy, diversified businessman. Cranach's investments included a paper mill and a trucking business for the distribution of books produced by the new printing consortium. In effect, Cranach built a vertically integrated printing firm to produce and sell Luther's works, and that was just one piece of his extensive investment portfolio.

Cranach's involvement went beyond capital and infrastructure. He was a pioneer in the production of decorative woodcuts, images that could drastically enhance the visual appeal of any printed product. Illustrated title pages made even Luther's humble pamphlets into works of art, beautiful material products that spoke to the gravity and importance of their message, and of the messenger himself. Luther's name was prominently displayed in the middle of an eye-catching image, precisely the kind of thing that leapt out at a potential reader passing by the bookseller's stall in the marketplace. As the historian Andrew Pettegree argues, this was an incredibly effective exercise in branding. A distinct visual style marked Luther's work, one in which Luther himself participated, and that gave his books and pamphlets instant recognition and appeal.[16]

The overall effect was a marriage of form and function that displayed Luther's—and his collaborators'—savvy understanding of the market. Much of his vast output was short, punchy, and accessible to lay readers in their own everyday language. Powered by this production apparatus and expert branding, Luther's ideas spread. The controversy that grew up around him and his message only heightened their appeal and encouraged additional would-be reformers or defenders of the Church to join the fray. Educated urbanites with an inclination for reform published their own pamphlets. So did Dominican theologians fighting a rearguard action against the tide of public opinion. Printing presses pumped out material of all sorts to meet this demand, cementing the survival of their industry and their profitability in the process.

Thanks to this alliance, Luther's output overwhelmed that of his contemporaries and rivals. Luther wrote, the printers produced his work on an increasingly vast scale, and the reading public gobbled it up. Luther responded with still more works, and the cycle continued, ad infinitum. This was the essence of the Reformation, both Luther's contribution to it and how it eventually spiraled beyond his control and understanding. As his works proliferated and audiences grew, his arguments became more and more extreme. He began openly challenging papal supremacy and the Church hierarchy, pushing the logical implications of his views ever further. More and more people were exposed to the reforming message. They soon developed their own ideas, which printers, sensing the opportunity for further profits, were happy to publish.

This dynamic rendered what had previously been unthinkable—a split within Christendom—increasingly likely. Like a runaway train careening downhill, gathering momentum as it descends, the effects of his writings went far beyond anything Luther had imagined or desired during his initial walk to the Wittenberg castle church on that first fateful day in 1517.

The Diet of Worms

Brother Martin did his best to keep his breathing calm and measured despite his pounding heart. Beads of sweat, raised by the heat and stuffiness of the cramped room, collected on his brow. Days of recent illness and the years of strain preceding them had further sharpened his protruding cheekbones and deepened the hollows around his dark brown eyes. His gaze, however, remained as piercing as ever as he scanned the packed room. Richly dressed nobles in furs and velvets sweated profusely, packed shoulder-to-shoulder with princes, counts, electors, and all the other high and mighty personages who made up this imperial diet—an assembly of the key decision makers of the Holy Roman Empire. Presiding over it all was the prominent jaw of twenty-one-year-old Emperor Charles V. Luther's eyes settled for a moment on the emperor, and he wondered whether it was true that the young man drooled, as he had heard.

The voice of the imperial spokesman snapped Luther back to attention. Were these his books, the man asked, and would Luther recant the messages therein, or not? He had already received two reprieves from that question. There would not be a third.

Brother Martin felt the crowd's eyes on him, the bald skin of his tonsure burning under the intensity of their staring. A sense of danger electrified the room: hostile glares, mouths twisted in anger and disgust, the emperor's clenched fist. But Brother Martin had made his choice long ago, long before the citizens of Worms had welcomed him with fanfare, before crowds gathered to see him on the long journey there from Wittenberg, before the imperial summons reached him in his humble monastery home. The tension squeezed the air from the room until the moment the monk began to speak. His words at first were precise and carefully chosen, before emerging in a rush as his emotions spilled over:

"I am bound by the Scriptures adduced by me, and my conscience has been taken captive by the Word of God, and I am neither able nor willing to recant, since it is neither safe nor right to act against conscience. God help me. Amen."[17]

The room exploded. The emperor's face twisted into an outraged snarl at the affront. Smiles and nods of approval from some observers clashed against others' rage. Brother Martin simply stood there, soaking it all in. One way or another, the verdict was now out of his hands.

The Diet of Worms was a moment of incredible drama, and it is usually understood as the climax of the first act of the Reformation. For Luther, it marked a point of no return—he was officially an outlaw and enemy of the Church and the emperor. Standing before Germany's most powerful lords and officials, both secular and ecclesiastic, at great personal risk, he had defined the conflict that would come to subsume every subsequent generation. Only the protection of Elector Frederick of Saxony, his guardian angel since the beginning of the indulgence controversy more than three years before, saved him from the fate that otherwise awaited all obstinate heretics: a fiery death at the stake.

Yet understanding the Diet of Worms as a culmination point misses something basic about the events of prior years and the underlying structural shifts that had accompanied them. Luther's actions at the Diet, as undeniably brave and public as they were, were a capstone, a bit of falling action after the fact rather than a genuine climax. The crux of the early Reformation had already passed: Luther scribbling text after text and walking them to Johann Rhau-Grunenberg's print shop in Wittenberg; dispatching letters and couriers with copies to the printers of Augsburg and Leipzig; printers working overtime to churn out thousands upon thousands of pamphlets and books; readers forking over cash and eagerly devouring Luther's latest works on everything from technical theology, to gentle pastoral works on the proper relationship between God and sinner, to vicious polemical attacks against any who dared criticize him.

Luther completely dominated the early Reformation in the years leading up to the Diet of Worms. By the time he arrived in the city for his fateful appearance, pictures of Martin Luther were treated with reverence. Nobles carried his books into Diet meetings. Crowds discussed his works in public. Alexander, the legate who came to Worms as papal representative to the Diet, was denied access to his lodgings. Strangers touched their swords, a significant gesture of respect, when he passed in the street. Printers published hostile pamphlets about him and the pope and suffered no consequences. "Nothing else is bought here except Luther's books even in the imperial court, for the people stick together remarkably and have lots of money," he wrote.[18]

Luther's domination was the result of his incredible output, his knack for writing different genres, his facility with both Latin and German, his notoriety, and the trust printers placed in him as a commercial brand. After the Diet, however, other voices began to compete with his for space and attention. Luther's was still by far the most important for the next several years, but after the Diet of Worms, and then especially after 1530, his monopoly shrank drastically. When he went into hiding in the Wartburg after Worms, other reformers—including his former close ally, Andreas Karlstadt—took up the cause and pushed the issues in directions, such as offering both bread and wine for Communion, that Luther was unwilling and unable to broach. While he was still a figure of immense importance, the Reformation was beginning to move beyond him.

We can see this effect in quantitative and geographic terms. Until 1525, Luther's works were printed and reprinted across 1,465 editions, eleven times more than the next most prolific author, Andreas Karlstadt, whose work clocked in at 125 editions. The famous and influential Swiss reformer Huldrych Zwingli, by contrast, managed just 70 editions in that same time. Even these numbers understate Luther's dominance, since most of the other Evangelicals who achieved print success in this period—like Karlstadt, at least early on, and Philipp Melanchthon—were associates and allies of the Wittenberg professor.

Yet despite the fact that he remained exceptionally prolific until he died in 1546, fully half of the lifetime printings of Luther's work took place in the eight years between the appearance of the *Ninety-Five Theses* in 1517 and 1525. Three-quarters were printed before 1530. Before 1525, his works were reprinted an average of six times for every original edition; afterward, this shrank to three reprintings. Cities like Strasbourg, Basel, and Augsburg had been major centers of reprinting for Luther in these early days; after 1525, their output of his works dropped by half to two-thirds. His readership was increasingly limited to northern and central Germany.[19]

The numbers tell a clear story: Luther's voice still mattered, but it mattered in fewer places for fewer readers. The landscape of reform shifted, and the reins of the movement slipped from Luther's grasp. Others were raising their own voices, disagreeing with him on issues of real importance—everything from the presence of Christ in the Eucharist during Mass to the nature of salvation. The general consensus that the Church required reform and that all the Evangelicals shared common goals and interests quickly disappeared.

Courteous disagreement was never one of Luther's strengths. A combative man by nature, he tended to see the world as one divided between enemies and allies. There was no real middle ground, and woe to the person who moved into the enemy camp. Conciliation was of no interest to him, either; he preferred submission to his point of view, which was obviously correct. Any opposition was evidence not of good-faith disagreement but of crass, wicked obstinacy. His long and increasingly nasty dispute with his formerly close friend Andreas Karlstadt ended only with Karlstadt's abject surrender.

Only those closest to Luther, people skilled in managing his temper and working with his strengths, could survive in his orbit. Most did not, at least not for long. It is ironic that one of the things that made Luther so effective in the early years of the Reformation, namely his willingness to fight and argue, also meant that he was incapable of serving as a uniting figure once the reform movement reached critical mass. In fact, his personality and tendencies effectively doomed even the remote possibility of a cohesive ideological front, just as his bravery, work ethic, and stubbornness had helped create the Reformation in the first place.

The End and Martin Luther

The Reformation inflamed the most deeply felt passions of Evangelicals and supporters of the church alike. Luther had issued a challenge to the authorities that governed society, both secular and religious. It took a long time for him to fully work out the implications of his challenge to papal supremacy and the established order, something he did mostly in the context of responses to attacks on his published beliefs. Others moved much further than he did, bringing his ideas to logical conclusions Brother Martin himself was unwilling to entertain. Luther opened a Pandora's box, not only through his ideas and their implications, but by proving that there was a market for printing still more radical material, with violence being the inevitable consequence.

Luther was always convinced he was right about everything. In one of his first sermons after returning to Wittenberg in 1522, for example, he told his parishioners, "Follow me. . . . I was the first whom God placed on this arena. It was also to me whom God first revealed to preach these, his words."[20] Yet the desire for change in the Church had never been limited to Luther himself, nor was his particular tradition of Augustinian reform and strict emphasis on Scripture the only possible route forward. Defenders of the traditional Church were not his only opponents, or his most important ones. As the years went on, new Evangelical challengers emerged.

The most formidable of these was Thomas Müntzer, a former devotee and correspondent of Luther's—he finished a letter by describing himself as someone "whom you brought to birth by the Gospel"—but one who soon moved in a drastically different direction. Müntzer's path was spiritual and apocalyptic: God actively spoke to the faithful through dreams and visions, not just through Scripture, and the time of reckoning was nigh. None of this came out of the blue. Mysticism was deeply rooted in medieval Christianity, and Luther and Müntzer shared their admiration for one of its more recent exponents, one Johannes Tauler.

Apocalyptic tendencies were never far from the surface, either. Müntzer's emphasis on them simply took him down a different, but still recognizable, path of reform. Parishioners flocked to hear his sermons by the hundreds and thousands. Printed copies of his fire-breathing orations circulated widely. The divine kingdom must be brought about here on Earth, Müntzer thundered, with violence if necessary. Luther grew to hate him even more than he did Karlstadt.[21]

As unrest festered among the German common folk, culminating in local strikes, alliances, and eventually a full-blown peasants' rebellion, Müntzer's message became increasingly extreme. He and a fellow radical preacher named Heinrich Pfeiffer turned the city of Mühlhausen into a miniature theocracy, ruled by what they saw as pure Christian ideals, and advocated violent confrontation with secular authorities. "God instructs all the birds of the heavens to consume the flesh of the princes; whilst the brute beasts are to drink the blood of the bigwigs," he wrote to Count Albrecht of Mansfeld in 1525.[22]

The German Peasants' War was one of the largest social rebellions of the era. In some ways, it was quite typical of the sort that had prevailed throughout the Middle Ages and up to the 1520s: Peasants demanded the abolition of serfdom, the free hunting of game, an end of onerous labor requirements on their lords' behalf, and so on. What made it different was the Evangelical, reforming, biblical language employed in support of the peasants' demands, and the explicit targeting of Church properties. Luther had directly influenced the masses with his social teachings and open rebellion against established authority—on this much the peasants were clear. The prologue to the Twelve Articles, the fundamental statement of the Peasants' War, leaves no doubt: The goal was "to hear the gospel and live accordingly," and all other demands flowed from that.[23] Some eighty-five printed editions of the various peasant manifestos and Müntzer's writings circulated across Germany, giving them an audience far beyond the active rebels.

Even among educated elites, there was sympathy for the rebels: "Although it seems terrible that the peasants destroyed certain monasteries," Erasmus wrote while stationed near one of the rebellion's outbreaks in Alsace, "the wickedness of the latter nevertheless provoked them to it."[24]

When Müntzer added a touch of apocalyptic violence to the mixture, the result was bloodshed on a staggering scale. Bands of rebels sacked castles, monasteries, and manor houses and eventually came into open battle with the armies of the German princes, clashes that ended poorly for the peasants. Following the slaughter of his supporters, Müntzer was taken captive and executed, his head displayed for all to see outside the walls of Mühlhausen.

Tens of thousands died across Germany, perhaps as many as one hundred thousand, in an orgy of social upheaval and destruction.

Luther wanted nothing to do with any of this. In his first writing on the peasants' uprisings, entitled *Admonition to Peace*, he deplored the violence and disorder, but also warned the princes that rebellion was a punishment for their own sins. This was a bold statement, as close as Luther ever came to attacking the established social order, and one he soon rescinded. As the Peasants' War grew bloodier, any sympathy he had for the rebels disappeared. In one of his most notorious works, a pamphlet entitled *Against the Robbing and Murdering Hordes of Peasants*, he took a clear stance: "Therefore let everyone who can smite, slay, and stab, secretly or openly, remembering that nothing can be more poisonous, hurtful, or devilish than a rebel. It is just as when one must kill a mad dog." It was the kind of language he had employed for years in his conflicts with the papacy, and occasionally other Evangelical reformers, but he had never before turned it against his supporters. The shift did not help his reputation.[25]

Unfortunately for Luther, *Against the Robbing and Murdering Hordes of Peasants* only appeared after the slaughter of some six thousand peasants and the execution of Müntzer himself. At best, this was in poor taste, considering the copious amount of blood that had been spilled; at worst, the sentiments he expressed in the pamphlet amounted to a fundamental rejection of what his audience understood him to be—a kind, thoughtful caretaker of his flock, concerned about both their spiritual health and material well-being. It was inevitable that the printed ideal of Luther would eventually clash with the polemical, obstinate reality. The Peasants' War brought that disconnect home.

Perhaps fittingly, it was the printers who made clear Luther's position on the matter. They printed and reprinted *Against the Robbing and Murdering Hordes of Peasants* across Germany. The pamphlets sold, and the printers profited, just as they had from Luther's previous works. But Luther's reputation never recovered.

Luther's years as the unquestioned leader of the Evangelical tides sweeping Europe were over. He had become but one voice among many, tarnishing his own legacy with vicious, full-throated expressions of bigotry and antisemitism. His followers eclipsed him, and so too did the second generation of reformers led by John Calvin.

The increasingly stout, parochial pastor of Wittenberg, no longer an ascetic monk but a married father of six, slowly faded into the background. Luther dispensed his earthy wisdom, theological insight, and occasional tirades from the comfort of his home. As his disciples collected his *Table Talk* and he continued to publish as the face of one of many reform movements, Christendom continued to splinter. Brother Martin, the now-corpulent elder statesman, had made possible the excesses, extremism, and violence of both his and the following age. Thousands of people had died in the gory Peasants' War. Still more would perish throughout the next century and beyond, culminating in the apocalyptic Thirty Years' War.

The world would never be the same in the wake of Martin Luther's small act of rebellion. As with so much else in this period, finance and credit had made it all possible: the future monk's education via the financialized mining industry; the indulgence controversy of Pope Leo, Bishop Albrecht, and Tetzel that set off the Reformation, driven by loans from the Fuggers and international financial transfers; and the printing presses, themselves the product of sophisticated speculative credit arrangements, that produced the millions of texts that powered the Reformation. Martin Luther was already a representative of that world as he walked toward the castle church of Wittenberg on October 31, 1517, and he pushed it further and further until it slipped over the edge of the approaching abyss.[26]

CHAPTER 8

———— ❧ ————

Suleiman the Magnificent and the Ottoman Superpower

August 31, 1526, Mohács, Kingdom of Hungary

Drops of rain poured onto the tent, thick sheets of water sluicing down from the sky to pound against the fine, intricately decorated red fabric.

The sound of splashing raindrops merged with the low buzz of conversation, an occasional laugh, and intermittent raised voices. The steady rhythm of heavy blade against flesh punctuated the ambient noise of that wet August day. Every once in a while, a shortened cry or painful howl pierced the veil of falling water. One after another, the heads of the prisoners fell to the ground, separated from their bodies by a single practiced stroke of a heavy, curved sword. Spraying arterial blood joined with the rain before falling into the churned, sucking mud of what had until recently been a battlefield.

Protected from the rain by his elaborate tent, Suleiman the Magnificent watched the beheadings from the comfort and majesty of his golden throne. An enormous white turban, crowned with a magnificent red plume, shaded his lean, pale face. Under an aquiline nose, his thin mustache spread outward onto angular cheekbones. This was the ruler of the Ottoman Empire, showing no signs of discomfort or emotion as the blades came down. He had witnessed countless executions, and he knew he would see many more.

The sultan exchanged glances with the sightless eyes of his dead Hungarian enemies in the moments before his Janissaries—professional slave-soldiers—picked up the decapitated heads and carefully placed them on sharp pikes in front of his tent. Others were used to form the rising layers of a growing pyramid, a monument of bloody horror. The sight of the dead did not disturb Suleiman, but the rain was an intolerable inconvenience. When he set down his account of the day in his campaign diary, the downpour and the decapitations received equal mention.

A crowd of viziers and beys, the powerful civil and military officials who ran the empire that belonged to the House of Osman, surrounded Suleiman, who—or more precisely his generals and armies—had won a great victory two days before here at Mohács, killing the king of Hungary and countless thousands of his soldiers and nobles. The two thousand wet, bedraggled, defeated prisoners now in the process of being paraded past Suleiman's fine red tent before being beheaded were simply the final flourishes on a masterpiece of military organization, logistics, and strategy. This was another in a long line of conquests for the sultan, an entry into the vastness of central Europe. Buda, the capital of Hungary, would be next, followed by Vienna. Rome would surely follow, and perhaps the rest of Europe after that. Suleiman's lands already stretched from the Red Sea to the Danube, from the mountains of western Iran to the deserts of North Africa. Now, with a single decisive blow, the plains of Hungary had fallen under his control. Why stop there?

In 1324, two centuries prior to Suleiman's crushing victory

at Mohács, his ancestor, Osman, had died a minor warlord in Anatolia. Eight members of that dynasty, direct descendants from father to son, followed Osman onto the throne. Suleiman was the ninth. In the process, the Ottoman dynasty transformed a tiny *beylik*—a frontier principality—eking out a living in the cracks between the Christian and Islamic worlds into a vast empire spanning three continents. Suleiman was still a warlord, perhaps the last of the Ottoman sultans to embody such a role, but his ambitions were set on the ruin of whole kingdoms, not the snatching of a few captives and some plunder from the next Anatolian *beylik*. His Ottoman Empire was to be the superpower of its day and age, every bit a match for the Trastámaras of Spain, the Valois of France, and the rapaciously acquisitive Habsburgs—more so, perhaps, than all of them put together.

Suleiman ruled the Ottoman Empire from 1520 to 1566, a golden age of territorial expansion, internal reform, cultural efflorescence, and global influence. Istanbul was the center of the world. It dwarfed London, Paris, and Madrid: impossibly wealthy, populous, ancient, and sophisticated. Suleiman's armies sat on the cutting edge of military development—there were no better practitioners of siege warfare, no more skilled artillerists, than those serving the sultan. The financial and demographic resources at the sultan's disposal dwarfed the perennially empty coffers and overstretched powers of his European rivals. Flourishing trade networks bound together Istanbul and Alexandria, Damascus and Algiers, Baghdad and Belgrade. And no ruler had access to a higher quality of servant than Suleiman with the *devşirme* system, which plucked talented boys from obscurity and raised them to prominence as bureaucrats, viziers, Janissary *aghas*, and cavalry commanders loyal only to the sultan. No Inquisition troubled the sultan's many Christian and Jewish subjects so long as they paid the requisite taxes. The Ottomans were the greatest power both in Europe and in the western reaches of Asia. In an era of rising states, none rose to greater heights than the Ottoman Empire.

Yet this begs a question. Suleiman's reign, golden age though it might have been, marked both an apex and a point of no return. If the Ottomans were the dominant power of this age, why did the roots of the future global order plant themselves in the indebted, war-torn, relatively impoverished soil of western Europe, rather than the fertile lands surrounding the Bosporus?[1]

The Wild Frontier

Anatolia was a volatile frontier zone at the beginning of the fourteenth century. This westernmost extension of Asia, across the Aegean Sea from the Balkans and Europe, was the intersection of three worlds: Byzantine, Muslim, and Latin Christian. The Greeks had been there the longest, with settlements dating back more than two millennia and fifteen hundred years of largely unbroken Roman and then Byzantine rule. The Muslim world had begun to impinge on Anatolia nearly five centuries before, when the Seljuk Turks ejected the Byzantines from the eastern parts of Asia Minor. Western Christians were the most recent arrivals, a combination of Italian merchants plying the coastal trading routes and crusading holy warriors attempting to carve out new and lucrative territories for God, glory, and material advancement.

This was the world in which the Ottomans emerged, a melting pot of cultural collision, migration, religious friction, and constant, vicious warfare. Muslim, Turkic-speaking nomads and semi-nomads called Turkomans, many of them recent arrivals from the open grassland of the great Eurasian steppe, provided the military muscle. Expert horsemen and archers, they made for a readily available pool of manpower that would-be warlords could tap into with the right combination of incentives. Charismatic holy men claiming divine inspiration regularly whipped up waves of religious fervor among the Turkomans, providing yet another impetus to war and conflict. Better still, Anatolia lay out of the direct control of any of the region's great powers—the Mongol-descended Ilkhans of Persia, the formerly ascendant Seljuk Sultanate, the Mamluks of Egypt and Syria, and the much-diminished Byzantines—all of whom could be played off against one another. In other words, this region offered a wealth of opportunities for those ambitious, violent, and lucky enough to exploit them.

Osman, the son of a Turkic tribal chieftain named Ertugrul, must have had all those qualities and more. We know little about him. His reign, which lasted until 1324, left behind almost no contemporary evidence. This is not surprising. Practically all of Osman's activities took place in a tiny corner of northwestern Anatolia, the region of Bithynia just east of Constantinople. His victories all occurred within an area measuring roughly 150 miles east to west and 100 north to south. Whatever Osman built, it must have been a small principality, a few fortified refuges from which he controlled a swathe of countryside and set out to raid and fight his neighbors, Christians and Muslims alike. There was very little that set Osman and his tiny *beylik* apart from dozens of similar warlords and tiny polities dotting the mountains, high plateaus, and rocky coastlines of Anatolia.

When Osman died in 1324, his territory passed to his son Orhan, who ruled until 1362. Far more than his father, it was Orhan who turned his small inheritance into the foundations of a genuine Ottoman state. Orhan took the city of Bursa in 1326, then Nicaea in 1331, both from the Byzantines, and Ankara from its Muslim rulers in 1356. He also defeated a Byzantine army in a major battle and conquered the Muslim emirate of Kareşi. These were serious accomplishments that made the Ottomans the dominant power in western Anatolia, but they paled in comparison to his most important action: In 1352, Ottoman soldiers—participants in a Byzantine civil war, thanks to Orhan's marriage to the Byzantine princess Theodora—crossed into Europe for the first time. They established themselves in a fortress on the rocky heights of the Gallipoli Peninsula, where their descendants would bleed the Allies white during the First World War 550 years later.

Rooted in that secure base along the Dardanelles, the Ottomans expanded farther and farther into Europe. Mobile raiders and armies of conquest fanned out from there, slicing into Greece, the plains of Thrace to the west of Constantinople, and deep into the Balkans. Treasure, tribute, and slaves, all the material rewards successful warfare offered, poured into the coffers of the Ottoman dynasts, their servants, and their allies.

A combination of factors drove this explosive growth. The first and most obvious of these was the possibility of material reward. The early Ottoman dynasts, and those they attracted to their service, were on a fundamental level predators. Their state, such as it actually existed, was a predatory one. They raided, first in neighboring Bithynia and western Anatolia, and then farther afield: Thrace, Greece, eastern Anatolia, and Serbia. Christians or Muslims, it mattered little who their targets might be, or their followers. The Ottomans attracted Muslim Turkomans in large numbers because they were the most convenient source of military manpower in western Anatolia, but they were happy to take supporters from any background. Through raiding and conquest, the Ottoman dynasts acquired riches and lands, which they used to pull in still more followers. Like a snowball rolling downhill, gathering mass and momentum as it descends, the Ottomans raided and conquered their way to regional relevance.

The second key factor was religion. Scholars used to believe that the early Ottomans rose to prominence as holy warriors for

Islam, *gazis* defeating the infidel and spreading their faith, but a reevaluation of the (extremely thin) evidence in this early period gives pride of place to material concerns. That does not mean that religious sentiment was irrelevant, but that it interacted with, and strengthened, other motivations in dynamic ways. *Gaza*, holy war, was effectively synonymous with *akin*, raiding for booty and glory. These pillagers, *akincis*, did not even have to be Muslim. In fact, at various points they were largely conscripted or recruited from Christian territories ruled by the Ottomans. Pious Muslims who carried war against the infidel expected and deserved material rewards; so too did the sultan's loyal Christian subjects. Both of these intertwined motivations—worldly gain and spiritual obligation—wound themselves into the DNA of the emerging Ottoman state.[2]

The Rising Ottoman Tide

The Ottoman dynasts—beys at first, then sultans, a far more exalted title that spoke to long traditions of Muslim rulership— built their state on predatory foundations. But states built on raiding and opportunism rarely last long if not reinforced with organization. Sitting at the intersection of three worlds, each with its own long institutional traditions, the Ottomans had plenty of options at their disposal.

The Ottomans simply took over existing Byzantine landholding systems, distributing holdings (*timars*) to their followers in return for cavalry service in their armies as *sipahis*. Revenue then flowed into Ottoman coffers instead of those of their former recipients. From their Ilkhanid neighbors, the Ottomans acquired bureaucratic practices, systems of tax registration and taxation, and organizational norms built around the sultan's household. "Households" comprised the servants at the very center of power, most of them enslaved people who owed their position to the generosity and approval of the ruler rather than independent operators who had to be wooed and appeased.

Muslim rulers had a long tradition of employing enslaved people as soldiers, imports from far away who would be dependent on the sultan rather than any local power broker. The Ottomans adopted this practice as well but added their own twist: Rather than buying Circassians from the Caucasus, as the Mamluks of Egypt had long done, or Turks from the steppe, the Ottomans levied a human tax on their Christian subjects.

The *devşirme*, as this practice was known, provided a massive pool of ambitious, upwardly mobile manpower that was directly dependent on the sultan. From this pool, the sultan recruited his fearsome Janissaries (*yeni çeri*, "new soldiers"), professional and loyal infantrymen. For poor peasant boys from a dusty Thracian village or shepherds from the rocky Balkan highlands, the *devşirme* was a chance to move up in the world, a way to earn an exalted place in society through talent rather than accidents of blood and birth. Ottoman slavery was not a gentle institution, but it differed in fundamental ways from chattel slavery of the kind growing increasingly prevalent in the Atlantic world, and that would take its mature form in the Americas in centuries to come. The most powerful person in the Ottoman Empire after the sultan himself—the grand vizier—might technically be enslaved. For those who were both gifted and extremely fortunate, enslavement in the sultan's household offered a path to power and wealth unimaginable given the circumstances of their birth. Driven by this meritocratic incentive, the Janissaries and the household provided a centralizing counterweight to the centrifugal forces of the frontier that constantly threatened to detach the expanding empire from its ruler.

Armed with the desire for plunder, an inchoate sense of

religious obligation, and an increasingly statelike organizational structure, the Ottomans rolled through the chaotic Balkans without meeting much effective resistance. They took Edirne, northwest of Constantinople, and made it their capital. Most of Thrace fell, along with large stretches of northern Greece and the central Balkans. Serbia was reduced to subservience—literal vassalage—after the cataclysmic Battle of Kosovo in 1389. Sultan Bayezid I laid siege to Constantinople itself, striking more of an ideological blow than a real one, and then crushed an army of French, Burgundian, German, and Hungarian crusaders at Nicopolis in 1396. Even an apocalyptic defeat at the hands of the infamous conqueror Timur Lenk (Tamerlane) at Ankara in 1402, complete with Sultan Bayezid's capture and humiliation and a devastating, decade-long civil war to decide his successor, could not stop the onward march of the expanding Ottoman Empire.[3]

By 1451, when nineteen-year-old Mehmet II took over the throne from his father, Murad, said empire stretched from the high peaks and lush green pastures of central Anatolia to the Danube and west to the edge of the Hungarian Plain. But Mehmet was not satisfied with these substantial holdings. Obsessed with Alexander the Great and world conquest since childhood, the young sultan turned his attention toward the grand city on the Bosporus: Constantinople. Slowly, methodically, turning the vast resources of his empire to this single task, Mehmet squeezed the Byzantine capital. With cutting-edge gunpowder artillery, mines to collapse the thousand-year-old city walls, full-sized oared galleys transported miles overland for surprise attacks in the harbor, and human wave assaults, he finally succeeded in capturing the city in May 1453. The meeting point of Europe and Asia was now his.[4]

Secure in his new capital, Mehmet made war practically every year for the rest of his reign. His armies fought Wallachians, Hungarians, Serbians, the White Sheep Turkomans (Aq Qoyunlu) of Iran, rebellious vassals in Anatolia, Albanians, and Venetians. The entirety of Greece and the Balkans, aside from a few minor enclaves, fell under Ottoman rule. Only Hungary, protected by the Danube River, was spared from conquest. During the devastating sixteen-year conflict with the maritime Republic of Venice, Ottoman raiders lit fires that could be seen from the city itself, took key ports along the Aegean and Adriatic, and nearly bankrupted one of the richest states in Christendom. In 1480, a year before Mehmet's death, an Ottoman force landed in southern Italy and sacked the port of Otranto, sending a clear message about his intentions for the future: Rome was next. Had Mehmet not died the following year under suspicious circumstances, he might have succeeded in taking it.

Mehmet's son Bayezid II (r. 1481–1512) was a less dedicated conqueror, though crushing exhaustion from his father's ceaseless campaigning and a less favorable political outlook in the west limited the possibilities. It was Selim, Bayezid II's son and Suleiman's father, known to posterity as "the Grim," who inherited his grandfather Mehmet's warmongering tendencies. Turning his attention to the Islamic world and the east, Selim crushed the expansive ambitions of the Safavids of Persia and their charismatic leader Ismail at the Battle of Chaldiran in 1514. Two years later, Selim's armies rolled over the Mamluks of Egypt, taking Syria, the Levant, Egypt, and guardianship over the holy cities of Mecca and Medina. In just a few years' time, Selim had doubled the size of the Ottoman Empire, transforming it from a bit player on the fringes of the Muslim world to its most prestigious power.

Facing Two Worlds

Suleiman, twenty-five years old when he inherited the throne upon his father's untimely death in 1520, was the beneficiary and result of centuries of aggressive conquest and expansion. The new sultan took a bit of everything from his predecessors: He bore a noticeable physical resemblance to his great-grandfather Mehmet, with an aquiline, slightly too large nose, lean profile, and keen gaze. The thin mustache that split Suleiman's face resembled Selim's, but where aggressive warmongering had defined the Grim, Suleiman had a bit more of his grandfather Bayezid's contemplative, deliberate nature.

Every member of the House of Osman, however, had the capacity for shocking, bloody cruelty. Mehmet had once impaled a Venetian ship captain who defied him on a dull stake in full view of passing maritime traffic along the Bosporus. Selim had ordered tens of thousands of executions of his own Turkoman subjects in Anatolia on the way to campaign against the Safavids of Iran, and probably the assassination of his own father, Bayezid, as well. Suleiman, as his supervision of the executions at Mohács proved, was far from a shrinking violet. The new sultan's noticeable pallor, a paleness on which observers regularly commented, was not the result of a weak stomach when it came to inflicting violence.

For most of its existence, Europe had been the focus of Ottoman expansion. Given a choice between fighting the mobile Turkomans of the southern Caucasus or the Mamluks of Egypt and the Serbians, Hungarians, or Venetians, sultan after sultan chose the western option. The material rewards were more enticing, it was easier to motivate Ottoman armies to fight Christians, and the apparatus of the Ottoman state was better suited to campaigns in the west. Selim the Grim had spent most of his eight-year rule reversing that trend, addressing first the religiously suspect Safavids and then the teetering Mamluks. This left Suleiman with a vastly larger, wealthier, and more cosmopolitan empire, but also one whose scale and structural faults were unlike those faced by rulers before him.

Mehmet had spent practically his entire reign campaigning, much of it in the thick of battle. So had Selim. Suleiman would have to campaign, both to maintain the all-important loyalty of his Janissaries and to appear in person before his key subjects. He would have to turn his military attention west toward the Christian world, to retain the Ottomans' newly acquired prestige within the Muslim world. At the same time, however, he would have to consolidate his new territories. Conquests on a global scale had been his father's calling card—some historians have actually referred to Selim's acquisitions as the beginning of a prolonged sixteenth-century world war—but actually ruling those lands would require a different approach. Suleiman would have to juggle all of these requirements simultaneously.[5]

Most European observers were happy to see Selim gone. With the absorption of Egypt and sidelining of the Safavids in the first years of his reign, most veteran Ottoman-watchers assumed that the Grim would return his attention to the west. He had long maintained an interest there. The sultan had recently accepted the vassalage of the fearsome Barbarossa brothers, the piratical corsairs who controlled the port of Algiers, the strategic key to the central and western Mediterranean. With the North African coast under Selim's nominal control, the entirety of the Mediterranean basin was open to Ottoman raiding, and perhaps even conquest. Even Spain itself was in grave danger. And with all of Europe's great powers embroiled in the increasingly expansive Italian Wars, there was little chance of a coordinated response to an Ottoman invasion. Despite the best efforts of popes and kings alike, they had accomplished nothing. Religious and secular rulers had made only sporadic efforts at containment and launched a few small-scale campaigns since the miserable, crushing failure of the last crusade at Varna in 1444. Anyone paying attention realized that Selim's conquests in the distant east made the Ottomans drastically more dangerous. The sultan's advances in Egypt and Persia were met with trepidation in the west, but no ruler wanted to be the one to incur the wrath of the mighty Selim.

Suleiman, in contrast to his father's fearsome reputation, was thought to be of lesser quality. "It seemed to all men," wrote the Italian historian and churchman Paolo Giovio, "that a gentle lamb had succeeded a fierce lion... since Suleiman himself was but young and of no experience... and altogether given to rest and quietness." On hearing the news of Selim's death, Pope Leo X "commanded that the Litany and common prayers should be sung throughout all Rome."[6]

Their elation was premature. Suleiman was already a mature man at the time of his accession, and years of officeholding and smaller-scale governance had prepared him well for his new role as sultan. Moreover—and rare for an Ottoman succession—he was his father's only potential heir. A sultan might have many sons, but none was automatically favored to succeed his father, and only one could emerge victorious. The result was a constant jockeying for position among the potential heirs to the Ottoman Empire, a shadowy, treacherous, and dangerous competition that could last years, even decades. Selim was more than forty years old at the time of his accession, and had spent decades carefully plotting his way to the throne, deposing his father and removing three brothers and a number of nephews to ensure his own succession in 1512.

This internal shadow war between potential heirs was a constant source of strife, a focus for all the tensions that lived within a vast and powerful empire. At the moment of a sultan's death, all of those fault lines—between the sultan's household and frontier lords, battle-hardened Janissaries and palace viziers, freedom-loving semi-nomads and tax collectors—ruptured. It was the moment of greatest weakness for the Ottoman Empire, of which its neighbors were well aware. Thanks to Selim's ruthless blood-letting, however, there was no question who would follow him, thus averting the usual civil war that accompanied the death of a ruler. Suleiman was spared a lengthy process of consolidation. He simply stepped into the role of sultan, paid off the Janissaries as was expected of a new ruler, and got to work.[7]

Said work took several forms. Selim had been a hard man, an aggressive conqueror, but that had not endeared him to his subjects. Suleiman's first intention as sultan was to remedy these ill feelings among the people. A revolt soon broke out in newly acquired Syria, stoked by the neighboring Shah Ismail of Persia, but Suleiman handled both his rebellious provincial governor and the potentially dangerous Safavids with a minimum of unneces-sary bloodshed. He released some Egyptian notables whom Selim had deported to Istanbul, restored freedom of trade with Iran and released a number of imprisoned merchants, and executed one of his father's least popular officials, Cafer Bey.

Launching his reign with the public execution of a man known as "the Bloodthirsty" sent a strong message to the people regard-ing Suleiman's desire to be seen as a just ruler. "My sublime com-mandment," he wrote to the governor of Egypt soon after taking the throne, "as inescapable and binding as fate, is that rich and poor, town and country, subjects and tribute-payers—everyone must hasten to obey you. If some are slow to accomplish the duty, be they emirs or fakirs, do not hesitate to inflict on them the ulti-mate punishment." In Suleiman's words, even the most exalted in society were subject to correction if they defied justice and the sultan's command.[8]

While the young Suleiman dispensed justice with a firm hand and still lacked his father's instinctive impulse toward warmonger-ing, all Ottoman rulers were expected to wage war. The Janissar-ies had to be kept busy. The *sipahi* cavalry had to assemble, equip themselves, and ride off on campaign. The Ottoman Empire still, in myriad important ways, revolved around conquest: Its state finances and social dynamics practically demanded military engagement and territorial acquisition. New lands and plunder sated the ambitions and demands of key stakeholders in the political order. Sultans had to put the restive *akincis*, frontier raiders, to work. Provincial governors and Janissary *aghas* had to be kept busy. The ideological weight of the sultan's position demanded war, and preferably against the Christian west rather than fellow Muslims.

Belgrade and Rhodes

Iron-shod hooves and heavy boots plodded over the flagstones leading out of Istanbul, a constant pounding that nearly drowned out the wailing pipes and beating drums that accompanied the military parade. *Sipahis* on horseback, drawn from the countryside of Anatolia, Thrace, and Greece, led the way; decorated quivers packed with arrows for their powerful recurve bows hung from their belts next to thick, crescent-bladed swords. The *sipahis* preceded the Janissaries in their tall, flat-fronted caps, hefting long arquebuses and vicious polearms. They were the core of the sultan's army. Masses of raiding cavalry, *akincis* on small, fast horses, and hordes of conscripted or volunteer infantry, *azabs* hefting axes and shields, followed. In the midst of it all rode Suleiman himself astride a magnificent mount, adorned in a massive white turban studded with precious gems and exotic feathers. The icy early morning sunshine of February 6, 1521, glinted off steel armor, naked blades, and cannon barrels that had been polished to a high shine for the occasion. By design, the Ottoman war machine in motion was a fearsome thing; Suleiman and his advisors knew that spies and ambassadors were watching, that they would compose their reports for the rulers of western Europe, and the message had to be loud and clear.

On taking the throne, Suleiman had dispatched an envoy to the young King Louis II of Hungary, demanding tribute in return for peace. Accounts vary—the Ottoman envoy later returned to Istanbul with his ears and nose cut off, or he was dead altogether. Either way, Suleiman had his justification for war.

And war with Hungary was inevitable, besides. It was a Christian kingdom bordering Ottoman territory in the volatile northern Balkans. The two states had over a century of shared conflict. Yet Hungary had fallen far from its halcyon days in the second half of the fifteenth century, when its powerful king Matthias Corvinus had lorded over central Europe. Louis II was a mere boy of fifteen, and the powerful Hungarian nobility had drained the treasury and destroyed much of the kingdom's military and fiscal capacity. The time would never be better for an attack.

Rather than charging straight into Hungary, Suleiman set his sights on the southern stronghold of Belgrade, now the capital of Serbia. Ottoman rulers had targeted the city for a long time: Even the great Sultan Mehmet II came close to death outside Belgrade's daunting walls in 1456, losing a desperate battle against a combined force of Hungarians and crusaders from the west. Mehmet had barely escaped with his life on that occasion, but Hungary in 1521 was nowhere near as imposing a foe as it had been in 1456. Suleiman's empire was not that of Mehmet the Conqueror. Times had changed, and so too would the outcome of this particular fight.

Suleiman proceeded through Serbia toward Belgrade in the heat of July, his path along the road shaded by the impaled heads of a Hungarian fortress garrison that had refused to surrender to the Ottomans. On the last day of the month, he arrived outside the walls of the city, where his army had been laying the groundwork for the siege for weeks. No state in Europe could match the Ottomans when it came to siege warfare. Hails of incessant bombardment from cannon, Janissaries sniping defenders on the walls, the relentless scraping of shovels and picks digging out trenches and underground mines, assault after assault on potential weak points: The Ottomans put continual pressure on the defenders of a walled city until the citadel fell or the defenders surrendered, well beyond anything their rivals could hope to match. In the case of Belgrade, a massive mining operation brought down a tower after a few preparatory attacks and a vicious, monthlong cannonade. The city's Serbian defenders surrendered at the end of August 1521, while the Hungarians fought on and were massacred to a man. With Belgrade in his hands, Suleiman's road north into central Europe was open.[9]

While the sultan hinted at a new campaign against Hungary in the spring of 1522, even telling a Venetian envoy that he had left his artillery in Belgrade for ease of transport, he had already decided on a different target for the following year: the island of Rhodes, headquarters of the Hospitaller Knights, for generations a painful thorn in the side of the Muslim world. Mehmet II had made an attempt to conquer Rhodes in 1480, shortly before his death, but even he had come up short against the well-fortified, resourceful, and disciplined Knights.

From their imposing fortifications and protected harbor, the Knights sent out fast, well-armed galleys to raid the shipping routes of the eastern Mediterranean. Captives and loot poured into Rhodes, as did donations from pious Christians in the west seeking to keep the order afloat long after the Crusades had ended. The Hospitallers' shipborne holy war disrupted trade, endangered the pilgrimage routes to Mecca, and generally embarrassed the rulers of the Muslim world.

More embarrassing and dangerous still: The Knights were

experienced Ottoman-watchers who grasped the subtleties of the empire's politics. It had been thanks to their intervention that Prince Cem, brother of Bayezid II, had escaped to Christian Europe back in the 1480s. The mere possibility that he might return to the Ottoman Empire with the backing of one or more Christian powers was enough of a threat to prevent Bayezid from launching a campaign against the west.

Suleiman was determined to succeed where his great-grandfather had failed and end this real and potential threat once and for all. After rolling through Belgrade, it was clear to him that no aid would be forthcoming from the west. The Holy Roman Emperor and king of Spain, Charles V, was busy with the Italian Wars. So was Francis I of France, who had promised to aid the Knights but quickly reneged. The pope had no resources to devote to a campaign in the distant east. The Hospitallers were on their own. However, unlike the disorganized Hungarians, who had been drained by decades of misrule and riven by internal conflict, the Hospitallers and their stronghold at Rhodes were a marvel of cutting-edge military fortification, built in various stages over the preceding centuries and updated repeatedly as gunpowder technology and defensive engineering developed in tandem.

When Suleiman arrived on the island on July 28, 1522, to command a force numbering somewhere north of one hundred thousand men, the sultan was immediately confronted by a series of formidable obstacles. Round towers laced with circular gun-ports jutted upward behind polygonal bulwarks; outer defensive towers connected to the towering main wall, which bristled with artillery and was as much as twelve meters thick in some places. Earthen ramparts placed in front of the more vulnerable stone structures soaked up the impact of incoming cannon fire. Angled bastions—yet another low structure projecting outward from the main wall—looked downward onto a wide, stone-faced ditch, which lay behind a second, wider, and still more inconvenient ditch fronted with an earthen bank called a *glacis*. Even if an attacking force managed to weather a hailstorm of cannon, gunfire, and crossbow bolts on their way to these ditches, they would still be staring upward at a series of high stone obstacles manned by experienced professional soldiers. Moreover, the four-kilometer course of the land walls flexed inward, allowing the projecting towers to provide flanking gun and cannon fire to any attackers unfortunate enough to have reached the main fortifications. The Hospitallers had turned their Rhodian fortress into a death trap designed to ensnare its besiegers, layer by layer, and bleed them dry.[10]

None of this was a mystery to Suleiman when he stepped foot on Rhodes's rocky shores, accompanied by tens of thousands of soldiers and laborers and hundreds of ships and cannon. The sultan knew taking Rhodes would require time, resources, and countless lives. The Knights repelled assault after assault, repaired breach after breach in their mine-blasted walls, and weathered ceaseless bombardment from the Ottoman guns. Thousands of the sultan's soldiers fell in fruitless attacks on the walls, each bloodier than the last. One last assault on November 30, carried out amid an apocalyptic rainstorm, left the waterlogged ditch full of dead Ottomans.

The Knights had suffered just as dearly, however, and after a few more inconclusive clashes, they accepted the offer of surrender. As such things went, the terms were generous: Aside from leaving behind a few hostages, the Knights were free to go wherever they pleased. Villiers de l'Isle Adam, grand master of the order, strapped on his armor, picked eighteen of his finest knights, and walked out to meet the sultan. He kissed Suleiman's hand, and the two men exchanged a long and poignant silence.

"I am really distressed to have thrown that man out of his palace," Suleiman later told his grand vizier. For his part, Villiers said of Suleiman, "He was a knight in the truest sense of the word."

On January 1, 1523, the Hospitaller Knights left Rhodes forever. Suleiman had his victory, albeit at a terrible cost. Far more than the easy victory at Belgrade, this siege showed precisely what the Ottomans were capable of. No other state in Europe could have kept that many men, a large supporting fleet, and hundreds of cannon supplied and fighting for more than five months against determined opposition, suffering tens of thousands of casualties in the process. Bankruptcy and disaster surely would have resulted if Charles V or Francis I had tried an equivalent task. But where others would have failed, Suleiman succeeded.

Mohács

While Martin Luther's Reformation continued to tear at the social and religious fabric of Christendom, and its princes and kings drained each other dry in a series of campaigns stretching from Pamplona to Milan to Picardy, Suleiman watched and waited. The costly siege of Rhodes had strained even his vast resources to the breaking point, and it would be some time before he was prepared for another outing. To complicate matters, one of his most trusted servants had launched a rebellion in Egypt, and nearly succeeded in detaching this wealthy, valuable territory before the sultan was able to restore order. Suleiman was forced to lean heavily on his new grand vizier, an enslaved man of Greek extraction named Ibrahim Pasha, who was both immensely talented and the sultan's closest friend. The rise and cataclysmic fall of Ibrahim Pasha makes for a saga in its own right, but at least for now, Suleiman was blessed to have the aid of exceptionally competent subordinates.

For the moment, Suleiman was not planning another campaign to the west. If anything, he had designs toward the east, where Shah Ismail, the founder of the Safavid dynasty of Persia, had died of dissipation and disappointment at the tender age of thirty-seven, leaving behind a ten-year-old son named Tahmasp as his successor. Suleiman sent a threatening letter to the new shah: "I have decided to bear arms to Tabriz and Azerbaijan, and to pitch my tent in Iran and Turan, at Samarkand and in Khorasan. . . . If you want to come and beg a crust of bread at my door for the love of God, I will be happy to oblige and you will lose nothing of your country. . . . I will keep you in my sights and, with the grace of God, seize on you and rid the world of your poisonous existence."[11]

Luckily for Tahmasp and Persia, the crushing French defeat at the Battle of Pavia in February 1525 opened up more promising strategic horizons in the west. The French king, Francis I, was captured in the fighting. His kingdom was in desperate need of allies in its ongoing struggle against Charles V of Spain and the Holy Roman Empire. Who could be a more valuable ally than the supremely powerful ruler of the Ottoman Empire, whose forces could intrude on Charles's vast domains everywhere from Spain to Naples to central Europe? One of the two envoys bearing the message asking for aid was killed in Bosnia, but the other made it to Istanbul, and made quite an impression on the sultan. In return, Suleiman offered the imprisoned Francis hope: "Keep your spirits high, do not be heartbroken," he wrote to the king of France. The Ottomans would make war on Charles V.[12]

The Janissaries needed a war. In the absence of consistent campaigning, they grew restless in their barracks, running amok in Istanbul in March 1525. After executing their *agha* and a few other ringleaders, Suleiman appeased the rest with a large cash gift, which quelled the disturbance for the meantime. That was a short-term solution, however, and Suleiman needed to put them to work on a new project. The project would be the conquest of Hungary, the last thing standing between the Ottomans and the soft underbelly of Charles's lands within the Holy Roman Empire. Beyond Hungary lay Vienna and Austria, the heartland of the Habsburg domains. If he could take Hungary and Austria, Suleiman might extend his rule from the Danube to the Rhine. That would keep the Janissaries busy for a good long while.

Louis II, the king of Hungary, was no better suited to repelling an Ottoman invasion in the spring of 1526 than he had been when Suleiman had marched on Belgrade five years earlier. The young, prematurely gray-haired Louis—he turned twenty years old during the campaigning season of 1526—looked even more pallid and deathly than usual in the hale shadow of his Muslim adversary. Louis appealed for aid to one brother-in-law, Charles V, who could offer none while faced with Francis I and an array of European allies. His other brother-in-law, Ferdinand, Archduke of Austria and brother of Charles V, begged the Diet of the Holy Roman Empire for funds and soldiers. They dithered and sent nothing. The Hungarian nobility, the core of any army with a prayer of turning back an invasion, were not chomping at the bit to face the battle-hardened Ottoman war machine. More worrisome, the Hungarian elite backstabbed and politicked against each other, as they had for generations, making any sort of united front against the advancing Ottomans impossible.[13]

At least some Hungarians were determined to fight. They chose the plain of Mohács as their battleground. It lay directly in the path of the Ottoman advance, a convenient mustering point for the dispersed Hungarians, and good ground for cavalry, which the defenders had in abundance. The Ottoman army arrived there in the evening of August 28, 1526, screened from the Hungarians' view by the marshes and thickets bordering the plain. They had somewhere around fifty thousand capable soldiers, roughly double what the Hungarians could put in the field, and a considerable advantage in artillery and gunpowder handguns. The Hungarians, by contrast, had large numbers of heavily armored men-at-arms, and while these descendants of the medieval knight were far from outmoded, the modern battlefield demanded that they be used in conjunction with professional infantry and artillery. Compared to the Ottomans, the Hungarians were sorely lacking in those departments.

If the Hungarians had sat back behind a defensive line and let the Ottomans throw themselves against a prepared position, their disadvantage in numbers and the composition of their forces might not have been fatal. If they had attacked immediately, as the Ottomans were struggling through the marsh and onto the plain of Mohács, they might have destroyed the invaders piecemeal. Instead, they waited for the Ottomans. A full third of the Ottoman army deployed on the field before the Hungarians made any move to stop them. They picked an opportune moment to attack, though: It was already early afternoon, and the deployed Ottomans had assumed that the Hungarians would sit tight. The Hungarians proved this assumption wrong, hoping to catch this segment of the Ottoman force before the rest could join the fight.

This was a sound enough plan. A wave of armored men on armored horses crashed into the ill-prepared left flank of the Ottoman line, forcing them back in disarray. Unfortunately for the Hungarians, Suleiman had brought up his Janissaries and artillery in support. Coming down a steep slope muddied by days of rain, Suleiman took in the scope of the battlefield. He looked out at his first division of troops, streaming backward, and saw the Hungarian men-at-arms hot on their heels. Hooves thundered against the ground. Screams and cries, the clash of steel on steel, the wet stab of blades into flesh, the occasional crack of an arquebus and roar of a cannon all rent the thick, humid summer air. The Janissaries leveled their handguns at the charging Hungarians, mustached faces obscured by whorls of smoke coming off the lit matches of their arquebuses. Artillerymen dragged their cannon into position, forcing shot and gunpowder down the barrels and aiming at the mass of armored opponents.

Suleiman's world exploded in a rippling wave of white smoke. Heavy arquebus shot punched through steel plate armor. Cannonballs disemboweled horses. Three or four times, the Janissaries reloaded, pouring volley after volley into the mass of men-at-arms milling in front of them. One group of Hungarian knights somehow survived the storm of lead and iron and made directly for Suleiman himself. The sultan could see them approaching, arrows and shot and the blades of swords and pole-arms clanging off their armor as they approached. Razor-sharp lances deflected off Suleiman's breastplate in the desperate, chaotic melee before the sultan's bodyguard succeeded in hamstringing the attackers' horses, dragging their riders to the ground, and finishing them with swords and daggers.

The Hungarian infantry, many of them experienced mercenaries who had clashed with the Ottomans before, advanced in the wake of their cavalry, but could not get through the Ottoman Janissaries and guns. They became trapped in the center of the battlefield, their men-at-arms shattered by gunfire. The Ottomans enveloped the Hungarian infantry on three sides and wiped them out almost to a man. "Shields cracked like the heart of a rose, helmets filled with blood like the lips of a rose-bud. Mists of blood rising like a purple cloud to the horizon were like a rosy sky above the head of victory's betrothed," poeticized Ottoman historian Kemalpaşadze, who was present at the battle.[14]

As night fell, a few pathetic survivors—King Louis among them—retreated toward safety. The twenty-year-old ruler nearly escaped, but his horse tripped and fell crossing a stream or ditch, trapping him underneath. Louis drowned. An independent kingdom of Hungary died with him.

The aftermath of the battle was gruesome. Thousands of corpses littered the plain of Mohács. Two thousand prisoners remained in Ottoman hands. These bedraggled survivors soon met the executioner, their heads destined to end up impaled on pikes or piled in a makeshift pyramid in front of Suleiman's red tent.

After another few days of torrential rain, the army moved on, capturing the Hungarian capital of Buda. Only a small slice of the kingdom remained outside Ottoman control. The sultan's rule now extended from the Nile across the great plain of Hungary, on the very doorstep of Austria and central Europe.

Vienna

Suleiman's next steps proved far more challenging than winning the Battle of Mohács. His ultimate opponent was always Charles V, king of Spain, Holy Roman Emperor, Duke of Burgundy, and effective head of the Habsburg dynasty. Charles's brother, Ferdinand, had been made Archduke of Austria and ruler of Carinthia, Styria, and the Tyrol, the territories bordering the now-overrun Hungary. For his part, Ferdinand was determined to add a couple of vacant thrones to his existing territories. With the death of his brother-in-law Louis II, the opportunity was open. The Diet of Bohemia elected Ferdinand king, so one of Louis's two thrones passed to the Habsburg; the Hungarians were a bit more recalcitrant, many of them preferring the Transylvanian magnate John Zápolya rather than a foreign prince.

That did not stop Ferdinand from pressing his claim, leading an army of professional German mercenaries into Hungary and occupying part of the kingdom. Zápolya went looking for help. He found it in the form of Suleiman, who much preferred a weakened Hungarian magnate on his borders over a grasping and ambitious Habsburg. For reasons of imperial prestige and great-power politics, Suleiman had always known a clash with the Habsburgs was coming. Now it was on the cusp of becoming a reality.

For several years after Mohács, Suleiman stayed on the sidelines while Ferdinand and Zápolya fought it out for themselves. He had a series of rebellions in Anatolia to deal with, and the campaigns of his early reign had drained him of money and manpower. Moreover, a campaign into the heart of central Europe, to the gates of Vienna itself, represented a logistical challenge that would stretch even the Ottomans to the breaking point.

Any force capable of taking a well-fortified city like Vienna would have to be large, larger even than the force Suleiman had led into Hungary in 1526. In addition to manpower and equipment, sieges required enormous stockpiles of gunpowder for cannon, arquebuses, and mines; iron and stone shot for the artillery; rations for soldiers and laborers; and fodder for thousands of horses and other beasts of burden. All of that would have to be transported more than a thousand miles from Istanbul across difficult terrain, including mountains and several major rivers. Some of the necessary supplies could be sourced from Ottoman territories closer to Vienna—Serbia, Bosnia, and occupied parts of Hungary—but coordinating the necessary amounts and delivery would still be a challenge. As if all that were not difficult enough, time was a fickle factor. Staying through the winter was out of the question, so the available window of operations was impossibly narrow. Leave too early in the year, and supplies and manpower would not be ready to deploy. Leave too late, and there would not be enough time to mount a proper siege of Vienna.

Suleiman and his massive force set out from Istanbul on May 10, 1529: thousands of Janissaries, rank after rank of *sipahis* from the provinces, hundreds of cannon, and uncountable masses of *akinci* raiders and auxiliaries. Almost immediately, however, the vagaries of weather slowed the sultan's forces in a way no enemy possibly could: Rains pounded the army's path, washing away bridges, flooding encampments, and turning the roads into churning muck. It took two full months to reach Belgrade, a month longer than expected. Suleiman did not reach Vienna until September 27. Bogged down by the incessant downpour, the big siege guns were even further behind schedule.

Even under perfect conditions, Vienna presented an imposing obstacle. With plenty of advance notice, the Austrians had reinforced the city's medieval walls to better resist bombardment. They had also cleared out and deepened the defensive ditch. To provide clear fields of fire for the seventy-two available cannon and thousands of hand gunners, the defenders had demolished hundreds of houses outside the city walls. Experienced German mercenaries and battle-hardened Spanish arquebusiers fresh from the blood-soaked battlefields of Italy rounded out the garrison, along with thousands of local levies. Ferdinand appointed an aged but accomplished soldier to lead the defense. Count Nicholas von Salm had more than five decades' experience on battlefields ranging from Flanders to Switzerland to Lombardy, and he knew his business well.

Suleiman watched the proceedings from his extravagant red tent, pitched on a hillside some three or four miles outside Vienna. With the big guns left behind, the sultan's miners tunneled underneath the walls to create a breach, but only succeeded in creating small openings. The light cannon could not break through the reinforced defenses. Continual rain lashed the Ottoman camp. Unseasonable frosts froze them at night. Every assault failed, leaving behind increasing casualties. The defenders held strong, and Ottoman morale plunged past the point of no return. One final assault, offering a king's ransom in gold as incentive for the first man over the battlements, failed with even heavier losses. The corpses of Janissaries from Albania and Greece, *sipahis* from the rolling hills of Anatolia, and Bosnian *akincis* littered the ground before Vienna's walls, their forces having made little impression on the defenders.

Finally, Suleiman ordered the retreat. He had no real choice. It was the middle of October. The weather was bad and getting worse. The Janissaries were near mutiny, but even they were in a better mood than the rest of the army. As the Ottomans burned their camp and set off for home, Suleiman and Ibrahim Pasha claimed victory, but there was no real doubt about the outcome. The Ottomans had reached their high tide.[15]

The Ottoman Way

On one hand, the siege of Vienna was the apogee of the Ottoman Empire. While Ottoman raiders continued to carry off captives, burn villages, and cause mayhem from northern Italy to Bohemia, the failure at Vienna blunted the threat of outright conquest. Suleiman's second attempt on Vienna, in 1532, was so slowed by a siege of a Hungarian fortress that he never even reached the city.

On the other hand, the setback in 1529 turned Ottoman attention in other, far more viable (and far more worrisome) directions. Ottoman involvement in the politics of Christendom deepened, culminating in an alliance with France against Charles V and his brother, Ferdinand. The Mediterranean became the arena for a decades-long struggle pitting Suleiman and his successors against the might of Spain and its allies. The alliance with Hayreddin Barbarossa and the corsairs of North Africa turned the shores of

Italy and Spain into a war zone. Opportunities in the Muslim world also beckoned. A series of campaigns against the Safavids added Baghdad, lower Mesopotamia, the mouths of the Tigris and the Euphrates Rivers, and the coast of the Persian Gulf to the sultan's domains. As their interests in this direction grew stronger, Ottoman naval forces appeared in the Indian Ocean, where the new arrivals clashed with the Portuguese for control of trade in the vast and lucrative sea. No less than the Europeans, the Ottomans were participants in the Age of Exploration, newcomers to a world that extended beyond their corner of Eurasia.[16]

Suleiman's empire was not invincible in the face of its contemporaries. The sultan did not make a run at global conquest in the tradition of Genghis Khan or Tamerlane before him. His Ottoman state, however, was the most powerful of its day by a substantial margin. Suleiman humiliated the Habsburgs—the only other real contender in terms of competition—during their second real conflict, between 1542 and 1544, at the very edges of Ottoman operational range against an opponent fighting much closer to home.

None of this was an accident, or the product of pure contingency; instead, Ottoman superiority in this age grew out of firm institutional and structural foundations laid down by generations of dedicated rulers and their skilled, talented subordinates. The Ottoman process of state-building grew out of much different antecedents, and took vastly different forms, than that of its Christian competitors. It was not, however, a fundamentally different process; the goal was to put more central power in the hands of the ruler, who wielded it in the form of revenue collection, bureaucratic muscle, and military capacity. Yet as potent as the Ottomans were in Suleiman's day (and they remained a superpower until the eighteenth century), their future weaknesses grew out of their very effectiveness in this period. Suleiman's reign was simultaneously a golden age and a time of transition, after which the structural differences between the Ottomans and their rivals looked less flattering for the sultan's successors.

At heart, the Ottoman Empire Suleiman inherited revolved around conquest and territorial acquisition. "War made the state, and the state made war," as Charles Tilly famously remarked about the states of western Europe, but that was no less true of the Ottomans. If anything, the connection was more direct. The fruits of conquest in plunder and enslaved people financed both the state apparatus and future war-making. New territorial acquisitions produced more *sipahis*, the cavalry backbone of the Ottoman army, each of whom received a *timar* landholding from the state to support them. Unlike fiefs in western Europe, a *timar* was not hereditary, but reverted to the state at its owner's death. Newly conquered Christians were subject to the *devşirme*, the human levy that provided talented recruits for the Janissaries and the sultan's household. Any land under Ottoman control could be tapped for military recruits, grain, livestock, timber, metal, or whatever else was deemed necessary for a single campaign or extended conflict. An Ottoman army on the move did not loot its own subjects, generally, relying instead on complex logistical arrangements. Suleiman noted in his diary on multiple occasions the beheading of a Janissary for this particular crime.

In short, successful conquests produced the means of more effective, larger-scale war-making for the Ottomans: more soldiers, more resources, and greater state capacity. They also produced profit for the state. The Ottoman tax system, far from being despotic or ramshackle, was efficient, effective, and generally well administered by bureaucratic professionals. Local officials produced regularly updated tax registers for their areas. Non-Muslim subjects had to pay the *jizya*, the poll tax, which was the single largest source of revenue for the state. All peasants were subject to some kind of taxation, usually to local *timar*-holders. In other regions, consortia of wealthy merchants pooled capital to buy the rights to taxation of particular areas or special products, providing ready cash to the state and then further outsourcing collection to local specialists. State bureaucrats kept a close handle on these tax farmers (*mukataat*), regularly punishing any overreach, updating their information on amounts owed, and renewing the contracts every few years to prevent financial stagnation. Mining and specialized resources, namely salt, provided another major chunk of revenue. All of this amounted to huge sums of ready cash for the sultan, which could then be put toward further conquest.

Unlike his perpetually penniless Christian rivals, Suleiman routinely enjoyed budget surpluses, as huge amounts of tax, tribute, and plunder flowed into the state's coffers. In 1527–28, for example, the treasury practically overflowed: The year's surplus amounted to 1,027,016,000 akça, roughly 2.35 million ducats. That was more than four times what Jakob Fugger loaned Charles V to pay for his election as Holy Roman Emperor, and Charles mortgaged years of future income to pay for it. That was an extraordinary year, but smaller surpluses were common, and one year of deficit rarely followed another. Beyond these ordinary sources of revenue, major military campaigns—such as those against Rhodes or Vienna—justified extraordinary taxes, further enriching the sultan.[17]

Even beyond the raw amounts of money involved, a high level of organization characterized the Ottoman tax system. Soldiers received their wages on time, with enough left over for bonuses and additional payments. When the Janissaries made trouble in 1525, Suleiman had their ringleaders executed, but also paid out 200,000 ducats—more than 10 million akça—as a bribe. At the siege of Vienna in 1529, Suleiman could offer a bonus of 1,000 akça per man as an inducement for a dangerous assault. That bonus, a relative pittance for Suleiman to offer in the hope of a swift victory, amounted to eight months' wages for one of Vienna's defenders. By contrast, the wages of *Landsknechte*, Swiss pikemen, and Spanish arquebusiers were constantly in arrears, precisely the situation that led to the Sack of Rome in 1527.

To prevent the unnecessary flow of coin out of local or regional circulation, officials coordinated tax receipts and revenues at multiple levels. Financial information flowed to the central bureaucracy and kept the sultan's key officials up to date on what was available and possible, but cash did not have to. A judge in a provincial village or town could order the repair of a bridge or the collection of supplies for an upcoming military campaign and draw on locally available funds. The official then relayed a notice of those funds' use to the central treasury in the interests of good accounting. The impressive budget figures and surpluses cited above did not even include these locally held revenues or the taxes distributed to *sipahis* through the *timar* system.

The resources available to the Ottoman state were staggering. Suleiman brought fifty thousand soldiers to Mohács, six hundred hard miles from his capital. The Hungarian army he faced was not small by the standards of the day; it was roughly the size of the contingent Francis I had brought to Pavia the year before. Suleiman's fifty thousand at Mohács was a force of great size and quality, and it was certainly smaller than what he had taken to Rhodes in 1522.

Beyond mere manpower, the sultan and his servants had a better grasp of precisely what those resources were, where they could be deployed, and how effectively, more than any other ruler of the age. The sultan did not have to rely on independent contractors of mercenaries or military suppliers of questionable quality; if he wanted artillery for a campaign, he could turn to the Istanbul Imperial Foundry. Between 1517 and 1519, for example, the foundry produced a total of 673 cannon and mortars, many of them among the largest guns in existence. State officials kept a close watch on the production of saltpeter, the key ingredient in gunpowder. While entrepreneurs did play a key role in Ottoman military supply, particularly as the sixteenth century wore on, the practice of war never became as privatized or expensive as it did farther west. There was no Ottoman equivalent to Götz von Berlichingen or Georg von Frundsberg. In an age where war was growing more expensive to wage and its scale ballooned beyond recognition, the Ottomans could spend more money, tap greater resources of materiel and manpower, and project power at greater distances than their rivals. None of this was perfect. The system required large numbers of administrators, local exactions could produce discontent among peasants or even relatively privileged *timar*-holders, and the Janissaries could be rapacious in their demands for gifts and bribes. Yet any Christian ruler of the age would have given an eye for a fiscal system half this efficient or lucrative. As Martin Luther disapprovingly noted in his *Address to the Christian Nobility of the German Nation*, he had even heard from Christians that "there is no better temporal rule than under the Turks."[18]

In the long run, however, the fact that the Christian rulers of western Europe had to scrape the bottom of the barrel for available funds gave them—and perhaps more importantly, their bankers—an increasingly sophisticated set of financial tools with which to operate. By virtue of their sheer wealth and power, and their tendency to run surpluses, the Ottomans did not have to develop a permanent, interest-bearing state debt of the kind that revolutionized state finance in western Europe. Loans from merchants and other wealthy creditors were a short-term affair to cover immediate costs, not the basis of a long-term, interdependent, and ultimately productive relationship between financiers and the state apparatus.

While the Ottomans did not have the rapacious, freewheeling military entrepreneurs of the type that characterized the Holy Roman Empire, they also lacked figures like Jakob Fugger and the Genoese moneymen who bankrolled the expansive ambitions of Spanish monarchs in the later sixteenth century. Debt, crushing interest payments, and bankruptcy were the eventual results of western Europe's barrel-scraping approach—fight the wars and let the financial chips fall where they may—but they laid essential groundwork. Increased reliance on tax farming and temporary, inefficient, high-interest loans from powerful court officials, the stopgap measures the Ottomans eventually adopted, were nowhere as viable in the long run. Eventually, these financial mechanisms allowed the states of Christian western Europe to invest in ever more expensive military technology, fight longer wars at greater distances from home, and surpass the mighty Ottomans.

No farsighted visionary saw this future on the horizon. Distance from core territories, far more than fiscal shortcomings, proved to be the limiting factor on Ottoman ambitions during Suleiman's reign and those of his successors. The failure to take Malta in 1565, the crushing naval defeat at Lepanto in 1571, even the stalemate against the Habsburgs in the Long War of 1593–1606: None of them marked the end of the line. What was clear, however—even by the end of Suleiman's reign in 1566—was that the Ottomans were no longer a conquest state. They could no longer depend on windfall revenues from territorial acquisitions. The wars would get longer, harder, and less lucrative, even if Ottoman performance in them did not actually suffer much. Yet under those circumstances, barring major and ongoing reforms, it was only a matter of time before the cracks in the Ottoman fiscal system began to show.

Suleiman's long reign marked the key process of transition.

The empire's last major territorial acquisitions came with his conquests of Hungary and Mesopotamia. He led his soldiers into battle on multiple occasions, embodying the personal leadership that had defined the Ottoman dynasty for centuries, but sultans after him rarely did so. The tremendous competence—born out of cutthroat competition for the throne—that had defined Ottoman rulers from Osman to Selim essentially disappeared after Suleiman; in fact, he had executed his most promising son, Mustafa, in 1553. Another son, Bayezid, fell victim after a failed rebellion in 1561. Selim II, Suleiman's last surviving son, was an even less impressive specimen. His successors were worse still.[19]

On the other hand, they did not have to be personally impressive. The Ottoman Empire had become an established, bureaucratic state staffed by career officials. The sultan did not have to be seen personally on campaign to get his soldiers to the battlefield or to actively direct policy. He had viziers, advisors, and other powerful officials for that. The Ottomans remained a first-rate power, but slowly and surely, the weaknesses laid down at the moments of greatest strength became fully manifest. In strength and weakness, the Ottomans always remained a fundamental part of Europe, no less than the Habsburgs of Spain and Germany or any other European dynasty of the time.

CHAPTER 9

———— ◦◦◦ ————

Charles V and Universal Rule

September 20, 1517

A stiff breeze stirred the deep blue waters, raising whitecaps that swelled as the waves neared the narrow beach and rocky shore. The air was punctuated by fat droplets of rain, driven nearly horizontal by the wind.

Several small boats struggled through the pitching surf. Craggy cliffs and tree-covered hills rose ahead of them, looming through the downpour and flanking the tiny river that emptied into an equally diminutive harbor. The cove was too small to offer much protection to the fleet of ships anchored behind the advance guard, brown masts barely visible through the mist.

A young man swathed in a heavy cloak, a fashionable wide-brimmed hat tilted rakishly to the side, sat in the lead boat. His name was Charles, an appellation passed down from a famously rash and brave grandfather. Absent a beard to hide it, the young man's prominent jaw jutted forward, leaving his mouth hanging slightly open as he breathed in the salt spray of the ocean. Straight hair, brownish blond, hung down toward his neck. He said nothing as the boat approached the river. He rarely did. Speaking was something of a chore for Charles, the result of an awkward tongue and his nearly deformed jaw, so he preferred to let others speak for him. Men in his position, even those barely on the cusp of adulthood, had that luxury.

So, this is Spain, Charles thought, pulling his hat down to protect against the driving rain. It was much different than the land in which he had grown up. The prominent hills and jagged rocks of the Asturian coast stood in stark contrast to the long, flat beaches and sprawling floodplains of the Low Countries. Come to think of it, Charles realized, he knew very little about Spain. This was his first visit, and it was not an auspicious view. This little cove, shrouded in low-lying clouds and obscured by rain, had not been his intended destination; the weather had unexpectedly driven them down the coast to this impoverished harbor. It was hardly a fitting place for the new king of Spain to arrive in his kingdom, especially a foreign one who had hoped to make a favorable impression on his subjects.

Charles was thankful to be in sight of land. Contrary winds had plagued the ten-day trip south from Zeeland. He coughed and felt a sneeze coming on. His constitution had never been especially strong despite a regular regimen of hunting and riding, and his friends and advisors regularly worried about his health. If Charles died, things would get complicated. All the many dynastic lines he embodied would come to an end. That was not a passing concern for this rather unremarkable seventeen-year-old; it was a fundamental question for the political future of the entire European continent.[1]

This new king of Spain was the grandson of Isabella of Castile and Ferdinand of Aragon, and the Holy Roman Emperor Maximilian and Mary of Burgundy. All of their vast lands—Granada and Asturias, Sicily and Naples, Flanders and Holland,

Austria and Tyrol—would belong to him. In a few short years, Jakob Fugger's money would buy him the throne of the Holy Roman Empire. The brutal, world-shaking subjugations of the New World empires, the Aztecs and the Inca, occurred under his oversight, and the material rewards of these genocidal conquests enriched his treasury. The not-so-humble Wittenberg professor and monk, Martin Luther, grew to incendiary fame in territories subject to the youthful emperor. His influence spread despite Charles's repeated efforts to stop it. Götz von Berlichingen took Charles's coin, and in return fought in his armies. Charles and his underlings faced off against Suleiman the Magnificent everywhere from the gates of Vienna to the sands of North Africa.

State-building and dynastic consolidation, the expansion of global empire, and the pervasive influence of financiers: These were the essential trends of the era, and Charles embodied them all. His actions—and perhaps more important, his inactions—fanned the flames of the Reformation and transformed Martin Luther into a living martyr for the cause. Charles's emergence as the most powerful Christian ruler of the age was both inevitable and incredibly contingent, the result of decades of deep structural transformations and complete accidents of birth, death, legal minutiae, and mental illness. The emperor himself was both the spider at the center of the web of causality and the victim hopelessly entrapped within it. He was capable of everything and nothing, simultaneously all-powerful and completely impotent amid the unstoppable wave of ongoing events.

In this sense, Charles personifies the Europe of this period. He was a Burgundian prince, a Spanish king, and a Holy Roman Emperor, bringing together a vast continent solely through his claims and bloodlines. He was the end of something and the beginning of another, both outcome and progenitor.

A Rather Unremarkable Young Man

By the time the twenty-one-year-old Charles faced down Martin Luther at the Diet of Worms in 1521, he was Duke of Burgundy, Brabant, Lothier, Limburg, and Luxemburg; Margrave of Namur; Count Palatine of Burgundy; Count of Artois, Charolais, Flanders, Hainaut, Holland, Zeeland, and Barcelona; king of Castile, Aragon, Sicily, and Naples; Holy Roman Emperor; and king of the Romans. He had recently handed over the title of Archduke of Austria, which had belonged to his grandfather Maximilian and a long line of Habsburg dynasts, to his younger brother Ferdinand. He owed this impressive bounty to the accidents and structural momentum of succession.

The combination of those titles, and the rights to land, revenues, and allegiance that went with them, made Charles the most powerful European ruler in centuries, if not ever. Aside from France, a few chunks of Italy, the British Isles, and Scandinavia, practically all of central and western Europe acknowledged him as its ultimate ruler.

How did a single person manage to accumulate so many titles, so many claims to rights, stretching from the great plains of the Danube to the rocky shores of the Strait of Gibraltar? The answer grew out of centuries of accumulation in two principal dynastic lines, the Habsburg and Trastámara, beginning in Austria and Spain, respectively.

Late medieval Europe was full of aggressively acquisitive noble families. All of them, from the lowliest country gentry in the English Midlands up to the jewel-bedecked rulers of France, fought over, bought, and especially married into new lands and titles as much as they could. Competing claims to these lands and titles caused wars on every scale from local feuds involving a few dozen combatants to international conflicts that called on tens of thousands of soldiers. Those lucky enough to have liquid funds, either for outright purchase from its current ruler or to bribe a representative body into recognizing a claim, could simply buy a new territory or title. A single marriage could tip the balance of power in a county, a kingdom, or the continent as a whole, depending on what claims came with the inheritance. This was both a deadly serious undertaking for nobles and effectively the way they amused and occupied themselves.

None of these families were more successful than the Habsburgs and the Trastámaras. The Habsburgs began with a single castle in what is now the Aargau of Switzerland. They then acquired the Duchy of Austria and never looked back. By the thirteenth century, members of the dynasty had been elected as Holy Roman Emperor. After 1438, Habsburgs held the imperial title continuously. Charles's grandfather Maximilian made the greatest leaps of all. In addition to his hereditary possessions, he acquired his cousin Sigismund's land in Tyrol, with its rich silver mines. More important, he married the heiress of Burgundy, Mary, the sole daughter and descendant of Duke Charles the Bold, inheritor of all the dead duke's scattered lands and claims around the fringes of France. At the death of his father, Frederick, in 1493, Maximilian was elected Holy Roman Emperor as well. It was a foregone conclusion.[2]

No slouches in their own right, the Trastámaras had acquired both of the major kingdoms of Spain, Castile and Aragon, along with a variety of claims elsewhere. The most notable of these were Sicily and Naples. Through the marriage of Isabella and Ferdinand, themselves cousins, these claims all came to be united in their eldest surviving child, Juana. After much clever maneuvering and sharp calculation, Juana married Philip the Handsome, the son of Maximilian and the now-deceased Mary of Burgundy, and perhaps the only Habsburg blessed with good looks.

Philip and Juana had a tumultuous and abusive relationship. Philip enjoyed numerous extramarital affairs, which deeply distressed Juana. Whether she was simply high-strung or suffered from some more or less severe mental illness is an open and much-debated question, with suppositions ranging from severe depression to schizophrenia; regardless, what is certain is that first her husband, and then after his death her ruthless, power-hungry father, Ferdinand, wanted her to be seen as too disturbed to rule in her own right. They benefited politically from this perception, as it meant that Philip and later Ferdinand could exploit her titles and rights without her—or anyone else's—interference.[3]

Charles was born in 1500, the eldest son of the union of Philip and Juana, and was immediately immersed in this profoundly dysfunctional mixture of personal relationships and dynastic power politics. He was raised almost entirely in the Burgundian Netherlands, and his parents figured only a little in his upbringing. Philip and Juana departed for Spain in 1506 to take the throne of Castile, left vacant by the death of Queen Isabella, where Philip died shortly thereafter. Juana, left bereft both emotionally and politically by her husband's death, did not see her eldest son again for more than a decade. Her father, Ferdinand, was unwilling to give up the rule of Castile, which he had held since his wife's death in 1504. The only way to guarantee that he had the continued use of Castile's resources to support his ambitions in Naples and Sicily was to declare his daughter unfit to exercise the power of her office as queen. He ordered Juana to be locked away in a monastery. She barely had any contact with the outside world, much less her young son, eight hundred miles away in Flanders.[4]

Despite remarrying after Isabella's death, Ferdinand had no more children who might inherit Aragon, Sicily, and Naples. Those crowns would instead pass to the young Charles, his eldest grandson, at his death. So would the throne of Castile, which Ferdinand was effectively exercising in trust for his imprisoned daughter. And as Charles was the eldest son of Philip the Handsome, all of the Burgundian lands—Holland, Brabant, Flanders, Hainaut, and the rest—had already come into his possession. The titles that would have passed to Philip on the death of his father, Maximilian, namely the Archduchy of Austria and the best chance at election as Holy Roman Emperor, would instead go to Maximilian's eldest grandson. That was, once again, Charles.

It had taken centuries of accumulation by two of Europe's most acquisitive dynasties to put a young boy in this position: decade after decade of war, purchase, and advantageous marriage. Powerful dynasties tended to become more powerful in the later Middle Ages, consolidating separate territories that had previously belonged to an array of different rulers. That was partially structural, the result of the centralizing forces that dominated the age and shifts in military and political technology. Yet the confluence of all these lines of inheritance in the person of Charles had also required a series of unforeseeable occurrences: Charles the Bold dying on a battlefield in 1477, the untimely death of Mary of Burgundy five years later after a riding accident, the sickliness and early demise of Isabella and Ferdinand's only son, Philip the Handsome's shockingly short reign as king of Castile, and the incapacitation of Queen Juana.

Charles himself, of course, had done nothing to earn the enormous resources and responsibilities that fell into his hands, aside from the accident of his birth. "Few," writes Charles's most recent and accomplished biographer, Geoffrey Parker, "found much of note to report about young Charles."[5]

This was not an especially auspicious start for a would-be global ruler.

Coming to Spain

As a young man, Charles did not show many signs of independence, or indeed much at all that any commentator thought was worth mentioning. Silence in public, whether at a meal or a formal audience, was his defining characteristic. It was difficult for observers to tell whether he was a bit slow or simply deeply reserved. A few snippets of personality emerge, but they do not give us much real insight. At age twelve, Charles told off a servant for trying to maneuver the young master into dismissing a rival. He did not care for swearing in his presence and always told the truth. Flattery and tale-telling did not appeal to him.

These were stock descriptions. Both of his grandfathers had ridden through danger to claim their brides like the teenaged heroes of chivalric romance, Maximilian to seize the moment with the heiress Mary of Burgundy in 1477, and Ferdinand with Isabella in 1469. Charles never did anything of the sort.

On the whole, he relied heavily—too heavily, some said—on a succession of advisors, including William de Croÿ, Lord of Chièvres, and Adrian of Utrecht, the future Pope Adrian VI. The only incident that gives a hint of his future intentions came when he used his dagger to carve the words *Plus oultre*, "still further," into the windowsill of his chambers in Brussels. Translated into Latin as *Plus Ultra*, it became his motto for the next four decades. The young man almost certainly picked up the phrase from a heroic romance about the Trojan War that had been read aloud to him.[6]

When he stepped off the ship onto the shores of his new kingdom of Spain in 1517, still mostly silent in the face of his subjects, Charles was not an especially striking youth. He was of medium height and fit, the product of endless rounds of hunting and riding, activities in which he delighted. His face, however, was not what anyone would call handsome. That prominent jaw jutted outward, leaving his mouth slightly agape below a sizable and sharp nose. No portraitist, no matter how skilled or inclined toward generosity for his patrons, could do much about any of that. Still, it does not seem to have diminished his popularity with the opposite sex; Charles was a prolific womanizer throughout his life, and like most high-ranking male nobles of the age, got an early start. His conquests included various ladies-in-waiting, noblewomen, burghers' wives and daughters, and household servants, leading to at least four illegitimate offspring. He also had a vigorous relationship with his wife, his first cousin Isabella of Portugal, that produced seven children, three of whom survived to adulthood.[7]

If he was not physically commanding, he was even less mentally striking. "He spoke little and was not a man of much intelligence," a Venetian diplomat commented at the time. An Englishman was even less charitable: "The king of Castell [Castile] is but an idiote." Charles was well educated by the noble standards of the day, if not an especially diligent or interested student, but he spoke no Castilian or Aragonese. His Latin was not particularly accomplished, despite years of instruction. French was his native tongue and the language in which he was most comfortable.[8]

He had never been to Spain and had no direct personal or political relationships with the key power brokers and nobility of his new kingdoms. His advisors and associates, for their part, were all from northern Europe, mostly French speakers or Flemings, with a few Dutch and Germans sprinkled throughout.

This was not especially promising. His new subjects had no idea what to expect from him, and the same was true for the reverse. In short, Charles arrived to places where he had much dynastic but little personal connection, in which his right to rule was unquestioned but his experience of governance null. This was the logical conclusion of centuries of political marriages and borderline incestuous noble interbreeding. It was not the first time that a ruler had arrived in a new land, but the sheer extent of Charles's lack of familiarity with his large, powerful, and internally complex kingdoms was unprecedented. This lack of familiarity created an escalating series of challenges that would have been difficult to manage even under the best of circumstances.

The mismanagement of his vast and recently acquired lands began even before Charles left his home in the Burgundian Netherlands. Despite the fact that his mother was still alive, Charles had immediately claimed the title of king at his grandfather Ferdinand's death, which upset the Royal Council in Aragon. "In our opinion Your Highness should not take this step," they wrote to him in February 1516. "It is not in accordance with divine or secular law. Your Highness is in peaceful possession of this kingdom; no one denies that it is yours to govern henceforth as you please and give orders high and low, so that there is no need to use the title of King in the lifetime of our lady, the Queen." This statement may have been unrealistic—Juana might live a long time, and a prince was not a king—but Charles and his advisors should have taken note of the reserve and resentment it expressed.

They did not. Moreover, rather than immediately setting out to take charge, the young king and his advisors sat tight in Brussels, where they received reports that the kingdom, from Granada to Naples, was well. This was not entirely misguided: Cardinal Jiménez de Cisneros, the powerful regent in Castile and longserving councilor to Isabella and Ferdinand, seemed to have things well in hand, and the viceroy of Naples put down a minor rebellion when news of Ferdinand's death arrived. Without ever setting foot in Spain, Charles felt confident enough to order an expedition against the port of Algiers in North Africa. He and his advisors, principally the Lord of Chièvres, were more concerned about the emboldened new king of France, Francis I, and the threat he posed to the Netherlands, than to what was happening a thousand miles away.[9]

It did not take long for things to fall apart. The attempted conquest of Algiers was a disaster. Cisneros did not, in fact, have total control of the situation in Castile; his imperiousness, greed, and lack of a clear mandate upset the powerful grandees. Some of them even traveled to Brussels to make their dissatisfaction clear to their new king. Unless he came to Spain by October 1517, Charles was told, the Cortes would convene without him. That could lead to a rebellion or worse.

That was how Charles ended up on the shores of northern Spain on September 20, 1517, far from his destination or anything resembling what he considered civilization. The journey from the tiny port of Villaviciosa to Tordesillas, where his long-absent mother was imprisoned, took months. Charles himself grew ill on the journey, and the attempts to treat him with powdered unicorn horn and a variety of other drugs were not successful. The accommodations and provisions were atrocious compared to the luxury of the Burgundian court in which he had grown up. The trip to Tordesillas meant that he did not immediately go to Valladolid, where the Cortes were assembled, so he kept the most powerful men in Spain waiting for his coronation and introduction. None of this immediately endeared Spain to Charles, or him to Spain.[10]

Cisneros died in early November 1517, shortly after Charles landed and traveled to Tordesillas. Whatever his shortcomings, Cisneros had been an institution in Spanish politics, a veteran of decades of administration and executive decision making, and a living link to the successful reigns of Charles's grandparents. The cardinal had also been archbishop of Toledo, the most important and lucrative diocese in Spain. With his death, the bishopric was vacant. Losing Cisneros was bad enough; nominating a disastrously inexperienced nineteen-year-old foreigner, the nephew of the Lord of Chièvres, to the 80,000-ducat-per-year post made matters far worse. This was a clear contravention of Isabella's will, which stipulated that no foreigners should be granted ecclesiastical offices. Charles had already violated this on a small scale, but Toledo was a much bigger affair. Just as important, one of the most powerful people in Spain—Alfonso de Aragón, illegitimate son of Ferdinand, archbishop of Zaragoza, and regent in Aragon since his father's death—wanted Toledo. Not only did Charles not give it to Alfonso, but he told his uncle not to bother coming to see him, which everyone agreed was rude and discourteous.[11]

This was all minor compared to how Charles treated his fourteen-year-old brother, Ferdinand. While Charles had been raised in Flanders, a Burgundian prince in every way, Ferdinand had spent his entire life in Spain. He had been named after his Machiavellian (literally—Machiavelli admired him greatly) grandfather Ferdinand and even shared a birthday with him. He was every bit as Spanish a prince as his brother Charles was Burgundian. The complex negotiations between Charles's representative Adrian of Utrecht and Ferdinand of Aragón that preceded the old king's death had made provisions for the young Ferdinand, his grandfather's favorite and protégé, but Charles disregarded them. On their way to Zaragoza, where he had promised to set up Ferdinand with his own court, the young king instead sent Ferdinand away to the Netherlands, a place Ferdinand had never seen. And in the process, Charles separated his brother from all his childhood companions. Aragon was proving difficult to manage, and there were hints that powerful Aragonese interests might try to raise Ferdinand as an alternative to Charles. The new king refused to take that risk, at the cost of his brother's comfort and general well-being.

If perhaps politically necessary, it was certainly heartless. Ferdinand, however, fared far better than Juana, whom Charles insisted on keeping imprisoned in an ever more elaborate fantasy world from which the queen could not escape. She was not told of her father Ferdinand's death, nor of anything important happening in the outside world. This was assuredly unnecessary—nobody was yet clamoring for Juana's return to an active life—and cruel in the extreme.

That was how the young Charles began his reign in Spain: by removing a prince with whom his new subjects were already familiar, isolating his mother, insulting his uncle the regent of Aragon, and filling his court with foreign advisors who despised the Spanish. If there were countervailing points, like the rapidity with which Charles learned Castilian and his increasing ability to speak on his own behalf in public, they paled in comparison to the missteps. He progressed slowly through his new kingdoms, meeting key people, wheedling grants of taxation from the representative bodies (Cortes of Castile, Corts of Aragon and Catalonia) and making promises in return. Whether any ruler could have successfully managed the forces bubbling under the surface in Spain, which had already dealt with more than a decade of conflict regarding precisely who was in charge, is questionable. Charles certainly could not, and within just a few years, a serious and open rebellion would break out. The Comuneros would soon threaten Charles's most important possessions in ways he could not have imagined before traveling to his new kingdoms.

Buying a Throne

Before the Comuneros set fire to Spain, other matters occupied the teenaged king. In late January 1519, a year and a half into his progress through his new kingdoms, Charles received word that his grandfather Maximilian had died.

This was a personal tragedy. Aside from his twice-widowed and exceptionally competent aunt Margaret, who acted as regent in the Burgundian lands and effectively raised the young prince, Maximilian had been the most important influence on Charles's life. The old emperor was a braggart. He was full of grand ambitions that far outstretched his ability to carry them out. Despite his occasional moments of inspired brilliance, he was often a fool, a fact well known to his contemporaries, his father, Frederick III, and his daughter Margaret. Maximilian had failed; he said as much himself. "You see that I have expended my blood, my money and my youth for the Empire, and got nothing for it," he told Frederick, Count Palatine, in 1513, his first attempt to secure the throne for his grandson. Charles was Maximilian's heir, his protégé, and the person in whom he had invested all his towering hopes for the future of his dynasty. With the resources of Spain and Burgundy at his disposal, Charles could succeed where Maximilian had fallen short. All the old fool's chivalric dreams, his relentless plotting and scheming, his backstabbing and often-failed maneuvering came to fruition in the figure of his eldest grandson.[12]

Maximilian's death was more than a personal blow to an eighteen-year-old who had lost one of the few adult figures in his life; it was also a political crisis of the highest order. The aggressive young king of France, Francis I, had covered himself in glory in his few brief years as ruler. He personally crushed a powerful Swiss army at Marignano, in northern Italy, in 1515. The battlefield victory ended that eight-year bout of the Italian Wars on terms favorable to France. His reputation burnished by his early accomplishments, Francis made it clear that he was more than willing to pay for the throne of the Holy Roman Empire as well.

The electors, no fools in their own right, were just as willing to listen to his proposition. If nothing else, they could leverage Francis's interest—and the somewhat less serious bid of King Henry VIII of England—into a bidding war for their votes.

Despite the fact that he could not speak a word of any German dialect—he was no more German than Francis or Henry, and had never set foot in the empire's vast German lands—Charles could not afford to allow his grandfather's throne to pass into the hands of his greatest rival. Francis had designs on Charles's interests in Italy, in both Milan and Naples. More seriously, at least from Charles's perspective, Francis would always be a threat to his possessions in the Burgundian Netherlands. The thought of Francis leading an army north into Artois, Flanders, and Brabant, like generations of French kings before him, was enough to inspire a visceral reaction in the young ruler. Charles had been raised there—he still thought (and would always think) of himself as a Burgundian prince, and those territories were always foremost in his mind.

Maximilian had been planning for this eventuality for years prior to his death. As his last campaigns in Italy turned into bitter farce and his health failed, he redoubled his efforts, pouring his last energies into securing the election for his grandson.

Seven electors chose the Holy Roman Emperor: the archbishops of Mainz, Cologne, and Trier; the king of Bohemia; the Margrave of Brandenburg; and the electors of the Palatinate, a haphazard collection of Rhineland territories, and Saxony. Each of them had a price tag, and Maximilian set about determining what that was and how it could be paid. Perpetually indebted and effectively penniless—Maximilian frequently resorted to taking comparatively tiny loans of 1,000 florins from Jakob Fugger just to pay his household expenses—the old emperor could not afford to front any of that cash himself. His grandson Charles, however, had two bright and shiny new kingdoms whose revenues he could tap for the task.

Charles initially granted his grandfather 100,000 florins, a massive sum, with which to buy the imperial title. It was not nearly enough. "If you aspire to gain this crown, you must not hold back any resource," Maximilian told him bluntly, demanding not only money but the authority to make marriage alliances as he saw fit. When a satisfactory reply had not arrived within a week, Maximilian wrote in terms still more blunt, and manipulative to boot. "If there is any fault or negligence, we will feel greatly displeased that we have gone to so much trouble and effort throughout our life to aggrandize and exalt our dynasty and our posterity, and yet by your negligence everything should collapse and jeopardize all our kingdoms, dominions and lordship, and thus our succession."[13]

Chièvres, who was by this point the chief financial official for both the Burgundian lands and Spain, received an even blunter message from Maximilian's treasurer, Jakob Villinger. "You already know the importance of this business, but let me refresh your memory," he wrote. Electing Charles would allow them "to subjugate our enemies and those who wish us ill, while the reverse would plunge us into total misery and confusion, which we would always bitterly regret.... Pay attention to what I have just said, otherwise we will be lost. Don't fall asleep on this!"[14]

Maximilian had spent his entire life working toward this, and he would spend every penny in his grandson's name if he had to. The old emperor had always been liberal with other people's money, and he saw no reason to change at the end of his life. Shortly before his death, Maximilian reached a tentative agreement with the electors, promising them half a million florins in up-front payments and tens of thousands more per year in pensions and assorted other inducements. Before it was signed, sealed, and delivered, however, Maximilian died on January 12, 1519.

With Maximilian dead, so too was any prior arrangement. Francis's diplomats pointedly reminded the elector Palatine, ruler of the Palatinate along the Rhine, of the French king's "strength, wealth, love of arms, expertise and experience in war," which simultaneously served as an inducement and a veiled threat. "You can only get what you want," Francis wrote to an agent in Germany, "by using bribes or force." He was prepared to employ both. Next to the strapping, accomplished Francis, the immature and not especially impressive Charles looked like a poor option. There was nothing stopping a French army from crossing into the empire in support of Francis's claim.[15]

Yet Charles was determined to spend whatever it took, and he had inherited the key to that pursuit from Maximilian: the confidence of Jakob Fugger. Fugger was nobody's fool. He had been in the Habsburg business for more than three decades, making eye-watering profits along the way. Serving as the financial agent for the purchase of the imperial crown would open up the door to wealth beyond any previous financier's wildest dreams. Why? Because the kingdoms of Spain and Naples, plus the hereditary lands in Austria and the Burgundian inheritance in the Low Countries, represented a financial base the likes of which no ruler in European history had ever commanded. Loaning that monarch money was the pathway to impossible riches. Fugger barely had to think twice about refusing to cash King Francis's letters of credit and instead extending more than half a million florins in immediate funds to Charles. The loans were secured with future Spanish tax revenues, estimated down to the maravedi by the skilled and precise denizens of Augsburg countinghouses.

This was the key to Charles's election: the resources of a large chunk of the continent, funneled through the financial networks centered on Augsburg. Charles's lofty ancestry and his ambitious grandfather had put him in position to become Holy Roman

Emperor, but the Fuggers, and the world of finance they represented, bought his crown.

Overreach

By 1520, Charles had acquired the titles and claims that would define the next thirty-five years of his life. Put together, they made him the most powerful ruler in the history of the continent since Charlemagne. The new emperor's lands touched the North Sea, the Baltic, the Adriatic, the Atlantic, and the Mediterranean, even the Caribbean and the Pacific in the distant and little-known lands of the New World. Some of Europe's wealthiest regions, including Flanders, southern Germany, and the bustling ports of Andalusia, fell under his rule. His election as Holy Roman Emperor had been as much about harnessing the wealth of those various regions, and their financial networks, for a common purpose as Charles's claim on the imperial crown.

For many observers, Charles represented the possibility of universal monarchy. Universal monarchy meant universal peace, the triumph of a deeply medieval worldview—albeit a multifaceted one, drawn from many different sources, including papal propaganda, Dante, and Roman law—centered on a universal faith and a universal Church to administer it. This universalizing tradition retained its currency and force with intellectuals across the continent, even as new humanist ideas of rulership and the role of the Church emerged. Charles's new chancellor, Mercurino de Gattinara, an experienced Italian lawyer and administrator, gave voice to these universalizing claims when he put this speech in Charles's mouth for the benefit of the Cortes of Castile: "At last to me empire (*imperium*) has been conferred by the single consent of Germany with God, as I deem, willing and commanding.... For from God himself alone is empire."[16]

Charles held more claims to rights than any ruler in history. Yet the collision of those rights was as much a straitjacket as it was a boon. They were not integrated in any way, except in the person of Charles himself, the man who held the title. The claim that made him Duke of Brabant had nothing to do with his claim to be king of Naples, and the subjects of the Kingdom of Naples conceived of their ruler differently than those of the Duchy of Brabant. Taxes from one could not easily be transferred to another, if at all. If he needed money for a war, he had to separately beg them from the Diet of the Holy Roman Empire, the Cortes of Castile, and the Corts of Aragon, and they were three of many, many more representative bodies in his lands. His subjects in each of these territories had their own ideas about what they wanted from their ruler, what their ruler owed them, and where their ultimate interests lay. Whatever his claims to universal monarchy, no matter the rituals and symbols of world rule he employed, despite his advisors' deeply ideological propagandizing, Charles could not make his subjects do what he wanted.

Why would the nobles of Brabant or the ecclesiastics of Saxony care about Charles's personal designs on the Duchy of Milan, or a campaign against the north African port of Algiers intended to safeguard the coasts of Granada and Sicily? How might the barons of Naples benefit from a campaign against the king of France in Picardy? Should the wool merchants of the Basque ports on the Spanish coast pay taxes to support a campaign against the Ottomans in Hungary? Put in these terms, the limitations of Charles's powers and abilities were clear.

This was the central conundrum of Charles's reign. No matter how powerful he appeared on paper, for one man to rule such a disparate collection of territories—each with its own nobles, hierarchies, issues, concerns, political structures, and peculiarities— was a herculean task. Charles was a diligent and relentless worker, rising early and attending to business throughout the day, but no single individual could handle such a workload on their own. As the meeting point between the checks imposed by patch-work multiplicity of medieval politics and the endless possibilities afforded by the rising state, these competing responsibilities and constituencies pulled Charles in a thousand directions at once.

Those contradictions and problems made themselves clear immediately. Charles departed from Spain early in 1520, head-ing for his new territories within the Holy Roman Empire. Within months, a massive rebellion spread across Castile, known as the Revolt of the Comuneros. Riots and disorder broke out in Toledo, Burgos, Valladolid, and many other cities. It was a wide-spread revolt, born of the cities' deep discontent with the ongoing situation and their powerful sense of identity, which gave them a means of showcasing their anger. In the countryside, by con-trast, the unrest took the form of an anti-elite uprising. The rebels marched on Tordesillas and freed Queen Juana, intending to use her to replace her son.

Far away in Germany, his mind occupied with other con-cerns, Charles failed to grasp the seriousness of the situation. His representative in Spain, Adrian of Utrecht, was not a native of Iberia and had no real idea of the roots or extent of the simmer-ing tensions the revolt had brought to the fore. Nor did Charles himself, for that matter, who continued to demand that his offi-cials send along Spanish tax revenues from areas that were under rebel control. In any other situation, this would have been down-right comical. Luckily for Charles, Juana refused to be used as a figurehead, and the young king eventually appointed competent deputies who raised an army to crush the rebels in open battle. If that were not enough, a simultaneous and almost equally serious disturbance broke out in Valencia. As in Castile, open battle was the only solution to the crisis. Severe repression in the aftermath, including mass executions in Valencia, the torture and garrotting of the bishop of Zamora, and enormous fines, brought them to an end. Harsh treatment could not solve the underlying issues of representation, taxation, and royal control that had caused the revolts in the first place.[17]

And Spain was just one of Charles's holdings. Almost simultaneously, the king and emperor had to deal with a certain Augustinian named Martin Luther, who was spreading his troublesome message far and wide. As the Comuneros of Castile and the *agermanats* of Valencia were launching their rebellions, Luther was making his stand at the Diet of Worms. It was no wonder that Charles was not especially interested in aiding his brother-in-law, King Louis II of Hungary, as Suleiman the Magnificent advanced on Belgrade. That was also happening at the same time. Charles simply did not have any attention to spare, whatever the strategic implications of the Ottoman advance into central Europe.

Important things fell through the cracks over and over again. The emperor only had so much attention to give. This was a repeated theme throughout Charles's life and rule, one that would sour as the years went on.

Making War, Making Peace

There were many obstructions to Charles's exercise of power, but when he set his mind and resources to a task, the possibilities were almost limitless. Charles, instructed by Gattinara and other theorists, bought into the idea of universal monarchy. He also believed that it was his duty to pursue the rights claimed by generations of Habsburg and Trastámara dynasts before him. But there was no grand strategy here, no unified goal or a careful weighing of the balance of power, no deep understanding of the risks and opportunities of peace or conflict. Charles and his advisors were not stupid—far from it—but their calculus was fundamentally different than our own. War was both the fundamental duty and the pastime of kings. It had a logic and reason all its own.[18]

Charles had plenty of outlets for his martial ambitions. He had acquired his thrones in Spain and the Holy Roman Empire during a lull in the Italian Wars, the series of conflicts afflicting both Italy and much of Europe from 1494 onward. Both of his grandfathers, Ferdinand and Maximilian, had been intimately involved in these wars at various stages. The Trastámara side of the family tree had been more successful in exploiting the possibilities of these endless wars than the Habsburg. Maximilian had spent a great deal of money, politicked and backstabbed and switched sides for years, without gaining any real advantage. Ferdinand, by contrast, had added the Kingdom of Naples, the initial cause of the conflict, to his possessions and given the dynasty a firm foothold in Italy. Naples now belonged to Charles, giving him a long-term interest in Italy. Significantly, however, his accession to a whole array of titles and lands meant that his territories bordered those of the French king Francis I everywhere from Picardy to Catalonia.

Even as the Comuneros were in revolt and Martin Luther was declaring his unwillingness to recant at Worms, a pair of French armies were on the move: one along the Meuse River in eastern France, the other into Navarre in northern Spain. To make matters worse, the king of France had encouraged the Duke of Guelders, a small but powerful lordship along the Rhine, to invade Charles's territories in Friesland. Charles would have to deal with all three threats, the first in a long line of military challenges threatening his lands and his authority.

Even though they took place far from the Italian Peninsula, these engagements were the opening confrontations of a new clash in the Italian Wars. The various powers had assembled themselves in a bewildering variety of configurations since 1494, stretching the theaters of war everywhere from sunbaked southern Italy to the moors of northern England. It had dragged in every major power in western Europe, including England and Scotland. At one point, the Republic of Venice had faced the combined might of France, Spain, the Holy Roman Empire, and the pope on its own. The emperor Maximilian had switched sides on several occasions, trying (and usually failing) to gain some advantage in the confusion. For the most part, however, the conflict had pitted France against Spain, and mostly on Italian battlefields. The French kings held a claim to Naples, as did the kings of Aragon. The powers of Italy were forced to pick sides. The end result meant that armies of mercenaries had rampaged through the peninsula for decades by 1521, looting, killing, sacking, burning, and occasionally slaughtering each other in enormous numbers.

It was time for Charles to take up the long struggle against France and do his own share of the damage, just as his grandfathers had done before him. The question of where to fight occupied Charles and his advisors at great length over the winter of 1521–22, though not enough to prevent the emperor from siring at least three illegitimate children and spending a great deal of time hunting and playing tennis. He took an extended visit to England, where Henry VIII was married to his aunt Catherine, and whose daughter Mary he was currently contracted to wed. Without Charles's direct involvement, an army of Spanish professionals and German mercenaries in his pay, led by an experienced Italian soldier of fortune named Prospero Colonna, crushed a French army in April of 1522 at Bicocca. By the end of the year, the emperor was in Spain, thoroughly enjoying himself and overseeing the punishment of the Comuneros. Things looked even better when the Duke of Bourbon, one of the most important nobles in France, defected from Francis I to the king of Spain and

Holy Roman Emperor. Francis I, insatiably greedy and strapped for cash like every other ruler of the period, had denied the duke lands that he otherwise would have inherited. That was enough to make Bourbon, a gifted soldier and powerful figure, a free agent. He sided with Charles.

A planned joint attack with Henry VIII never came to fruition, but through 1524, Charles held the initiative. His viceroy of Naples, Charles de Lannoy, drove the French garrisons from most of northern Italy. Bourbon had failed to carry off a conspiracy against Francis within France, but he invaded Provence with an imperial army, besieging Marseilles and torching the gorgeous countryside. That was when things went south. Francis I cut off Bourbon's line of retreat, crossing into northern Italy with a powerful army and laying siege to the imperial garrison in Pavia in February, 1525. Charles was practically out of money. His forces were on the retreat. The English alliance was done. He would lose his position in Italy, possibly even the Kingdom of Naples, and worse was still to come. Charles and his court brooded, sure that any news would be bad news.

The emperor was discussing the dire situation in Italy with a clutch of advisors around noon on March 10, 1525, when a breathless messenger rode a tired horse into the royal palace in Madrid. The courier relayed his message; frozen, Charles said nothing for a moment, then repeated the words back. "The king of France is a prisoner in my power, and we won the battle?" The emperor fell silent again, then retreated to his quarters, where he fell to his knees before an image of the Virgin Mary and gave thanks in prayer for half an hour before finally emerging to celebrate his victory.[19]

The Battle of Pavia was a disaster of epic proportions for France, their worst defeat since the Battle of Agincourt in 1415. The French army had been crushed. Their strategic position in

northern Italy was hopelessly lost. The cream of the French nobility was dead on the battlefield. Francis himself was a prisoner,
the ultimate leverage in an age of dynastic rulers who personally embodied the state. Whatever Charles wanted—the dismissal
of Francis's claims to lands, the outright granting of territory, a
literal king's ransom—was within his grasp. Charles held all the
cards and had but to play them.[20]

Perhaps predictably, it did not take long for all of these grand
possibilities to melt away into chaos and disaster.

Coming Together, Coming Apart

Just a few days before Charles's German mercenaries and Spanish arquebusiers cut the French army to pieces at Pavia, peasants
living in the territory belonging to the Bavarian city of Memmingen presented a long, detailed list of demands to the city's
ruling magistrates. The waves of Evangelical, reforming religious
sentiment roiling Germany played a part: The villagers asked to
elect their own preachers rather than remaining beholden to the
Church. This was radical enough, but far more than that, egali-
tarian Christian brotherhood was the logical endpoint of reforming religion. The villagers of Memmingen wanted to remake the
whole hierarchical structure that oppressed them and kept them
subservient to their social betters.

They were hardly alone in this. Over the course of the harvest season of 1524 and the early months of 1525, southwestern
Germany had been engulfed in an enormous peasants' revolt, the
largest to occur across Europe in generations. The rebellion spread
across western and central Germany in the months after the Battle
of Pavia, reaching the Palatinate along the Rhine, Baden, Württemburg, and Thuringia. Open battles between the peasants and
the forces of the German princes soon followed. The situation

deteriorated from there. The more militant peasants murdered nobles and looted their castles. The German princes retaliated by hiring armies of hardened *Landsknechte* who carried out wholesale slaughter, torture, and mass executions. Luther's influence might have helped cause the rebellion, but he disavowed it in inflammatory and callous terms. All of this took place in territories ultimately subject to Charles as Holy Roman Emperor, including a few of the Habsburg hereditary lands. But Charles was busy elsewhere, relying on his brother, Ferdinand, and the nobles of the Swabian League to handle matters for him. He simply hoped the peasant problem would go away.[21]

It did go away, but not without leaving countless thousands dead and swathes of horrific destruction across Germany. The Peasants' War did not directly affect Charles, ensconced a thousand miles away in Spain and trying to discern how to best exploit his victory over Francis, but it was a sign of issues to come.

By the spring of 1526, Charles had mostly managed to squander any advantages he had gained from Francis's capture. The imprisoned king agreed to Charles's demands in return for his freedom, including handing over his two sons and heirs as hostages, but repudiated it all as soon as he was back over the border. In the meantime, Francis's capable mother had been busily assembling an alliance to take the fight to the emperor. Pope Clement VII, the Republic of Venice, Florence, and the deposed Duke of Milan, Francesco Sforza, with Henry VIII of England acting as guarantor, joined Francis in the League of Cognac. Their demands were staggering, including the return of the French princes, the repayment of 800,000 ducats in debts to Henry VIII, and various guarantees regarding the settlement of territories in Italy.[22]

This was just the beginning of Charles's woes. Increasingly desperate pleas for aid from Louis II, the king of Hungary, reached his Habsburg brothers-in-law. Sultan Suleiman was on the move, his eyes locked on Hungary. Charles and Ferdinand refused to offer any aid to their distraught brother-in-law against the encroaching Ottomans. Ferdinand, now the Archduke of Austria and currently working in his brother's place to manage the troublesome Lutheran reformers and snuff out the last embers of the peasants' revolt, understood perfectly the threat at hand. Charles, still far away in Spain, would do nothing. "If we could have peace, you can be sure that I would deploy everything I have to Hungary," he wrote to Ferdinand. "But if the wars concerning my own possessions are going to continue—and I see for sure that they will—I leave you to judge whether I should not look to my own defence and deploy all my resources for that." Charles instead suggested that Ferdinand offer to sell toleration to the German Lutherans in return for troops to meet the Ottoman threat. Even when a final plea from Louis arrived, Charles still would not budge. "I already have a tiresome Turk to deal with: the king of France," he wrote to the Hungarian king.[23]

Absent any soldiers or funds from his Habsburg relatives, Suleiman rolled over the Hungarian king at Mohács, killing him and much of the Hungarian nobility. The path into central Europe—into the ancestral Habsburg lands of Styria, Austria, and Tyrol—opened to the Ottomans. Whatever effort and funds it would have cost to fight the Ottomans in Hungary in 1526, it would cost far more to do so on the Habsburg doorstep in the ensuing years.[24]

The bills for Charles's divided attention, to say nothing of the literal costs of governance and war, had come due. Could the emperor have settled them? Therein lay the intertwined problems. Charles was not convinced that the Ottomans were more of a danger to him than the immediate, and very real, peril posed by the League of Cognac. Even as Suleiman advanced into Hungary, Ferdinand was raising mercenaries in Germany on his brother's orders and sending them south to fight for Charles in Italy. Even if Louis and Ferdinand could have convinced Charles that the biggest threat lay in Hungary—a tall order, considering the Christian forces arrayed against his lands, including the pope himself—his resources were stretched too thin. "I had already raised and sent to Italy the last ducat in cash that I could find," he wrote as the news of the fall of Hungary reached him. It was only after the disaster at Mohács that Charles decided the Ottomans were the greatest threat, and by then it was too late.

There was still plenty of room for things to worsen. Charles had enough funds to assemble a large and imposing army in Italy, including sixteen thousand expensive *Landsknechte* brought south from Germany by the old soldier Georg von Frundsberg, but not enough to keep that army paid. Some of the Spanish soldiers from the Naples garrison attached to the army had not seen any coin in twenty months. The Germans had not been paid since leaving home months before. To complicate matters, Charles had never specified who was actually in command of the army. Was it the Duke of Bourbon? Or Frundsberg, who commanded the largest bloc of soldiers? Or the viceroy of Naples, Charles de Lannoy?

The stage was set for a catastrophe. The soldiers refused to follow orders until they were paid. Frundsberg, the most respected and experienced commander among them, had an apoplectic fit at the sight of the mutiny and could no longer lead. Lannoy cut a deal with Pope Clement, but he could not enforce it on an army that did not care to listen to him. The troops liked Bourbon, who promised them plunder in return for loyalty, but that meant a rampaging trip south from Lombardy to Rome. On May 6, 1527, the starving and enraged army assaulted the Eternal City, leaving thousands dead in the streets and the entire city looted and pillaged beyond recognition.[25]

The Sack of Rome was the logical endpoint of an overstretched emperor's attempts to have it all. Two years later, Suleiman the Magnificent appeared outside the gates of Vienna itself with an army; Charles could do only a little to protect his family's ancestral possessions. Vienna's survival and the Ottoman retreat owed as much to bad weather and limited logistical support as anything Charles did or could have done. The bankers would lend to him, their repayment guaranteed with the future revenues of the emperor's vast holdings, but there was not enough coin in all of Europe to pay for everything he needed to do.

Global Empire

Luckily for Charles, the emperor also had access to sources of windfall revenues from across the Atlantic. Following Columbus's expeditions, a variety of colonizing and conquering projects sprouted up in the Caribbean under the nominal suzerainty of the Spanish crown. When the new king arrived in Spain for the first time, these possessions did not amount to much: several islands in the Caribbean and a few forlorn outposts on the Isthmus of Panama, none of which were particularly wealthy or promising. Only five thousand or so Spaniards resided there, along with several hundred enslaved Africans and the much greater number of indigenous peoples. Over the course of Charles's reign, however, Spanish territory in the New World would more than quadruple in size, taking in Mexico, Peru, and huge swathes of territory, all of which were governed directly by the crown of Castile. From a great distance, and with only cursory attention paid to his marauding subjects who carried it out, Charles supervised one of the most extensive, horrifying, and lucrative projects of conquest in human history.[26]

The combination of new diseases and almost unimaginably

exploitative brutality devastated the indigenous inhabitants. Within two generations of Columbus's arrival, the indigenous population of the Caribbean had declined to almost nothing everywhere the Spanish touched. A thriving regional trade in enslaved people had grown up to ensure a labor supply for the new colonies, with predictably lethal results: Of the fifteen thousand indigenous people forcibly transported to the island of Hispaniola, for example, all but two thousand died within a decade. According to one estimate, roughly two hundred thousand people died on the four largest Caribbean islands under Spanish control between 1493 and 1518. Spanish steel, European diseases, emotional devastation, malnutrition, and overwork, all of them driven by the incentives for profit built into the process of exploration from the very beginning, took a staggering human toll.[27]

This process did not begin with Charles, and his successors were no better, but the extension of Spanish rule over vast territories of the American mainland fundamentally changed the scale of the violence and exploitation. Hernán Cortés, the savvy and exceptionally ruthless freebooter who led the conquest of Mexico, massacred (by his own account) more than three thousand people in a single incident at the town of Cholula in 1519. He and his men did far worse at Tenochtitlan, the capital of the Mexica, in subsequent years.[28]

Charles retained an abiding interest in the exotic plants and animals of his new lands; he delighted in colorful feathers and a parrot that had belonged to his grandfather Ferdinand. The emperor displayed occasional care for the well-being of the indigenous inhabitants, which ironically—and unfortunately—led him to push for the large-scale importation of enslaved Africans. In the final reckoning, however, Charles was only consistently concerned with the treasure his American possessions could provide. He needed money to pay soldiers, build ships, bribe foreign

rulers, and satisfy his many creditors. The New World could provide it in spades.

The first infusions of cash from the New World arrived in
March 1520. Cortés sent a large shipment of treasure, much of
it gathered during the horrific massacre at Cholula, to sweeten
Charles's opinion of him during the conquistador's dispute with
the governor of Cuba. Charles promptly spent every last penny of
it to pay for a voyage to England and the Netherlands, Cholulan
blood funding the emperor's European adventures.

This quickly became a pattern. When money arrived, Charles
found a way to spend it almost as soon as it hit land. The 120,000
gold pesos Cortés sent in 1524, following his barbarous conquest
of Tenochtitlan and the Mexica heartland, immediately went to
pay for the ongoing war in Italy. The brutal deaths of tens of
thousands of indigenous Americans was enough to fund Charles's
martial habits for a few months, after which the emperor was once
again out of money.[29]

Charles tapped into the immense sources of wealth his subjects
in the Americas were looting, but he failed to exercise any genuine control. Consider his instructions to Francisco Pizarro, issued
in 1529, prior to the adventurer's departure from Panama to Peru:
"According to the available information about the area, its inhabitants possess the intelligence and capacity to understand our Holy
Catholic Faith, so there is no need to conquer and subjugate them
by force of arms. Instead they should be treated with love and
generosity." Needless to say, that was not how Pizarro actually
behaved. In November 1532, Pizarro and his small cohort blasted
an assembled gathering of Inca notables with cannon and used
cavalry to ride them down. More than two thousand people were
killed, and the emperor, Atahualpa, was taken prisoner. His ransom amounted to more than six tons of gold and twelve tons of
silver. After it arrived, Pizarro had Atahualpa strangled.[30]

By 1535, Charles could lay claim to a genuine global empire. He had paid for Magellan's circumnavigation of the world, which produced a claim on the Spice Islands of the Moluccas. As with everything else in Charles's life, that too was fungible: He sold it to the king of Portugal for a large sum when the emperor needed cash to pay for the defense of Vienna from the Ottomans. Mexico's mines and fields became a source of regular shipments of treasure, produced by the blood and sweat of forced indigenous laborers, but it was never enough.

When the first batch of incredible Inca treasures arrived in Seville in 1534, Charles did not marvel at them; instead, he kept only the most striking pieces of the plunder and had the rest melted down into coin. As always, he needed the money. The emperor had turned his attention to Tunis, a key port on the North African coast, and directed all of his substantial energies and resources toward its capture.

Tunis

Sweat drenched Charles V's short, golden hair and ran down into his neatly trimmed beard, plastering it to his prominent jaw. This defeated the purpose of the beard, which Charles had grown to mask precisely how much his chin protruded from the rest of his face. At least here, in the midst of a battle, nobody was paying much attention to the emperor's underbite. Roaring cannon, spitting arquebuses, the clash of steel on steel: The thousands of soldiers gathered outside the walls of La Goletta, the port of Tunis in North Africa, made their assault on the town. In the harbor, where the blue waters of the sea met the dusty brown of the shore, a fleet of low, lean galleys and high-sided galleons unleashed cannon fire onto the town's defenders. July 14, 1535 was a fine day for Charles, one of his first experiences of battle, and it made him feel alive and worthwhile in a way no other experience in his thirty-five years possibly could. Decades of paying for warfare on a vast scale, directing it from palaces and field camps, had finally given way to open battle. It was what he had always wanted, and now he had it. In fact, against the advice and judgment of his advisors, Charles had insisted on being present, on personally leading his men against the Muslim foe. As cannonballs blasted through masonry and blades found their homes in vulnerable flesh, the emperor looked on with approval. He had made this happen.

This army and the ships that carried them had gathered from the vast corners of Charles's empire: *Landsknecht* mercenaries from Germany, marched south over the Alps and embarked near Genoa; veteran Spaniards who had spent years of service in Naples and Sicily, carrying well-worn arquebuses and dented armor; experienced Italian soldiers of fortune, heirs to decades of military tradition in the peninsula's ceaseless wars; Hospitaller Knights based on the island of Malta, descendants of the crusading knights of holy wars long past; fine Portuguese warships provided by one of Charles's brothers-in-law, the king of Portugal, paid for with profits made from voyages to the Indies. Some twenty-six thousand fighting men aboard four hundred ships, carrying perhaps another twenty-five thousand crewmen, converged on this hotbed of Muslim piracy from all over the European Christian world. Treasures robbed from murdered Inca paid for the whole enormous expedition, blood money begetting yet more blood.

Charles's finest hour came at the capture of La Goletta, followed shortly by the fall of Tunis itself and the flight of its fearsome ruler, the infamous corsair Barbarossa. His soldiers took huge quantities of plunder in movable treasure and enslaved people. The terrible threat of corsairing raids on the coasts of Spain and France had for the moment been neutralized.

Charles V spent enormous amounts of treasure fighting his

fellow Christian rulers. His preoccupation with Italy had led him to neglect his responsibilities in central Europe, leading to the death of one brother-in-law and a series of far more costly campaigns to defend Austria and Bohemia against the Ottoman threat. In Tunis, all agreed, Charles had found the proper enemy to fight—Muslims—and finally turned all his vast resources toward a worthy cause. It was even enough to produce a grudging, temporary truce with King Francis I of France, Charles's lifelong enemy.[31]

As with all of Charles's endeavors, however, the expedition's success proved temporary, even illusory. Barbarossa fled to Algiers, reinforced his burgeoning alliance with Suleiman the Magnificent, and took command of the entire Ottoman fleet, expanding his powers tenfold. His raids on Italy in the following years, which killed thousands and took enormous numbers of captives to flood the slave markets of the Muslim world, made his prior excursions seem like mere pinpricks. The cost of the campaign was ruinous: 1,076,652 ducats, according to one estimate, even more than Charles had spent purchasing his throne.

Inca treasure propelled this entire campaign. Charles assembled his forces in Barcelona, and among those summoned to Catalonia were all the mint masters in his kingdom. They were needed to quickly turn every ounce of that bloody windfall into coinage to pay the soldiers, sailors, shipmasters, armorers, biscuit makers, salt-meat preparers, and, of course, the bankers. Even the profits of the Andes were mere security for other, larger expenditures, all funneled through the increasingly labyrinthine financial arrangements of the time. Nobody stretched their resources further or drew more creatively and extensively on financiers than Charles V, and the Tunis expedition was a microcosm of how and why.

By 1535, no state in Europe (aside from Venice, a mercantile city-state with an overseas empire) had more experience or better tools for financing large-scale military expeditions than Spain. Castile and Aragon had been at war more or less continuously since 1482, when the campaign to conquer Granada began; since then, only a few years of peace had interrupted the constant drumbeat of conflict. Naples, Milan, the Veneto, the Romagna, Genoa, Provence, Catalonia, Navarre, the coast of Greece: Those were just a few of the places where the resources of Spain had paid for campaigns. Charles's ambitions pushed even further than his already grasping grandparents, and luckily for him, he had a clutch of skilled financial advisors to help him in the task. The most prominent of these was Francisco de los Cobos, perhaps the only person alive who fully understood the convoluted finances of the crown of Castile, the backbone of Charles's many kingdoms.

When the Inca treasure began to arrive in 1534, its total value amounted to around 2 million ducats. Charles, as king of Spain, was entitled to his customary royal fifth, which would have been somewhere in the range of 400,000 ducats. That was a huge amount of ready cash, but still nowhere near enough for the planned expedition. Nevertheless, Cobos had some ideas for how to get the rest. He drew on the fundamental tool of Spanish state finance: the *juro*. These were bonds that offered long-term returns at low interest rates in return for immediate cash payments. In this case, Charles and Cobos simply sequestered all of the arriving Inca treasure and required the intended recipients to accept *juros* in return. This was a creative combination of two sources of revenue that allowed Charles and his advisors to drum up most of the funds necessary for the Tunis expedition. But this was still insufficient, and a stopgap measure in the form of a large loan from the Fuggers was necessary to bridge the gap and keep the preparations for the campaign moving while the rest of the treasure was in transit. Another 120,000 ducats' worth was remitted to Antwerp bankers, who transferred the funds to Charles's aunt and regent in the Low Countries, the exceptionally gifted and stable Margaret of Austria. This guarded against the possibility that King Francis would try to test the Habsburgs during the supposed truce.[32]

The Tunis campaign utilized every financial tool developed in the prior decades and centuries, drawing on the treasures of the Americas as security. Money flowed from Augsburg to Spain to Antwerp, drawing on the services of the most prominent bankers of the age. The campaign it bankrolled pulled soldiers from all over the vast dynastic lands united in Charles's person, the end of a long process of accumulation and consolidation. Those soldiers, using pikes, gunpowder handguns, and large quantities of artillery, represented the cutting edge of warfare in an age of transformation. Printed propaganda portraying Charles as defender of the faith, "Destroyer of the Turks," and "Tamer of Africa" circulated widely after the campaign, broadcasting the emperor's victory across Europe in word and engraved or woodcut image. The sheer scale of what Charles accomplished, and then made sure everybody knew about, reflected the scale of transformation in the age as a whole.[33]

Charles and the End

Tunis and the victory lap Charles took through Italy afterward, celebrating triumphal entries across the peninsula as he made his way via Sicily to Naples, Rome, and Florence, marked the high point of the emperor's reign. The triumph did not last long. Within the year, Francis I and Charles had already started another round of devastating wars. The Ottoman threat was growing and became drastically more dangerous when the elusive corsair Barbarossa—whom Charles had failed to contain at Tunis—took command. At the Battle of Preveza in 1538, Barbarossa crushed a Christian fleet led by Charles's subordinates, causing tens of thousands of casualties. It only worsened from there: Charles's two great enemies, Suleiman the Magnificent and Francis I, had already signed a formal alliance in 1536 and combined their efforts against his vulnerable territories. The emperor's 1542 campaign against the Ottomans in central Europe (with Götz von Berlichingen and a troop of men-at-arms in tow) was an expensive debacle. He managed to defeat the Protestant Schmalkaldic League of German princes later in the 1540s, but there was no more glory to be found. The wars grew longer and more expensive, a drained emperor rushing to address one crisis after the next.

Now a broken man, Charles abdicated his throne in 1555. He handed over his German responsibilities to his brother, Ferdinand, and Spain and the Netherlands to his son, Philip. The emperor, his jutting jaw now covered in an iron-gray beard, his face thinned and drawn by decades of stress, lived out his three remaining years in a fine Spanish monastery. He did not survive to see the end of the Italian Wars that had occupied so much of his life. The struggle with the Ottomans continued for decades, flaring up in both the Mediterranean and central Europe. Charles's beloved Low Countries fell into rebellion a decade after his death, launching an on-again, off-again war that lasted for eighty years.

Charles was not the most talented man, but neither was he stupid; most observers agreed that he was a diligent worker and rarely did anything that amounted to outright incompetence. He did have a ruthless streak, a genuine necessity for rulers of the age. Among noblemen of the time, his bravery, commitment to martial pursuits and hunting, and his belief in himself and the righteousness of his claims to rights were all completely run-of-the-mill. Nobody ever accused him of brilliance, but intellectual brilliance was not what men of his class sought.

All of Charles's grand plans and aspirations to universal rulership eventually came to naught, but that's not to say he was a failure; he had tried—and failed—to ice-skate uphill. No ruler, no matter how prodigious their talents, could have met every challenge Charles faced: uniting Christian Europe against the Ottoman threat; reaching an accommodation with or snuffing out the religious reformers in Germany and beyond; overseeing his subjects' vicious, self-serving actions in the Americas; and coming to a long-term settlement over the question of Italy and the broader Habsburg-French conflict.

In that sense, Charles V serves as an emblematic stand-in for Europe as a whole in this period, an embodiment of what it could and could not do—the foundations of states, financial systems, technology to produce and disseminate the written word, transformative military developments, and key religious innovations. The world was full of new horizons, from the Moluccas to Peru. For better and worse, but always impactfully, Charles had his hands in all of them. While his hands mostly remained clean, tucked away in the highest European luxury, those of his subordinates came away soaked in blood and guilt.

CONCLUSION

———— ✧ ————

The bewildering ups and downs of Charles V's reign defined the age as a whole. The emperor embodied all the major trends of the era: the growth of the state and voyages of exploration, the violent potential of voyages of exploration and gunpowder warfare, the emergence of the Reformation, and above all, the power of money.

Simultaneously, the emperor represented both unity and division: unity, as the man who ultimately ruled more of western Europe than anybody for centuries before or after and represented its greatest hope of universal monarchy since the end of the Roman Empire; and division, as the man who presided over its religious disintegration and its most prolonged and destructive wars to date.

A simmering tension underscores Charles's royal tenure and this era as a whole. Europeans from the sheepfolds of Gloucestershire to the bustling canals of Venice had a great deal in common. Their Church was a universal one, with a single hierarchy (at least in theory) stretching upward from the lowliest parish priest to the pope himself. Their respective political structures even bore a strong resemblance to one another thanks to centuries of contact and exchange.

Most of all, Europeans shared a common conception of how to do business. They approached money, credit, investment, and profit from similar perspectives and employed much the same tools.

Aldus Manutius could not have spoken a word of John Heritage's English language, but he absolutely would have understood the nature of the wool trader's account book, what it recorded, and how he operated. The credit arrangements and delayed payment cycles that defined Götz von Berlichingen's military enterprise were entirely familiar to John Heritage, even if the mercenary's Swabian dialect was unintelligible. The frameworks and institutions that made their activities possible, the understandings that shaped how they transacted, borrowed, lent, and invested, were everywhere. The differences from industry to industry and region to region were minor compared to what they shared.

Those similarities were the driving force behind the rapid spread of the major processes of the era: voyages of exploration, rising states and state finance, printing presses, gunpowder warfare, and the Reformation. After Isabella and Ferdinand turned to long-term debt to finance Spain's wars, the French would follow suit within a generation. Christopher Columbus, a born and bred Genoese, used a language of mercantile investment that resonated with the wealthy merchants of Seville and court financiers of Castile and Aragon. Jakob Fugger's agents made staggering profits in Lisbon, Antwerp, and Venice. The wool from John Heritage's sheep might be woven into finished cloth in the Low Countries and then turned into a finished garment in Italy, spawning a web of transactions stretching from a Milanese artisan's cloak to a Gloucestershire shepherd paying his running tab at the alehouse. The major processes of this era took hold so quickly, and circulated so far, because the mechanisms that paid for them had already disseminated across western Europe.

But if these economic institutions pulled Europe together, their consequences split it apart at the seams.

Charles V's dream of universal empire shattered when confronted by the reality of ceaseless, destructive gunpowder warfare

waged by a coterie of quarrelsome states. New financial mechanisms found innovative ways of paying for all of it, sustaining
the violence for generation after generation. The printing presses
that had set up shop all over Europe did not immediately unite
the continent in a new age of easily accessible learning; instead,
religious polemics proved to be the most lucrative products, fueling the mass disturbances of the Reformation. The deaths of millions of people in the Americas, the immiseration of countless
more across the globe, and the Indian Ocean's introduction to
the savagery of maritime trade conducted at sword- and gun-
point resulted directly from voyages of exploration. All of these
transformative processes converged in the first few decades of the
sixteenth century. This was an era of unprecedented disruption
and upheaval, one that remade an entire continent and shaped the
entire world.

This age did not witness the beginning of western European
dominance. The Ottoman Empire was the most powerful force
in this particular corner of Eurasia; Charles V's perennial indebt-
edness looks laughable in comparison to Suleiman's overflowing
budget surpluses. The emperor's failure to find the funds to pay
the army that sacked Rome stands in stark contrast with Suleiman's bonus offers of 1,000 akça per Janissary to make one last
attempt on the walls of Vienna; that was more than six months'
pay for an impoverished Spanish pikeman. Money that Charles
couldn't hope to find was relative pocket change to the sultan.

But these four decisive decades laid the essential groundwork
for European global dominance. Within three centuries, Charles's
successors—and those of his rivals—would come to outright control much of the globe. The blurry outlines of that future, inconceivable in 1490, were beginning to come into focus.

The changes hardly stalled in 1530, but we can trace many
of the major developments of the next several centuries back to

those eventful years between Columbus's first expedition and the Sack of Rome. The North Sea's emergence as first Europe's and then the world's center of economic gravity definitively happened during this period, mostly thanks to the myriad financial activities of the Fuggers and the Portuguese decision to use Antwerp as the transshipment point for spices. Though its precise home shifted from Antwerp to Amsterdam to London, the North Sea remained the center of global finance for the next four centuries. It was here that everything from negotiable and transferable bills of exchange to the joint stock corporation were pioneered, before finally crossing the Atlantic to Wall Street amid the seismic upheavals of the First World War.[1]

This was the root of the "Little Divergence" of the Low Countries and Britain, the essential predecessor of the Great Divergence that still defines our world today. It went hand in hand with the Dutch Revolt, in which the northern Low Countries— the modern-day Netherlands—split away from Spanish Habsburg rule and became the Dutch Republic. This grew out of the dynastic machinations of the Habsburgs and the religious turmoil that went along with the Reformation, both of which came to fruition in the decades around 1500.

It is impossible to imagine the decades-long cataclysms of the Thirty Years' War (1618–48) without either the religious schisms of the Reformation or the dramatically increased state and fiscal capacity that spread between 1490 and 1530. This was the logical culmination of a century of sectarian violence overlaid onto the dynastic rivalries of Europe, all of it paid for by tools of state finance first established during the Italian Wars. The era of the Thirty Years' War gave way to the fiscal-military states of the later seventeenth and eighteenth centuries, the backbone of both incessant intra-European conflict and the birth of true global empires. This was the stew of ingredients that eventually produced the

Industrial Revolution, from which the Great Divergence proper emerged as the nineteenth century dawned.

This enormous superstructure still towers over the twenty-first century. Its legacies are everywhere: in cricket games played in India, post-apartheid truth and reconciliation commissions in South Africa, flocks of wool sheep grazing among the desert rock formations of the Navajo Nation, salaryman culture in Japan, and apocalyptic environmental degradation in the Arctic. All of these things grew upward from foundations laid down during this seemingly distant era.

Capital lives at the heart of this story. States taxed their subjects to make war. Soldiers demanded pay at the barrel of a gun or the tip of a pike. Voyages from Lisbon, Amsterdam, and London to the spice-rich ports of the Indian Ocean or the sugar-producing islands of the Caribbean were pricey ventures. Everything had a cost, and the peculiar advantage of Europe lay not so much in resources or some particular cultural genius, but in economic institutions that happened to be helpful for these particular purposes at this specific moment in time. Everything had a cost, and in this forty-year period, Europeans excelled at finding ways to pay.

This period inaugurated a seismic shift in world history, but at a staggering price to the people of Europe, and dramatically more so for those they encountered elsewhere. The corpses piled high in the streets of Rome were a mere taste of what the Dutch Revolt and the Thirty Years' War would bring, with their lethal combination of unpaid soldiery and religious enmity. The thousands of enslaved people who were forced onto early Portuguese voyages to the Canaries and West Africa were harbingers of far more commodified bodies to come, shipped across the Atlantic by the millions under horrifying circumstances.

An account book looks at first glance like a sterile, lifeless thing: numbers in rows and columns, arcane systems of notation impenetrable to the uninitiated. This seeming sterility is an illusion, as it is for the endless streams of spreadsheets that increasingly define life in the twenty-first century. Real things and real people lie behind those numbers, dates, and short descriptions. The papers of a Lisbon merchant recorded human lives bought and sold, people's suffering transmuted into assets. *Landsknecht* paymasters documented wages paid for violence meted out at swordpoint. The local wool merchant registered sheep grazing in pastures made empty by the dispossession of their prior owners. Bankers chronicled investments in overseas voyages that profited thanks to silks and spices seized under the looming barrel of a cannon.

All told, these accounts were written not in ink, but in blood.

Acknowledgments

This book wouldn't exist without a huge number of people. I'm thankful for all of them, and incredibly lucky to have them in my life.

I owe a debt of gratitude to all of the listeners of *Tides of History* over the years. Thanks to you, I got to explore the fifteenth and sixteenth centuries to my heart's content in episode after episode. The infinite curiosity of *Tides* listeners, your perceptive questions, and your endless support mean so much to me.

Judith Bennett introduced me to the later Middle Ages, to economic and social history, and how to plan a lecture. Deb Harkness was my guide to early modernity and the art of narrative. I'm eternally grateful for both of them: The lessons they taught me in graduate school are the bedrock of my life as a writer and historian.

Dan Jones, not just a fine historian and TV presenter but also a great dude, guided me through the process of writing a book proposal. This book wouldn't exist without his invaluable advice. The same goes for my agent, William Callahan. Rachel Kambury, the editor, made everything about this book better; working with her has been one of the great pleasures of my writing life.

Good friends are hard to come by, and I've got more than my fair share. Keith Pluymers, a fantastic historian and even better person, has been there at every stage of the book. Albro Lundy is an impossibly perceptive commentator and sounding board, the best writer I've ever known. Eduardo Ariño de la Rubia and J. Eatedali have offered the best advice and kept me sane in these trying times.

Most of all, I'm grateful for my family. My parents have supported me far too kindly and generously on the path to doing real history since childhood, indulging every visit to museums, battlefields, and bookstores along the way. My kids are a source of constant joy; I'm sorry for the constant refrains of "Daddy's writing right now." My wife is just the best. I'm so impossibly grateful that I get to spend every single day with her.

Bibliography

Abu-Lughod, Janet L. *Before European Hegemony: The World System, A.D. 1250–1350.* Oxford: Oxford University Press, 1989.

Ágoston, Gábor. *Guns for the Sultan: Military Power and the Weapons Industry in the Ottoman Empire.* Cambridge, UK: Cambridge University Press, 2005.

Aland, Kurt, ed. *Martin Luther's Ninety-Five Theses: With the Pertinent Documents from the History of the Reformation.* St. Louis: Concordia Publishing, 1967.

Andreau, Jean. *Banking and Business in the Roman World.* Cambridge, UK: Cambridge University Press, 1999.

Aram, Bethany. *Juana the Mad: Sovereignty and Dynasty in Renaissance Europe.* Baltimore: Johns Hopkins University Press, 2005.

———. *La reina Juana: Gobierno, piedad y dinastía.* Madrid: Marcial Pons, 2001.

Asch, Ronald G. "Monarchy in Western and Central Europe," pp. 355–83 in Hamish Scott, ed., *The Oxford Handbook of Early Modern European History, 1350–1750.* Vol. 2, *Cultures and Power.* Oxford: Oxford University Press, 2015.

Aston, T. H., ed. *The Brenner Debate: Agrarian Class Structure and Economic Development in Pre-Industrial Europe.* Cambridge, UK: Cambridge University Press, 1987.

Ayton, Andrew, and J. L. Price, eds. *The Medieval Military Revolution: State, Society, and Military Change in Medieval and Early Modern Europe.* New York: St. Martin's Press, 1995.

Babinger, Franz. *Mehmed the Conqueror and His Time.* Edited by William C. Hickman. Translated by Ralph Manheim. Princeton, NJ: Princeton University Press, 1978 (original German ed. 1953).

Bagchi, David. "Luther's *Ninety-Five Theses* and the Contemporary Criticism of Indulgences," pp. 331–56 in R. N. Swanson, ed., *Promissory Notes on the Treasury of Merits: Indulgences in Late Medieval Europe.* Leiden: Brill, 2006.

Bailey, Mark, and Stephen Rigby, eds. *Town and Countryside in the Age of the Black Death: Essays in Honour of John Hatcher.* Turnhout, Belgium: Brepols, 2011.

Barron, Caroline. *London in the Later Middle Ages: Government and People, 1200–1500.* Oxford: Oxford University Press, 2005.

Baumann, Reinhard. *Georg von Frundsberg: Der Vater der Landsknechte und Feldhauptmann von Tirol.* Munich: Süddeutsscher Verlag, 1984.

Belich, James. *Replenishing the Earth: The Settler Revolution and the Rise of the Angloworld.* Oxford: Oxford University Press, 2009.

Benecke, Gerhard. *Maximilian I, 1459–1519: An Analytical Biography.* London: Routledge, 1982.

Benedictow, Ole J. *The Black Death, 1346–1353: The Complete History.* Woodbridge, UK: Boydell Press, 2004.

Bergier, Jean-François. "From the Fifteenth Century in Italy to the Sixteenth Century in Germany: A New Banking Concept?," pp. 105–29 in *The Dawn of Modern Banking.* New Haven, CT: Yale University Press, 1979.

Berlichingen, Götz von. *Götz von Berlichingen: The Autobiography of a 16th-Century German Knight.* Translated Dirk Rottgardt. West Chester, OH: The Nafziger Collection, 2014.

———. *Mein Fehd und Handlungen.* Edited by Helgard Ulmschneider. Sigmaringen, Germany: Thorbecke, 1981.

Blickle, Peter. *The Revolution of 1525: The German Peasants' War from a New Perspective.* Baltimore: Johns Hopkins University Press, 1981.

Bonney, Richard, ed. *Economic Systems and State Finance.* Oxford: Clarendon Press, 1995.

Bowd, Stephen D. *Renaissance Mass Murder: Civilians and Soldiers During the Italian Wars*. Oxford: Oxford University Press, 2019.

Brandi, Karl. *The Emperor Charles V: The Growth and Destiny of a Man and of a World-Empire*. Translated by C. V. Wedgwood. London: Jonathan Cape, 1965.

Braudel, Fernand. *Civilization and Capitalism, 15th–18th Century: The Structures of Everyday Life: The Limits of the Possible*. Translated by Sian Reynolds. Berkeley and Los Angeles: University of California Press, 1992 (1st ed. 1981).

————. *The Perspective of the World*. Translated by Sian Reynolds. Berkeley and Los Angeles: University of California Press, 1992 (1st ed. 1982).

————. *The Wheels of Commerce*. Translated by Sian Reynolds. Berkeley and Los Angeles: University of California Press, 1992 (1st ed. 1982).

Brecht, Martin. *Martin Luther: His Road to Reformation, 1483–1521*. Minneapolis: Fortress Press, 1985.

Britnell, Richard H. *The Commercialisation of English Society, 1000–1500*. Cambridge, UK: Cambridge University Press, 1993.

Britnell, Richard, and Ben Dobbs, eds. *Agriculture and Rural Society After the Black Death: Common Themes and Regional Variations*. Hatfield, UK: University of Hertfordshire Press, 2008.

Cameron, Euan. "Dissent and Heresy," pp. 3–21 in R. Po-chia Hsia, ed., *A Companion to the Reformation World*. Malden, MA: Blackwell, 2004.

Campbell, Bruce M. S. *The Great Transition: Climate, Disease, and Society in the Late-Medieval World*. Cambridge, UK: Cambridge University Press, 2016.

Capoccia, Giovanni. "Critical Junctures," pp. 89–106 in Orfeo Fioretos, Tulia G. Falleti, and Adam Sheingate, eds., *The Oxford Handbook of Historical Institutionalism*. Oxford: Oxford University Press, 2016.

Carpenter, Christine. *The Wars of the Roses: Politics and the Constitution in England, c. 1437–1509*. Cambridge, UK: Cambridge University Press, 1997.

Carus-Wilson, Eleonora Mary, and Olive Coleman. *England's Export Trade, 1275–1547.* Oxford: Clarendon Press, 1963.

Casale, Giancarlo. *The Ottoman Age of Exploration.* Oxford: Oxford University Press, 2010.

Chaudhuri, K. N. *Trade and Civilisation in the Indian Ocean: An Economic History from the Rise of Islam to 1750.* Cambridge, UK: Cambridge University Press, 1985.

Çipa, H. Erdem. *The Making of Selim: Succession, Legitimacy, and Memory in the Early Modern Ottoman World.* Bloomington: Indiana University Press, 2017.

Clemons, G. Scott. "Pressing Business: The Economics of the Aldine Press," pp. 11–24 in Natale Vacalebre, ed., *Five Centuries Later. Aldus Manutius: Culture, Typography and Philology.* Milan: Biblioteca Ambrosiana, 2019.

Clot, André. *Suleiman the Magnificent.* Translated by Matthew J. Reisz. London: Saki, 2005 (original French ed. 1989).

Crosby, Alfred W. *The Measure of Reality: Quantification and Western Society, 1250–1600.* Cambridge, UK: Cambridge University Press, 1997.

Crouzet-Pavan, Elisabeth. "Toward an Ecological Understanding of the Myth of Venice," pp. 39–64 in John Martin and Dennis Romano, eds., *Venice Reconsidered: The History and Civilization of an Italian City-State, 1297–1797.* Baltimore: Johns Hopkins University Press, 2000.

Crowley, Roger. *Conquerors: How Portugal Forged the First Global Empire.* New York: Random House, 2015.

Davies, Martin. *Aldus Manutius: Printer and Publisher of Renaissance Venice.* Malibu, CA: J. Paul Getty Museum, 1995.

De la Rosa Olivera, Leopoldo. "Francisco de Riberol y la colonia genovesa en Canarias." *Anuario de Estudios Atlanticos* 18 (1972): 61–129.

De las Casas, Bartolomé. *The Diario of Christopher Columbus's First Voyage to America, 1492–1493.* Translated by Oliver Dunn and James E. Kelly Jr. Norman: University of Oklahoma Press, 1989.

De Roover, Raymond. *The Rise and Decline of the Medici Bank, 1397–1494.* New York: Norton, 1966.

Desan, Christine. *Making Money: Coin, Currency, and the Coming of Capitalism.* Oxford: Oxford University Press, 2014.

De Valera, Diego. *Memorial de diversas hazañas.* Edited by Juan de Mata Carriazo. Madrid: Espasa-Calpe, 1941.

De Zurara, Gomes Eanes. *Chronicle of the Discovery and Conquest of Guinea.* Edited and translated by Sir Charles Raymond Beazley and Edgar Prestage. London: Hakluyt Society, 1896.

Dimmock, Spencer. *The Origin of Capitalism in England, 1400–1600.* Leiden: Brill, 2014.

Disney, A. R. *A History of Portugal and the Portuguese Empire.* Vol. 2, *The Portuguese Empire.* Cambridge, UK: Cambridge University Press, 2009.

Duffy, Christopher. *Siege Warfare: The Fortress in the Early Modern World, 1494–1660.* London: Routledge & Kegan Paul, 1979.

Dyer, Christopher. *An Age of Transition? Economy and Society in the Later Middle Ages.* Oxford: Oxford University Press, 2005.

———. *A Country Merchant, 1495–1520: Trading and Farming at the End of the Middle Ages.* Oxford: Oxford University Press, 2012.

Edwards, John. "*España es Diferente*"? Indulgences and the Spiritual Economy in Late Medieval Spain," pp. 147–68 in R. N. Swanson, ed., *Promissory Notes on the Treasury of Merits: Indulgences in Late Medieval Europe.* Leiden: Brill, 2006.

———. *Torquemada and the Inquisitors.* Stroud, UK: Tempus, 2005.

Edwards, Mark U. *Printing, Propaganda, and Martin Luther.* Minneapolis: Fortress Press, 1994.

Ehrenberg, Richard. *Capital and Finance in the Age of the Renaissance: A Study of the Fuggers, and Their Connections.* Translated by H. M. Lucas. New York: Harcourt, 1928.

Eisenstein, Elizabeth. *The Printing Press as an Agent of Change.* Cambridge, UK: Cambridge University Press, 1980.

Eisermann, Falk. "The Indulgence as a Media Event: Developments in Communication Through Broadsides in the Fifteenth Century," pp. 309–30 in R. N. Swanson, ed., *Promissory Notes on the Treasury of Merits: Indulgences in Late Medieval Europe*. Leiden: Brill, 2006.

Elbl, Ivana. "The King's Business in Africa: Decisions and Strategies of the Portuguese Crown," pp. 89–118 in Lawrin Armstrong, Ivana Elbl, and Martin M. Elbl, eds., *Money, Markets and Trade in Late Medieval Europe: Essays in Honour of John H. A. Munro*. Leiden: Brill, 2013.

Elgger, Carl von. *Kriegswesen und Kriegskunst der schweizerischen Eidgenossen im XIV., XV. und XVI. Jahrhundert*. Lucerne: Militärisches Verlagsbureau, 1873.

Elliott, J. H. "A Europe of Composite Monarchies." *Past and Present* 137 (1992): 48–71.

Epstein, Steven. *Genoa and the Genoese, 958–1528*. Chapel Hill: University of North Carolina Press, 1996.

Erasmus, Desiderius. *Colloquies*. Vol. 1. Translated by Craig R. Thompson. Toronto: University of Toronto Press, 1997.

Erikson, Erik. *Young Man Luther: A Study in Psychoanalysis and History*. New York: Norton, 1958.

Espinosa, Aurelio. *The Empire of the Cities: Emperor Charles V, the Comunero Revolt, and the Transformation of the Spanish System*. Leiden: Brill, 2009.

Faroqhi, Suraiya. *The Ottoman Empire and the World Around It*. London: I. B. Tauris, 2007.

Fernández-Armesto, Felipe. *Before Columbus: Exploration and Colonization from the Mediterranean to the Atlantic, 1229–1492*. Philadelphia: University of Pennsylvania Press, 1987.

———. *Columbus*. Oxford: Oxford University Press, 1991.

———. "La financiación de la conquista de las islas Canarias durante el reinado de los Reyes Católicos." *Anuario de Estudios Atlánticos* 28 (1982): 343–78.

Ferreira, Susannah Humble. *The Crown, the Court, and the Casa da Índia: Political Centralization in Portugal, 1479–1521*. Leiden: Brill, 2015.

Flint, Valerie. *The Imaginative Landscape of Christopher Columbus*. Princeton, NJ: Princeton University Press, 1992.

Francisco, Adam. *Martin Luther and Islam: A Study in Sixteenth-Century Polemics and Apologetics*. Leiden: Brill, 2007.

Freedman, Paul. *Out of the East: Spices and the Medieval Imagination*. New Haven, CT: Yale University Press, 2009.

Füssel, Stephan. *Gutenberg and the Impact of Printing*. Translated by Douglas Martin. Aldershot, UK: Ashgate, 2003.

Geffcken, Peter. "Jakob Fuggers frühe Jahre," pp. 4–7 in Martin Kluger, ed., *Jakob Fugger (1459–1525): Sein Leben in Bildern*. Augsburg: Context-Medien und -Verlag, 2009.

Gerulaitis, Leonardas Vytautas. *Printing and Publishing in Fifteenth-Century Venice*. Chicago: American Library Association, 1976.

Ghosh, Shami. "Rural Economies and Transitions to Capitalism: Germany and England Compared (c.1200–1800)." *Journal of Agrarian Change* 16, no. 2 (2016): 255–90.

Goffman, Daniel. *The Ottoman Empire and Early Modern Europe*. Cambridge, UK: Cambridge University Press, 2002.

Goldthwaite, Paul. *The Economy of Renaissance Florence*. Baltimore: Johns Hopkins University Press, 2011.

Gordon, Bruce. "Conciliarism in Late Mediaeval Europe," pp. 31–50 in Andrew Pettegree, ed., *The Reformation World*. London: Routledge, 2000.

Granovetter, Mark. "The Impact of Social Structure on Economic Outcomes." *Journal of Economic Perspectives* 19, no. 1 (2005): 33–50.

Green, Toby. *A Fistful of Shells: West Africa from the Rise of the Slave Trade to the Age of Revolution*. Chicago: University of Chicago Press, 2019.

Greif, Avner. *Institutions and the Path to the Modern Economy: Lessons from Medieval Trade*. Cambridge, UK: Cambridge University Press, 2006.

Grendler, Paul F. *Schooling in Renaissance Italy: Literacy and Learning, 1300–1600*. Baltimore: Johns Hopkins University Press, 1989.

Gritsch, Eric W. *Thomas Müntzer: A Tragedy of Errors*. Minneapolis: Fortress Press, 1989.

Guardiola-Griffiths, Cristina. *Legitimizing the Queen: Propaganda and Ideology in the Reign of Isabel I of Castile*. Lewisburg, PA: Bucknell University Press, 2011.

Häberlein, Mark. *The Fuggers of Augsburg: Pursuing Wealth and Honor in Renaissance Germany*. Charlottesville: University of Virginia Press, 2012.

Hall, Bert. *Weapons and Warfare in Renaissance Europe*. Baltimore: Johns Hopkins University Press, 1997.

Hanawalt, Barbara. *The Wealth of Wives: Women, Law, and Economy in Late Medieval London*. Oxford: Oxford University Press, 2007.

Harreld, Donald J. *High Germans in the Low Countries: German Merchants and Commerce in Golden Age Antwerp*. Leiden: Brill, 2004.

Harris, Ron. *Going the Distance: Eurasian Trade and the Rise of the Business Corporation, 1400–1700*. Princeton, NJ: Princeton University Press, 2020.

Headley, John M. *The Emperor and His Chancellor: A Study of the Imperial Chancellery Under Gattinara*. Cambridge, UK: Cambridge University Press, 1983.

Hess, Andrew. "The Ottoman Conquest of Egypt and the Beginning of the Sixteenth-Century World War." *International Journal of Middle East Studies* 4, no. 1 (January 1973): 55–76.

Hirsch, Rudolf. *Printing, Selling and Reading, 1450–1550*. Wiesbaden: Otto Harrassowitz, 1967.

Hoffman, Philip T. *Why Did Europe Conquer the World?* Princeton, NJ: Princeton University Press, 2015.

Hook, Judith. *The Sack of Rome: 1527*. 2nd ed. New York: Palgrave Macmillan, 2004.

Howell, Martha C. *Commerce Before Capitalism in Europe, 1300–1600*. Cambridge, UK: Cambridge University Press, 2010.

Hunt, Edwin S., and James M. Murray. *A History of Business in Medieval Europe, 1200–1550*. Cambridge, UK: Cambridge University Press, 2010.

Imber, Colin. *The Ottoman Empire: The Structure of Power, 1300–1650*. 2nd ed. New York: Palgrave Macmillan, 2009.

Inalcik, Halil. *An Economic and Social History of the Ottoman Empire*. Vol. 1, *1300–1600*. Cambridge, UK: Cambridge University Press, 1994.

Jacob, Frank, and Gilmar Visoni-Alonzo. *The Military Revolution in Early Modern Europe: A Revision*. London: Palgrave Pivot, 2016.

Jacobs, C. M., trans. *Works of Martin Luther: With Introduction and Notes*. Vol. 1. Philadelphia: Holman, 1915.

Kaebler, Lutz. "Max Weber and Usury," pp. 59–86 in Lawrin Armstrong, Ivana Elbl, and Martin M. Elbl, eds., *Money, Markets and Trade in Late Medieval Europe: Essays in Honour of John H. A. Munro*. Leiden: Brill, 2013.

Kaeuper, Richard. *Medieval Chivalry*. Cambridge, UK: Cambridge University Press, 2016.

———. *War, Justice, and Public Order: England and France in the Later Middle Ages*. Oxford: Clarendon Press, 1988.

Kafadar, Cemal. *Between Two Worlds: The Construction of the Ottoman State*. Berkeley: University of California Press, 1995.

Kamen, Henry. *The Spanish Inquisition: A Historical Revision*. New Haven, CT: Yale University Press, 1997.

Kapr, Albert. *Gutenberg: The Man and His Invention*. Translated by Douglas Martin. Aldershot, UK: Scolar Press, 1996.

Kastritis, Dimitris J. *The Sons of Bayezid: Empire Building and Representation in the Ottoman Civil War of 1402–1413*. Leiden: Brill, 2007.

Kleinschmidt, Harald. *Charles V: The World Emperor*. Stroud, UK: Sutton, 2004.

Knecht, R. J. *Renaissance Warrior and Patron: The Reign of Francis I*. Cambridge, UK: Cambridge University Press, 1994.

Koenigsberger, H. G. "*Dominium Regale* or *Dominium Politicum et Regale*: Monarchies and Parliaments in Early Modern Europe," pp. 1–26 in H. G. Koenigsberger, *Politicians and Virtuosi: Essays in Early Modern History*. London: Hambledon, 1986.

Kowaleski, Maryanne. *Local Markets and Regional Trade in Medieval Exeter*. Cambridge, UK: Cambridge University Press, 1995.

Ladero Quesada, Miguel Ángel. *La Haciendia Real de Castilla, 1369–1504*. Madrid: Real Academia de la Historia, 2009.

Lane, Frederic C. *Venice: A Maritime Republic*. Baltimore: Johns Hopkins University Press, 1973.

Le Goff, Jacques. "The Usurer and Purgatory," pp. 25–52 in *The Dawn of Modern Banking*. New Haven, CT: Yale University Press, 1979.

L'Héritier, Maxime, and Florian Téreygeol. "From Copper to Silver: Understanding the *Saigerprozess* Through Experimental Liquation and Drying." *Historical Metallurgy* 44, no. 2 (2010): 136–52.

Liss, Peggy K. "Isabel, Myth and History," pp. 57–78 in David A. Boruchoff, ed., *Isabel la Católica, Queen of Castile: Critical Essays*. New York: Palgrave Macmillan, 2003.

———. *Isabel the Queen: Life and Times*. 2nd ed. Philadelphia: University of Pennsylvania Press, 2004.

Lopez, Robert S. *The Commercial Revolution of the Middle Ages, 950–1350*. Cambridge, UK: Cambridge University Press, 1976.

———. "The Dawn of Medieval Banking," pp. 1–24 in *The Dawn of Modern Banking*. New Haven, CT: Yale University Press, 1979.

Lowry, Heath W. *The Nature of the Early Ottoman State*. Albany: State University of New York Press, 2003.

Lowry, Martin. *Nicholas Jenson and the Rise of Venetian Publishing in Renaissance Europe*. Oxford: Basil Blackwell, 1991.

———. *The World of Aldus Manutius: Business and Scholarship in Renaissance Venice*. Ithaca, NY: Cornell University Press, 1979.

MacCulloch, Diarmaid. *The Reformation: A History*. New York: Penguin, 2003.

Mahoney, James, Khairunnisa Mohamedali, and Christopher Nguyen. "Causality and Time in Historical Institutionalism," pp. 71–88 in Orfeo Fioretos, Tulia G. Falleti, and Adam Sheingate, eds., *The Oxford Handbook of Historical Institutionalism*. Oxford: Oxford University Press, 2016.

Mallett, Michael. *Mercenaries and Their Masters: Warfare in Renaissance Italy*. 2nd ed. Barnsley, UK: Pen & Sword Military, 2009.

Mallett, Michael, and Christine Shaw. *The Italian Wars, 1494–1559: War, State and Society in Early Modern Europe*. New York: Routledge, 2012.

Mann, Nicholas. "The Origins of Humanism," pp. 1–19 in Jill Kraye, ed., *The Cambridge Companion to Renaissance Humanism*. Cambridge, UK: Cambridge University Press, 1996.

Marius, Richard. *Martin Luther: The Christian Between God and Death.* Cambridge, MA: Belknap, 1999.

Marshall, Richard K. *The Local Merchants of Prato: Small Entrepreneurs in the Late Medieval Economy.* Baltimore: Johns Hopkins University Press, 1999.

McCormick, Michael. *Origins of the European Economy: Communications and Commerce, AD 300–900.* Cambridge, UK: Cambridge University Press, 2001.

McGrath, Alister E. *The Intellectual Origins of the European Reformation.* 2nd ed. Malden, MA: Blackwell, 2004.

Merriman, Roger Bigelow. *Suleiman the Magnificent, 1520–1566.* Cambridge, MA: Harvard University Press, 1944.

Mokyr, Joel. *A Culture of Growth: The Origins of the Modern Economy.* Princeton, NJ: Princeton University Press, 2016.

Morris, Ian. *Why the West Rules—For Now: The Patterns of History, and What They Reveal About the Future.* New York: Farrar, Straus & Giroux, 2010.

Muldrew, Craig. *The Economy of Obligation: The Culture of Credit and Social Obligation in Early Modern England.* New York: St. Martin's Press, 1998.

Munro, John. "The Monetary Origins of the 'Price Revolution': South German Silver-Mining, Merchant-Banking, and Venetian Commerce, 1470–1540." University of Toronto working paper, 2003.

Nauert, Charles G. *Humanism and the Culture of Renaissance Europe.* Cambridge, UK: Cambridge University Press, 1995.

Newitt, Malyn. *A History of Portuguese Overseas Expansion, 1400–1668.* New York: Routledge, 2005.

Nightingale, P. "Monetary Contraction and Mercantile Credit in Later Medieval England." *Economic History Review* 43 (1990): 560–75.

Nossov, Konstantin, and Brian Delf. *The Fortress of Rhodes 1309–1522.* Oxford: Osprey, 2010.

Oberman, Heiko. *Luther: Man Between God and the Devil.* New Haven, CT: Yale University Press, 1989.

O'Callaghan, Joseph F. *The Gibraltar Crusade: Castile and the Battle for the Strait.* Philadelphia: University of Pennsylvania Press, 2011.

————. *The Last Crusade in the West: Castile and the Conquest of Granada.* Philadelphia: University of Pennsylvania Press, 2014.

————. *Reconquest and Crusade in Medieval Spain.* Philadelphia: University of Pennsylvania Press, 2003.

Ocker, Christopher. *Luther, Conflict, and Christendom.* Cambridge, UK: Cambridge University Press, 2018.

Ogilvie, Sheilagh. *Institutions and European Trade: Merchant Guilds, 1000–1800.* Cambridge, UK: Cambridge University Press, 2011.

Oldland, John. *The English Woollen Industry, c.1200–c.1560.* New York: Routledge, 2019.

Oliva Herrer, Hipólito Rafael. "Interpreting Large-Scale Revolts: Some Evidence from the War of the Communities of Castile," pp. 330–48 in Justine Firnhaber-Baker and Dirk Schoenaers, eds., *The Routledge History Handbook of Medieval Revolts.* New York: Routledge, 2017.

Oro, José García. *El Cardenal Cisneros: Vida y impresas.* 2 vols. Madrid: Biblioteca de Autores Cristianos, 1992–93.

Özbaran, Salih. "Ottoman Naval Policy in the South," pp. 55–70 in Metin Kunt and Christine Woodhead, eds., *Süleyman the Magnificent and His Age: The Ottoman Empire in the Early Modern World.* London: Longman, 1995.

Pálffy, Géza. *The Kingdom of Hungary and the Habsburg Monarchy in the Sixteenth Century.* Translated by Thomas J. DeKornfeld and Helen D. DeKornfeld. New York: Columbia University Press, 2009.

Pamuk, Şevket. "In the Absence of Domestic Currency: Debased European Coinage in the Seventeenth-Century Ottoman Empire." *Journal of Economic History* 57, no. 2 (June 1997): 345–66.

Parker, Geoffrey. *Emperor: A New Life of Charles V.* New Haven, CT: Yale University Press, 2019.

————. *The Military Revolution: Military Innovation and the Rise of the West, 1500–1800.* 2nd ed. Cambridge, UK: Cambridge University Press, 1996.

Parrott, David. *The Business of War: Military Enterprise and Military Innovation in Early Modern Europe.* Cambridge, UK: Cambridge University Press, 2012.

Perjés, Géza. *The Fall of the Medieval Kingdom of Hungary: Mohács 1526–Buda 1541*. Vol. 26 of *War and Society in East Central Europe*. New York: Columbia University Press, 1989.

Pettegree, Andrew. *The Book in the Renaissance*. New Haven, CT: Yale University Press, 2010.

———. *Brand Luther: 1517, Printing, and the Making of the Reformation*. New York: Penguin, 2015.

———. *The Invention of News: How the World Came to Know About Itself*. New Haven, CT: Yale University Press, 2014.

Pike, Ruth. *Enterprise and Adventure: The Genoese in Seville and the Opening of the New World*. Ithaca, NY: Cornell University Press, 1966.

Pomeranz, Kenneth. *The Great Divergence: China, Europe, and the Making of the Modern World Economy*. Princeton, NJ: Princeton University Press, 2000.

Poos, L. R. *A Rural Society After the Black Death: Essex 1350–1525*. Cambridge, UK: Cambridge University Press, 1991.

Potter, David. *Renaissance France at War*. Woodbridge, UK: Boydell Press, 2008.

Preda, Alex. "Legitimacy and Status Groups in Financial Markets." *British Journal of Sociology* 56, no. 3 (2005): 451–71.

Redlich, Fritz. *The German Military Enterpriser and His Work Force: A Study in European Economic and Social History*. Vol. 1. Wiesbaden: Franz Steiner Verlag, 1964.

Reeve, Michael D. "Classical Scholarship," pp. 20–46 in Jill Kraye, ed., *The Cambridge Companion to Renaissance Humanism*. Cambridge, UK: Cambridge University Press, 1996.

Reston, James. *Defenders of the Faith: Christianity and Islam Battle for the Soul of Europe, 1520–1536*. New York: Penguin, 2009.

Rex, Richard. "Humanism," pp. 51–71 in Andrew Pettegree, ed., *The Reformation World*. London: Routledge, 2000.

Rogers, Clifford J., ed. *The Military Revolution Debate: Readings on the Military Transformation of Early Modern Europe*. Boulder, CO: Westview Press, 1995.

————. "The Military Revolution of the Hundred Years War," pp. 55–93 in Clifford J. Rogers, ed., *The Military Revolution Debate: Readings on the Military Transformation of Early Modern Europe*. Boulder, CO: Westview Press, 1995.

Roper, Lyndal. *Martin Luther: Renegade and Prophet*. New York: Random House, 2016.

Rösch, Gerhard. "The *Serrata* of the Great Council and Venetian Society, 1286–1323," pp. 67–88 in John Martin and Dennis Romano, eds., *Venice Reconsidered: The History and Civilization of an Italian City-State, 1297–1797*. Baltimore: Johns Hopkins University Press, 2000.

Roth, Norman. *Conversos, Inquisition, and the Expulsion of the Jews from Spain*. Madison: University of Wisconsin Press, 1995.

Ruggiero, Guido. *The Renaissance in Italy: A Social and Cultural History of the Rinascimento*. Cambridge, UK: Cambridge University Press, 2015.

Ruiz, Teofilo R. *Crisis and Continuity: Land and Town in Late Medieval Castile*. Philadelphia: University of Pennsylvania Press, 1994.

Rummel, Erika. *Jiménez de Cisneros: On the Threshold of Spain's Golden Age*. Tempe: Arizona Center for Medieval and Renaissance Studies, 1999.

Russell, Peter. *Prince Henry "the Navigator": A Life*. New Haven, CT: Yale University Press, 2000.

Saak, Eric Leland. *Luther and the Reformation of the Later Middle Ages*. Cambridge, MA: Cambridge University Press, 2017.

Safley, Thomas Max. *Family Firms and Merchant Capitalism in Early Modern Europe: The Business, Bankruptcy, and Resilience of the Höchstetters of Augsburg*. New York: Routledge, 2020.

Şahin, Kaya. *Empire and Power in the Reign of Süleyman: Narrating the Sixteenth-Century Ottoman World*. Cambridge, UK: Cambridge University Press, 2013.

Scheidel, Walter. *Escape from Rome: The Failure of Empire and the Road to Prosperity*. Princeton, NJ: Princeton University Press, 2019.

Scott, Jonathan. *How the Old World Ended: The Anglo-Dutch-American Revolution, 1500–1800*. New Haven, CT: Yale University Press, 2019.

Scott, Tom. *Thomas Müntzer: Theology and Revolution in the German Reformation.* New York: St. Martin's Press, 1989.

Scott, Tom, and Bob Scribner, eds. *The German Peasants' War: A History in Documents.* New York: Humanities Books, 1991.

Shaffern, Robert W. "The Medieval Theology of Indulgences," pp. 37–64 in R. N. Swanson, ed., *Promissory Notes on the Treasury of Merits: Indulgences in Late Medieval Europe.* Leiden: Brill, 2006.

Shepard, Alexandra. *Accounting for Oneself: Worth, Status, and the Social Order in Early Modern England.* Oxford: Oxford University Press, 2015.

Sherer, Idan. *Warriors for a Living: The Experience of the Spanish Infantry During the Italian Wars, 1494–1559.* Leiden: Brill, 2017.

Silver, Larry. *Marketing Maximilian: The Visual Ideology of a Holy Roman Emperor.* Princeton, NJ: Princeton University Press, 2008.

Simonsfeld, Henry. *Der Fondaco dei Tedeschi in Venedig und die deutsch-venetianischen Handelsbeziehungen.* Stuttgart: Cotta, 1887.

Spruyt, Hendrik. *The Sovereign State and Its Competitors: An Analysis of Systems Change.* Princeton, NJ: Princeton University Press, 1994.

Spufford, Peter. *Money and Its Use in Medieval Europe.* Cambridge, UK: Cambridge University Press, 1988.

———. *Power and Profit: The Merchant in Medieval Europe.* London: Thames & Hudson, 2002.

Stasavage, David. *States of Credit: Size, Power, and the Development of European Polities.* Princeton, NJ: Princeton University Press, 2011.

Stayer, James M. "The German Peasants' War and the Rural Reformation," pp. 127–45 in Andrew Pettegree, ed., *The Reformation World.* London: Routledge, 2000.

Stein, Robert. *Magnanimous Dukes and Rising States: The Unification of the Burgundian Netherlands, 1380–1480.* Oxford: Oxford University Press, 2017.

Steinmetz, Greg. *The Richest Man Who Ever Lived: The Life and Times of Jacob Fugger.* New York: Simon & Schuster, 2015.

Strayer, Joseph R. *On the Medieval Origins of the Modern State.* Princeton, NJ: Princeton University Press, 1970.

Strieder, Jacob. *Jacob Fugger the Rich.* New York: Adelphi Press, 1931.

Studer, Roman. *The Great Divergence Reconsidered: Europe, India, and the Rise of Global Economic Power*. Cambridge, UK: Cambridge University Press, 2015.

Subrahmanyam, Sanjay. *The Career and Legend of Vasco da Gama*. Cambridge, UK: Cambridge University Press, 1997.

Swanson, R. N. "The Pre-Reformation Church," pp. 9–30 in Andrew Pettegree, ed., *The Reformation World*. London: Routledge, 2000.

Taylor, Larissa. "Society and Piety," pp. 22–36 in R. Po-chia Hsia, ed., *A Companion to the Reformation World*. Malden, MA: Blackwell, 2004.

Thomas, Hugh. *Conquest: Montezuma, Cortés, and the Fall of Old Mexico*. New York: Touchstone, 1993.

Thrupp, Sylvia L. *The Merchant Class of Medieval London, 1300–1500*. Ann Arbor: University of Michigan Press, 1948.

Tilly, Charles. *Coercion, Capital, and European States, AD 990–1992*. Malden, MA: Blackwell, 1992.

———. *The Formation of National States in Western Europe*. Princeton, NJ: Princeton University Press, 1975.

Tooze, Adam. *The Deluge: The Great War, America and the Remaking of the Global Order, 1916–1931*. New York: Viking, 2014.

Tracy, James D. *Emperor Charles V, Impresario of War: Campaign Strategy, International Finance, and Domestic Politics*. Cambridge, UK: Cambridge University Press, 2002.

Trim, David J. B., ed. *The Chivalric Ethos and the Development of Military Professionalism*. Leiden: Brill, 2003.

Usher, Abbott Payson. *The Early History of Deposit Banking in Mediterranean Europe*. Cambridge, MA: Harvard University Press, 1943.

Val Valdivieso, María Isabel del. "Isabel, *Infanta* and Princess of Castile," pp. 41–56 in David A. Boruchoff, ed., *Isabel la Católica, Queen of Castile: Critical Essays*. New York: Palgrave Macmillan, 2003.

Van der Wee, Herman. *The Growth of the Antwerp Market and the European Economy, 1400s–1600s*. The Hague: Nijhoff, 1963.

Van Doosselaere, Quentin. *Commercial Agreements and Social Dynamics in Medieval Genoa*. Cambridge, UK: Cambridge University Press, 2009.

Varela, Consuelo. *Colón y los Florentinos*. Madrid: Alianza, 1989.

Vaughan, Richard. *Charles the Bold*. Woodbridge, UK: Boydell Press, 2002 (1st ed. 1973).

Verlinden, Charles. "The Italian Colony of Lisbon and the Development of Portuguese Metropolitan and Colonial Economy," pp. 98–113 in Charles Verlinden, *The Beginnings of Modern Colonization*. Ithaca, NY: Cornell University Press, 1970.

———. "A Precursor of Columbus: The Fleming Ferdinand van Olmen," pp. 181–95 in Charles Verlinden, *The Beginnings of Modern Colonization*. Ithaca, NY: Cornell University Press, 1970.

Watts, John. *The Making of Polities: Europe, 1300–1500*. Cambridge, UK: Cambridge University Press, 2009.

Weissberger, Barbara F. *Isabel Rules: Constructing Queenship, Wielding Power*. Minneapolis: University of Minnesota Press, 2004.

Wickham, Chris. *Framing the Early Middle Ages*. Oxford: Oxford University Press, 2005.

Williams, Ann. "Mediterranean Conflict," pp. 39–54 in Metin Kunt and Christine Woodhead, eds., *Süleyman the Magnificent and His Age: The Ottoman Empire in the Early Modern World*. London: Longman, 1995.

Wilson, Peter. *The Thirty Years War: Europe's Tragedy*. Cambridge, MA: Harvard University Press, 2011.

Wood, Diana. *Medieval Economic Thought*. Cambridge, UK: Cambridge University Press, 2002.

Woodhead, Christine. "Perspectives on Süleyman," pp. 164–90 in Metin Kunt and Christine Woodhead, eds., *Süleyman the Magnificent and His Age: The Ottoman Empire in the Early Modern World*. London: Longman, 1995.

Wyman, Patrick (host). "Interview: Historian Christopher Dyer on Peasants and the Medieval Economy." *Tides of History*, September 27, 2018.

Zmora, Hillay. *The Feud in Early Modern Germany*. Cambridge, UK: Cambridge University Press, 2011.

———. *State and Nobility in Early Modern Germany: The Knightly Feud in Franconia, 1440–1567*. Cambridge, UK: Cambridge University Press, 2003.

Endnotes

A Note on Money and Currencies

1　Peter Spufford, *Money and Its Use in Medieval Europe* (Cambridge, UK: Cambridge University Press, 1988), pp. 291–93 and 400–414.

2　Martha C. Howell, *Commerce Before Capitalism in Europe, 1300–1600* (Cambridge, UK: Cambridge University Press, 2010), pp. 303–6.

3　Idan Sherer, *Warriors for a Living: The Experience of the Spanish Infantry During the Italian Wars, 1494–1559* (Leiden: Brill, 2017), p. 25.

4　Paul Goldthwaite, *The Economy of Renaissance Florence* (Baltimore: Johns Hopkins University Press, 2011), p. 613.

Introduction

1　Judith Hook, *The Sack of Rome: 1527*, 2nd ed. (New York: Palgrave Macmillan, 2004), pp. 161–66.

2　Quoted in Hook, *Sack of Rome*, p. 163.

3　Quoted in Hook, *Sack of Rome*, p. 167, and see pp. 166–76; Kenneth Gouwens, *Remembering the Renaissance: Humanist Narratives of the Sack of Rome* (Leiden: Brill, 1998), pp. xvii–xix and 1–5.

4　On Europe as backwater, see Janet L. Abu-Lughod, *Before European Hegemony: The World System, A.D. 1250–1350* (Oxford: Oxford University Press, 1989).

5　On the multipolar system: Walter Scheidel, *Escape from Rome: The Failure of Empire and the Road to Prosperity* (Princeton, NJ: Princeton University Press, 2019); deep divergence: Ian Morris, *Why the West Rules—For Now: The Patterns of History, and What They Reveal About the Future* (New York: Farrar, Straus & Giroux, 2010); culture: Joel Mokyr, *A Culture of Growth: The Origins of the Modern Economy* (Princeton, NJ: Princeton University Press, 2016); the Anglo-Dutch: Jonathan Scott, *How the Old World Ended: The Anglo-Dutch-American Revolution, 1500–1800* (New Haven, CT: Yale University Press, 2019), and James Belich, *Replenishing the Earth: The Settler Revolution and the*

Rise of the Angloworld (Oxford: Oxford University Press, 2009); China: Kenneth Pomeranz, *The Great Divergence: China, Europe, and the Making of the Modern World Economy* (Princeton, NJ: Princeton University Press, 2000); military: Philip T. Hoffman, *Why Did Europe Conquer the World?* (Princeton, NJ: Princeton University Press, 2015); India and markets: Roman Studer, *The Great Divergence Reconsidered: Europe, India, and the Rise of Global Economic Power* (Cambridge, UK: Cambridge University Press, 2015). This is just a brief selection of recent works; there are many, many more.

6   For the classic works on the *longue durée*, the long-term processes that remodel social structures on a large scale, see Fernand Braudel's three-volume series *Civilization and Capitalism, 15th–18th Century: The Structures of Everyday Life: The Limits of the Possible*, trans. Sian Reynolds (Berkeley and Los Angeles: University of California Press, 1992 [1st ed. 1981]); *The Wheels of Commerce*, trans. Sian Reynolds (Berkeley and Los Angeles: University of California Press, 1992 [1st ed. 1982]); and *The Perspective of the World*, trans. Sian Reynolds (Berkeley and Los Angeles: University of California Press, 1992 [1st ed. 1982]).

7   Avner Greif, *Institutions and the Path to the Modern Economy: Lessons From Medieval Trade* (Cambridge, UK: Cambridge University Press, 2006), especially pp. 14–23; Sheilagh Ogilvie, *Institutions and European Trade: Merchant Guilds, 1000–1800* (Cambridge, UK: Cambridge University Press, 2011), especially pp. 414–33.

8   Bruce M. S. Campbell, *The Great Transition: Climate, Disease, and Society in the Late-Medieval World* (Cambridge, UK: Cambridge University Press, 2016).

9   See fundamentally Craig Muldrew, *The Economy of Obligation: The Culture of Credit and Social Obligation in Early Modern England* (New York: St. Martin's Press, 1998), pp. 1–3. Muldrew's arguments apply far more broadly than his English case study. See also Thomas Max Safley, *Family Firms and Merchant Capitalism in Early Modern Europe: The Business, Bankruptcy, and Resilience of the Höchstetters of Augsburg* (New York: Routledge, 2020); Alexandra Shepard, *Accounting for Oneself: Worth, Status, and the Social Order in Early Modern England* (Oxford: Oxford University Press, 2015). On markets and social networks more generally, see Mark Granovetter, "The Impact of Social Structure on Economic Outcomes," *Journal of Economic Perspectives* 19, no. 1 (2005): 33–50; Alex Preda, "Legitimacy and Status Groups in Financial Markets," *British Journal of Sociology* 56, no. 3 (2005): 451–71.

10 Greif, *Institutions and the Path to the Modern Economy*, pp. 338–49; see also Ron Harris, *Going the Distance: Eurasian Trade and the Rise of the Business Corporation, 1400–1700* (Princeton, NJ: Princeton University Press, 2020), pp. 173–233.

11 On the theoretical framework of institutional migration, see Harris, *Going the Distance*, pp. 57–62; on differences in credit regimes throughout Europe, and its

extreme prevalence in England, see Christine Desan, *Making Money: Coin, Currency, and the Coming of Capitalism* (Oxford: Oxford University Press, 2014), pp. 205–30; on credit's centrality to business in a small Italian market, see Richard K. Marshall, *The Local Merchants of Prato: Small Entrepreneurs in the Late Medieval Economy* (Baltimore: Johns Hopkins University Press, 1999), pp. 71–100.

12 Peter Spufford, *Money and Its Use in Medieval Europe* (Cambridge: Cambridge University Press, 1988), especially pp. 339–62; on the shortage of coin and the accompanying shortage of credit, see Desan, *Making Money*, p. 206.

13 Stephen D. Bowd, *Renaissance Mass Murder: Civilians and Soldiers During the Italian Wars* (Oxford: Oxford University Press, 2019), table on p. 6.

14 For an introduction to the concepts, see James Mahoney, Khairunnisa Mohamedali, and Christopher Nguyen, "Causality and Time in Historical Institutionalism," pp. 71–88 in Orfeo Fioretos, Tulia G. Falleti, and Adam Sheingate, eds., *The Oxford Handbook of Historical Institutionalism* (Oxford: Oxford University Press, 2016), especially pp. 77–87; and Giovanni Capoccia, "Critical Junctures," pp. 89–106 in Fioretos, Falleti, and Sheingate eds., *The Oxford Handbook of Historical Institutionalism*.

Chapter 1: Christopher Columbus and Exploration

1 Bartolome de las Casas, *The* Diario *of Christopher Columbus's First Voyage to America, 1492–1493*, trans. Oliver Dunn and James E. Kelly Jr. (Norman: University of Oklahoma Press, 1989), pp. 391–93.

2 Felipe Fernández-Armesto, *Before Columbus: Exploration and Colonization from the Mediterranean to the Atlantic, 1229–1492* (Philadelphia: University of Pennsylvania Press, 1987), pp. 151–202.

3 Peter Russell, *Prince Henry "the Navigator": A Life* (New Haven, CT: Yale University Press, 2000).

4 Russell, *Prince Henry*, pp. 73–74.

5 Russell, *Prince Henry*, p. 84.

6 On the West African gold trade, see Toby Green, *A Fistful of Shells: West Africa from the Rise of the Slave Trade to the Age of Revolution* (Chicago: University of Chicago Press, 2019), pp. 31–67.

7 Green, *A Fistful of Shells*, pp. 37–59.

8 Malyn Newitt, *A History of Portuguese Overseas Expansion, 1400–1668* (New York: Routledge, 2005), pp. 26–32.

9 Gomes Eanes de Zurara, *Chronicle of the Discovery and Conquest of Guinea*, ed. and trans. Sir Charles Raymond Beazley and Edgar Prestage (London: Hakluyt Society, 1896), p. 6.

10 Ivana Elbl, "The King's Business in Africa: Decisions and Strategies of the Portuguese Crown," pp. 89–118 in Lawrin Armstrong, Ivana Elbl, and

Martin M. Elbl, eds., *Money, Markets and Trade in Late Medieval Europe: Essays in Honour of John H. A. Munro* (Leiden: Brill, 2013), pp. 106–7.

11 Charles Verlinden, "The Italian Colony of Lisbon and the Development of Portuguese Metropolitan and Colonial Economy," pp. 98–113 in Verlinden, *The Beginnings of Modern Colonization* (Ithaca, NY: Cornell University Press, 1970), p. 104. See also A. R. Disney, *A History of Portugal and the Portuguese Empire*, vol. 2, *The Portuguese Empire* (Cambridge, UK: Cambridge University Press, 2009), pp. 33–34.

12 Quentin van Doosselaere, *Commercial Agreements and Social Dynamics in Medieval Genoa* (Cambridge, UK: Cambridge University Press, 2009).

13 Steven Epstein, *Genoa and the Genoese, 958–1528* (Chapel Hill: University of North Carolina Press, 1996), pp. 242–62.

14 Fernández-Armesto, *Before Columbus*, pp. 105–20; see also Ruth Pike, *Enterprise and Adventure: The Genoese in Seville and the Opening of the New World* (Ithaca, NY: Cornell University Press, 1966), pp. 1–19.

15 Felipe Fernández-Armesto, *Columbus* (Oxford: Oxford University Press, 1991), pp. 1–7. Quote cited in ibid., p. 5.

16 Quote cited in Fernández-Armesto, *Columbus*, p. 5.

17 On Isabella and Ferdinand and the War of the Castilian Succession, see Peggy K. Liss, *Isabel the Queen: Life and Times*, 2nd ed. (Philadelphia: University of Pennsylvania Press, 2004), pp. 115–65.

18 Newitt, *A History of Portuguese Overseas Expansion*, pp. 39–41.

19 Consuelo Varela, *Colón y los Florentinos* (Madrid: Alianza, 1989), pp. 25–26.

20 Valerie Flint, *The Imaginative Landscape of Christopher Columbus* (Princeton, NJ: Princeton University Press, 1992), pp. 44–46 and 66–67.

21 Fernández-Armesto, *Columbus*, pp. 33–43; Flint, *Imaginative Landscape*, pp. 43–78.

22 Newitt, *A History of Portuguese Overseas Expansion*, pp. 44–48; more generally, Susannah Humble Ferreira, *The Crown, the Court, and the Casa da Índia: Political Centralization in Portugal, 1479–1521* (Leiden: Brill, 2015).

23 Disney, *A History of Portugal and the Portuguese Empire*, pp. 35–37.

24 Paul Freedman, *Out of the East: Spices and the Medieval Imagination* (New Haven, CT: Yale University Press, 2009).

25 On Van Olmen and his possible influence on Columbus, see Charles Verlinden, "A Precursor of Columbus: The Fleming Ferdinand van Olmen," pp. 181–95 in Verlinden, *The Beginnings of Modern Colonization*.

26 Fernández-Armesto, *Columbus*, p. 54.

27 Fernández-Armesto, *Columbus*, pp. 54–65. On the Canary Islands angle, see Felipe Fernández-Armesto, "La financiación de la conquista de las islas Canarias durante el reinado de los Reyes Católicos," *Anuario de Estudios*

Atlánticos 28 (1982): 343–78. On the Rivarolos, see Leopoldo de la Rosa Olivera, "Francisco de Riberol y la colonia genovesa en Canarias," *Anuario de Estudios Atlanticos* 18 (1972): 61–129.

28 Liss, *Isabel the Queen*, pp. 325–26.

29 Fernández-Armesto, *Columbus*, pp. 61–63; Pike, *Enterprise and Adventure*, p. 3.

30 Quoted in Fernández-Armesto, *Columbus*, p. 93.

31 Liss, *Isabel the Queen*, p. 326. Only a safe-conduct (a pass explaining Columbus's affiliation with the Crown) in early 1492 made any mention of a religious purpose.

32 Sanjay Subrahmanyam, *The Career and Legend of Vasco da Gama* (Cambridge, UK: Cambridge University Press, 1997), pp. 47–54.

33 Newitt, *A History of Portuguese Overseas Expansion*, pp. 46–52; on the Marchionni, see also Paul Goldthwaite, *The Economy of Renaissance Florence* (Baltimore: Johns Hopkins University Press, 2011), pp. 155–60.

34 Subrahmanyam, *The Career and Legend of Vasco da Gama*, pp. 54–57.

35 On da Gama's first voyage, see Subrahmanyam, *The Career and Legend of Vasco da Gama*, pp. 79–163; estimate: Roger Crowley, *Conquerors: How Portugal Forged the First Global Empire* (New York: Random House, 2015), p. 130; on the Indian Ocean more broadly, see K. N. Chaudhuri, *Trade and Civilisation in the Indian Ocean: An Economic History from the Rise of Islam to 1750* (Cambridge, UK: Cambridge University Press, 1985), pp. 52–62.

36 Subrahmanyam, *Vasco da Gama*, pp. 181–84; Newitt, *A History of Portuguese Overseas Expansion*, pp. 66–70.

37 Thomé Lopes, cited in Crowley, *Conquerors*, pp. 108–9.

38 Quoted in Fernández-Armesto, *Columbus*, p. 138; on slavery and Columbus, see Epstein, *Genoa and the Genoese*, pp. 310–12.

39 Newitt, *A History of Portuguese Overseas Expansion*, pp. 68–70 and 99.

40 Elbl, "The King's Business in Africa," pp. 112–14.

41 Hugh Thomas, *Conquest: Montezuma, Cortés, and the Fall of Old Mexico* (New York: Touchstone, 1993), pp. 65–69.

Chapter 2: Isabella of Castile and the Rise of the State

1 The incident is chronicled by Diego de Valera, *Memorial de diversas hazañas*, ed. Juan de Mata Carriazo (Madrid: Espasa-Calpe, 1941), cap. 36.

2 De Valera, *Memorial*, trans. and quoted in Peggy K. Liss, *Isabel the Queen: Life and Times* (Philadelphia: University of Pennsylvania Press, 2004), pp. 47–48.

3 For useful overviews of this narrative, see John Watts, *The Making of Polities: Europe, 1300-1500* (Cambridge, UK: Cambridge University Press, 2009), pp. 23–33, and Ronald G. Asch, "Monarchy in Western and Central Europe," pp. 355–83 in Hamish Scott, ed., *The Oxford Handbook of Early*

Modern European History, vol. 2, *Cultures and Power* (Oxford: Oxford University Press, 2015). The classic formulations are Joseph R. Strayer, *On the Medieval Origins of the Modern State* (Princeton, NJ: Princeton University Press, 1970), and Charles Tilly, *The Formation of National States in Western Europe* (Princeton, NJ: Princeton University Press, 1975).

4 Watts, *The Making of Polities*, pp. 29–32 and 376ff.

5 Hendrik Spruyt, *The Sovereign State and Its Competitors: An Analysis of Systems Change* (Princeton, NJ: Princeton University Press, 1994).

6 Liss, *Isabel the Queen*, pp. 11–25 and 37–50; María Isabel del Val Valdivieso, "Isabel, *Infanta* and Princess of Castile," pp. 41–56 in David A. Boruchoff, ed., *Isabel la Católica, Queen of Castile: Critical Essays* (New York: Palgrave Macmillan, 2003).

7 Quoted in Liss, *Isabel the Queen*, p. 54, from a letter to Gonzalo Chacón, her mayordomo.

8 J. H. Elliott, "A Europe of Composite Monarchies," *Past and Present* 137 (1992): 48–71; H. G. Koenigsberger, "*Dominium Regale* or *Dominium Politicum et Regale*: Monarchies and Parliaments in Early Modern Europe," pp. 1–26 in H. G. Koenigsberger, *Politicians and Virtuosi: Essays in Early Modern History* (London: Hambledon, 1986).

9 Liss, *Isabel the Queen*, pp. 58–62; letter to Enrique quoted on p. 61.

10 Liss, *Isabel the Queen*, pp. 62–67; letter to Enrique quoted on p. 65.

11 Richard Kaeuper, *War, Justice, and Public Order: England and France in the Later Middle Ages* (Oxford: Clarendon Press, 1988).

12 See Watts, *The Making of Polities*, pp. 340–52.

13 Liss, *Isabel the Queen*, pp. 105–8; on Isabel and legitimacy, see Cristina Guardiola-Griffiths, *Legitimizing the Queen: Propaganda and Ideology in the Reign of Isabel I of Castile* (Lewisburg, PA: Bucknell University Press, 2011); Barbara F. Weissberger, *Isabel Rules: Constructing Queenship, Wielding Power* (Minneapolis: University of Minnesota Press, 2004).

14 Liss, *Isabel the Queen*, pp. 113–15.

15 Liss, *Isabel the Queen*, 202–6.

16 Charles Tilly, *Coercion, Capital, and European States, AD 990–1992* (Malden, MA: Blackwell, 1992), pp. 82–90; for the quote, Tilly, *The Formation of National States in Western Europe*, p. 42.

17 Joseph F. O'Callaghan, *Reconquest and Crusade in Medieval Spain* (Philadelphia: University of Pennsylvania Press, 2003), pp. 3–8.

18 Joseph F. O'Callaghan, *The Gibraltar Crusade: Castile and the Battle for the Strait* (Philadelphia: University of Pennsylvania Press, 2011).

19 Liss, *Isabel the Queen*, pp. 101–9; Peggy K. Liss, "Isabel, Myth and History," pp. 57–78 in Boruchoff, ed., *Isabel la Católica*.

20 Quoted in Liss, *Isabel the Queen*, p. 212.

21 Quoted in Joseph F. O'Callaghan, *The Last Crusade in the West: Castile and the Conquest of Granada* (Philadelphia: University of Pennsylvania Press, 2014), p. 127.

22 O'Callaghan, *The Last Crusade in the West*, p. 134.

23 O'Callaghan, *The Last Crusade in the West*, pp. 142–45 and 184–95.

24 See, e.g., Christine Carpenter, *The Wars of the Roses: Politics and the Constitution in England, c. 1437–1509* (Cambridge, UK: Cambridge University Press, 1997), pp. 104–5.

25 Robert Stein, *Magnanimous Dukes and Rising States: The Unification of the Burgundian Netherlands, 1380–1480* (Oxford: Oxford University Press, 2017), pp. 226–54.

26 Miguel Ángel Ladero Quesada, La Haciendia Real de Castilla, 1369–1504 (Madrid: Real Academia de la Historia, 2009), pp. 233–40; O'Callaghan, *The Last Crusade in the West*, pp. 222–24.

27 Liss, *Isabel the Queen*, p. 247.

28 O'Callaghan, *The Last Crusade in the West*, pp. 220–25.

29 On the Bardi and Peruzzi, see Edwin S. Hunt and James M. Murray, *A History of Business in Medieval Europe, 1200–1550* (Cambridge, UK: Cambridge University Press, 2010), pp. 116–21; on the Medici, see Raymond de Roover, *The Rise and Decline of the Medici Bank, 1397–1494* (New York: Norton, 1966), pp. 346–57.

30 Liss, *Isabel the Queen*, pp. 250–53.

31 David Stasavage, *States of Credit: Size, Power, and the Development of European Polities* (Princeton: Princeton University Press, 2011), pp. 9–38.

32 Richard Bonney, ed., *Economic Systems and State Finance* (Oxford: Clarendon Press, 1995).

33 Liss, *Isabel the Queen*, p. 258.

34 Liss, *Isabel the Queen*, pp. 101–9, 177–96, and 278–79; Norman Roth, *Conversos, Inquisition, and the Expulsion of the Jews from Spain* (Madison: University of Wisconsin Press, 1995); Henry Kamen, *The Spanish Inquisition: A Historical Revision* (New Haven, CT: Yale University Press, 1997); John Edwards, *Torquemada and the Inquisitors* (Stroud, UK: Tempus, 2005).

35 Liss, *Isabel the Queen*, pp. 396–99.

Chapter 3: Jakob Fugger and Banking

1 Quoted in Greg Steinmetz, *The Richest Man Who Ever Lived: The Life and Times of Jacob Fugger* (New York: Simon & Schuster, 2015), p. xiii.

2 Jean Andreau, *Banking and Business in the Roman World* (Cambridge, UK: Cambridge University Press, 1999); Chris Wickham, *Framing the Early Middle Ages*

(Oxford: Oxford University Press, 2005), pp. 693–831; Michael McCormick, *Origins of the European Economy: Communications and Commerce, AD 300–900* (Cambridge, UK: Cambridge University Press, 2001), pp. 27–122.

3 Robert S. Lopez, *The Commercial Revolution of the Middle Ages, 950–1350* (Cambridge, UK: Cambridge University Press, 1976).

4 Robert S. Lopez, "The Dawn of Medieval Banking," pp. 1–24 in *The Dawn of Modern Banking* (New Haven, CT: Yale University Press, 1979); see also Abbott Payson Usher, *The Early History of Deposit Banking in Mediterranean Europe* (Cambridge, MA: Harvard University Press, 1943, especially pp. 110–20.

5 Raymond de Roover, *The Rise and Decline of the Medici Bank, 1397–1494* (New York: Norton, 1966).

6 Quoted in Lutz Kaebler, "Max Weber and Usury," pp. 59–86 in Lawrin Armstrong, Ivana Elbl, and Martin M. Elbl, eds., *Money, Markets and Trade in Late Medieval Europe: Essays in Honour of John H. A. Munro* (Leiden: Brill, 2013), p. 87.

7 On the usury prohibition, see de Roover, *The Rise and Decline of the Medici Bank*, pp. 10–12; Jacques Le Goff, "The Usurer and Purgatory," pp. 25–52 in *The Dawn of Modern Banking*; Kaebler, "Max Weber and Usury," pp. 79–86; Diana Wood, *Medieval Economic Thought* (Cambridge, UK: Cambridge University Press, 2002), pp. 181–205.

8 Mark Häberlein, *The Fuggers of Augsburg: Pursuing Wealth and Honor in Renaissance Germany* (Charlottesville: University of Virginia Press, 2012), pp. 22–25; Jean-François Bergier, "From the Fifteenth Century in Italy to the Sixteenth Century in Germany: A New Banking Concept?," pp. 105–29 in *The Dawn of Modern Banking*.

9 Paul Goldthwaite, *The Economy of Renaissance Florence* (Baltimore: Johns Hopkins University Press, 2011), pp. 37ff.

10 Häberlein, *The Fuggers of Augsburg*, pp. 9–12.

11 For a parallel elsewhere, see Barbara Hanawalt, *The Wealth of Wives: Women, Law, and Economy in Late Medieval London* (Oxford: Oxford University Press, 2007).

12 Häberlein, *The Fuggers of Augsburg*, pp. 29–30, and Peter Geffcken, "Jakob Fuggers frühe Jahre," pp. 4–7 in Martin Kluger, ed., *Jakob Fugger (1459–1525): Sein Leben in Bildern* (Augsburg: Context-Medien und -Verlag, 2009).

13 On the Fondaco, see Henry Simonsfeld, *Der Fondaco dei Tedeschi in Venedig und die deutsch-venetianischen Handelsbeziehungen* (Stuttgart: Cotta, 1887), pp. 61–62.

14 Jacob Strieder, *Jacob Fugger the Rich* (New York: Adelphi Press, 1931), pp. 15–19; quote on p. 16, from Schwarz's famous costume book.

15 Häberlein, *The Fuggers of Augsburg*, pp. 35–36.

16 Strieder, *Jacob Fugger the Rich*, pp. 18–19.

17 Strieder, *Jacob Fugger the Rich*, pp. 16–17.

18 Quoted in Richard Ehrenberg, *Capital and Finance in the Age of the Renaissance: A Study of the Fuggers, and Their Connections*, trans. H. M. Lucas (New York: Harcourt, 1928), p. 60.

19 On Maximilian's use of printed propaganda, see Larry Silver, *Marketing Maximilian: The Visual Ideology of a Holy Roman Emperor* (Princeton, NJ: Princeton University Press, 2008); on Maximilian in general, see Gerhard Benecke, *Maximilian I, 1459–1519: An Analytical Biography* (London: Routledge, 1982).

20 Häberlein, *The Fuggers of Augsburg*, pp. 36–37.

21 Ehrenberg, *Capital and Finance in the Age of the Renaissance*, p. 67.

22 Maxime L'Héritier and Florian Téreygeol, "From Copper to Silver: Understanding the *Saigerprozess* Through Experimental Liquation and Drying," *Historical Metallurgy* 44, no. 2 (2010): 136–52.

23 John Munro, "The Monetary Origins of the 'Price Revolution': South German Silver-Mining, Merchant-Banking, and Venetian Commerce, 1470–1540," University of Toronto working paper, 2003, pp. 10–12.

24 Häberlein, *The Fuggers of Augsburg*, p. 58.

25 Häberlein, *The Fuggers of Augsburg*, pp. 40–45; on commerce and information flows, see Andrew Pettegree, *The Invention of News: How the World Came to Know About Itself* (New Haven, CT: Yale University Press, 2014), pp. 40–57.

26 Häberlein, *The Fuggers of Augsburg*, pp. 44 and 53; on the Fuggers in Antwerp, see Donald J. Harreld, *High Germans in the Low Countries: German Merchants and Commerce in Golden Age Antwerp* (Leiden: Brill, 2004), pp. 131–33.

27 Häberlein, *The Fuggers of Augsburg*, pp. 31–35; quoted in Strieder, *Jacob Fugger the Rich*, pp. 192–93.

28 Häberlein, *The Fuggers of Augsburg*, pp. 20–21 and 58–59.

29 Ehrenberg, *Capital and Finance in the Age of the Renaissance*, pp. 137–55.

30 Ehrenberg, *Capital and Finance in the Age of the Renaissance*, pp. 151–52; Häberlein, *The Fuggers of Augsburg*, pp. 40 and 60–62.

31 On Antwerp, see Herman van der Wee, *The Growth of the Antwerp Market and the European Economy, 1400s–1600s* (The Hague: Nijhoff, 1963), especially pp. 89–142, and Harreld, *High Germans in the Low Countries*, pp. 17–39.

32 Quoted in Strieder, *Jacob Fugger the Rich*, pp. 207–8.

33 Häberlein, *The Fuggers of Augsburg*, pp. 45–49.

34 Michael Mallett and Christine Shaw, *The Italian Wars, 1494–1559: War, State and Society in Early Modern Europe* (New York: Routledge, 2012), pp. 85–136; Häberlein, *The Fuggers of Augsburg*.

374

Endnotes

35 On the Frescobaldi, see Ehrenberg, *Capital and Finance*, p. 71; quoted in Strieder, *Jacob Fugger the Rich*, p. 202.
36 Ehrenberg, *Capital and Finance in the Age of the Renaissance*, p. 74.
37 Ehrenberg, *Capital and Finance in the Age of the Renaissance*, pp. 74–79; Häberlein, *The Fuggers of Augsburg*, pp. 64–65.
38 Ehrenberg, *Capital and Finance in the Age of the Renaissance*, p. 80.
39 Steinmetz, *The Richest Man Who Ever Lived*, pp. 227–30.
40 Ehrenberg, *Capital and Finance in the Age of the Renaissance*, pp. 83–86; Häberlein, *The Fuggers of Augsburg*, p. 67.

Chapter 4: Götz von Berlichingen and the Military Revolution

1 Götz von Berlichingen, *Götz von Berlichingen: The Autobiography of a 16th-Century German Knight*, trans. Dirk Rottgardt (West Chester, OH: The Nafziger Collection, 2014), p. 21; Götz von Berlichingen, *Mein Fehd und Handlungen*, ed. Helgard Ulmschneider (Sigmaringen, Germany: Thorbecke, 1981).
2 See fundamentally Geoffrey Parker, *The Military Revolution: Military Innovation and the Rise of the West, 1500–1800*, 2nd ed. (Cambridge, UK: Cambridge University Press, 1996), pp. 1–2 and especially 155–76; for a wholesale and not entirely convincing rejection, see Frank Jacob and Gilmar Visoni-Alonzo, *The Military Revolution in Early Modern Europe: A Revision* (London: Palgrave Pivot, 2016); Clifford J. Rogers, ed., *The Military Revolution Debate: Readings on the Military Transformation of Early Modern Europe* (Boulder, CO: Westview Press, 1995); on the Thirty Years' War, see Peter Wilson, *The Thirty Years War: Europe's Tragedy* (Cambridge, MA: Harvard University Press, 2011), pp. 786ff.
3 Clifford J. Rogers, "The Military Revolution of the Hundred Years War," pp. 55–93 in Rogers, ed., *The Military Revolution Debate*; Andrew Ayton and J. L. Price, eds., *The Medieval Military Revolution: State, Society, and Military Change in Medieval and Early Modern Europe* (New York: St. Martin's Press, 1995).
4 David Parrott, *The Business of War: Military Enterprise and Military Innovation in Early Modern Europe* (Cambridge, UK: Cambridge University Press, 2012).
5 Berlichingen, *Autobiography*, p. 3.
6 Richard Kaeuper, *Medieval Chivalry* (Cambridge, UK: Cambridge University Press, 2016), pp. 155–207 and 353–83.
7 Berlichingen, *Autobiography*, p. 12; David J. B. Trim, ed., *The Chivalric Ethos and the Development of Military Professionalism* (Leiden: Brill, 2003).
8 Berlichingen, *Autobiography*, pp. 11–16.
9 Berlichingen, *Autobiography*, p. 12. Götz's three men-at-arms were contracted in a feud and took captive eleven rich peasants.

10 Berlichingen, *Autobiography*, pp. 19–21.

11 Berlichingen, *Autobiography*, pp. 22–23; Reinhard Baumann, *Georg von Frundsberg: Der Vater der Landsknechte und Feldhauptmann von Tirol* (Munich: Süddeutsscher Verlag, 1984), pp. 80–81.

12 Fritz Redlich, *The German Military Enterpriser and His Work Force: A Study in European Economic and Social History*, vol. 1 (Wiesbaden: Franz Steiner Verlag, 1964), pp. 8–13 and 18–29; on retaining in England, see Christine Carpenter's summary of the literature in *The Wars of the Roses: Politics and the Constitution in England, c.1437–1509* (Cambridge, UK: Cambridge University Press, 1997), pp. 16–26; on Italy and the *condotta*, see fundamentally Michael Mallett, *Mercenaries and Their Masters: Warfare in Renaissance Italy*, 2nd ed. (Barnsley, UK: Pen & Sword Military, 2009), pp. 76–87.

13 On the mercenary market, see Parrott, *The Business of War*, pp. 29–31 and 40–69.

14 Berlichingen, *Autobiography*, pp. 42–44.

15 On the *condottieri*, see Mallett, *Mercenaries and Their Masters*, pp. 146–206.

16 Carl von Elgger, *Kriegswesen und Kriegskunst der schweizerischen Eidgenossen im XIV., XV. und XVI. Jahrhundert* (Luzern: Militärisches Verlagsbureau, 1873); Parrott, *The Business of War*, pp. 46–47.

17 On Charles's loss to the Swiss, see Richard Vaughan, *Charles the Bold* (Woodbridge, UK: Boydell Press, 2002 [1st ed. 1973]), pp. 292–93, 360–97, and 426–32; David Potter, *Renaissance France at War* (Woodbridge, UK: Boydell Press, 2008), pp. 125–31; and Parrott, *The Business of War*, pp. 48–54.

18 Parrott, *The Business of War*, pp. 54–62.

19 Berlichingen, *Autobiography*, p. 21 and p. 5, e.g.

20 Berlichingen, *Autobiography*, pp. 20, 30, and 36.

21 On the origins of the arquebus, see Bert Hall, *Weapons and Warfare in Renaissance Europe* (Baltimore: Johns Hopkins University Press, 1997), pp. 95–100.

22 On Cerignola, see Michael Mallett and Christine Shaw, *The Italian Wars, 1494–1559: War, State and Society in Early Modern Europe* (New York: Routledge, 2012), pp. 64–66; on its debatable importance and the employment of arquebuses, see Hall, *Weapons and Warfare in Renaissance Europe*, pp. 167–71. The exception that proves the rule was 1513's Battle of Flodden, between the English and the Scots.

23 Parker, *The Military Revolution*, pp. 8–16; Christopher Duffy, *Siege Warfare: The Fortress in the Early Modern World, 1494–1660* (London: Routledge & Kegan Paul, 1979), pp. 1–22.

24 Berlichingen, *Autobiography*, pp. 33–37.

25 On feuds, see Hillay Zmora, *State and Nobility in Early Modern Germany: The Knightly Feud in Franconia, 1440–1567* (Cambridge, UK: Cambridge

University Press, 2003); Hillay Zmora, *The Feud in Early Modern Germany* (Cambridge, UK: Cambridge University Press, 2011).

26 Baumann, *Georg von Frundsberg*, pp. 180–98.

27 For Götz's account of his participation in the Peasants' War, see Berlichingen, *Autobiography*, pp. 57–68. He explicitly says that it was not just what he did in that conflict, whatever it was, but the sum total of all his past acts that led to his long imprisonment.

28 Berlichingen, *Autobiography*, p. 72.

Chapter 5: Aldus Manutius and Printing

1 Elizabeth Eisenstein, *The Printing Press as an Agent of Change* (Cambridge, UK: Cambridge University Press, 1980).

2 Andrew Pettegree, *The Book in the Renaissance* (New Haven, CT: Yale University Press, 2010), pp. 7–20.

3 Stephan Füssel, *Gutenberg and the Impact of Printing*, trans. Douglas Martin (Aldershot, UK: Ashgate, 2003), pp. 10–13; Albert Kapr, *Gutenberg: The Man and his Invention*, trans. Douglas Martin (Aldershot, UK: Scolar Press, 1996), pp. 29–73.

4 On the Gutenberg Bible, see Füssel, *Gutenberg and the Impact of Printing*, pp. 18–25 and 51–52; Pettegree, *The Book in the Renaissance*, pp. 23–29.

5 Pettegree, *The Book in the Renaissance*, pp. 32–33 and 45–50.

6 On Venice, see fundamentally Frederic C. Lane, *Venice: A Maritime Republic* (Baltimore: Johns Hopkins University Press, 1973), pp. 136–53 and 224–49; Elisabeth Crouzet-Pavan, "Toward an Ecological Understanding of the Myth of Venice," pp. 39–64 in John Martin and Dennis Romano, eds., *Venice Reconsidered: The History and Civilization of an Italian City-State, 1297–1797* (Baltimore: Johns Hopkins University Press, 2000); Gerhard Rösch, "The *Serrata* of the Great Council and Venetian Society, 1286–1323," pp. 67–88 in Martin and Romano, eds., *Venice Reconsidered*; on the Medici in Venice, see Raymond de Roover, *The Rise and Decline of the Medici Bank, 1397–1494* (New York: Norton, 1966), pp. 240–53.

7 On the background to early Venetian printing, see Martin Lowry, *Nicholas Jenson and the Rise of Venetian Publishing in Renaissance Europe* (Oxford: Basil Blackwell, 1991), pp. 49–71; Leonardas Vytautas Gerulaitis, *Printing and Publishing in Fifteenth-Century Venice* (Chicago: American Library Association, 1976), pp. 1–30.

8 On the crash of 1473, see Gerulaitis, *Printing and Publishing in Fifteenth-Century Venice*, p. 23.

9 Martin Lowry, *The World of Aldus Manutius: Business and Scholarship in Renaissance Venice* (Ithaca, NY: Cornell University Press, 1979), p. 52.

10 Lowry, *The World of Aldus Manutius*, pp. 52–64.

11 For an overview of the complexities of the Renaissance, see Guido Ruggiero, *The Renaissance in Italy: A Social and Cultural History of the Rinascimento* (Cambridge, UK: Cambridge University Press, 2015), pp. 6–18.

12 Charles G. Nauert, *Humanism and the Culture of Renaissance Europe* (Cambridge, UK: Cambridge University Press, 1995), pp. 8–13; Nicholas Mann, "The Origins of Humanism," pp. 1–19 in Jill Kraye, ed., *The Cambridge Companion to Renaissance Humanism* (Cambridge, UK: Cambridge University Press, 1996); Michael D. Reeve, "Classical Scholarship," pp. 20–46 in Kraye, ed., *The Cambridge Companion to Renaissance Humanism*.

13 Nauert, *Humanism and the Culture of Renaissance Europe*, pp. 26–35; Ruggiero, *The Renaissance in Italy*, pp. 15–18 and 229–49.

14 Paul F. Grendler, *Schooling in Renaissance Italy: Literacy and Learning, 1300–1600* (Baltimore: Johns Hopkins University Press, 1989); Vergerio quoted on p. 118, and see more generally pp. 111–41.

15 Lowry, *The World of Aldus Manutius*, pp. 58–66; quoted on p. 66.

16 Quoted in Lowry, *The World of Aldus Manutius*, p. 59.

17 Desiderius Erasmus, *Colloquies*, vol. 1, trans. Craig R. Thompson (Toronto: University of Toronto Press, 1997), pp. 979–91; Lowry, *The World of Aldus Manutius*, pp. 76–83.

18 Lowry, *The World of Aldus Manutius*, pp. 80–86.

19 G. Scott Clemons, "Pressing Business: The Economics of the Aldine Press," pp. 11–24 in Natale Vacalebre, ed., *Five Centuries Later. Aldus Manutius: Culture, Typography and Philology* (Milan: Biblioteca Ambrosiana, 2019); Rudolf Hirsch, *Printing, Selling and Reading, 1450–1550* (Wiesbaden: Otto Harrassowitz, 1967).

20 Lowry, *The World of Aldus Manutius*, pp. 110-15; Clemons, "Pressing Business," pp. 15–17.

21 Lowry, *The World of Aldus Manutius*, pp. 115–16; Clemons, "Pressing Business," p. 17.

22 Lowry, *The World of Aldus Manutius*, pp. 137–46.

23 Hirsch, *Printing, Selling and Reading*, pp. 128–29.

24 Pettegree, *The Book in the Renaissance*, pp. 58–62; Lowry, *The World of Aldus Manutius*, pp. 78, 113, 125, and 147–67.

25 Lowry, *The World of Aldus Manutius*, pp. 98–100.

26 Lowry, *The World of Aldus Manutius*, pp. 257–90.

27 Pettegree, *The Book in the Renaissance*, pp. 65–82.

28 This incident, recounted by Erasmus himself, is detailed in Martin Davies, *Aldus Manutius: Printer and Publisher of Renaissance Venice* (Malibu, CA: J. Paul Getty Museum, 1995), p. 58.

29 Hirsch, *Printing, Selling and Reading*, p. 105; Andrew Pettegree, *The Invention of News: How the World Came to Know About Itself* (New Haven, CT: Yale University Press, 2014).

Chapter 6: John Heritage and Everyday Capitalism

1 The essential work on John Heritage is Christopher Dyer, *A Country Merchant, 1495–1520: Trading and Farming at the End of the Middle Ages* (Oxford: Oxford University Press, 2012); see also Patrick Wyman, host, "Interview: Historian Christopher Dyer on Peasants and the Medieval Economy," *Tides of History*, September 27, 2018.

2 On the plague, see fundamentally Ole J. Benedictow, *The Black Death, 1346–1353: The Complete History* (Woodbridge, UK: Boydell Press, 2004); Bruce M. S. Campbell, *The Great Transition: Climate, Disease and Society in the Late-Medieval World* (Cambridge, UK: Cambridge University Press, 2016), especially pp. 267–331; on deserted villages in Heritage's area, see Dyer, *A Country Merchant*, pp. 230–31.

3 Campbell, *The Great Transition*, pp. 30–133.

4 Campbell, *The Great Transition*, pp. 355–63.

5 On these processes, see L. R. Poos, *A Rural Society After the Black Death: Essex 1350–1525* (Cambridge, UK: Cambridge University Press, 1991); Richard Britnell and Ben Dobbs, eds., *Agriculture and Rural Society after the Black Death: Common Themes and Regional Variations* (Hatfield, UK: University of Hertfordshire Press, 2008); Mark Bailey and Stephen Rigby, eds., *Town and Countryside in the Age of the Black Death: Essays in Honour of John Hatcher* (Turnhout, Belgium: Brepols, 2011); Christopher Dyer, *An Age of Transition? Economy and Society in the Later Middle Ages* (Oxford: Oxford University Press, 2005).

6 Dyer, *A Country Merchant*, pp. 25–27.

7 Dyer, *A Country Merchant*, p. 29.

8 Dyer, *A Country Merchant*, pp. 29–33.

9 Dyer, *A Country Merchant*, p. 34.

10 On the Brenner debate, as this dustup is known, see T. H. Aston, ed., *The Brenner Debate: Agrarian Class Structure and Economic Development in Pre-Industrial Europe* (Cambridge, UK: Cambridge University Press, 1987); Spencer Dimmock, *The Origin of Capitalism in England, 1400–1600* (Leiden: Brill, 2014); Shami Ghosh, "Rural Economies and Transitions to Capitalism: Germany and England Compared (c.1200–1800)," *Journal of Agrarian Change* 16, no. 2 (2016): 255–90; Dyer, *An Age of Transition*, pp. 66–85.

11 Dyer, *A Country Merchant*, pp. v–vi and 90; Wyman, "Interview: Historian Christopher Dyer." For a similarly rare survival, see Richard K. Marshall,

The Local Merchants of Prato: Small Entrepreneurs in the Late Medieval Economy (Baltimore: Johns Hopkins University Press, 1999).

12 On the rising need for bookkeeping in this period, see Alfred W. Crosby, *The Measure of Reality: Quantification and Western Society, 1250–1600* (Cambridge, UK: Cambridge University Press, 1997), pp. 199–224; on Medici methods, see Raymond de Roover, *The Rise and Decline of the Medici Bank, 1397–1494* (New York: Norton, 1966), pp. 96–100.

13 Recorded in Dyer, *A Country Merchant*, p. 226.

14 Dyer, *A Country Merchant*, pp. 91–99; quote on p. 93.

15 Dyer, *A Country Merchant*, pp. 17–18; Eleonora Mary Carus-Wilson and Olive Coleman, *England's Export Trade, 1275–1547* (Oxford: Clarendon Press, 1963), pp. 48–72; John Oldland, *The English Woollen Industry, c.1200–c.1560* (New York: Routledge, 2019), especially pp. 215–36.

16 Dyer, *A Country Merchant*, pp. 100–107.

17 Dyer, *A Country Merchant*, pp. 117–20.

18 See fundamentally Richard H. Britnell, *The Commercialisation of English Society, 1000–1500* (Cambridge, UK: Cambridge University Press, 1993); see also Dyer, *An Age of Transition*, pp. 173–210, for a somewhat less but still quite optimistic assessment of commercialization in England.

19 Maryanne Kowaleski, *Local Markets and Regional Trade in Medieval Exeter* (Cambridge, UK: Cambridge University Press, 1995), pp. 328–30, for a summation of the overall arguments.

20 Sylvia L. Thrupp, *The Merchant Class of Medieval London, 1300–1500* (Ann Arbor: University of Michigan Press, 1948), especially pp. 4–52; on merchant guilds, see fundamentally Sheilagh Ogilvie, *Institutions and European Trade: Merchant Guilds, 1000–1800* (Cambridge, UK: Cambridge University Press, 2011); Peter Spufford, *Power and Profit: The Merchant in Medieval Europe* (London: Thames & Hudson, 2002); on London, see Caroline Barron, *London in the Later Middle Ages: Government and People, 1200–1500* (Oxford: Oxford University Press, 2005).

21 Teofilo F. Ruiz, *Crisis and Continuity: Land and Town in Late Medieval Castile* (Philadelphia: University of Pennsylvania Press, 1994). On the rise of commerce in this period more generally, see Martha C. Howell, *Commerce Before Capitalism in Europe, 1300–1600* (Cambridge, UK: Cambridge University Press, 2010).

22 See Craig Mulgrew, *The Economy of Obligation: The Culture of Credit and Social Relations in Early Modern England* (Houndmills, UK: Palgrave, 1998), especially pp. 95ff.; Howell, *Commerce*, pp. 24–29 and 70–78; P. Nightingale, "Monetary Contraction and Mercantile Credit in Later Medieval England," *Economic History Review* 43 (1990): 560–75.

23 Dyer, *A Country Merchant*, pp. 35–39 and 129–31.

Chapter 7: Martin Luther, the Printing Press, and Disrupting the Church

1   Much ink has been spilled over whether Luther actually posted the *Ninety-Five Theses* on the castle church's door or not, but it would have been standard practice—the church door was Wittenberg's unofficial bulletin board—and there is no good reason to doubt that it happened. For a summation of the arguments on the topic, see Andrew Pettegree, *Brand Luther: 1517, Printing, and the Making of the Reformation* (New York: Penguin, 2015), pp. 70–72; for a full accounting, see Kurt Aland, ed., *Martin Luther's Ninety-Five Theses: With the Pertinent Documents from the History of the Reformation* (St. Louis: Concordia Publishing, 1967), p. 62.

2   C. M. Jacobs, trans., *Works of Martin Luther: With Introduction and Notes*, vol. 1 (Philadelphia: Holman, 1915), p. 27.

3   Pettegree, *Brand Luther*, pp. 73–75; Martin Brecht, *Martin Luther: His Road to Reformation, 1483–1521* (Minneapolis: Fortress Press, 1985), pp. 190–221; Heiko Oberman, *Luther: Man Between God and the Devil* (New Haven, CT: Yale University Press, 1989), pp. 192–97.

4   Much has been written about Luther's early life, ranging from straightforward description to complex psychobiography, but key recent works include Lyndal Roper, *Martin Luther: Renegade and Prophet* (New York: Random House, 2016), pp. 3–36; Oberman, *Luther*, pp. 82–115; Brecht, *Martin Luther*, pp. 1–50; Richard Marius, *Martin Luther: The Christian Between God and Death* (Cambridge, MA: Belknap, 1999), pp. 19–42; for the now-discredited but still often provocative psychobiographical approach, see Erik Erikson, *Young Man Luther: A Study in Psychoanalysis and History* (New York: Norton, 1958), pp. 13–97.

5   Roper, *Martin Luther*, pp. 16–17.

6   On Luther in the monastery, see Roper, *Martin Luther*, pp. 37–62; Brecht, *Martin Luther*, pp. 51–82.

7   On the Church in Luther's day, see Diarmaid MacCulloch, *The Reformation: A History* (New York: Penguin, 2003), pp. 3–52; R. N. Swanson, "The Pre-Reformation Church," pp. 9–30 in Andrew Pettegree, ed., *The Reformation World* (London: Routledge, 2000); Alister E. McGrath, *The Intellectual Origins of the European Reformation*, 2nd ed. (Malden, MA: Blackwell, 2004), pp. 11–33; Larissa Taylor, "Society and Piety," pp. 22–36 in R. Po-chia Hsia, ed., *A Companion to the Reformation World* (Malden, MA: Blackwell, 2004).

8   On reform, see Bruce Gordon, "Conciliarism in Late Mediaeval Europe," pp. 31–50 in Pettegree, ed., *The Reformation World*; Richard Rex, "Humanism," pp. 51–71 in Pettegree, ed., *The Reformation World*; Eric Leland Saak, *Luther and the Reformation of the Later Middle Ages* (Cambridge, MA: Cambridge University Press, 2017), especially pp. 11–63; Euan Cameron, "Dissent and Heresy," pp. 3–21 in Hsia, ed., *A Companion to the Reformation World*.

9   On the theological underpinnings of indulgences, see Robert W. Shaffern, "The Medieval Theology of Indulgences," pp. 37–64 in R. N. Swanson, ed., *Promissory Notes on the Treasury of Merits: Indulgences in Late Medieval Europe* (Leiden: Brill, 2006); on indulgences in Spain, see John Edwards, "*España es Diferente*"? Indulgences and the Spiritual Economy in Late Medieval Spain," pp. 147–68 in Swanson, ed., *Promissory Notes*; Pettegree, *Brand Luther*, pp. 54–64.

10 On the indulgence campaign, see Pettegree, *Brand Luther*, pp. 63–67.

11 Pettegree, *Brand Luther*, pp. 56–66; Falk Eisermann, "The Indulgence as a Media Event: Developments in Communication through Broadsides in the Fifteenth Century," pp. 309–30 in Swanson, ed., *Promissory Notes*; David Bagchi, "Luther's *Ninety-Five Theses* and the Contemporary Criticism of Indulgences," pp. 331–56 in Swanson, ed., *Promissory Notes*.

12 Pettegree, *Brand Luther*, pp. 105–9; this is a point that in its most developed form fundamentally belongs to Andrew Pettegree in *Brand Luther*; see also Mark U. Edwards Jr., *Printing, Propaganda, and Martin Luther* (Minneapolis: Fortress Press, 1994), and see notes on pp. 2–4.

13 On this back-and-forth, see Pettegree, *Brand Luther*, pp. 78–83.

14 Pettegree, *Brand Luther*, pp. 104–31; Edwards, *Printing, Propaganda, and Martin Luther*, pp. 14–37.

15 Pettegree, *Brand Luther*, pp. 11–14.

16 Pettegree, *Brand Luther*, pp. 157–63.

17 Quoted in Pettegree, *Brand Luther*, p. 136; on Worms more generally, see Roper, *Martin Luther*, pp. 160–82; Brecht, *Martin Luther*, pp. 448–76.

18 Quoted in Pettegree, *Brand Luther*, pp. 210–11.

19 Edwards, *Printing, Propaganda, and Martin Luther*, pp. 14–28; Pettegree, *Brand Luther*, pp. 206–10.

20 Quoted in Roper, *Martin Luther*, p. 223.

21 On Müntzer, see fundamentally Eric W. Gritsch, *Thomas Müntzer: A Tragedy of Errors* (Minneapolis: Fortress Press, 1989); Tom Scott, *Thomas Müntzer: Theology and Revolution in the German Reformation* (New York: St. Martin's Press, 1989).

22 Quoted in Roper, *Martin Luther*, p. 253.

23 Quoted in James M. Stayer, "The German Peasants' War and the Rural Reformation," pp. 127–45, p. 131, in Pettegree, ed., *The Reformation World*; on the Peasants' War, see Tom Scott and Bob Scribner, eds., *The German Peasants' War: A History in Documents* (New York: Humanities Books, 1991); Peter Blickle, *The Revolution of 1525: The German Peasants' War from a New Perspective* (Baltimore: Johns Hopkins University Press, 1981).

24 Quoted in Stayer, "The German Peasants' War and the Rural Reformation," pp. 129–30.

25 Quoted in Pettegree, *Brand Luther*, p. 242.
26 On the nuanced question of Luther's personal impact, see, e.g. Christopher Ocker, *Luther, Conflict, and Christendom* (Cambridge, UK: Cambridge University Press, 2018).

Chapter 8: Suleiman the Magnificent and the Ottoman Superpower

1 On the Ottoman Empire as fundamentally "European," see Daniel Goffman, *The Ottoman Empire and Early Modern Europe* (Cambridge, UK: Cambridge University Press, 2002).
2 On the early roots of the Ottoman Empire, see Cemal Kafadar, *Between Two Worlds: The Construction of the Ottoman State* (Berkeley: University of California Press, 1995); Heath W. Lowry, *The Nature of the Early Ottoman State* (Albany: State University of New York Press, 2003); Colin Imber, *The Ottoman Empire: The Structure of Power, 1300–1650*, 2nd ed. (New York: Palgrave Macmillan, 2009), pp. 3–24.
3 On Ankara and its aftermath, see Dimitris J. Kastritis, *The Sons of Bayezid: Empire Building and Representation in the Ottoman Civil War of 1402–1413* (Leiden: Brill, 2007).
4 The standard account of Mehmet's reign remains Franz Babinger, *Mehmed the Conqueror and His Time*, ed. William C. Hickman, trans. Ralph Manheim (Princeton, NJ: Princeton University Press, 1978 [orig. German ed. 1953]).
5 On Selim's legacy to his son, see Kaya Şahin, *Empire and Power in the Reign of Süleyman: Narrating the Sixteenth-Century Ottoman World* (Cambridge, UK: Cambridge University Press, 2013), pp. 27–34; Andrew Hess, "The Ottoman Conquest of Egypt and the Beginning of the Sixteenth-Century World War," *International Journal of Middle East Studies* 4, no. 1 (January 1973): 55–76.
6 Quoted in Roger Bigelow Merriman, *Suleiman the Magnificent, 1520–1566* (Cambridge, MA: Harvard University Press, 1944), p. 37.
7 On Selim's accession, see H. Erdem Çipa, *The Making of Selim: Succession, Legitimacy, and Memory in the Early Modern Ottoman World* (Bloomington: Indiana University Press, 2017), pp. 29–61.
8 Quoted in André Clot, *Suleiman the Magnificent*, trans. Matthew J. Reisz (London: Saki, 2005 [orig. French ed. 1989]), p. 30.
9 On the Belgrade campaign, see Clot, *Suleiman the Magnificent*, pp. 37–38; Merriman, *Suleiman the Magnificent*, pp. 56–58.
10 Konstantin Nossov and Brian Delf, *The Fortress of Rhodes 1309–1522* (Oxford: Osprey, 2010).
11 Quoted in Clot, *Suleiman the Magnificent*, p. 55.
12 Quoted in James Reston Jr., *Defenders of the Faith: Christianity and Islam Battle for the Soul of Europe, 1520–1536* (New York: Penguin, 2009), p. 171.

13 On the early relationship between the Habsburgs and Hungary, see Géza Pálffy, *The Kingdom of Hungary and the Habsburg Monarchy in the Sixteenth Century*, trans. Thomas J. DeKornfeld and Helen D. DeKornfeld (New York: Columbia University Press, 2009), pp. 17–51.

14 Quoted in Clot, *Suleiman the Magnificent*, p. 58. For further discussion of the battle, see Merriman, *Suleiman the Magnificent*, pp. 87–93; Reston, *Defenders of the Faith*, pp. 186–94; Géza Perjés, *The Fall of the Medieval Kingdom of Hungary: Mohács 1526–Buda 1541*, vol. 26 of *War and Society in East Central Europe* (New York: Columbia University Press, 1989), pp. 225–65.

15 On the siege of Vienna, see Clot, *Suleiman the Magnificent*, pp. 64–68; Merriman, *Suleiman the Magnificent*, pp. 103–8.

16 Ann Williams, "Mediterranean Conflict," pp. 39–54 in Metin Kunt and Christine Woodhead, eds., *Süleyman the Magnificent and His Age: The Ottoman Empire in the Early Modern World* (London: Longman, 1995); Giancarlo Casale, *The Ottoman Age of Exploration* (Oxford: Oxford University Press, 2010); Salih Özbaran, "Ottoman Naval Policy in the South," pp. 55–70 in Kunt and Woodhead, eds., *Süleyman the Magnificent and His Age*.

17 Halil Inalcik, *An Economic and Social History of the Ottoman Empire*, vol. 1, *1300–1600* (Cambridge, UK: Cambridge University Press, 1994), pp. 55–74, and for these figures, pp. 98–99; Şevket Pamuk, "In the Absence of Domestic Currency: Debased European Coinage in the Seventeenth-Century Ottoman Empire," *Journal of Economic History* 57, no. 2 (June 1997): 345–66, pp. 354–55. Pamuk's figure for that budget year differs, but seems to be a misprint.

18 Gábor Ágoston, *Guns for the Sultan: Military Power and the Weapons Industry in the Ottoman Empire* (Cambridge, UK: Cambridge University Press, 2005), pp. 70 and 96–127; Suraiya Faroqhi, *The Ottoman Empire and the World Around It* (London: I. B. Tauris, 2007), pp. 98–118; quote cited in Adam Francisco, *Martin Luther and Islam: A Study in Sixteenth-Century Polemics and Apologetics* (Leiden: Brill, 2007), p. 86.

19 On the image of Suleiman, see Christine Woodhead, "Perspectives on Süleyman," pp. 164–90 in Kunt and Woodhead, eds., *Süleyman the Magnificent and His Age*.

Chapter 9: Charles V and Universal Rule

1 On Charles's arrival in Spain, see Karl Brandi, *The Emperor Charles V: The Growth and Destiny of a Man and of a World-Empire*, trans. C. V. Wedgwood (London: Jonathan Cape, 1965), pp. 78–80; Geoffrey Parker, *Emperor: A New Life of Charles V* (New Haven, CT: Yale University Press, 2019), pp. 75–77.

2 Benecke, *Maximilian*, pp. 31–45.

3   On the profoundly dysfunctional Trastámara family dynamics, see, for example, Parker, *Emperor*, pp. 51–56.

4   On Juana, see fundamentally Bethany Aram, *La reina Juana: Gobierno, piedad y dinastía* (Madrid: Marcial Pons, 2001); and Bethany Aram, *Juana the Mad: Sovereignty and Dynasty in Renaissance Europe* (Baltimore: Johns Hopkins University Press, 2005).

5   Parker, *Emperor*, p. 68.

6   Parker, *Emperor*, pp. 68–69.

7   There is no reason to think, contrary to many recent assertions, that Charles fathered an illegitimate child with his stepgrandmother Germaine de Foix; see Parker, *Emperor*, pp. 545–46, for a conclusive debunking.

8   Quoted in Parker, *Emperor*, p. 70.

9   On Cisneros, see fundamentally José García Oro, *El Cardenal Cisneros: Vida y impresas*, 2 vols. (Madrid: Biblioteca de Autores Cristianos, 1992–93); Erika Rummel, *Jiménez de Cisneros: On the Threshold of Spain's Golden Age* (Tempe: Arizona Center for Medieval and Renaissance Studies, 1999). Letter quoted in Rummel, *Jiménez de Cisneros*, p. 85.

10 On the journey, see Parker, *Emperor*, pp. 76–79; Brandi, *The Emperor Charles V*, pp. 80–81.

11 On these events, see Parker, *Emperor*, pp. 81–83, and Brandi, *The Emperor Charles V*, pp. 81–83.

12 Quoted in Parker, *Emperor*, p. 87.

13 Quoted in Parker, *Emperor*, p. 89. More generally, see Parker, *Emperor*, pp. 87–94; Brandi, *The Emperor Charles V*, pp. 99–112.

14 Quoted in Parker, *Emperor*, pp. 89–90.

15 Quoted in Parker, *Emperor*, p. 91.

16 On the ideals of universal rulership, see John M. Headley, *The Emperor and His Chancellor: A Study of the Imperial Chancellery Under Gattinara* (Cambridge, UK: Cambridge University Press, 1983), especially pp. 10–12, and the quote on p. 10; see also Harald Kleinschmidt, *Charles V: The World Emperor* (Stroud, UK: Sutton, 2004), pp. 81–89.

17 On Juana's role in the Comunero revolt, see Aram, *Juana the Mad*, pp. 123–28. On the revolt, see Aurelio Espinosa, *The Empire of the Cities: Emperor Charles V, the* Comunero *Revolt, and the Transformation of the Spanish System* (Leiden: Brill, 2009), pp. 65–82; Hipólito Rafael Oliva Herrer, "Interpreting Large-Scale Revolts: Some Evidence from the War of the Communities of Castile," pp. 330–48 in Justine Firnhaber-Baker and Dirk Schoenaers, eds., *The Routledge History Handbook of Medieval Revolts* (New York: Routledge, 2017).

18 James D. Tracy, *Emperor Charles V, Impresario of War: Campaign Strategy, International Finance, and Domestic Politics* (Cambridge, UK: Cambridge University

Press, 2002), pp. 20–28; Wim Blockmans, *Emperor Charles V, 1500–1558*, pp. 25–45.

19   Parker, *Emperor*, pp. 148–51.

20   Parker, *Emperor*, pp. 153–62; R. J. Knecht, *Renaissance Warrior and Patron: The Reign of Francis I* (Cambridge, UK: Cambridge University Press, 1994), pp. 218–36.

21   On Charles and the Peasants' War, see Parker, *Emperor*, p. 194.

22   Knecht, *Renaissance Warrior and Patron*, pp. 239–56.

23   Quoted in Parker, *Emperor*, pp. 167–68.

24   See chapter 8.

25   On which see Judith Hook, *The Sack of Rome: 1527*, 2nd ed. (New York: Palgrave Macmillan, 2004), pp. 107–80.

26   Parker, *Emperor*, pp. 342–58.

27   Hugh Thomas, *Conquest: Montezuma, Cortés, and the Fall of Old Mexico* (New York: Touchstone, 1993), pp. 65–69.

28   Thomas, *Conquest*, pp. 260–62.

29   On the conquest of Mexico, see Thomas, *Conquest*.

30   Quoted in Parker, *Emperor*, p. 355; see pp. 355–57.

31   On these events, see Parker, *Emperor*, pp. 237–43; Brandi, *The Emperor Charles V*, pp. 365–71.

32   On the financial arrangements, see fundamentally Tracy, *Emperor Charles V, Impresario of War*, pp. 154–57.

33   Parker, *Emperor*, pp. 246–47.

Conclusion

1   Adam Tooze, *The Deluge: The Great War, America and the Remaking of the Global Order, 1916–1931* (New York: Viking, 2014).

Index

387